BUILDING BUSINESS WEB SITES

BUILDING BUSINESS WEB SITES

ADAM BLUM

A Subsidiary of
Henry Holt and Co., Inc.

First Edition—1996

Printed in the United States of America.

ISBN: 1-55828-431-1

10 9 8 7 6 5 4 3 2

MIS:Press books are available at special discounts for bulk purchases for sales promotions, premiums, fund-raising, or educational use. Special editions or book excerpts can also be created to specification.

For details contact: Special Sales Director
MIS:Press
a subsidiary of Henry Holt and Company, Inc.
115 West 18th Street
New York, New York 10011

Associate Publisher: Paul Farrell **Managing Editor:** Cary Sullivan

Copy Edit Manager: Shari Chapell **Copy Editor:** Jack Donner

Editor: Debra Williams Cauley **Technical Editor:** Bob Kline

Production Editor: Maya Riddick

Dedication

To Elizabeth Alice

ACKNOWLEDGMENTS:

I would like thank Bob Kline for the thorough technical review of the material and good ideas for additional content. Thanks to Matt Holmes and Noam Chopak for coming through with a very informative security chapter. Thanks to Debra Williams Cauley for the detailed editing and assistance in bringing aboard all the companies that participated in the Webmaster's Toolbox. Finally, I'd like to thank my wife, Jennifer for her support and indulgence over the last several months spent closeted in my office with a bunch of NT servers.

TABLE OF CONTENTS

PART 2: BUILDING YOUR WEB CONTENT

CHAPTER 7: HTML CONVERTERS: CREATING HTML FROM EXISTING SOURCES 145

PART 3: SETTING UP YOUR WEB SERVER

CHAPTER 8: SETTING UP YOUR INTERNET SERVER 183

CHAPTER 10: GATEWAYS: CONVERTING INFORMATION TO HTML ON DEMAND 249

CHAPTER 11: WEB PROGRAMMING CGI GATEWAYS AND MORE 275

PART 1

WHAT CAN YOU DO

WITH THE WEB

## CHAPTER 1

INTRODUCTION

There are many books available today that describe the World Wide Web—how to use Mosaic and other Web browsers to access the vast amount of information available via the Web. In fact, it is possible to get most of the information necessary to be a proficient Web surfer exclusively from popular periodicals, without ever cracking a book. Rarely in recent memory has any technical subject been so ferociously hyped. It's not hard to understand this, however. The Web is becoming an enormously important marketplace, and it is changing the paradigm of how information is distributed. It's not surprising that the media is engrossed by the phenomenon of the World Wide Web.

But our goal is not to discuss the Web phenomenon. Though we introduce the Web briefly in this chapter, we assume that you have read at least something about this craze, or you would not be reading this book. Web browser usage, even Web surfing for business, will not even be covered by this book. This book shows businesses how to create Web sites for their business needs, particularly for electronic commerce. Though there are now a few HTML reference guides, there is little information cohesively and *comprehensively* organized on this subject. In my efforts helping large organizations use Web servers for electronic commerce and information distribution, this was a common problem all of my clients faced. This book began as a whitepaper to give my clients enough background on the fundamentals of Web publishing so that I could concentrate on helping them with the really hard problems.

Besides serving as a collecting area for the large amount of information necessary to successfully create Web sites for publishing and commerce, this book acts as a filter narrowing is vast information to that relevant for most business Web sites. For example, there is a wealth of material scattered around the Internet on HTML. Putting it together here in one place certainly has value, but the greater value is narrowing down the information professionals planning Web servers for their businesses need. This should be the only book you need to keep on your shelf as you pursue your authoring efforts. We will cover all aspects of web creation. Where more depth is needed, if the appendices don't supply it, references to relevant WWW pages will be presented every time. Early drafts of the book served as a roadmap to WWW material on Web authoring for myself and my clients. I hope it performs the same service for you.

The focus of this book is entirely on the server side of the Web, and even more narrowly: *creating Web sites for business*. The book has very much an implementation flavor to it. We assume that you are interested in creating your own Web server, and the book contains the level of detail and specificity necessary to that goal. The first part (Chapters 1 and 2) presents a survey of Web servers for publishing and electronic commerce, then presents in detail publishing and electronic commerce applications. The second part (Chapters 3 to 7) is devoted to creating Web content: a discussion of HTML is followed by chapters on HTML authoring and conversion tools. The third part (Chapters 8 to 12) describes how to set up Web servers: how to get Internet connectivity, how to choose and set up Web server software, and how to do some of the more intricate Web server techniques, such as setting up gateways from your Web server to other information sources. Chapter 11 presents information on how to program gateways for yourself, but you can easily skip or skim this chapter if you are not a programmer, or prefer to restrict yourself to off-the-shelf products in your webmastering efforts. Chapter 12 presents general Internet security information structured to allow you to develop a security policy for your commercial Web host.

The CD-ROM contains a variety of tools useful in creating Web servers, and also contains the complete HTML for the example just mentioned. In fact, for many of you, the CD-ROM will contain *everything* you need (beyond the operating system itself) to create a functioning Web server. The value of this should not be underestimated—there are many tools necessary to create a modern, bidirectional Web server with real-time data access and multimedia objects. This will likely be the first time they are collected in one place. You can still surf the Web to get these tools, and evaluate them one by one. But using this book should let you get your Web server up and running (content and all) in days rather than weeks.

The vast majority of these tools are for Windows and Windows NT. Indeed the coverage of tools in the book is focused on this market as well. The reason for this bias is twofold: in my opinion, Windows NT makes a great platform for hosting Internet servers in general and particularly for Web servers; and it leverages the skill base of most businesses. In the early days of the Web, and to some degree still at this writing it is more common to have Web servers running on UNIX platforms. But the tool set for Web authoring is already much richer on Windows and Windows NT. By the time you read this, a version of Windows NT even more focused on acting as an Internet server will have appeared with a built-in firewall, Web server software, and other components necessary to create a successful commercial Web server. I believe that by the end of

1995, Windows NT will be the predominant Web server platform for creating new Web servers for businesses.

Another unique aspect of this book is to present coding techniques, and some code, for the various aspects of Web server creation that still require it. For the most part, the tool set has evolved so that coding often is not necessary. This is good, since Web server coding issues (CGI scripts and HTML conversion facilities) have rarely, if ever, been covered in print. However, for bidirectional applications where the user is supplying information to the Web server (such as ordering a product, or registering as a user), this is still required. It is also (usually) necessary for applications that require real time access to data. It is even necessary sometime for one-time static conversion of information into Web server content, if no conversion tool has yet been written for the data you need to make available (for example, with proprietary legacy databases that you may have to deal with). But I *don't* assume that you are a developer. The coding sections are restricted almost exclusively to Chapter 11, and you can skip over them if they are not of interest, without missing any information crucial to understanding the technology. For example, I will supply you with scripts that allow you to process forms submitted by the user. If your need is relatively generic you may be able to work with the supplied scripts. Nevertheless, as the needs of your Web server evolve, you may want to refer back to the coding portions. The techniques presented there will allow you to push the envelope of your Web server's capabilities. Eventually the Web marketplace will be competitive enough that only the best implemented, fastest, and most innovative sites will thrive.

Origins of the World Wide Web

The World Wide Web was an initiative begun at the CERN, the European Laboratory for Particle Physics. The goal was to share information among researchers scattered around the globe. Tim Berners-Lee proposed a system which would allow incorporation of various types of information objects (e.g. text, images, sound) linked into structured documents that could also be linked to other documents. The hypertext document aspect allowed use of various types of data in the documents, as well as allowing information to be coalesced from many different, potentially geographically-distributed, sources.

In late 1990, the project began in earnest, with the first primitive text browser appearing in 1991. CERN went public to the rest of the world in 1991 with the availability of this technology, spurring crucial software development in 1992. In 1993, the first real graphical browsers appeared, showing the world what was possible with the Web: Viola for X Windows, CERN's Mac browser, and the National Center for Supercomputing Application's (NCSA) Mosaic for X Windows. The emergence of these browsers sparked the initial popularity of the Web. The introduction of Mosaic for Microsoft Windows fueled that growth. Other browsers for Windows and other systems also began to appear, but Mosaic certainly dominated the field.

In 1994, the emergence of the Web as a business phenomenon began to take hold. More and more companies established beachheads on the Web, usually in the form of a simple home page with perhaps a few links to auxiliary pages. The other phenomenon was the commercialization of Web tools and tool builders. Spyglass Communications formed to market Mosaic licenses. Marc Andreesen and several other developers on the Mosaic team left NCSA to form Netscape Communications along with Jim Clark, the founder of Silicon Graphics. Netscape's browser had several performance advantages over the then-current version of Mosaic. By the end of 1994, Netscape had gained widespread initial acceptance and rivaled Mosaic in popularity.

One of Netscape's other goals (besides building a better Web browser) was to introduce standards for secure Web server access. By the end of 1994, several competing solutions for solving the problem of Web security had begun to appear. This development should be particularly interesting to the audience of this book, and we will cover them in detail.

Another recent development is the relocation of the "Web home." The Web initiative began at CERN, but is now run by the W3 Consortium (W3C). W3C (**http://www.w3.org/hypertext/WWW/Consortium/Prospectus/**) is a cooperative venture between CERN, MIT, and Institut National de Recherche en Informatique et en Automatique (INRIA). W3C's main purpose is the World-Wide Web Core Development (WebCore) project, which will evolve the Web standard. You should reference this site often to keep up with late-breaking developments in the standard.

What It Is Today

At this writing, the tools are finally available to begin to use the Web for business in earnest—not just for putting signposts on the information highway. It is now feasible for businesses to put whatever information they might distribute through print media (newspapers, magazines, direct mail) via the Web. The information dissemination and display capabilities of Web servers and browsers combined are now a strict superset of conventional media (with the exception of full motion video media right now). The demographics for Internet information distribution don't yet rival print media, but the installed base is estimated to be doubling every six months.

The current installed based of Web browser users is estimated to be in the tens of millions of users. Windows 95 is now available and not only includes a Web browser called Internet Explorer (based on Mosaic, and licensed from Spyglass Communications), but also includes an easily accessible Internet connection through the Microsoft Network. OS/2 3.0 (Warp) already includes both a Web browser and an 800 number for access to the Internet. Technical information for both Windows and OS/2 is already distributed from Web servers. With the introduction of Internet Explorer in Windows 95, a Web browser will be standard for anyone purchasing new equipment.

Other new developments include the emergence of secure servers, and standards for transmitting and receiving sensitive information (such as credit card numbers) over the Internet from Web browser to Web server. This critical mass of potential market, and recent technological advances have made it practical to not just distribute your business's information via the Web, but to actually conduct commerce over it. In later chapters, we present technology that makes Web-based commerce both feasible and secure. Let's begin by examining in detail the types of businesses appearing on the Web, what they're doing on the Web (what type of commerce or information distribution), and the methods that they are bringing to bear in doing it.

CHAPTER 2

THE WORLD OF BUSINESS WEB SERVERS: A BRIEF SURVEY OF BUSINESS APPLICATIONS

This chapter presents an overview of all current business uses of Web servers with samples of almost every type of existing business Web server used for publishing information and performing electronic commerce. These samples also show the potential designs of Web servers that might be used as a basis for the design of your business Web server. This survey is not meant to be anything like a tour guide of cool sites. There's just too much good content available now to make this practical in a book not devoted exclusively to Web browsing. The intent is not even to present a hot list of cool sites for business. The purpose is to give ideas on what is possible to do with a Web server.

First this chapter presents a list of good starting places to find Web sites. Several good indexes are provided that allow you to find Web sites in many categories of interest. Then, you learn how to search for Web resources without necessarily going through these clearinghouses. Finally a survey of interesting Web sites is presented that should yield good ideas for the kinds of applications that can be done via the Web, types of businesses on the Web, and emerging Web malls devoted to electronic commerce.

WEB INDEXES: ROADMAPS TO EVERYWHERE

Your discovery of what business resources are available on the Web has to begin somewhere. These sites are good places to start. This book is not a Web browser guide nor is it a Web site survey, but knowledge of the major Web server indexes is essential. You should be familiar with *every* Web site offering in your planned area of business. This is a constant struggle—thousands of new Web servers appearing monthly. More importantly, you should be aware of all Web sites in your area of business and of innovation in Web server content on no matter the type of business. This field is changing at breakneck speed: Web servers that seemed fresh and innovative a year ago look hopelessly dated now. You are faced with a large, growing and affluent audience, a dream demographic, but one that has a short attention span, patience, and is just a couple mouse clicks away from your nearest competitor.

Your Web surfing skills are just as much a part of being an effective webmaster as indepth knowledge of HTML or secure Web server standards. There are dozens of good books on available Web sites, but they are all hopelessly dated by the time they get in print. The indexes presented here, and the search sites shown in the next section are your best method of staying current.

W3 Consortium

The W3C (**http://www.w3.org**) site is essential background for the budding webmaster. There, the intricacies of HTML are documented (albeit in fragments amongst several disjoint hypertext links). These hypertext links are also a good jumping off point for most of the interesting Web servers. W3C has several excellent indexes to a wide variety of Web sites. W3C is distinguished by its multiple index approach, which organizes the site alphabetically, by subject, and by geography.

The Web Registry

W3C is the home of the Web registry (**http://www.w3.org/hypertext/DataSources/ WWW/Servers.html**) where all Web servers participating in the World Wide Web are listed (see Figure 2.1). When you get to the point of registering your Web site, check the site listed as the registration host for your region. In the United States, this is done on a state by state basis. Details of the registration process are presented in Chapter 16. In the meantime, if you know the approximate region of the site you are looking for, or if you are interested in listing all of the sites in a particular area, this is an excellent resource.

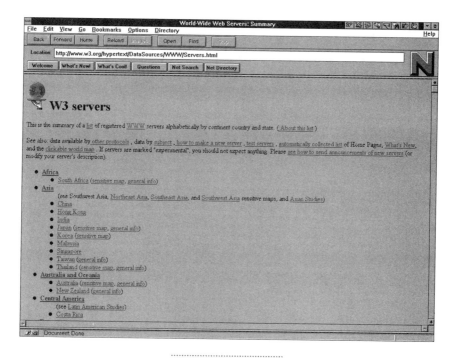

FIGURE 2.1 W3 CONSORTIUM

The WWW Virtual Library

The Virtual Library (**http://www.w3.org/hypertext/DataSources/bySubject/Overview.html**) has an excellent catalog of Web servers organized by subject (see Figure 2.2). It has multiple indexes: by subject, by subject, by Library of Congress standard. It also has a listing by Virtual Library which has a pretty good shot at being comprehensive since it is on the site where the Web Registry is located.

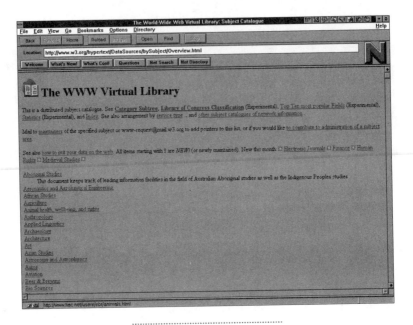

FIGURE 2.2 THE WWW VIRTUAL LIBRARY

NCSA Mosaic What's New and Starting Points Pages

The Mosaic new page (**http://www.ncsa.uiuc.edu/SDG/Software/Mosaic/Docs/ whats-new.html**) is one of the oldest on the net, and should certainly be on the list that a site should register itself with. It's still referenced by many Mosaic users. However, it has been superseded in thoroughness and currency by sites such as Yahoo.

The Starting Points page (**http://www.ncsa.uiuc.edu/SDG/Software/ Mosaic/StartingPoints/NetworkStartingPoints.html**) is much more relevant to beginning Web browser users than to people planning a Web site (see Figure 2.3). Nevertheless if your site is likely to draw Web newbies, you may want to include a link to this site where appropriate (such as an answer on a FAQ page).

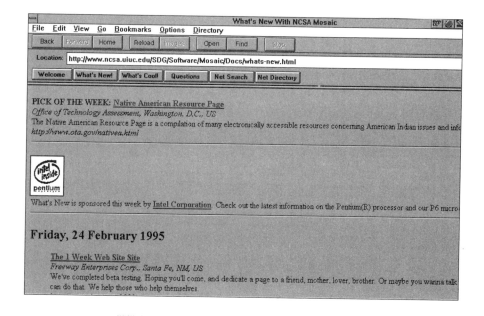

FIGURE 2.3 NCSA MOSAIC WHAT'S NEW AND STARTING POINTS PAGES

Yahoo

This is the motherlode. Yahoo (**http://www.yahoo.com**) is the most comprehensive manually-maintained site listing available, with over 50,000 sites now indexed (see Figure 2.4). One sign of this is that many other sites that used to maintain their own directories now just point to Yahoo. For example, Netscape Communications (authors of the enormously popular Netscape Web browser) used to maintain a What's New page; now they just point to Yahoo. Mosaic has completely removed their What's New page. This should be your first stop in browsing for a particular subject.

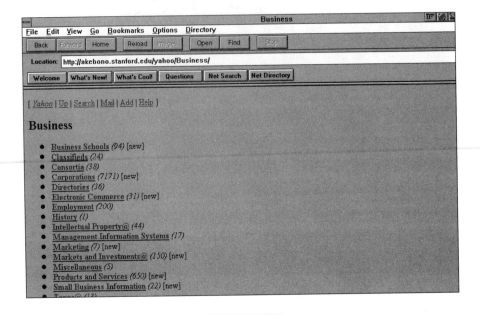

FIGURE 2.4 YAHOO

In just the business area alone Yahoo has over 10,000 links. The entire Yahoo site is very structured. Categories have subcategories to make them manageable, resulting in a site where there is rarely more than one entry per page. In keeping with its status as a functional tool, Yahoo makes minimal use of graphics or long textual descriptions. The content is the list itself.

The Yahoo index is also searchable with Boolean AND/OR combinations and can be searched by title, URL, or comments. Finally, despite the fact the Yahoo is the best index, it includes links to all of the other major indexes (including the one's listed here). Its search facility includes links to other searchable indexes (see Figure 2.5). Yahoo's quality may lead you to only stop there on your way to venturing to other Web sites. This is not a bad approach, but you should continue to be aware of the other indexes that may be more focused on business topics.

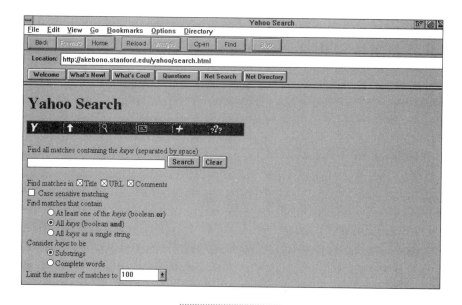

FIGURE 2.5 YAHOO SEARCH

Open Market's Commercial Sites Index

The most focused index of sites for our purposes is probably Open Market's Commercial Sites Index (**http://www.directory.net/**). This site used to be located at MIT, but was moved to this commercial site recently. This site provides a comprehensive list of business-related Web sites. The directory has a What's New page, is searchable by alphabetic keyword, or can be browsed alphabetically (see Figure 2.6). The alphabetical listing is divided into sections for Business and Commercial; Government; Organizations and Non-Profits; States, Cities, and Towns; Other Indexes. Some of the categories seem questionable for a commercial sites index. Indeed the vast majority of the approximately 2500 links are in the Business and Commerce area. Finer distinctions among the thousands of commercial links should be made to make this index truly useful.

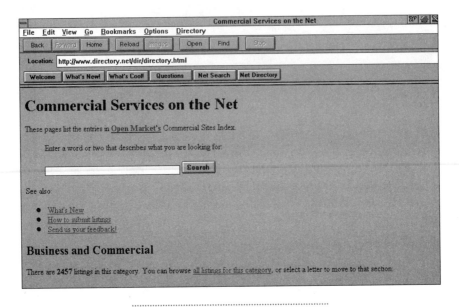

FIGURE 2.6 OPEN MARKET'S COMMERCIAL SIRES INDEX

Open Market may need more work now, but its status as a business-focused index means that you should continue to check it from time to time. As the content available on the Web explodes, it may be the only special purpose index that remains truly comprehensive.

EINet Galaxy

EINet Galaxy (**http://www.einet.net/galaxy.html**) maintains a subject index that is also searchable (see Figure 2.7). In contrast to Open Market's directory, EINet Galaxy's directory has a business section that is broken up into a very sensible division of subjects:

Business Administration	Business General Resources Consortia and Research Centers
Consumer Products and Services	Electronic Commerce General Products and Services
Investment Sources	Management Marketing and Sales

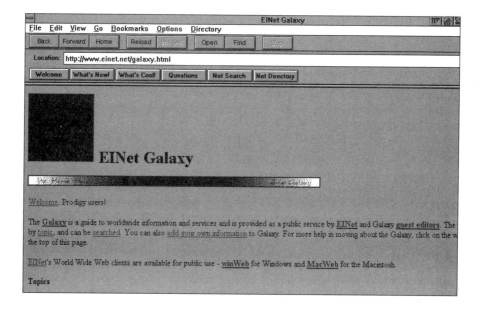

FIGURE 2.7 EINet Galaxy

FINDING RESOURCES ON THE WEB

If a site isn't listed directly on one of the clearinghouses and you need to find information on a topic, you will have to search for it somehow. Various Web searching tools are presented here. Utilizing these search resources effectively is an art and one that you will need to practice if you are to have any hope of remaining even remotely current with the methods and content of other Web sites in your field.

For each of the sites a fair amount of detail on the techniques used to do automatic retrieval and indexing of information is presented. The goal of presenting this detail on search strategy employed by these web crawlers is not to make you an expert in networked information retrieval, but to show you how to be an effective Web searcher. Understanding how the various crawlers operate will make you familiar with the limitations of each technique. Understanding those limitations should give you a better idea of what other search indexes to try, with what keywords, when a search on one index comes up empty.

CUI W3 Catalog

This site (**http://cuiwww.unige.ch/w3catalog**) is the first Web searcher and so has historical importance. But the technology used to maintain this catalog is a bit dated. It simply indexes the contents of the following catalogs (see Figure 2.8).

- NCSA What's New (nwn)
- NCSA's NCSA Starting Points (nsp)
- CERN's W3 Virtual Library Subject Catalog and selected sub-lists (cvl)
- Martijn Koster's Aliweb Archie-like Indexing for the Web (ali)
- Scott Yanoff's Internet Services List (isl)
- Simon Gibbs' list of Multimedia Information Sources (mis)
- John December's list of Computer-Mediated Communication Information Sources (cmc) and Internet Tools Summary (its)
- Marcus Speh's User Documents for DESY and HEP (msp)

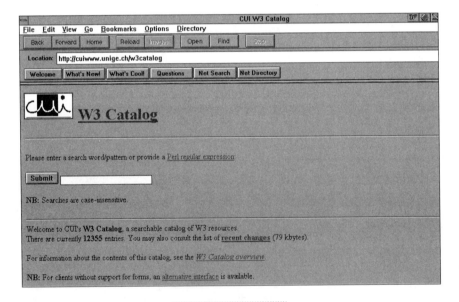

FIGURE 2.8 CUI W3 CATALOG

These catalogs are not comprehensive, however (some of them fall far short and thus were not listed in my list of the best indexes above). A better approach is to capitalize on the structure of the Web and its interconnectedness to build a truly comprehensive searchable index without human intervention.

World Wide Web Worm

Developed by Oliver McBryan at the University of Colorado, this site (**http://www.cs.colorado.edu/home/mcbryan/WWWW.html**) is the grandfather of the automatic searching tools (see Figure 2.9). The Worm lets you search by title of document, names of citing documents, citation text (linking text within the document you're searching for), and the URLs themselves that a document is linking to. The flexibility of the varied search approaches is very useful.

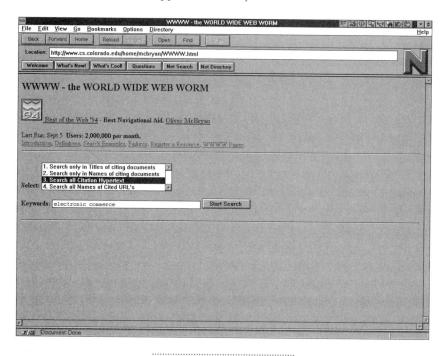

FIGURE 2.9 WORLD WIDE WEB WORM

The Worm builds its index by traversing the Web itself and indexing all the documents it finds. It indexes only the names of documents, the linking text within the documents, the URLs that that text links to, and the titles of documents. It turns out that this is a pretty good heuristic for the salient information in the document. But it's not perfect—many documents have important information and terms in them that aren't contained at all in link text, URLs, the title of the document, or the name (URL) of the document. An example is a leaf document, a document that is at the bottom level of a hierarchical tree of information, and doesn't link to anything else. Unless your search term is in the title or name, it is missed altogether. There are better approaches to searching. At a casual level, it would seem that heading and subheading names would be a useful approximation of significant content. Suffice it to say that if a search turns up empty on the Worm you should certainly not end your search there. You should also know that whatever search results you receive there are likely to be incomplete. Figure 2.10 shows the returned list from the search performed in Figure 2.9.

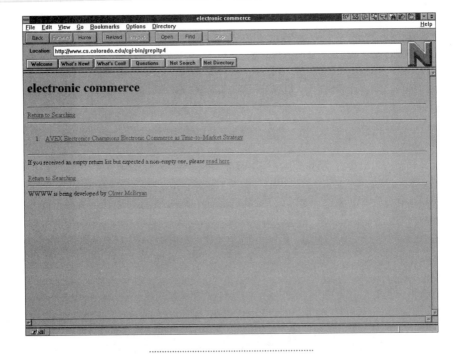

FIGURE 2.10 WORLD WIDE WEB WORM LIST

The Worm's status as one of the first automated searching mechanisms means that it is frequently very overloaded. This is not so bad actually, since Web automatic indexing technology has evolved a bit since McBryan's initial effort. There are now better sites to start your searches from.

Lycos

Lycos (**http://lycos.cs.cmu.edu/**) is an excellent indexer, probably the best available (see Figure 2.11). Due to its popularity it is also frequently overloaded. Lycos has resolved some of this problem by making available several Lycos servers, all of them linked to each other. If one server is overloaded, just click over to one of the other available servers.

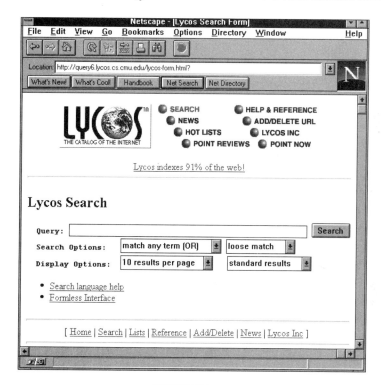

FIGURE 2.11 LYCOS

Lycos presents the user with a simple query field and the ability to restrict the number of hits to a specified number of the most relevant. The default search is to combine the keywords with ORs to search for documents containing any of the supplied words. However, documents containing occurrences of all presented terms will have higher relevancy scores, yielding something approaching an AND-style search. Lycos also has the capability of doing negation (all documents not containing a specified word), which is usually only useful in combination with a positive search for another term. Lycos also allows forcing exact matching by appending a period to the search term (only full word matching is returned). Quoted queries (of multiple search terms) and adjacency search is not supported.

The returned list is the most thorough of any of the search methods presented here (see Figure 2.12). Instead of just a list of sites or document URLs, Lycos returns a list of documents in relevance order, with a variety of information about each document, including an outline and an excerpt of the document to summarize the document content—very impressive.

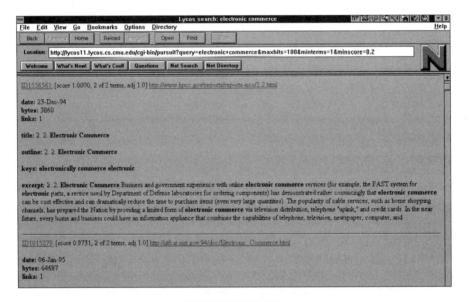

FIGURE 2.12 LYCOS LIST

To give you a better sense of what information Lycos is likely to find the following information is indexed by Lycos: title, headings and subheadings, important words, first 20 lines of the document. Important words are determined by their frequency in the document adjusted by how common a word it is. For example, very rare words that appear frequently in the document are weighted highest. Another nice innovation is that Lycos uses its own search results to build word frequency counts, rather than relying on static word frequency data (a more common technique).

Lycos narrows its search by only linking to http (Web server), ftp, and gopher URLs—the ones likely to have document content. Lycos also prunes its web constantly by clipping off paths it has already traversed and summarizes their content with a list of important words. This is a significant thing to know. It means that if the content of documents that you are searching for changes often (such as an online magazine), Lycos' summary of those documents might be obsolete. Lycos is a great tool, but that limitation means that you should still be aware of other search mechanisms, especially for information that might appear on sites whose content is changed frequently.

Harvest

Harvest is an Internet information gathering technology rather than a specific index to the Web. It can be used to index a wide variety of information. However, there are Harvest Brokers set up to search Webspace. One such site is **http://harvest.cs.colorado.edu/ brokers/www-home-pages/query.html** (shown in Figure 2.13).

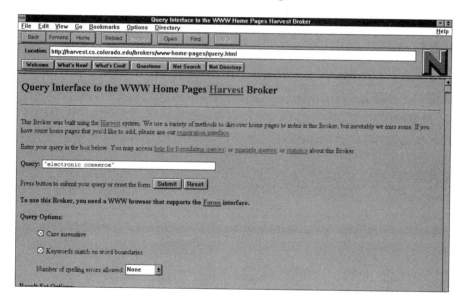

FIGURE 2.13 HARVEST

The returned list of sites is much terser, and I think more readable, than the Lycos list. It doesn't show relevancy ranking scores, but does return hits in relevance order. The only information it shows beyond the site and file address is the matched line, but that's probably enough to tell you whether the hit is truly significant or not (see Figure 2.14). In some cases it won't be. For each search you perform you will have to make a judgment about the most effective search method. Often Lycos will work best, many times Harvest will. In my experience, these two methods are the best.

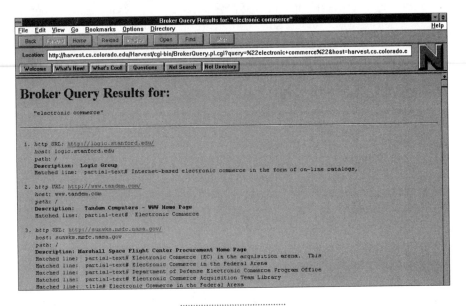

FIGURE 2.14 HARVEST LIST

Web Crawler

WebCrawler (**http://webcrawler.com**) was originally developed by Brian Pinkerton at the University of Washington in early 1994. This service is now owned by America Online. I don't find that I get quite the depth or precision with WebCrawler's limited search options, but it's significant in other ways. WebCrawler was one of the earliest spiders, and AOL's purchase of it represents the earliest large corporate acquisition of a Web spider and Web-related technology. It was also one of the first spiders to describe its architecture well.

The WebCrawler consists of three components:

- The database, which contains a list of documents and a fulltext index on the content of those documents.

- The search engine which finds additional documents to add to the database. It searches for additional documents using unvisited links from its existing database. WebCrawler's search engine works in breadth-first order—traversing the oldest unvisited links in order, rather than depth-first traversal down a specific document's link hierarchy. WebCrawler's search engine can also execute directed searches, traversing the links indicated by a user or administrator search, and adding those documents to the database.

- A group of agents. The agents perform the actual document retrieval as directed by the search engine. Typically several agents operate simultaneously. This architecture, and naming convention, is shared by many successor spider technologies.

FIGURE 2.15 WEB CRAWLER

Architext Excite

Architext's Excite searching service (**http://www.excite.com**) is distinguished by its concept-based searching—the ability to retrieve sites and documents without necessarily matching the words you supply. For example, a search for "online bookseller" (as shown in Figure 2.16) returns several documents where bookseller isn't mentioned at all, but bookstores are mentioned. You will want to use this service if your area of interest can't be neatly defined by a standard boolean keyword search. However, I have found that when a keyword search is appropriate, Lycos tends to produce more hits for a given search than Excite. Another distinguishing feature of Architext's site is the indexing of recent Usenet News postings and classified ads.

Architext's technology also promises to make the Web spider process of adding sites to a searchable database much more efficient. Architext proposes that each site does its own indexing, using Architext supplied software, so that the Architext spider can retrieve the information already indexed. This alleviates the burden of the spider servers doing the work to index the content of the thousands of servers that they access. The Architext engine is freely downloadable from Architext's Web site (**http://www.architext.com**), but is only available for Unix platforms at this writing.

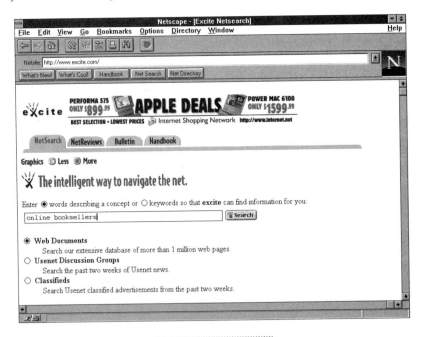

FIGURE 2.16 ARCHITEXT EXCITE

CYBERCASTING: PUBLISHING ON THE WEB

In the early years of the Web, before recent innovations in security, business use was really only providing information. So Web publishing actually has one of the richer traditions of Web use to survey and discuss. This section briefly surveys the various types of publishing already done on the Web.

The focus is on technique rather than content here. We want to show the gamut of possible uses of Web sites for providing information, different media and styles of providing that information, and different models for selling that information. There is now an incredible variety of news and information being published on the Web. The vast majority of it does not leverage strengths and capabilities of the Web platform fully. This results in many undoubtedly useful services, but since much of the information available via the Web is duplicated, there will soon be a shakeout where the commercial providers of Web information that survive are those that truly make use of the power of the Web.

For example, subscriber-based services (i.e. those that you need to join before using) should make use of their knowledge of the user to tailor information to the user (see the following on Quote.Com). Magazines that review products should link to the Web servers of the products they are reviewing (and the —company Web servers should link to reviews of their products). All publications should take advantage of the interactivity of the Web to allow both public and private feedback to the issues they are discussing. This makes interactive media, something that has been anticipated and promised and hyped for a long time now, a reality.

Next publishing services are described along with some of the best examples of services in each of those areas. These examples are chosen because out of the dozens of possible entrants in each category, they are both higher in overall quality and attempt to truly make use of the Web's publishing capabilities.

The Daily News

San Jose Mercury News

This is the first daily newspaper to hit the Web (**http://www.sjmercury.com/**) and they have had time to really get it right by now. Notice the unobtrusive method of advertising in the paper's contents (see Figure 2.17). In keeping with what we mentioned about utilized the hypertext nature of the Web, the *San Jose Mercury News* has links to a stock quote site, the DowVision WAIS server, and Lasser's Income Tax information Web site from the business section. They are annoying labeled hyperlinks (what else would they be?), but are nevertheless what online newspapers should all be doing. *San Jose Mercury News* also has feedback links to click on at the bottom of articles, which invokes the Web browser mail interface to send email to the paper. Again this could be done on a per author basis, but its presence is valuable.

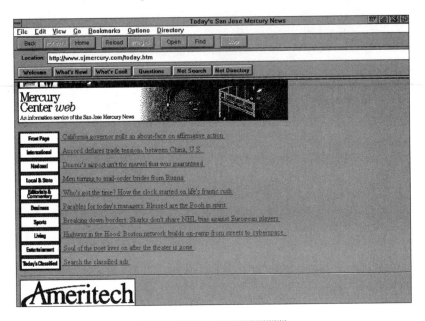

FIGURE 2.17 *SAN JOSE MERCURY NEWS*

My only complaint is that the articles themselves could make better use of the medium. They could have:

- **More structure.** Use HTML headings and subheadings.
- **More formatting.** Use what facilities are available in HTML to relieve the drab monotony of the presented text by using lists (ordered, unordered, and indented) and bold and italics for emphasis
- **More hypertext.** Containing links to related material in the current issue of the paper, back issues, and other electronic publications

Another missing features from the news sections is searchability. To their credit, there really is quite a bit of content on *San Jose Mercury News*. They do offer a news profiling service known as NewsHound, that actively searches for articles matching a user's configurable set of search terms, and emails those articles to the user. However, the ability to search it by keyword is really necessary. The lack of keyword searching may help to drive usage of the NewsHound service. Still its an omission to not have keyword searching available from the Web browser. If you have a large amount of information on your Web server don't make the same mistake.

The *San Jose Mercury News* has an extensive classified advertising section, drawn no doubt from the print version. However, it's not browsable without searching, as the print version would be. It's also impossible to submit your own ad from your Web browser. Even an email address would help. If you are planning a newsletter or newspaper-like site with classifieds, you will definitely want to allow Web browser-based ad submission. Browsing of the ads without searching is also potentially valuable, but a truly huge ad base might make the Mercury News approach more sensible.

The Gate: the *San Francisco Chronicle* and the *San Francisco Examiner*

The Gate is a newer online newspaper entry and it shows. The Gate combines content from San Francisco's dailies, but its content is only a small subset of the real paper's. A look at the top level of the Gate gives a good clue as to how thin the content might be (see Figure 2.18).

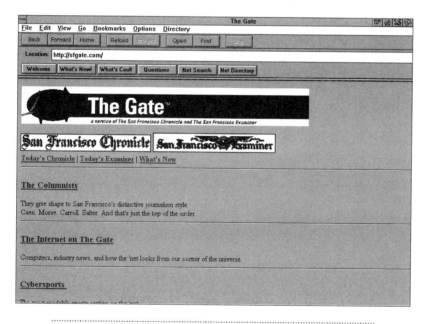

FIGURE 2.18 THE GATE: THE *SAN FRANCISCO CHRONICLE* AND THE *SAN FRANSICSO EXAMINER*

The *Chronicle's* approach is to give out content dynamically via CGI gateways (more on that subject later), presumably from some master database of articles. The idea behind this approach is to insure currency of the article and to eliminate duplicate storage. In practice this seems to yield some problems with performance and reliability. Response times on several ventures to this site were atrocious (mostly on the CGI-generated content). Also, many holes and idiosyncrasies in the data appeared. In the chapters on implementation, I'll discuss the pros and cons of generating content on-the-fly via gateways.

Notice in Figure 2.19 the stark simplicity of the layout. In the world of the Web where much more is possible, such simplicity is not a virtue. *The Chronicle* does have some nice features: their classifieds (in contrast to *Mercury News*) are browsable. Also they have a search feature, originally implemented with the Lycos Web searching code. The search feature is now offline, but will presumably be upgraded to a full text searchable WAIS server some time in the near future. In summary, this effort has a few nice features that you may want to investigate, but the site as a whole is unsatisfying and not to be emulated.

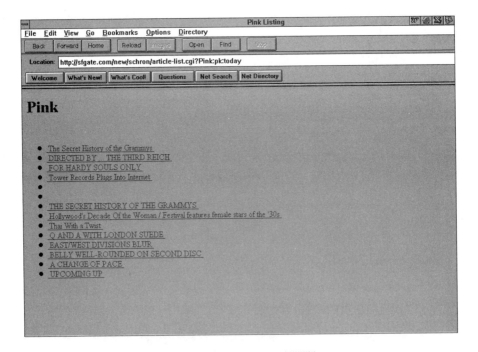

FIGURE 2.19 SAN FRANCISCO CHRONICLE

Nando Times

Although non-commercial, Nando is a particularly well-designed site for publishing newsbriefs. At the top level, a blurb of about a dozen late-breaking stories is presented in five areas: world news, U.S. news, financial, technology, and sports. Clicking on any of these areas presents a list of news headlines in reverse chronological order. About five or so new headlines are presented each day.

Webmasters that are planning some form of frequently updated news or information publishing should monitor this site for a period of time.

Periodicals

PCWeek

Ziff Davis puts out their weekly trade rag (**http://www.ziff.com/~pcweek/-Welcome.html**) in close to its full text form, free to any Web browser. The layout is not incredibly creative: very little use of graphics and no links to other Internet sites within articles (see Figure 2.20). Also, initially *PCWeek* had a FreeWAIS interface allowing searching for articles, but this was removed. A more compelling example of a Ziff Web site in terms of design and layout is their *PC Magazine* Web site.

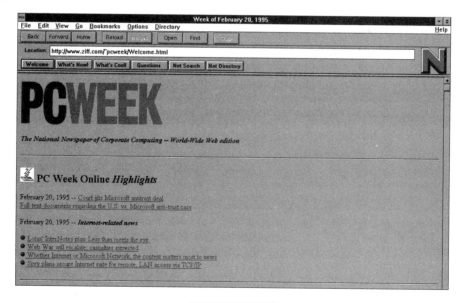

FIGURE 2.20 PCWEEK

PC Magazine

More compelling is another Ziff publication, *PC Magazine* (**http://www.ziff.-com/~pcmag/**). Each page has a high degree of navigability, with links to the PC Mag home page, the issue home page, and other relevant articles (see Figure 2.21). Files associated with articles have ftp links. Articles also have links to subscription information, which can be done via Web form or fax. A form for user feedback is presented with links to each *PC Magazine* editor. Clicking on these links (within any browser that supports the mailto HTML extension) invokes an email form. Its great, but the feedback link should email back to the author of each article, rather than the webmaster. They have even maintained a semblance of the *PC Magazine* layout, with pictures of the columnists centered above each column.

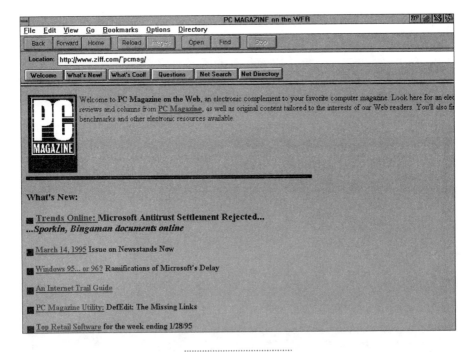

FIGURE 2.21 PC MAGAZINE

PC Magazine balances the tradeoff between a free electronic version that adds value to the paper version, and the need to make the paper version have value that is not presented in the free electronic version. There is a section called News Watch that provides daily updates of late-breaking news in the PC industry, truly leveraging the Web site for its unique strengths. But they withhold some content from Web version, while listing the article names in the online table of contents. They also list summaries of the feature stories, but withhold many of the features for the paper version.

This site is a model of how to put a magazine online. The following basic ideas can be imitated by any online publication.

- Lots of navigational links.
- Index of back issues.
- Clickable invocation of email for feedback.
- Easy subscription ordering to the paper equivalent (preferably with a Web-based form).
- Frequent news updates in areas of interest.
- Withholding some information for the print version.

HotWired

Wired Magazine's Web equivalent is HotWired (**http://www.hotwired.com**), although HotWired is really a magazine unto itself (see Figure 2.22). The people at *Wired* planned the electronic version to supplement rather than replace the print version—and it's done well. HotWired does not contain all of the articles from the print version. It contains some content from the print version and includes advance previews of forthcoming content, including several articles that never make their way into the print *Wired*. It's also a vehicle for presenting very timely, late-breaking stories. The Signal section houses most of the online articles. Within signal, the Flux column presents late-breaking Internet development with an irreverent tone. What Flux does do that none of the other publishing providers here do, is present hypertext links within the articles. They seem to have a rule of thumb of one link for every paragraph. That's great! It's how it should be done. It doesn't cost anything (except the mental bandwidth of the page designer) to put those links there.

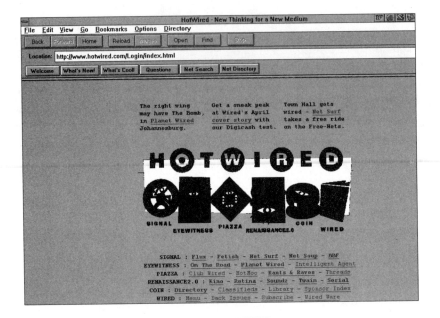

FIGURE 2.22 HOTWIRED

The NetSurf column surveys recent new Web URLs and other net happenings, with hypertext links to those sites of course. NetSoup contains a sampling of Usenet posts. But what's really innovative about these columns, and others on HotWired, is that at the bottom of the columns are links to a Web-based discussion medium—essentially a Usenet News-like forum for discussing the content (or topics loosely related to the content) of the article. The beauty of HotWired's approach is that the discussion areas are tied directly to the article content. Not everyone does things this way, but its the way to do it. This yields greater possibilities than conventional Usenet newsgroups or CompuServe forums. Discussions take place in the context of their subject matter. If you are going to have interactive discussion on your site (we will show you later some of the technology that enables this), you owe it to yourself to evaluate the way Wired implemented their discussions threads. Figure 2.23 is a sample thread that was attached to the Flux column (Netscape's Andreessen responding to a Flux generated rumor). Notice that the postings themselves have hypertext links embedded.

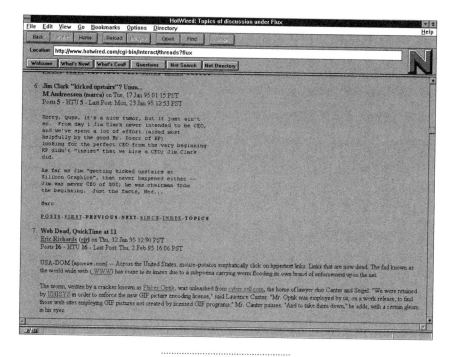

FIGURE 2.23 HOTWIRED THREADS

HotWired also has a gallery of images, sounds and video, to which readers can contribute to from their Web browser. There is also an electronic marketplace, that accepts digital cash (specifically a trial version of DigiCash's eCash) for a few sample items. For example, you can purchase an article from a future issue with 50 cents of eCash. One third of the proceeds from that purchase go to the author. You can get $100 of eCash free from the DigiCash Web server by setting up an account on a test basis. The marketplace contains advertisements for HotWired's sponsors to supplement the sponsor logos that appear on most article pages. There are also classifieds ads in a number of areas (see Figure 2.24). They're not incredibly high in content but reasonably well assembled with some nice features. Finally there is a section devoted to Wired's print products and Wired-related merchandise. You can order back issues, subscribe, and purchase Wired paraphernalia from this area.

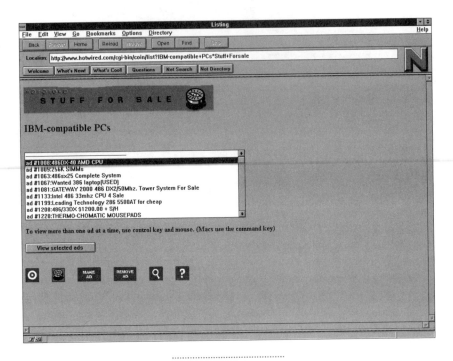

FIGURE 2.24 HOTWIRED ADS

In summary, HotWired serves two purposes that *Wired* can't: interactive discussion and an online marketplace. These goals add value that doesn't exist in the print version, yet the print version is still profitable by containing more content and (right now) more precise and creative graphics and layout. If you need to achieve the same kind of balance between print and electronic versions—leveraging the strengths of both environments by opening new market opportunities with your electronic version, yet keeping your printed material commercially viable, you owe it to yourself to study HotWired's approach thoroughly.

O'Reilly's Global Network Navigator

At the other extreme of the print to electronic medium spectrum is the Web-only based magazine about the Internet and the Web called Global Network Navigator (see Figure 2.25) now owned by America Online. GNN asks its readers to subscribe by registering on a form, but the subscription itself is free (available at **http://nearnet.gnn.com/gnn/index.html**). Advertising is sold on GNN, presumably at profitable prices that reflect the demographics GNN can provide to advertisers about each reader. GNN has great coverage of news about the Internet itself and links to their own online store which primarily sells O'Reilly's UNIX and Internet publications.

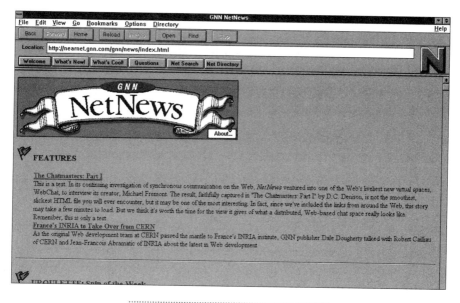

FIGURE 2.25 O'REILLY'S GLOBAL NETWORK NAVIGATOR

The business model here is simple: make money from advertising alone, not by supplementing a print-based product. There is no print-versus-Web content tradeoff to manage. Also, since GNN authored for the Web from the beginning there is more hypertext in the articles than with the converted magazines such as *PC Week* and *PC Magazine*.

Search Services

Table-of-Contents, Inc.

ToC, Inc. (**http://www.mag-browse.com/**) provides a very useful publishing related service and is a good example of providing valuable collections of other's content. ToC contains the table of contents of current editions of dozens of popular periodicals (see Figure 2.26). It's a great way to perform quick research on current topics or stay current on a wide variety of technical publications to the point of knowing when an article of interest is published. ToC is WAIS indexed and searchable from your Web browsers. So if you want to remain current on some topic, you only need to surf over to the ToC, search for some keywords, and make sure that you purchase periodicals with high relevance ranking to your search criteria.

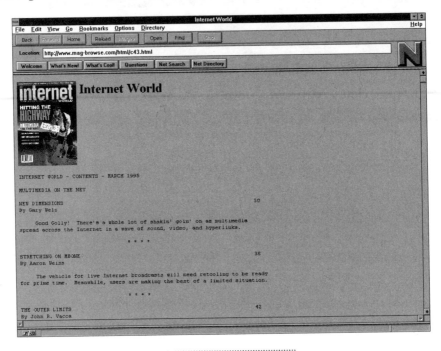

FIGURE 2.26 TABLE-OF CONTENTS, INC.

I include this site here as the canonical example of an online resource that *completely* supplements print content. It doesn't replace any similar print resource (which couldn't remain nearly as current on a real-time basis), and it actually creates demand for those periodicals for which it provides outlines and summaries. If you are asked to create an online version of an existing information base, a searchable, indexed collection of summaries and outlines of those resources may be a good approach, especially if supplanting the print resource is a financial risk. Other search services however are becoming more aggressive about providing greater capabilities electronically than are available in print medium.

Dow Vision WAIS Interface

For more complete searching of available news stories, Dow Jones now offers a free Web-accessible WAIS interface to their DowVision news product (**http://dowvision.wais.net**) that contains full text of many information sources, including of course Dow Jones News Service (see Figure 2.27). Other sources include *The Wall Street Journal* itself, *Business Wire*, and *The New York Times*, though only the current day's content of the Times is carried.

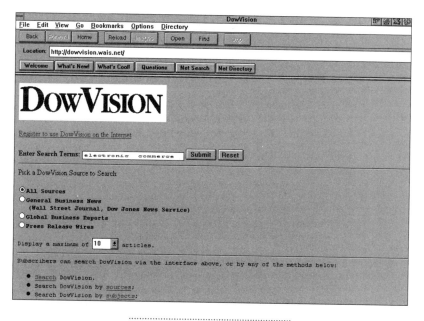

FIGURE 2.27 DOW VISION WAIS INTERFACE

The search interface allows control of news sources searched, which can reduce duplication of story content. It also allows a maximum number of hits to be set, in which case only the most relevant stories are returned. The resulting hit list indicates the headline, date, size of story, and relevancy score (see Figure 2.28). Notice however that the stories are not retrieved in order of relevance, a major drawback when many stories are retrieved but you only wish to review the top few. Also note that the list does not indicate news source. If your site will include a searchable index of information you should pay attention to such details.

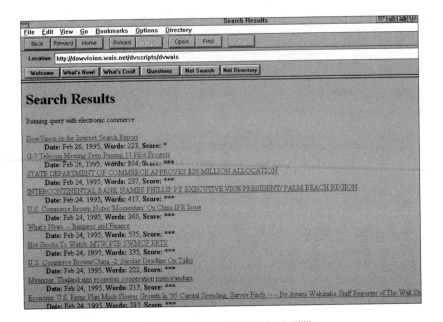

FIGURE 2.28 DOW VISION WAIS INTERFACE LIST

Quote.Com

An example of a membership-based searchable information service is Quote.Com. This service (**http://www.quote.com**) offers news and stock information to paid subscribers. A high quality selection of wire service information is presented: PR Newswire, Business Wire, and S&P MarketScope to name a few (see Figure 2.29). Users search these services by ticker symbol. Quote.Com and the wire services they supply have solved the dilemma of how to earn money from electronic versions of their information by restricting access to subscribers only. Subscribers log on to Quote.Com with a user ID and password, and are limited to a fixed amount of searches per day.

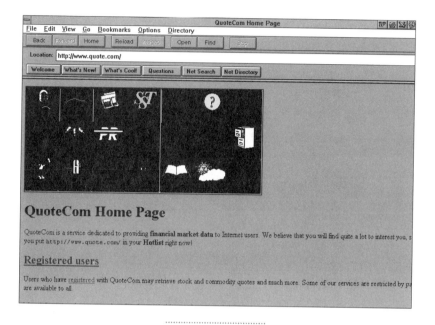

Quote.Com's basic service ($9.95 per month) provides up to 100 stock quotes per day, maintenance of up to a 50 stock portfolio on the Quote.Com system, retrieval of up to 25 Hoover Company Profiles per day, and the ability to order annual reports (up to 20 per day). PR NewsWire and BusinessWire are available for $9.95 per month and also allow a limited number of searches per day (see Figure 2.30). For basic service subscribers, news items are emailed on all stocks in their portfolio. S&P MarketScope is a comprehensive daily update on the market (earnings estimate updates, new issues, takeover activity, headlines) priced at $14.95 per month. The Standard & Poor's Stock Guide is available for $24.95 per month and allows retrieval of balance sheet data for up to 25 companies per day.

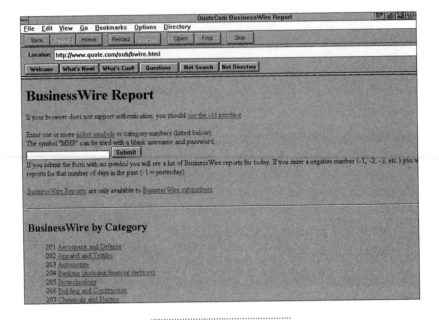

FIGURE 2.30 BUSINESS WIRE REPORT

Quote.Com is an excellent example of repackaging existing electronic information sources into a synergistic whole that is greater than the sum of its parts. Subscribers to the basic service get an innovative useful service, the online portfolio builder with automatic daily valuation. The premium services (the various wire services) build upon this basic service (specifically the portfolio information) to provide their information in a more useful format than the native wire services themselves. Its a lot more useful to get PR News and Business Wire emails on just the stocks in my portfolio automatically each day, than it is for me to work directly with either of those wire services to get more information on my own.

Whether or not you are planning a financial service Web server, the model Quote.Com provides can work for any Web provider, as long as you do the following.

- Provide a useful application to the end user at little or no cost, and
- Use the information you get from that to provide higher cost services in a manner tailored to the user based on the information you have acquired about them

A natural extension of this philosophy would be for Quote.Com to offer stock trading from the same service, with a similar level of integration.

BUSINESSES ON THE WEB

By this time there are thousands of businesses of the Web and I don't attempt to catalog them all here. Instead I focus on the types of uses that businesses are making of the Web, and the uses that are closest to the spirit of electronic commerce. A condition for being included in this list is that whatever each of these businesses do can actually be conducted over the Web—online advertisement sites are not included. Also, these are individual businesses that provide their own Web servers, as distinguished from the online malls described in the next section.

Finance: Aufhauser WealthWEB

Aufhauser (**http://www.aufhauser.com**) is a deep discount broker. This service provides online stock trading at very inexpensive rates. The site itself is pretty plain but very functional, and it highlights well the advantages of a Web-based online commercial service versus other online options (see Figure 2.31). Why? Because online trading has been possible through other venues for years. E*Trade and Quick & Reilly provide online trading through CompuServe. Schwab has their own proprietary electronic trading interface that has been very successful. Advantages of Web-based trading over these other methods include the following.

- Attractive appearance.
- No need for custom software to access.
- No online charges.
- Access to the service using the same application you use for the rest of your Web surfing.
- Access from anywhere in the world where you can get an Internet connection.
- Most importantly—quick access (via a few hypertext clicks) to the information necessary to make intelligent decisions. Even where Aufhauser doesn't provide links to relevant background material, you are just a bookmark away from Quote.Com and other information sources on the Web.

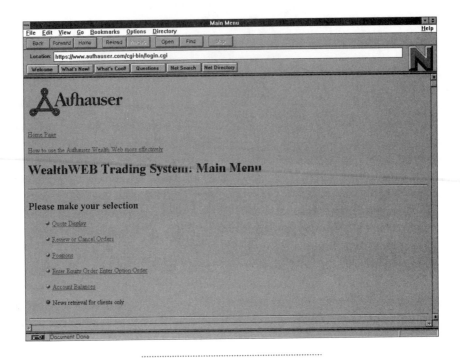

FIGURE 2.31 FINANCE: AUFHAUSER WEALTH WEB

Aufhauser is also significant in their early adoption of emerging security standards for electronic commerce. Aufhauser takes advantage of Netscape's Secure Sockets Library interface when talking to Netsite servers. That is, Aufhauser is running their Web server off of Netscape's Netsite commercial secure Web server. (These topics are covered in detail in Chapter 12 on security and Chapter 9 on Web server software.) When sending information back to Aufhauser, such as logon id and password, or when placing trades, the information is encrypted by the Netscape Web browser and decrypted by the server. Aufhauser is one of the first commercial sites to begin doing this. They are worth monitoring closely, since they will likely remain on the leading edge of deploying Web security solutions.

Software: The Internet Software Store

This store (**http://software.net**) sells thousands of software titles from its Web server, including electronic software delivery (see Figure 2.32). The Software Store also uses the

Netsite Secure Server for protection of credit card data. Thus they don't have to take the approach of Internet Shopping Network (another Web-based vendor that sells a lot of software that we describe later) where one has to join via a manual fax process for security.

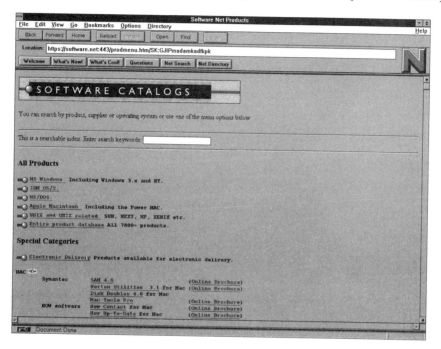

FIGURE 2.32 SOFTWARE: THE INTERNET SOFTWARE STORE

Music: Sound Wire

An online CD store (**http://soundwire.com/**), Sound Wire allows transactions to be submitted via PGP encrypted mail, through the use of electronic cash (specifically NetCash), and through the use of First Virtual's electronic payment scheme. Sound Wire also is one of the few sites, possibly the only commercial site, to use sound in their content (for, you guessed it, album samples). They've managed to overcome the uniformity that the Web imposes to some degree to create their own graphical style (see Figure 2.33). They really should have a search facility—the lettered selection mechanism to navigate to artists is awkward and doesn't scale well. Its very popular on the Web—but I wouldn't recommend it.

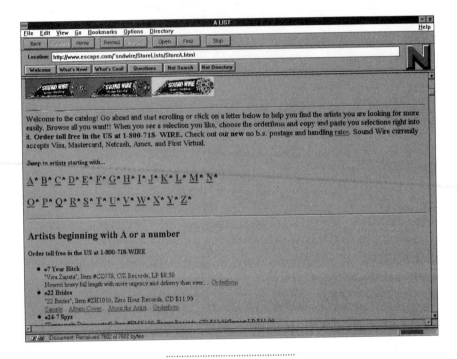

FIGURE 2.33 MUSIC SOUND WIRE

Sound Wire's shop is a model of high information content and innovative options in purchasing.

Books: O'Reilly's Online Bookstore

O'Reilly is a leading publisher (and certainly the most focused) of Internet and UNIX-related information (see Figure 2.34). Though billing themselves as a mall, O'Reilly's site (**http://www.ora.com/gnn/bus/ora/catalog/index.html**) is really too narrow in content to be considered as such. At this writing, the stores are limited to O'Reilly's books; Nolo Press, a publisher of legal self-help books; and a coffee merchant. O'Reilly has a lot of content about each product, with links to full descriptions and reviews. In fact, that's the reason for its inclusion here: high information content and lots of links on all their carried products. Unfortunately other aspects of O'Reilly Direct aren't really exemplary. It doesn't currently allow ordering from Web-based forms: only email, fax, or phone. They don't even offer PGP-encrypted email to place the order, despite the fact that the book on PGP is an O'Reilly title!

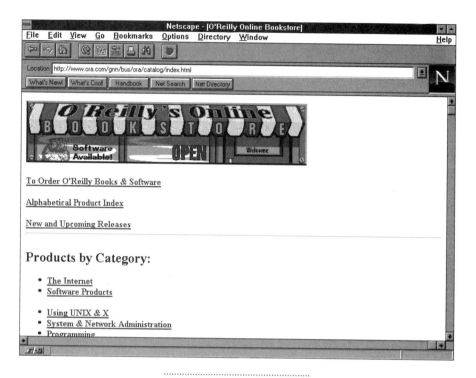

FIGURE 2.34 BOOKS: O'REILLY DIRECT

Wine: Virtual Vineyards

This site (**http://virtualvin.com**) is a well executed focused product store (selling wine of course) that has an exemplary level of information content (crucial in an online store). It is beautifully laid out by a very competent HTML author, who among other tricks has concocted an innovative order entry system (see Figure 2.35). Virtual Vineyards also follows another golden rule of Web design (more on those later): many different views on the same content. You can browse the available wines by varietal, label, or category. Yet another nice feature (again mentioned in our guidelines for good Web content): to supplement the large amount of information content virtualvin has an interactive section "Ask the Cork Dork." The interactive aspect isn't fully automated yet (it should allow users to post directly to the site as with HotWired), but emailing to post articles is clickable from the interactive content page.

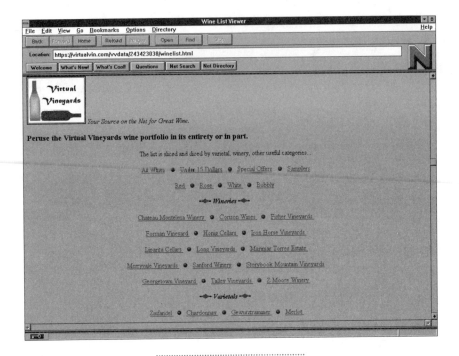

FIGURE 2.35 WINE: VIRTUAL VINEYARDS

One missing feature however is a search facility. Perhaps there isn't enough content to justify it yet, but its easy to imagine it growing large enough to do so. That brings up the other complaint: lack of selection. All the nice features of this system aren't enough if it's not used because serious wine shoppers (the type that would hit this site) go elsewhere for their purchases.

Pizza Hut

This site (**http://www.pizzahut.com**) is an experimental online pizza delivery service, now operating only in Santa Clara, California. What distinguishes Pizza Hut's site is the ordering interface tailored to their product (see Figure 2.36). Users design their pizza from a series of combo boxes. This approach is still relatively unique—most ordering forms just list all the products and allow the user to click on the items they want, but it's the way to do almost any service-like product (a category which most restaurant food falls into).

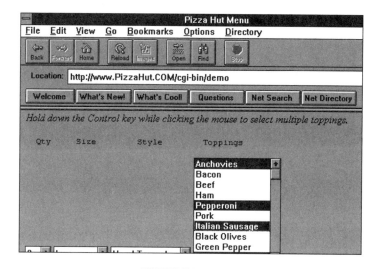

FIGURE 2.36 PIZZA HUT

This highlights one of the strengths of the Web for commerce. Custom interfaces for individual products are relatively easy to assemble via HTML forms—it would be much more work to create a custom Windows app and no one would use it anyway. With HTML, forms can be tailored to a very fine level of detail, but anyone can access the form from their Web browser.

Waiters on Wheels

Waiters on Wheels (**http://www.sunnyside.com**) is another restaurant delivery service; one that operates in a dozen cities. It's the same concept as Takeout Taxi and other services affiliated with a selection of local restaurants to offer call-in meal delivery. What's unique about Waiters on Wheels is that they're allowing online access to the service via a Web server (see Figure 2.37).

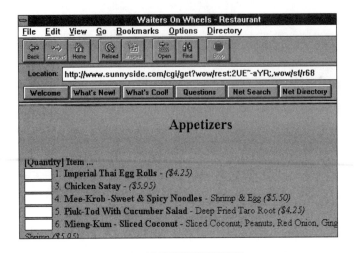

FIGURE 2.37 WAITERS ON WHEELS

As an example, the San Francisco WoW site has over two dozen restaurants. Each restaurant's menu is custom prepared as a Web-based form. It doesn't have the same fine-grained approach to each selection—one just picks a quantity of each menu item. When finished selecting, click on **Tally Selected Items** and your order is summarized. You are then prompted for the specific information about your order, including credit card information which is (gasp!) transmitted in the clear over the Internet. Despite that major faux pas, this a fairly innovative site that you should pay close attention to if you are contemplating any form of delivery-oriented service.

WEB MALLS

Although we admire the efforts of individual stores to appear on the Web, the sites mentioned above are really the best of an otherwise largely mediocre field. The fact is it currently takes a fair amount of expertise both in HTML authoring and programming (for those sites using CGI gateways for real-time data access) and in the design and graphical layout skills to do an attractive site. So despite the fact that you will leave this book with enough knowledge to create your own site, you may still want to assign that responsibility down to a full-time Web author, and perhaps to a full-time Web hosting facility as well.

In this section we will present some of the commerce clearinghouses that have started to emerge. You may be interested in them as just a service to host your content (keeping authoring to yourself), or as complete one-stop shopping for getting quick presence on the Web (you just supply them raw data). There is one other major factor in favor of the Web-based malls: secure methods for payment information (credit card encryption and electronic cash). This is still a difficult issue to plan and implement. Use of a commercial Web service may allow multiple vendors to share the effort in creating a very easy to use and secure payment infrastructure. Unfortunately, as we will see, not every site does a good job in this regard.

NetMarket

NetMarket (**http://www.netmarket.com**) is certainly among the earliest to recognize the promise of the Web as a venue for electronic commerce. Founded in early 1994, it was possibly the first Web mall to exist. It also incorporated use of PGP very early.

However the content is a bit thin. As of this writing, a CD catalog and a flower delivery service is the entire list of storefronts. The CD catalog is functional, but there are no album reviews and few sound bites. However, they have recently been acquired by CUC International and as a result supposedly much more content is now on the way.

One of the unique features of this site is that on many pages no savable HTML is returned. All presented information is output from CGI gateways (it's generated on the fly), and the Save As in your browser has no effect. It's not really generated on the fly. This technique might be useful if you have some HTML presentation techniques that you think are really innovative. I'm not sure that this applies to NetMarket, but they have security for whatever cool tricks they might come up with in the future. However, many browsers can circumvent this technique and save the content regardless. So don't depend too much on the privacy of your HTML. NetMarket recognizes this and they state in comments in their HTML source: "Thanks for reading our sources!"

Though an early entry into this field, their interface now seems plain vanilla in comparison to other sites (see Figure 2.38). Although they do have graphical and text equivalents of each page, their graphics are for the most part limited to two color buttons for command selections. Also note in the example below of the main "market" page, that the vast majority of the page is header content before finally presenting the icons of the two lonely vendors. In fairness, the low level of content doesn't yield too many opportunities for interface creativity. For example, if they had more stores, opportunities for graphical information maps might present themselves.

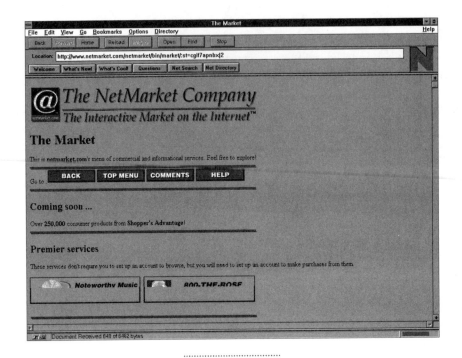

FIGURE 2.38 NETMAKER

Finally, with regard to payment methods, NetMarket allows payment via PGP-encrypted email and a secure Web browser. PGP is a public-private key encryption technology that we'll cover in detail in Chapter 8. It's great that they offer PGP-encrypted email, however, currently there are not any PGP email clients (a huge business opportunity if there are any developers reading this!). This means that the user must manually generate a text file, encrypt it by invoking the PGP command line program with the public key of NetMarket (that they make available as clear text), and paste the text file into their email client. This is a lot of work to do on a per transaction basis, and I doubt they have many users doing this.

The other option is a secure Web browser. Unfortunately they are using the httpd secure Web server (more information on this in the Web server chapter). This means that they can only use the Mosaic for X Windows Web browser to get secure transmission (Mosaic for Windows does not yet have secure transmission). Really what these two facts mean is that there are not yet any good options for secure payment on this Web Mall. Of course they do offer all of the offline secure options to set up an account, such as fax, phone, and snail mail. But in my opinion the commercial hosting services that succeed will be those that offer secure payment methods to a wide group of users. As we shall see, this is still an emerging capability.

Internet Shopping Network

At the other end of the scale in breadth of content lies the Internet Shopping Network (**http://shop.internet.net/**). ISN is a subsidiary of the Home Shopping Network, giving them a leg up on the ability to attract merchants and products. But this is not the cubic zirconia and porcelain figures hocked by online talkmeisters. ISN has recognized their core user base and restricted the products to computer-related wares, and has really taken advantage of the online medium in planning the offering. The products are divided into categories such as Windows products, CD-ROM products, Macintosh products, hard disks, modems, and games. ISN has also included a few outside vendors: FTD Florists and Hammacher Schlemmer (see Figure 2.39).

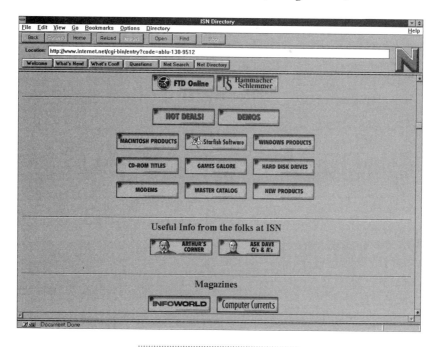

FIGURE 2.39 INTERNET SHOPPING NETWORK

You can search for the desired product via HTML forms (see Figure 2.40). The search has a useful degree of customizability: you can limit it by category, product name, company name, and price. This capability doesn't exist elsewhere (now) among the commercial Web vendors, and it's incredibly useful. If you have any breadth of content at all on your commercially oriented server, you should have a similar capability.

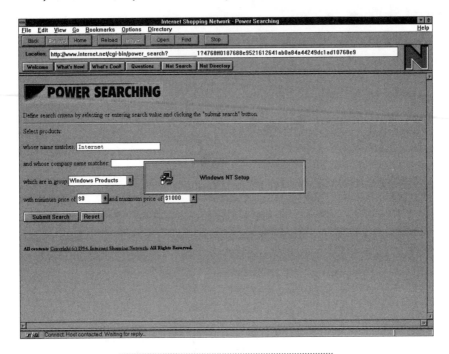

FIGURE 2.40 INTERNET SHOPPING NETWORK POWER SEARCH

Once the product listing is retrieved, you can read the product description, search for InfoWorld reviews on the product, or search for related software demos. Again, the tie to other related online material is invaluable. Figure 2.41 is an example search return for reviews on O'Reilly's Internet-in-a-Box. If you want to allow such searchability of large document bases, read Chapter 10 on WAIS integration closely.

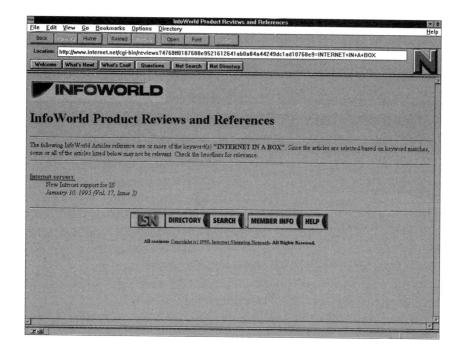

FIGURE 2.41 INFOWORLD REVIEWS

Despite all of ISN's strengths you cannot become a member online. You must fill out a form and fax it in. The reason they give is, correctly, insecurity of credit card information. But no plans for the use of PGP for a more automated approach to security are given. Also, they do not incorporate or mention any plans to incorporate electronic cash into their service. Electronic cash may not be appropriate for their computer hardware and software offerings, but it's certainly appropriate for the gift and flower shops that they host.

Right now ISN is the model for the multiproduct Web-based store. Calling them a mall is a small stretch because it's mostly their products, but they do host a couple other stores. Also the content they create for these other stores is carefully tuned for the products they sell. The forms to order flowers have options in their pick lists such as choosing the color of flowers. Their page layouts incorporate graphics where appropriate (in most content) but they're always small for speed of download and they don't get in the way.

Open Market

Strictly speaking Open Market (**http://www.openmarket.com**) is more than just a mall, its primary mission is software to assist in creating Web-based stores. Nevertheless, they do provide a marketplace as well. The content however is very thin, and the layout is nothing to get excited about, especially for a site that claims they offer software with which to create Web stores (see Figure 2.42). They do a better job in their role as a directory of commercial Web sites as listed earlier, although still not yet as good as Yahoo. We include this as a warning to potential Web mall creators: have enough content to earn the title or you will reduce your credibility enormously, especially if part of your role is to act as a software or services provider to other vendors.

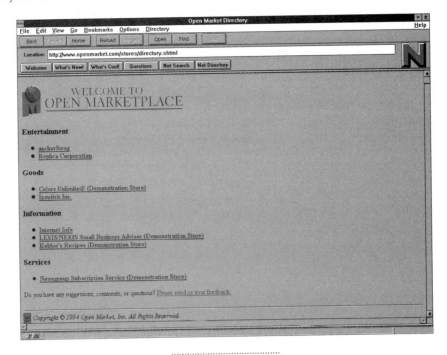

FIGURE 2.42 OPEN MARKET

CyberMalls

This is a nationwide network of regional Web-based malls. As an example, we review Rocky Mountain CyberMalls. RMCM (**http://www.hardiman.com/malls/rmcm/#directory**) is another site relatively light on content (see Figure 2.42). It contains the vast sum of:

- A department store with limited selections of a few types of merchandise.

- A travel agency that lists three cruise packages and two travel clubs. The U.S. travel club description does not even describe how to join or contact the travel club.

- A business/financial services page all of whose links went nowhere at the time I tried them

The only thing remotely innovative at this site is an electronic town hall. Paying $20 allows you the glorious privilege of browsing an all text description (the whole voting area is one big gob of unformatted text) of a bill for Congress, and voting for or against.

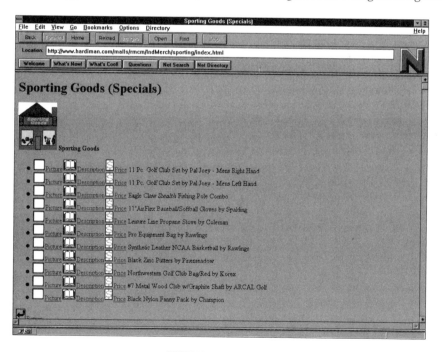

FIGURE 2.43 CYBERMALLS

Many if not most of the CyberMall's lower level pages have links that in some cases go nowhere and in other cases inform the user that the page is still under construction (how's that for consistency?) The department store layout has the labeling text misaligned under the graphic images (perhaps assuming a fixed pitch font?). The product listings force the user to click one icon for a picture, another for a description, and another for a price.

It's a Web browser's nightmare. No user has the patience to click three times just to get information on a product. This site is my nomination for the Web Hall of Lame. Perhaps the content and presentation of RMCM will improve over time, but not many users are going to be checking back to find that out. I include it here to give budding webmasters a great example of what not to do. The one redeeming feature of the entire site is the index to other more presentable Web malls.

Despite the missteps in this category, we believe that the Web-based mall is the best vehicle to getting businesses content online, be it for electronic commerce or publishing information. Nevertheless, you will finish this book with enough information to outdo many of the Web-based malls, so this assessment may not apply to you by the time you're finished reading. To that end, lets begin giving you the information you need to create these commercial applications.

PART 2

BUILDING YOUR WEB CONTENT

## CHAPTER 3

DESIGNING YOUR WEB

A FRAMEWORK FOR PLANNING YOUR WEB

Now that you've seen the diversity of content that other webmasters in your field have created, you're probably eager to start building your own site. Before you begin that task in earnest, step back for a moment and take time to formally plan your content. The chapter begins with a methodology for designing your Web server content. I have found the guidelines presented here to be useful in planning a wide variety of Web sites. But the commandments here are not written in stone. It's most important that you have a plan before implementation, and some orderly way of developing that plan.

Outline Your Content

While a good Web server doesn't have to be strictly hierarchical for navigation, the content should have a clear hierarchy to it. At the top level, there should be less than seven major functions to perform. An example of a commercial site is the following.

Welcome to the Web Book Store

- Browse our store in graphical form
- Shop the store in text form
- Establish an account with our store
- Send us feedback
- More background on our store
- Recent book reviews
- Links to Internet literary resources

We don't claim this is a particularly good home page structure, but it is similar to the general outline of most commercial sites, and it lays out a clear path for development of your server. It's also a good mechanism to communicate the structure of a site as multiple people work on developing content for it.

Although you may be developing your content bottom-up and may not finalize your home page until your content is developed, you should craft an initial home page to communicate the structure of your content development. You will probably want to start with at least two levels of pages to really communicate the structure. In the previous example, text form might link down to:

- Computer Books
- Business Books
- Periodicals
- History
- Literature
- Art
- Fiction
- Science Fiction/Fantasy

Each of these will link down to pages which will probably list individual titles each on a row. These rows will then be linked to "leaf" pages describing the books themselves. Note that it is not necessary to have a strict hierarchical structure. You can have linear relationships among peers in a hierarchy and have the parent pages link down to a location with a large document. For example, you might have all the books listed in a large document. The section listings shown in the previous list navigate the Web user to a location within that large document.

There will inevitably be large amounts of non-hierarchical and non-linear links within your content and to other Internet resources. For example, one book in your collection might reference another book altogether from another area. Or it may link to a Usenet newsgroup devoted to the author of the book. You should include these links as well in your outline since it makes the data dependencies of your content clear.

Establish a Page Style

Your pages may be linked to and from other sites. You need to have a style that distinguishes your site so that Web readers know where they are when they link to your cool content. The best sites on the Web now all have their own distinctive appearance—you know when you've hit a page on Netscape Communications Web site.

You will want to establish some form of page style to give your site stylistic unity and let surfers know when they've hit your server. Some of the issues here will be mentioned in the next sections on style guidelines (including email addresses, links to your top page). The important thing is that the way in which you incorporate these elements should distinguish your site from the rest. For example, links to the home page could be identified with an icon representing your site.

Choose Your Toolset

You need to decide what tools you will be using to do authoring and to create content on the fly. The availability of the toolset for the content you have in mind will affect how you lay out your site. We strongly recommend limiting yourself to one or two tools for static authoring, and a single gateway for each type of dynamically-created data. This is especially important in a team environment. HTML authoring packages are not yet nearly as interoperable as they should be. HoTMetaL is particularly egregious in its refusal to work with sources that it considers flawed. Notice that I do say one or two authoring packages, because, as we will see, many of the higher level authoring packages do not give sufficient access to the underlying HTML to make them truly capable of doing any necessary task. But the standard can be as simple as saying, for example, to use Word Internet Assistant for most of the work, and a text editor of choice for the details that WIA won't give access.

Plan Your Document Management Strategy

If you have any level of real volume of content, you will need to have a methodology for managing that content. This can range from a Notes or Access database to contain all of your documents to a version control system that you use to check in HTML. Again, the idea is not to just hack out some HTML, copy it to the Web server directory, and restart the server.

In a real commercial Web server effort, there will probably be multiple people involved in content production, and even more dependency on data providers. In an environment where impromptu linking of all of this content in non-hierarchical ways is encouraged, this can be a huge logistical challenge to coordinate. That explains the frequency with which Web browsers see the message "URL not found." It also explains why so many sites don't exploit the potential of having large amounts of highly-linked material, where such material might be really valuable.

The point is, you will be able to accomplish much more ambitious Web site content efforts if you develop a methodology that includes at least the following elements.

- Directory and file format standards for data providers.
- Directory and file format standards for HTML authoring.
- Version control standards for HTML files
- Notification standards for members of the data providing team in the event of source data changes. This can be as simple as email informing authors of a new source file and its location.
- Notification standards for the authoring team of new or revised HTML pages and their location. This last point is crucial since it will be what determines how effectively links are kept updated.

Timeline Your Web Deployment Effort

This is just basic project management, but a large Web deployment effort is a classic example of the complexity of coordinating people, resources, and schedules. You should have a Gantt chart to make sure that, for example, when your beautiful home page with its snazzy HTML+ forms is up online and ready to access your WAIS database of information, that the WAIS gateway is actually functional and that there is content ready to be searched.

Once you've planned your Web development effort, you're ready to start authoring. But before you're introduced to HTML in Chapter 6, here are some guidelines for creating good Web content.

CONTENT AND STYLE GUIDELINES FOR WEB SERVER AUTHORING

Most of this is opinion, but for IS professionals not steeped in the lore of the World Wide Web, background on what makes a good Web server is essential. Even webmasters that are frequent Web surfers should benefit from this material. Here are some guidelines on what makes good Web content. The inspiration for this material comes from: involvement in a number of large Web site development efforts, browsing other Web sites, and reading other style guides. These other guides are far more comprehensive than what I try to present here, so I'll start out by referring you to them.

I present this information now, even before you start to learn HTML, because it will help you to understand the introduction to HTML better and focus on the parts of

HTML that you need to learn. You should probably refer back to this section after learning HTML and before beginning your Web authoring process in earnest.

NCSA has a pretty complete listing of online Web style guides (**http://-union.ncsa.uiuc.edu:80/HyperNews/get/www/html/guides.html**). The oldest and most complete of the guides listed there is Tim Berners-Lee's "Style Guide for Online Hypertext" (**http://www.w3.org/hypertext/WWW/Provider/Style/Overview.html**). A couple of good sources that aren't presented there are the Yale C/AIM WWW Style Manual (**http://info.med.yale.edu/caim/StyleManual_Top.HTML**) and the CERN Guide (**http://www.w3.org/hypertext/WWW/Provider/Style/Introduction.html**).

In other words, *a lot* has been written about what makes good Web style. But a brief surf around the Web makes it clear that maybe these sites aren't getting a lot of hits. In fairness, there's a lot of information there to digest. Much of the information can be simplified, because not everything there applies to the commercial sites you are trying to build. For example, the sites you will be creating are much more oriented to the finished product mindset. So, for example, some of Berners-Lee's style guidelines about how to make current status and versions of your content visible to readers are not extremely relevant. In general, most of the style guides are oriented to how to present large amounts of relatively deep technical information.

Structure of Your Site

The clear hierarchical structure that you outlined when planning your site is not just useful for planning. Organizing all of your content with such a structure will make your content much easier for the reader to understand. You may supplement this structure with links amongst your pages, but the overall plan should still be clear. Take advantage of the tools available to you in HTML: keep the structure simple, and put background or optional information in links whose purpose is clearly indicated to the user.

Well-structured HTML content is much more approachable than its print equivalent. You can keep the content to its simplest form, with links to explanatory, background, or supplementary information. If your site is well structured in general, the ability to devolve nonessential content out to supporting documents makes your site even easier to understand.

Just as important as clear structure, is the capability for the reader to navigate well within your site once they understand the structure you are putting forth. You should not assume facilities of your reader's Web browser such as history, bookmarks, or rewind buttons. I'll discuss what elements should be part of any Web page in the next section, but we mention here that your structure design should include explicit links among your material between pages.

Do's (What to Include in Your Web Pages)

As you start planning your site, consider the positive guidelines first: what content you should have. You can always honor the prohibitions in the editing phase. Your individual Web pages should include at least the following elements:

- Address to respond to with feedback.
- Document link standards.
- Context free document titles.

Address to respond to with feedback

I recommend that the sites you create not be tied to an individual. The person responsible for a site may change over time, and you don't want to have to change these links on every page of your content. A good address for feedback might be webmaster@superstore.com.

Document link standards

Include links to parent documents, "forward" documents (in a progression if appropriate), and "backwards" documents (again if appropriate) set off from the main document body. For example, each page could have these links always presented at the top or bottom of the document. Choose whatever standard you want for this—just be consistent! These "link" frameworks can be useful parts of establishing your site's consistent style.

Context free document titles

This is straight from Berners-Lee, but it's one of his few guidelines that I felt was strongly relevant to this audience. Something not mentioned in the Style Guide is the fact that context free titles encourage linking to your relevant content, because they make it clear what a page is related to without navigating down from your top level. Although you may prefer that other sites link to your home page, this is not likely to happen if the content that is relevant to them is buried a few levels down. Thus expect many more links to your lower level pages than to your top page.

If your page title is "CyberBooks – Airport Novel Section – One Word Title Bestsellers," the context is much clearer than a page title "The Works of Danielle Steele and John Grisham." You have made it clear that this page is part of an electronic bookstore, your bookstore, not just a list of great literature of the 1980s and 90s. When a university English department's Web page devoted to analyzing Steele's corpus links to this page, you will have created a new marketing channel for your store, and casual Web surfers will know when they've hit the CyberBooks site by the title you have chosen. This is not to say that you need to put your business name in every document title. But there should be enough information in any document to allow it be linked to directly and for the reader to still understand the context in which that page appears on your site.

Don'ts (What to Avoid)

To create an effective and professional-looking Web page follow this list of don'ts—surfers are much more likely to stick around and browse.

- Don't concentrate on document appearance versus document structure.
- Don't use character styles (such as bold or italic) often.
- Don't <u>click here.</u>
- Don't leave links unimplemented.
- Avoid proprietary tags where possible.
- Don't include large objects in the main structure.
- Don't ignore your raw HTML content.

Don't concentrate on document appearance versus document structure

This is a controversial statement, especially to the community we are addressing. Many business will engage graphic artists to assist in developing their Web page layouts. These people are used to having very definite control over how images appear. Combine this with the tendency of businesses to associate Web technology with the client they use most (e.g. "we're going to put up a Mosaic server," "that's a great looking Netscape home page"), and you have a recipe for disaster.

For example, it's very common nowadays on the Web for authors to use heading levels at whenever they see fit in order to force a certain contrast between font sizes. I have seen some of the most knowledgeable Web pundits defend this practice. In fact, in this example, the results are not too bad with either Mosaic or Netscape. But the problem here is that Web technology in terms of specific browsers or server implementation is moving incredibly rapidly. If you stick to standard HTML and the guidelines that are presented here, you should be fine. If you try to "mine the implementation" and use the features present in HTML in unplanned ways that yield the appearance you seek on the browser you're viewing with you will most likely get burned and have to redo your content. If these mistakes are in your overall style templates, your rework will be even more costly.

Lets take the previous example of skipping heading levels and imagine how a new browser could make this widely used practice break the appearance on this new browser. As documents get larger and more information is presented it becomes increasingly difficult to manage that information. We might build a browser that addresses this issue, by having a mode of this browser that displays only the first level headings. To view each successive level of heading, one would click on the heading of interest. If a Web author mixes heading numbers with abandon to achieve a specific look, the results on this browser oriented to document structure will be meaningless.

There are many other sins of using structural markup tags to achieve (hoped for) cosmetic effects. They are too numerous and specific to present here. We will mention them in the discussion of individual HTML markup tags.

Don't use character styles (such as bold or italic) often.

Instead, use the logical character styles, such as strong, emphasis, or citation.

> <strong> **Better than bold** </strong>
>
> <em> especially when dealing with character mode browsers </em>
>
> <cite> so sayeth the HTML prophets </cite>
>
> Even better, if you are using bold to indicate document structure (a new section, subsection, or list element), use heading levels or lists instead.

Don't use click here

Don't refer to the navigating process itself with sentences such as:

```
For more information on this subject, click here.
```

First, the user may not be using a mouse. Second, l, this style, and any other that refers to the mechanisms of browsing the Web itself, don't take advantage of the architecture of HTML and the Web. They were invented to allow the hypertext capability to rest in the background and be applied to documents that were not written with the Web in mind. Take advantage of that capability and create documents that when printed you will not know were from a Web site.

Many otherwise fine webspaces are marred by the awkward introduction of webisms into otherwise laudable prose. Your prose should read just as printed prose would (with perhaps less online supplementary material and parenthetical phrases). The hypertext links should appear as if they have been overlaid on top of otherwise generic text. The only Web artifacts that should appear are the underlines themselves.

Don't leave links unimplemented

Many, many Web sites appear as works in progress—links that give error 404 (indicating that the destination document is unavailable) or link to pages that say "under construction—check back later." This is inevitable given the Web's background as a vehicle to facilitate research, and the fact that every other computer science student now has their own home page. This freewheeling expression and creativity is great and has certainly contributed to the growth and success of the Web. But it's exactly what you as a business want to avoid. If you want to identify a phrase as a future link, just underline it. Don't link anything until the destination document is ready.

In your role conducting business over the Web, you will want to set a much higher standard for polish and finish that exists elsewhere on the Web. Many innovative, excellent sites are rife with such occurrences, but in this regard set a higher standard by having a fully completed hypertext link web.

Avoid proprietary tags where possible

Although Netscape is great software, Netscape Communications by no means owns the browser market. One of the reasons for the success of the Web has been the openness of the standard. Writing HTML using Netscape tags usually won't affect other browsers negatively, but whatever meaning you were trying to convey with that information is obscured from a large percentage of Web browser users.

If you want to make aggressive use of emerging HTML standards, write to HTML 3.0. There's plenty of cool stuff there that will distinguish your site, that at least every browser will eventually support. For example, Netscape as of this writing doesn't support HTML 3.0 tables, but you can be sure it will soon. Aggressive incorporation of new HTML standard tags is acceptable when you know that the browser your audience uses will support it, because other browsers that your audience may use later will eventually catch up and support those features.

Don't include large objects in the main structure

Judicious use of small graphics for buttons, signature icons, mastheads, and the like is great. Any medium- to large-size graphic, however, should appear linked off of your main content, with it clearly indicated it requires a large download to retrieve. We discussed earlier planning the structure of your site carefully. Don't include large graphics or other files in your main structure.

Don't ignore your raw HTML content

You should treat HTML authoring like writing software code. Although you may use a tool to author your content, you should be aware of the HTML content that you generate. A conversion tool that allows authoring from another environment altogether, such as Microsoft Word Internet Assistant or Lotus Web Publisher, can be very useful, and we will review several of these. However, you need to be aware of the HTML that these tools create. You will want to have a text editor (such as Windows Notepad or Wordpad) handy to examine the HTML text that these tools generate. Further, you will want to jump in on occasion and make changes to the HTML to exploit features that may not be present in the conversion tools. For example, you might use Word Internet Assistant to author most of your content, but you may jump down to HTML directly to author your user registration form since WIA doesn't currently doesn't have very fine-grained control over HTML forms.

You should intersperse your HTML with comments to make clear what you are doing for your own use and those who maintain your content. At the very least, you should include version control information such as when you created the file, who the author was, what tools were used, and what level of HTML you are writing to. Note that here again you will probably need to use a text editor to do so.

Now that we are starting to talk about raw HTML, it's about to introduce you to authoring it. Even if you use one of the higher-level tools presented later that insulate you to some degree from the HTML, you will need to understand HTML at some level, as we have just described. In the next chapter, we present all the HTML you will need to know to perform a successful Web authoring effort.

## CHAPTER 4

WEB SERVER CONTENT: HTML

In this chapter we begin our Web authoring efforts in earnest by presenting the basics of HTML with enough information for you to immediately create useful, content-rich, attractive Web sites. We withhold some of the more advanced techniques used for interactive Web sites for Chapter 5 on advanced HTML. In the meantime, Chapter 4 presents everything you need to know to start writing HTML and build content for your Web site.

Even if you are planning on using a tool that isolates you from the native HTML, you will need to understand at least the basics of HTML to use those tools effectively. In fact, as stated in the "Don'ts" section of the previous chapter, in the current state of the art of HTML conversion tools, it is not practical to completely ignore your HTML output. If you are planning to use a higher-level tool (such as one that allows you to author from Microsoft Word) or if you are planning a relatively simple *billboard* site (my term for an informational site with a relatively small amount of content), you may be able to skip Chapter 5, at least initially, in your early Web server authoring efforts.

As mentioned earlier, HTML (both the current standard and emerging ones) is not documented well in one place. Despite the quality of the HTML Primer located on the W3 Org server, various emerging topics, such as forms, tables, and other proposed extensions, are documented at other sites. This is especially appropriate now that commercial Web vendors such as Netscape Communications are unilaterally proposing (actually more like independently introducing) significant enhancements to the standard. Potential webmasters need to be aware of the implications of these enhancements versus the existing standard. For example, many IS managers may inherit the responsibility for putting up a Web server and a copy of Netscape's Netsite Web server software. They may not be aware that certain HTML extensions render their Web server content usable only by Netscape.

Further, once the information is all gathered on one site, its volume can be staggering. We make a conscious effort here to focus on the tags and techniques that you will use. The entire grammar of HTML is documented thoroughly in Appendix B of this book, and you should refer to it. But in this chapter, you will learn all the HTML you need to begin your authoring efforts for most types of sites. In the next chapter, we will present everything that we've left out here that you will need to know for more advanced Web authoring efforts. We filter out elements of HTML that you are unlikely to use or that have been made obsolete by newer methods.

BACKGROUND ON HYPERTEXT MARKUP LANGUAGE

Just reading this chapter and using the supplied template will give you enough information to begin creating useful pages. But for more basic HTML information, check out NCSA's "A Beginner's Guide to HTML" (**http://www.ncsa.uiuc.edu/General/ Internet/WWW/HTMLPrimer.html**). Another, briefer, reference is the strangely titled "HTML Documents: A Mosaic Tutorial" (**http://fire.clarkson.edu/doc/html/htut.html**). The full HTML specification is on W3 Org (the former CERN site) as "The HTML Specification," (**http://www.w3.org/hypertext/WWW/MarkUp/MarkUp.html**), but we don't recommend this as a gentle introduction. In Appendix B, we include sections 5 through 8 of the September 22, 1995 draft of the HTML 2.0 specification by Tim Berners-Lee.

HTML is a dialect of SGML that facilitates the proposal that Berners-Lee put forth for a World Wide Web of information. *SGML* stands for Standard Generalized MarkUp Language, which is a language for specifying other document markup languages, including HTML. Thus all HTML documents are SGML documents, if they are perfectly formatted. Since, as discussed at length in this book, most HTML documents aren't, most HTML documents will not be accepted by rigorous SGML parsers. If you follow the guidelines set forth in this book, your documents should be fully SGML compliant.

THE BASIC HTML DOCUMENT TEMPLATE

You will make your job much easier if you begin all authoring efforts from a basic document template. At the very least, that template should contain:

- A head portion, containing the document title.
- A body portion, containing at least one header of structural information.
- Some content separated by paragraphs.
- Sign your work at the bottom.

Let's make a template that embodies these suggestions.

```
<HTML>
    <HEAD>
    <TITLE>Your Title Here</TITLE>
    </HEAD>
    <BODY>
    <H1>Your Heading Here</H1>
    Now put in some of your content.
    <P>Separate paragraphs as shown.
    <P>And sign your work at the bottom as shown below.
    <HR>
    <ADDRESS>ouraddress@ourstore.com</ADDRESS>
    </BODY>
    </HTML>
```

That's it! With just this template in hand and a text editor, you are now ready to create your Web home page! Figure 4.1 shows what this will look like within a Web browser.

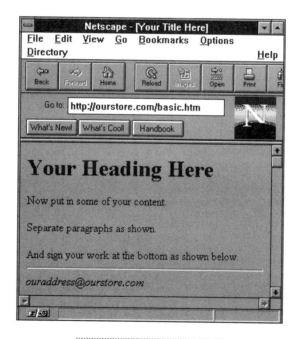

FIGURE 4.1 BASIC DOCUMENT TEMPLATE

Using this as the basis of your content, you can craft a respectable Web page. There are several elements here that are not present in every Web page on the 'Net. As a bad example of an even more minimalist Web page, lets look at the following.

```
<TITLE>Fast and Loose Web Authoring</TITLE>
<H1>How to Succeed With HTML Without Really Trying</H1>
Hey this stuff's pretty easy.
<P>
Just fire up your text editor and blast out the text.
```

NCSA's "Beginner's Guide to HTML" actually has this (that is, this structure) as a first example of simple Web content. But this isn't really a good base with which to begin your Web development. Continued innovations in Web browser development will take advantage of the HTML standard to do things you don't even see today. Just because current browsers accept the above example, doesn't mean that all Web browsers in the future will.

BASIC HTML ELEMENTS

You will want to learn a few more primitives before beginning your authoring efforts in earnest.

Head Elements

You should always have a head element within your document. If you start with our minimalist document template, you will always have this. The head element should at least contain a *<TITLE>* element, which you will also get with the document template. Some or all of the following elements may also prove useful. Don't feel overwhelmed by this list. All you really need is the *<TITLE>* element within your *<HEAD>*. The rest of the options may prove useful as you progress in your authoring efforts.

<TITLE>

The head element should contain at least a title. As discussed in the style guidelines, that title should be sufficient to identify your content outside the context of your Web site.

<ISINDEX>

This indicates to the server that the document is searchable. That is, when entering the Uniform Resource Locator (URL) of the document, the user may append a query string to search for a particular keyword or phrase within the document. If you want to allow this capability you should include this tag. For many documents with a lot of data, such as product catalogs, you will want to use this.

<BASE>

This element takes an attribute called *HREF* which indicates the URL of this page. For example

```
<BASE HREF="http://ourstore.com/home/">
```

<OWNER NAME>

This is a useful tag especially within a multi-author group web development effort. For example:

```
<OWNER NAME="John Doe">
```

<LINK REV>

The Link Rev attribute indicates where to get information about revisions of this document. *<LINK REV>* takes one attribute *HREF*, which can be any URL, but is typically either mail or http (another Web page). For example:

```
<LINK REV="versions" HREF="mailto:jdoe@ourstore.com">
```

<META>

This head element allows information that is not covered by any of the other elements to be included in the head. The syntax is:

```
<META NAME="YourElement" CONTENT="Your value text">
```

Here's an example head element that incorporates all of these elements:

```
<HEAD>
<TITLE>CyberBooks Home Page</TITLE>
<BASE HREF="http://cyberbooks.com">
<OWNER NAME="John Doe">
<LINK REV="versions" HREF="mailto:webmaster@cyberbooks.com">
</HEAD>
```

Headings

You should have at least one heading in your document labeled *<H1>*, hence its inclusion in the basic template. You can create lower level-headings under each higher-level heading by labeling subsequent levels *<H2>*, *<H3>*, etc. up to six levels. Each successive level of heading is typically sized smaller on the user's Web browser. Many Web authors have taken to using heading levels to get different font sizes, skipping around in heading levels with abandon to give their pages a "handcrafted" look. *Don't do this.* It by no means guarantees that you will get the font size effects you seek. In future Web browsers, this may cause unanticipated negative side effects.

Concentrate on the structure of your document. If there is any length to your document at all, give it some structure beyond the *<H1>* tag we've already given you in the minimal document template. Below is an example body section structured to two levels. For now don't worry about the tags that we have not yet discussed (*<LI>*, *<UL>*, and *<CITE>*). *<UL>* are *<LI>* are for building unordered lists which you will be shown you shortly. *<CITE>* is just a way of getting italics for the book titles without using physical character formatting (see the style guide where logical character formatting is emphasized).

```
<HTML>
        <HEAD>
        <TITLE>CyberBooks Monthly Specials</TITLE>
        </HEAD>
        <BODY>
        <H1>Nonfiction</H1>
        <H2>Science</H2>
        Make time for physics.
        <UL>
```

```
            <LI><CITE>Wrinkles in Time</CITE>, George Smoot
            <LI><CITE>Brief History of Time</CITE>, Stephen
Hawking
            <LI><CITE>The First Three Minutes<CITE>,Steven
Weinberg
            </UL>
            <H2>Computer</H2>
            Get ready for Windows NT
            <UL>
<LI><CITE>Inside Windows NT</CITE>, Helen Custer
<LI><CITE>Advanced Windows</CITE>, Jeffrey Richter
<LI><CITE>Inside OLE2, 2nd. Edition</CITE>, Kraig Brockschmidt
</UL>
<H2>Business</H2>
<H3>Investing</H3>
The classics.
<UL>
<LI><CITE>The Intelligent Investor</CITE>, Ben Graham
<LI><CITE>Random Walk Down Wall Street</CITE>, Burton Malkiel
<LI><CITE>One Up On Wall Street</CITE>, Peter Lynch
</UL>
<H3>Management</H3>
<UL>
<LI><CITE>Leadership Secrets of Attila the Hun</CITE>, Wes Roberts
<LI><CITE>Reengineering the Corporation</CITE>, Hammer and Champy
<LI><CITE>Reengineering Management</CITE>, Champy
</UL>
            <H1>Fiction</H1>
            Russian authors on sale this month.
            <H2>Classics</H2>
            <LI><CITE>Brothers Karamazov</CITE>, Dostoyevsky
            <LI><CITE>Anna Karenina</CITE>, Tolstoy
            <LI><CITE>And Quiet Flows the Don</CITE>, Sholokhov
            </UL>
            <H2>Science Fiction </H2>
            The future of Mars, past and present.
<UL>
            <LI><CITE>Blue Mars</CITE>, Kim Stanley Robinson
            <LI><CITE>Green Mars</CITE>, Kim Stanley Robinson
```

```
                <LI><CITE>The Martian Chronicles</CITE>, Ray Bradbury
                <LI>
                </UL>
                <ADDRESS>webmaster@cyberbooks.com</ADDRESS>
        </BODY>
    </HTML>
```

Figure 4.2 shows what this looks like.

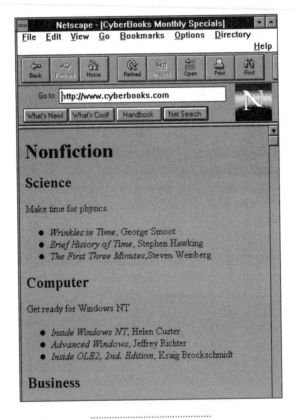

FIGURE 4.2 HEADINGS EXAMPLE

Lists

In the previous example, once we got to the bottom level we started building lists. This is a very useful capability, and HTML provides several ways of doing this.

Unordered lists

In the example above, the unordered list was built, which were displayed as bullets. Unordered lists are built by starting the list with the <UL> tag, putting each item after a <LI> tag, and closing the list with </UL>. Note that it is not necessary to "close" a list item with </LI>. For example (from the previous Web page):

```
<UL>
<LI><CITE>Wrinkles in Time</CITE>, George Smoot
<LI><CITE>Brief History of Time</CITE>, Stephen Hawking
<LI><CITE>The First Three Minutes</CITE>,Steven Weinberg
</UL>
```

Ordered lists

You can also build ordered lists. The Web browser will then display each item labeled with a successive number. Do this by using <OL> as the beginning tag and </OL> as the ending tag.

```
<OL>
<LI><CITE>Wrinkles in Time</CITE>, George Smoot
<LI><CITE>Brief History of Time</CITE>, Stephen Hawking
<LI><CITE>The First Three Minutes</CITE>,Steven Weinberg
</OL>
```

Definition lists

This feature might ordinarily seem somewhat obscure, but it turns out that definition lists are widely used, mainly to provide content where a title is presented for a list item and the text associated with the title is indented below it. The list is started with <DL> and ends with </DL>.

For example:

```
<DL>
<DT>Wrinkles in Time<DD>By George Smoot, presents his pioneering
research into finding evidence for the Big Bang in cosmic
background radiation.
<DT>Brief History of Time<DD>Stephen Hawking, our age's foremost
cosmologist, presents relativity theory, quantum mechanics, and
the search for a unified theory.
```

```
<DT>The First Three Minutes<DD>Steven Weinberg presents theories
of the early origin of the universe.
</DL>
```

Definition lists are often used (probably most of the time) in contexts that have nothing to do with definitions. For example, they are often used just to get the indented subsidiary text. Also, pictures can be embedded (using the *IMG SRC* tag, to be presented shortly) in the DT element to allow the effect on clicking on an icon to select a menu item.

Menu lists

This is very similar in syntax to an unordered list but is intended for situations where the list is used as a menu for navigation to other pages. The functionality is often identical, but it conveys to the HTML source reader the purpose of the construct. Also, some browsers will dispense with bullets for menu lists. For example,

```
<MENU>
<LI><A HREF="wrinkles.htm">Wrinkles in Time</A>
<LI><A HREF="histime.htm">Brief History of Time</A>
<LI><A HREF="1st3mins.htm">The First Three Minutes</A>
</MENU>
```

Directory lists

Directory lists are similar to menu lists, except that they are intended for very short items (fewer than 20 characters), such as file names. For example:

```
<DIRECTORY>
<LI><A HREF="wrinkles.htm">Wrinkles</A>
<LI><A HREF="brief.htm">Brief</A>
<LI><A HREF="first.htm">First</A>
</DIRECTORY>
```

Directory lists are not in widespread use.

Spacing

Unless you plan to write Joycean stream-of-consciousness Web content, you will probably want some way of spacing out text in the areas where you plan to create more than a sentence of prose.

<P>

This tag separates paragraphs in your body content. There is a close paragraph tag </P>, but it is really not necessary. Just be sure to separate your paragraphs with this tag. Separating your paragraphs with white space (as you might do in a word processor) will not work.

Sometimes you need to force a line break without incurring the spacing caused by a true paragraph break. For example, when formatting addresses you typically want all the lines closely spaced but each address on a line. Use this only for such special needs.

```
CyberBooks<BR>
webmaster@cyberbooks.com<BR>
1-800-CYBOOKS<BR>
```

<HR>

This results in the chiseled horizontal line you may have seen in your Web surfing expeditions. <HR> options take three attributes as arguments, SIZE, ALIGN, and WIDTH:

```
<HR size=6 align="center" width=60%>
```

Some sites really go wild with them, using them multiple times per page and changing their width. It's probably best to restrict your use to one or two per page. You should use them when it has logical meaning: to separate a top-level heading from the rest of the content, to finish off a page above an email signature, or to separate disparate parts of content. Whatever you use them for, be consistent across your site. See the above examples and the minimal document template we started with for examples of using <HR>.

Images

One of the strengths of HTML is that it's not just hypertext, but *multimedia* hypertext, which means, at the very least, images. For other multimedia content types besides images, and for some image formats, this is accomplished by launching a separate viewer application to view that content. The way to author these is to create links to the objects (I'll show you how to do this in the next section). However, for a limited set of image types (currently just JPEG and GIF format images), it is possible to embed the image directly in your document.

This is done with the *<IMG>* tag. The *<IMG>* tag requires an attribute of SRC, and has optional attributes of ALT, ALIGN, or ISMAP. The SRC attribute should be supplied with the URL of the image to incorporate. ALT should have some text that can be shown when the image won't display. ALIGN allows the image to be aligned with the top, middle, or bottom of the associated text. The ISMAP attribute allows the image to be a clickable image map used for navigation, covered in the "Advanced HTML". An example of an embedded image HTML is:

```
<IMG SRC="http://cyberbooks.com/wrinkles.gif" ALT="Cover not
displayable in text mode" ALIGN="bottom">
```

Note that it is necessary to convert your images into either JPEG or GIF format before they can be included in your document (though you can *link* to images in a much wider variety of formats, as long as the Web browser user has a viewer defined for that type of document). The tools and techniques for doing these conversions will be discussed in Chapter 7. Specifically, for converting your images from common PC image formats such as .BMP files and .PCX files, I recommend LViewPro, which is covered in the section on conversion tools in Chapter 7.

You can also use an embedded image as the anchor for a link. One common use of this technique is to link a small thumbnail version of an image to the full-screen version of an image. For example, an online gallery of photographs or paintings will typically have a directory of thumbnail images, each of which is linked to full-page displays of those pictures.

Special Characters

One of the problems with a tagged markup language is that all sorts of special characters have to be set aside for the tags. For example, with less than (<) and greater than (>) used for tags, what do you use when you really want to use the less than character? The mechanism for this is special characters. See the Appendix B on HTML grammar for a complete list. Here are some of the more common ones:

```
"    &quot
&    &amp
<    &lt
>    &gt
```

This is one of the most difficult things to remember when starting to author HTML directly in a text editor. But as long as you test your output frequently you should catch your slipups quickly.

Comments

Especially on large multiauthor projects, you should intersperse comments liberally in your HTML code. An example comment is:

```
<!- use these a lot ->
```

You may not, however, nest comments.

Character Formatting

You should avoid physical character formatting in favor of logical character formatting. What are these attributes? Below is a list of the more popular ones. Each tag must have a closing tag, e.g. *<CITE>* needs *</CITE>* to close the citation.

```
<CITE>      used for citations, typically displayed in italics
<CODE>      displayed in Courier or other fixed pitch font
<EM>        emphasis, typically in italics
<STRONG>    strong emphasis, usually in bold
<KBD>       keyboard input
<SAMP>      sequence of literal characters
```

Those are the popular logical formatting attributes, and you should be able to use them to get bold or italics or fixed pitch font. However, if you feel that the tags are misleading in some context, you can use the physical formatting tags:

```
<B>        bold
<I>        italics
<TT>       fixed pitch font
```

Other proprietary extensions have been introduced by Netscape Communications, these will be covered in Chapter 5 on advanced HTML.

Block Formatting

HTML provides a number of tags for formatting blocks of information. Typically, the block is identified as having a logical attribute, and it is up to the browser to determine how the logical attribute is displayed. For example, <ADDRESS> is often displayed in italics but that is not required. Three common block formatting tages are presented here.

<ADDRESS> tag

Used to list any type of address, postal or email, that you wish to set off as separate when displayed in a user's Web browser. It is often used at the bottom of a document to indicate how to contact the document author. It must be closed with </ADDRESS>.

<BLOCKQUOTE> tag

Used to set off quoted material. It results in text appearing indented in a separate paragraph.

<PRE> tag

Allows text to be displayed with a fixed pitch font and uses tab characters for columnar formatting. Its primary legitimate use is for tabular data. Since most browsers now support HTML 3.0 tables, this tag is not really necessary anymore.

An exception to this is processing forms. Often you will want to have field entry areas line up on top of each other. A table may not be the appropriate method to do this. See the example in Chapter 5 on forms, where the <PRE> tag is used for these purposes.

UNIFORM RESOURCE LOCATORS AND BUILDING LINKS

One of the foundations of the Web is hypertext, and to create hypertext you will need to know how to build links to your Web content, to other Web resources on the Internet, and in general to any Internet resource.

URLs

You should be at least familiar with the basic idea of a *Uniform Resource Locator*, which is a way to refer to an Internet resource so that a browser can retrieve it by supplying dialog or clicking on HTML links that have that address embedded. That's why they have been presented in earlier chapters without undue introduction.

But as you begin authoring hypertext links within your own documents, you will need a more rigorous understanding of URLs than you may already have. The general syntax of a URL is the type of resource (e.g., http, ftp, file, news) followed by a colon, followed by the server name or IP address, followed by the path to the resource. For example:

```
http://ourhost.com/home.html
```

Note that http identifies the resource type, ourhost.com identifies the host name, and home.html identies the file on the given host. Full grammar for URLs is presented in Appendix B on HTML grammar. Here are examples for the most common type of URL linking.

Hypertext transfer protocol

To link to data from another Web server, exploit the hypertext transfer protocol (http). Supply the host name and path name after *http://*. An example of linking to another http resource is:

```
http://cybermags.com:88/lists/maglist.html
```

The number following the host name is an optional port name that services http requests on the destination. By default, the http port is considered to be 80. If it is any other number, the number must be supplied explicitly as shown above. http URLs of searchable index pages (more on those later) or CGI programs can also take a search string argument by appending a question mark followed by individual keywords separated by + signs. For example:

```
http://cybermags.com/srch4title?web+HTML+book
```

This technique can be applied to linking to other resources that take search arguments such as WAIS servers.

File transfer protocol

To retrieve files from other sites, use file transfer protocol (*ftp*). Specify *ftp://* followed by the host name and path name. For example, to allow the user to pull down a GIF file from another site, use:

```
ftp://cybermags.com/photos/cover.gif
```

Files

For an internal network Web deployment, you can use a URL to link to a file on this site. List *file:* followed by the full path and file to link to. If you preface the path with two slashes (*//*), it is assumed that the first string is a host name. An example file link is:

```
file:/photos/gifs/wrinkle.gif
```

Unless you are planning deployment of an internal web (which is certainly possible), you should avoid this URL type.

Usenet News

You can even link or refer to Usenet News, both newsgroups and individual articles. To link to a newsgroup, enter *news:* followed by the newsgroup name. To link to a specific article, enter *news:* followed by the article identifier. However, it is rarely appropriate to link to an individual article, unless you are committed to updating your content *very* frequently, or your HTML is generated programmatically.

For example, to link to the misc.invest.stocks newsgroup:

```
news:misc.invest.stocks
```

email

You can also build a URL to send email. At the bottom of each page that you author, you may wish to allow the Web browser reader to send feedback on the content to you. This is done with *mailto:* followed by the address. For example, the following URL could be linked to by the phrase "send feedback to the webmaster."

```
mailto:webmaster@ourstore.com
```

mailto URLs can also be used as the "poor man's form processors" to accept input from user form data and send it to the interested party (see Chapter 5 on forms processing). This isn't the recommended long-term technique, but it can be useful to quickly make a form page available and active.

Building Hypertext Links

Now that you know how to build URLs, you will want to use this knowledge to build links from your text to those resources. The way to build links is to build an anchor by placing the anchor begin and anchor end tags around a linking phrase. The anchor begin tag is *<A>* and takes an HREF attribute. The HREF attribute takes as its argument the URL (in quotes) of the destination to link to. If the destination is on the current host, an access method and host name are not necessary. In fact, it is likely that most of your links will not be to other hosts. If you specify a link without a host name, it is said to be a *relative reference* or a *relative URL*. The advantage of relative URLs is that they do not have to be changed if you change the host of your web. Bear in mind that in some contexts (such as with clickable image maps discussed later) full (versus relative) URLs are required. To end an anchor end just type *</A>*.

Linking HTML on other sites

The following example links a description of a book on our site to its review on Dr. Dobb's Journal's hypothetical site.

```
A review of <CITE>Design Patterns</CITE> was recently published in <A
HREF="http://www.ddj.com/Design_Patterns.html">Dr. Dobb's Journal.</A>
```

Note that the filename on the DDJ site is **Design_Patterns.html**. Don't assume all files that you link to follow the "DOS 8.3" convention (8 characters for the base filename and 3 for the extension). Many other Web servers run on UNIX machines. Many NT-based Web servers are running on NTFS file systems (which we recommend as well for security reasons). NTFS supports longer than 8.3 file names so these may have long filenames as well.

Linking to HTML on our site

When we decided to link to our own review located on our site, the HREF attribute is simplified considerably. In this case, the full "resource type:host name" syntax is not necessary. In fact, most of your links are likely to be to local files.

```
We recently reviewed <A HREF="reviews/patterns.htm">
<CITE>Design Patterns</CITE></A>
```

This links to the file **patterns.htm** in the directory **reviews** off of our main directory (the one that our Web server is configured to talk to, which we discuss in the chapter on Web server setup).

Linking to non-HTML files

We can also link to non-Web content; For example, to refer to a picture and then link to that image. This is often a more effective technique than incorporating images directly into documents, since the image will slow down download and display of the main document. For images of any size, a much more effective technique is to refer to them in the main document and then anchor the reference with a hypertext link. For example:

```
<A HREF="images/bluemars.jpg">Blue Mars</A>third in Robinson's
trilogy on the colonization of Mars</A>
```

The title appears underlined in the Web browser. Clicking on it retrieves a JPEG image of the cover of the book.

Linking to document locations (named anchors)

Of course, links can be built to more than just whole files. You can link to locations within your current document or files on your host. To do this you must have a named anchor for the destination location in the document. A *named anchor* is built with the anchor tag (<A>) but with a NAME attribute added. The NAME attribute can be used at the same time as the HREF attribute, but this is rare. A named location is then linked to with an HREF attribute in another anchor. The name is prepended with a pound sign (#) in the linking anchor.

For example, the following would be a named location in the document.

```
<A NAME="Conclusion">Conclusion</A>
```

You link to this location in the document by referring to it as *#Conclusion*.

```
We discuss this further in the <A HREF="#Conclusion">Conclusion</A>
```

As discussed earlier, this last capability is quite exciting. It provides the capability to create long documents that are much more navigable and understandable than their paper equivalents. How many times have you read a book that said, "please refer to chapter 8, section 5, paragraph 4, where we really explain this"? With named anchors, a key phrase can be linked directly to the supplementary information. Named anchors also let you build a hypertext table of contents *without* making each section that the ToC links to its own page. Documents can be maintained as long continuous streams, with the Contents page providing both structure and accessibility to large amounts of information presented as continuous chapters.

HTML Summary

Once you have mastered the material in this chapter you are ready to begin real HTML authoring. We haven't shown you any tools to do so yet. But with this knowledge and a text editor (such as Notepad or WordPad) you can make a credible start. You are especially prepared for authoring efforts that are oriented to information publishing as opposed to Web applications that need to be interactive. For interactive applications, such as electronic commerce, read Chapter 5 on advanced HTML.

Before starting the next chapter however, I encourage you to create some basic HTML content. You can use your Web browser viewer to view the content. You should become familiar with all the HTML tags presented in this chapter. Again, if you are not planning an interactive Web site, this chapter should be a sufficient introduction to begin your authoring efforts, and you may want to skip ahead to Chapter 6 to learn about the tools that will help you in this.

References

- "The HTML Specification"
  (**http://www.w3.org/hypertext/WWW/MarkUp/MarkUp.html**)
- "Beginner's Guide to HTML"
  (**http: //www.ncsa.uiuc.edu/demoweb/html-primer.html**)
- "Web Etiquette"
  (**http://www.w3.org/hypertext/WWW/Provider/Etiquette.htm**)
- "HTML Documents: A Mosaic Tutorial"
  (**http://fire.clarkson.edu/doc/html/htut.html**)

## CHAPTER 5

ADVANCED HTML

To create interactive Web applications, you need to learn more advanced HTML techniques. After reading Chapter 4 on basic HTML, Web publishers can use HTML productively for sites publishing information outbound only. This chapter teaches you how to build interactive Web sites and should deepen your understanding of HTML, allowing you to become a more accomplished webmaster.

I'll begin by discussing necessary HTML features for interactive Web sites. These sites are distinguished by: user interaction with HTML forms and (often) clickable image maps. After that we delve into some other advanced HTML topics including forthcoming features of HTML 3.0 and private extensions to the standard.

FORMS

HTML 2.0 allows forms user input through the use of forms. Its important to mention ahead of time that to do anything useful with the data coming back from these forms, you will need to have some program (typically referred to as a *gateway*) to intercept the values and do something with them. These programs are often referred to as *CGI gateways*. CGI stands for Common Gateway Interface, a standard developed by CERN (now the W3 Organization) for programs to interact with HTTP servers. The standard is a bit loose—each Web server has its own slight variation. CGI gateways, both configuration of off-the-shelf programs and writing your own gateways, is discussed in Chapters 10 and 11.

THE **FORM** TAG

To allow the Web browser user to enter forms requires just creating the necessary HTML syntax. The syntax for the form tags is presented in Appendix B on HTML grammar. The tag to create a form is <FORM>. The ACTION attribute specifies the name of the program that will process the form. The ACTION attribute defaults to the current document, but that is not usually appropriate, so you should treat ACTION as a required attribute with no default.

The METHOD attribute specifies how the data is sent back. A method of GET (the default) sends the data to the program specified by the action URL, via the QUERY_STRING environment variable. This means that the data in the GET string may exceed the space available in the environment or the maximum length of an environment variable.

Since this makes GET very vulnerable to idiosyncracies of system installation, and data that is just too large to fit in the environment, the POST method is preferred. The POST method gives the data to the form-processing application as the standard input of the application.

Query arguments are appended to the ACTION URL with a question mark before the arguments (?) and plus signs (+) separating the query arguments. These parameters are passed as command-line arguments to the program.

As another method of passing parameters to form processing applications, you may append arguments to the program with just a slash (/) after the program name. The arguments are then available in the PATH_INFO environment variable.

Again more information on the specifics of this are presented in Chapters 10 and 11 on CGI gateways. The important things to remember here (while we are starting to author forms) are: use the POST method and you may use command-line arguments to pass to the form processing applications.

The ENCTYPE attribute specifies the encoding type and defaults to www-form-encoded, which is also the only legitimate value right now.

An example form element is:

```
<FORM ACTION="cgi-bin/procform.exe/store.txt" METHOD=POST>
<H1>Membership Application</H1>
Enter the information below.
First Name <INPUT TYPE="text" NAME="FirstName">
Last Name <INPUT TYPE="text" NAME="LastName">
```

```
<INPUT TYPE="submit" VALUE="SEND">
<INPUT TYPE="reset" VALUE="CLEAR">
</FORM>
```

For the sake of creating a working example, we showed you some tags above we have not introduced. We will rectify that problem right away.

The INPUT Tag

The <INPUT> tag is placed within form elements and allows you to create input fields (as shown above) of many types using the TYPE attribute. The TYPE attribute can have any of the following values. Some browsers require the types to be represented as lowercase; they are listed that way here.

"text"

This is the default input type and allows text fields to be entered. It (and all other INPUT field types which take data) requires a NAME attribute. This allows the data that it contains to be distinguished in the stream of data that the gateway program will receive. The SIZE attribute specifies the width of the field on the form. It is optional and also available for the "password" type tag. The optional MAXLENGTH attribute specifies the maximum width that may be entered by the user when editing the field. If not specified, there is no maximum width for the field.

An example would be:

```
<INPUT TYPE="text" NAME="FirstName" SIZE=20 MAXLENGTH=30>
```

"checkbox"

This allows checkbox fields to be created. The CHECKBOX input type takes a NAME attribute and a VALUE attribute. The value attribute specifies what value the field takes if the box is checked. The value attribute can also be modified with the CHECKED keyword to indicate that the checkbox is checked by default when the form is first displayed.

For example:

```
Would you like to be on our mailing list?<p>
<INPUT TYPE="checkbox" NAME="Email" VALUE="Yes" CHECKED>Yes, send
me information once a month via e-mail.<p>
```

"radio"

This allows the form author to create radio button fields. It requires the creation of several INPUT fields of RADIO type all with the same NAME attribute. It also has a VALUE attribute with an optional CHECKED keyword, but only one of the INPUT TYPE tags in the radio button group should have the checked attribute.

Please indicate what type of credit card you wish to use:

```
<INPUT TYPE="radio" NAME="CredType" VALUE="VISA" CHECKED>VISA
<INPUT TYPE="radio" NAME="CredType" VALUE="MC">MasterCard
<INPUT TYPE="radio" NAME="CredType" VALUE="AMEX">American Express
```

"submit"

Each form must should have an input tag of type "submit". No more than one should be provided. Its location determines the location of the Submit button on the form. The name attribute of the input tag is optional with no default. The value attribute controls the text that labels the Submit button. It is optional and defaults to Submit. For example, from the HTML fragment above, the following tag causes a submit button labeled SEND to be placed in the form.

```
<INPUT TYPE="submit" VALUE="SEND">
```

When the Web browser user clicks on the Send button all of the data in the form is sent to the program specified in the FORM tag ACTION attribute. If a "submit" tag is not provided, most browsers will allow the Enter key to trigger form submission.

"image"

An even slicker way to allow users to submit forms is to create *image buttons*. Image buttons are defined with the INPUT tag of type "image". This allows an image to be displayed as the submit button in lieu of the text label shown above. The image file is specified with the SRC attribute, and alignment of the image can be specified with the ALIGN attribute.

The coordinates of the user click are also sent as the data associated with this field. This yields a poor mans image map capability (real image maps are discussed in the next section). For many forms, an image may be an effective way of allowing choices from various alternatives. For example, an image of several products might be used in a form requesting more information about a company. The product clicked on in the image will result in the user receiving information back about that particular product.

Note that this method can only be used to perform form submission. It might would be nice to allow individual field values to be filled in by clicking on images, but that is not currently possible.

An example image button element would be:

```
<INPUT TYPE="image" NAME="sendit" SRC="images/bigbuttn.gif"
ALIGN="middle">
```

You may have noticed that this element type doesn't do much that the "submit" type doesn't do. Eventually the two types will be combined.

"reset"

The reset input tag allows the user to clear the form of values and reenter them. It is not required, but is a good feature to provide in your forms. As with the submit input tag, the NAME attribute is optional, and the VALUE attribute causes the label to be changed from its default of RESET. For example,

```
<INPUT TYPE="reset" VALUE="CLEAR">
```

"password"

This INPUT type is the same as the TEXT type but the letters are not echoed to the screen when the user types them. This tag is not included in the HTML 2.0 specification. It is deemed relatively insecure since the data is transmitted back to the server as clear text.

"hidden"

This allows data to be to be placed in the document by CGI gateways only for the purposes of sending the data back to other gateways—you do not wish that data to be displayed to the user. In effect, it maintains state information about the document.

The SELECT Tag

You may have noticed that the repetition of those tags in the above example seemed duplicative. <SELECT> allows a shorthand method of defining radio or checkbox fields. The related options can be explicitly grouped together. A SELECT element takes a NAME attribute, and an optional MULTIPLE attribute. MULTIPLE indicates that several options may be selected.

SELECT elements may contain many OPTION elements. OPTION elements do not require termination (</OPTION>), the next <OPTION> tag closes the option. The SELECTED attribute makes the option initially turned on by default. An OPTION element may be given a VALUE attribute that determines what data is sent if the option is selected. If the VALUE attribute is left out, the text following the option will be transmitted when an option is selected. For example, the following is a multiple selection set of check boxes.

```
<SELECT NAME="toppings" MULTIPLE>
<OPTION SELECTED>Cheese
<OPTION>Pepperoni
<OPTION>Mushrooms
</SELECT>
```

If the second option is selected, the string "Pepperoni" is sent in the form data packet.

The TEXTAREA Tag

This tag is used to define fields where multiple lines of text are required. Otherwise it is very similar to an INPUT field of text type. The TEXTAREA element takes attributes of ROWS and COLS, which specify the field's height and width in number of lines and number of characters. If the supplied text is too large, the browser supplies the field with scroll bars.

A Complete Form

Below is the HTML for a complete form that incorporates many of these elements. This form prompts the user for information necessary to join a Web-based store. The idea behind the form is that the customer joins the store one time, providing all of the information necessary to allow the online merchant to bill the customer and ship the goods to them.

IMPORTANT: We strongly urge you NOT to accept credit card information directly via the Internet unless you have a secure Web server such as Netsite from Netscape Communications based on Netscape's Secure Sockets Layer or Spry's Web server based on Secure-HTTP.

We will discuss the reasons for this at length in our chapter on Web security. In the meantime, do not just cut and paste this form for your own use if you are using EMWAC's HTTPS or another non-secure Web server.

```
<HTML>
<HEAD><TITLE>Account Application</TITLE></HEAD>
<BODY>
<H1>Join Our Store</H1>
<FORM METHOD=POST ACTION="cgi-bin/procapp.exe">
<HR>
<PRE>
Name <INPUT SIZE=20 NAME="Name">
Street <INPUT SIZE=30 NAME="Street">
City <INPUT SIZE=20 NAME="City"> State <INPUT SIZE=2 NAME="State"> ZIP
<INPUT SIZE=10 NAME="ZIP"> Country <INPUT SIZE=9 NAME="Country">
Phone <INPUT SIZE=15 NAME="Phone ">
Email <INPUT SIZE=25 NAME="Email_Address
</PRE>
<!- only accept credit card information over the Internet if you have a
secure Web server ->
<P>
Select a method of payment that will be used for all of your orders.
<SELECT NAME="PayMethod">
<OPTION SELECTED>VISA
<OPTION>MasterCard
<OPTION>American Express
<OPTION>COD
</SELECT><P>
Credit card number <INPUT SIZE=20 NAME="CardNumber"> Expiration <INPUT
SIZE=5 NAME="Expires"><P>
Based on what you've seen so far, please give us suggestions on how we can
make our store better.<P>
<TEXTAREA NAME="Suggestions" ROWS=5 COLS=40>
Some default text
</TEXTAREA><P>
Would you like to be on our mailing list?<p>
<INPUT TYPE="checkbox" NAME="Email" VALUE="Yes">Yes, send me information
once a month via e-mail.<P>
<INPUT TYPE="submit" VALUE="Submit Application"> <INPUT TYPE="reset"
value="Clear Form"><p>
</FORM>
<HR>
<ADDRESS><A
HREF="mailto:webmaster@ourstore.com">webmaster@ourstore.com</A></ADDRESS>
</BODY>
</HTML>
```

This is a reasonable template for allowing Web customers to join a store. Notice that we use the <PRE> tag to surround our name and address area. We needed to do this to get the field areas to line up for aesthetic (and user readability) reasons. We could have used tables for this as well, but, as of this writing, tables are not universally supported. <PRE> results in a Courier-like font which is not always attractive, but it gives us the easy readibility of having the field entry areas line up.

This form will result in all of the contents being submitted to the CGI program PROCAPP.EXE in the cgi-bin directory. We will cover how to build CGI programs to process form data in a later chapter. Figure 5.1 shows how the template appears.

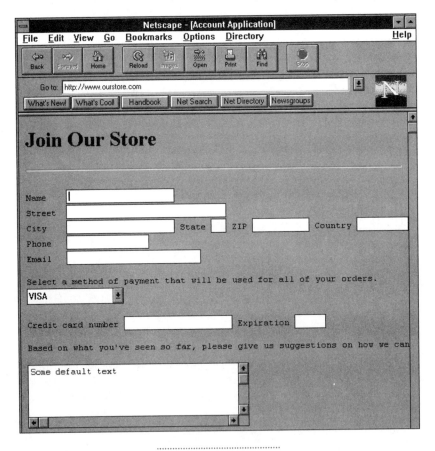

FIGURE 5.1 SIMPLE HTML FORM

Processing Forms

Note that we have just given you half of the ammunition you need to really process user input. The form shown above will allow you to prompt the user for all kinds of useful information that you may want to process. In the previous example all of that information is sent to a program called PROCAPP.EXE. However, you will need to have that program available before you can capture the information. This means that you must invest the effort to configure or build a program to process the data that you are providing these input facilities for. An exception to this rule is if the form is intended for human processing via email. In that case, just list the action as "mailto:username@domain.com" (substitute the email address as appropriate). Otherwise, you will need to list the URL of a gateway program to process the information.

If your storage mechanism for this data is a popular off-the-shelf database package, you may be able to use an off-the-shelf gateway program to take the values from the form and store them in your database. In Chapter 10 on CGI Gateways, we cover several such gateways including ones for Microsoft SQL Server and for Lotus Notes. Be forewarned now, however, that it is an effort unto itself to configure these programs for your needs. The Web is still in its infancy and the tools that exist are just that: tools, not comprehensive applications. Once you are finished with this book however, you should have ample knowledge to be able to effectively integrate these tools into a cohesive whole.

If you cannot find such a tool for your anticipated database store, you will have to write a gateway, or have one developed. This can be done in a script-like language such as Perl or Awk, or in a 3GL such as C. Most gateways are in fact written in Perl or C, with a handful developed in Visual Basic (mostly for Bob Denny's httpd for Windows Web server). Details of CGI gateway development are also presented in Chapter 10.

The ISINDEX Tag—A Poor Man's Web Search Facility

Forms (combined with CGI scripts) are certainly the best way to search for information via a Web server. But some browsers may not have forms support, and there is certainly an authoring effort associated with creating them. The other way to performs searches is to have the CGI script that generates a document generate an <ISINDEX> tag in the <HEAD> element. This will result in a field appearing in the user's browser, informing them that the document is a searchable index, and that it can be searched with keywords. If the user fills in the field, those keyword values are appended to the URL with a question mark separator. This results in the server reinvoking the same CGI script search program specified by that URL, with the specified search terms as arguments. A different result set will come back the second time of just the search hits. This time the resulting HTML will not contain the *<ISINDEX>* tag (see Figure 5.2).

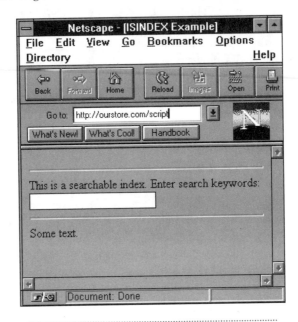

FIGURE 5.2 WEB BROWSER SCREEN FOR SEARCHABLE INDEX DOCUMENT

See **http://www.utirc.utoronto.ca/HTMLdocs/NewHTML/server-isindex.html** for more information on using ISINDEX for server-side searches.

CLICKABLE IMAGE MAPS AND IMAGE PROCESSING

Many of the most attractive Web sites use a clickable image map to facilitate navigation. *Image maps* are embedded images in HTML documents that allow navigation to other HTML documents based on which part of the image the user clicks on.

The general outline of creating image maps is:

- Embed an image in a document as you do normally and link the image to the image map specification file (which you create when you define the image map).

- Define an "mage map for the embedded image with association from various regions to the other documents using a map editing tool.
- Place the controlling document, embedded image file, and image map definition file on the Web server, and configured the Web server as necessary.

Unfortunately the details of this process still vary somewhat from server to server.

Embedding the Image

Image maps are defined just as an embedded image is defined, using the *<IMG>* tag. The IMG element is embedded in an anchor. This should link to the image map specification file. When the user clicks somewhere in the image, the URL specified in the anchor and the coordinates within the image are sent to the server. An example of the HTML necessary to link to the image map is:

Click on which product you are interested in.

```
<A HREF="/products.map"><IMG SRC="products.gif" ISMAP></A>
```

For example, when the user clicks on location (100,50) in the image, the following text is sent to the Web server:

```
cgi-bin/imagemap/products?100,50
```

The Web server will retrieve the document associated with that area. Now we need to learn how to associate various regions with various documents, or how to build the image map.

Map File Formats

In many places in this book where server-specific examples must be given, we will start with the European Microsoft Windows Academic Centre (EMWAC) https server as a reasonable default. EMWAC's server (discussed in more detail in Chapter 9) runs on Windows NT (a bias of this book), is free, is shipped on the Windows NT 3.5 Resource Kit, and has many other features to recommend it. Map file formats vary by server so we will present the https format first for discussion purposes.

An https map file is a text file with multiple lines each defining a region of an image. Comments may be created by beginning the line with a pound sign (#). A *circle* region is defined with a line in the map file beginning with the keyword *circle* followed by an x coordinate, y coordinate, a radius, and a uniform resource locator that that circular region should link to. A *rectangle* region is defined by the keyword *rectangle* followed by the coordinates of the upper left hand and lower right hand corners of the rectangle followed by the URL of what document to link to. A *polygonal region* is defined by the keyword *polygon* followed by a sequence of x,y coordinate pairs followed by the URL of what to link to. The default line indicates what to link to if no region matches occur. Of course you may simply list the current document to make default have no effect. You must always have a default line in your image map file.

To summarize, the possible line formats are:

```
circle x y r URL
rectangle x0 y0 x1 y1 URL
polygon x0 y0 x1 y1 x2 y2 ... URL
default URL
```

URL here refers to the *full* URL to the resource, including resource type and hostname. Relative references do not work. The URL should not be enclosed in quotes (a natural reflex from building HTML links). If you are using a tool, you need not worry about quoting the URL. You do need to remember to include the full URL, however, and not just a relative reference.

Also note that this format is not the same as other Web servers. In fact, it's different than the first two primary Web server platforms: the NCSA and CERN servers. The format of map file formats for those servers follows. The CERN server uses a program called *htimage* to handle its clickable images. But all you need to know is the format that htimage accepts. Its somewhat similar to https' format, except that x,y coordinates are grouped together in parentheses and separated by commas. The format is thus

```
circle (x,y) r URL
rectangle (x0,y0) (x1,y1) URL
polygon (x0,y0) (x1,y1) (x2,y2) ... URL
default URL
```

Again the URL must be a full URL and not relative references. Before you relax and assume that map formats are basically similar, be careful! The format of clickable images for NCSA's httpd server is very different from both of these. The httpd server is the basis of the httpd for Windows server and the WebSite for Windows NT server. The same scheme is used to present each region on a line, but the keywords are slightly different, and the point specifications are even more different. A circle is defined with a point in the center and any point on the circumference. Most significantly, a point directive is added which is not supplied by the other servers. When the browser user clicks on a point outside a defined shape area, the point closest to the click is selected. NCSA also doesn't require a default directive to be used, and disallows its use when a point specification is supplied.

```
circle URL x0,y0 x1,y1
rect URL x0,y0 x1,y1
poly URL x0,y0 x1,y1 x2,y2 ...
point URL x,y
default URL
```

Finally, though this should cover most of the basic formats used for images, don't assume so. Read your server documentation carefully on this issue. You will want to author image maps that are portable across all platforms that you may need to support. That may seem impossible, because of the many different formats, but you will not likely be authoring image maps directly, you will be using an image map authoring tool.

We review several image map tools in the next chapter on HTML authoring tools: MapEdit and HTMLMap are particularly useful. This will allow you to define your regions once and the tools will generate various image map formats as output. However you must still know the information above, because there is still no standard and you can not be certain that the generated map output will work on your server without reading your server documentation. In fact, MapEdit only directly supports the CERN and NCSA image map formats. It will not generate map output that is directly usable by EMWAC's https or Process Software's Purveyor.

Example Image Map

Figure 5.3 shows a clickable image map.

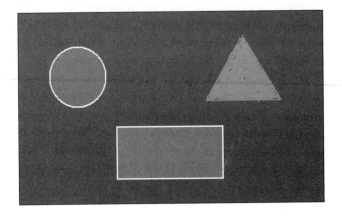

FIGURE 5.3 CLICKABLE IMAGE MAP

The following is the image map (in https format) corresponding to the marked regions in the image above.

```
circle 94 99 45 http://ourstore.com/circle.htm
rectangle 154 175 319 250 http://ourstore.com/rect.htm
polygon 350 39 291 137 412 137 349 37 http://ourstore.com/poly.htm
```

References for Image Maps

- Graphical Information Map Tutorial (**http://wintermute.ncsa.uiuc.edu:8080/ map-tutorial/image-maps.html**).
- CERN Server Clickable Image Support (**http://www.w3.org/hypertext/WWW/ Daemon/User/CGI/HTImageDoc.html**)
- Information for Imagemaps (**http://blake.oit.unc.edu/~duncan/mapex.html**)

HTML 3.0

All features of HTML that we have talked about thus far are reasonably solidified. The features that we have covered are basically HTML up through HTML 2.0. However, HTML 3.0 is still under development. HTML 3.0 is sometimes referred to as HTML+ although strictly speaking there are differences. It is very important that webmasters be aware of what is in the pipeline in Web development. Otherwise, they may work unnecessarily hard on enhancement to their Web server that are superceded by one of the emerging features. We will concentrate on the features likely to be relevant to our envisioned applications.

The major features of HTML 3.0 likely to be of greatest relevance for our purposes are tables, figures, stylesheets, and various enhancements for forms and interactive applications.

Tables

This is the big one. It solves a major weakness of current HTML 2.0—poor display of tabular data, or any data where lining up successive rows of data in the same column was important. In our previous examples, you saw where we needed to use the *<PRE>* (preformatted) tag to allow the fields of a user's address to line up above each other. This would not be necessary if tables were universally available. The data fields could just be presented in the second column of a table, with the first column used for field names.

A table is defined with the *<TABLE>* tag. The BORDER attribute indicates that lines should enclose each cell. The *<TH>* tag is used to separate table headers. The *<TR>* tag separates table rows. After the table headers, data elements are each introduced with the *<TD>* tag. No closing tags for any of the internal elements are necessary (no *</TH>*, *</TR>*, or *</TD>*). The following is an example of a simple table (using our bookstore example introduced earlier)

```
<TABLE BORDER>
<CAPTION>Classics On Sale This Month In Paperback</CAPTION>
<TH>Title<TH>Author<TH>Cost<TR>
<TD>Brothers Karamazov<TD>Dosteyevsky<TD>$7.95<TR>
<TD>Anna Karenina<TD>Tolstoy<TD>$9.95<TR>
<TD>And Quiet Flows the Don<td>Sholokhov<td>$14.95<TR>
</TABLE>
```

Figure 5.4 shows the table.

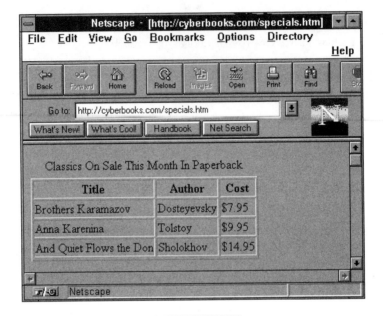

FIGURE 5.4 SIMPLE TABLE

The example above is the simple case. We can also create tables with more advanced features such as multiple row or column cells. This is done by supplying a ROWSPAN or COLSPAN attribute to the TH tag. Also, both TH and TD elements may be positioned using an ALIGN attribute. The ALIGN attribute may have a value of LEFT, CENTER, or RIGHT, with a default value of CENTER.

As of this writing only the Mosaic 2.0, Cello, and Arena browsers support tables. Netscape supports tables in their latest beta (1.1N at this writing) but there are a number of problems with them. Since Web browsers ignore tags they don't understand, we urge you to author appropriate material using the TABLE feature.

Figures

The FIG element has been proposed to support figures in HTML. The <FIG> has a required attribute of SRC (as IMG does) which specifies the image used to build the figure. The <FIG> tag takes an optional attribute of ALIGN. The browser may move the figure to a more convenient location, resize it, and flow text and other elements around it. In fact, this is a key difference between figures and straight embedded images. An embedded image is literal in its placement. A figure can be placed in the vicinity of associated text, leaving options open to the browser for more attractive display.

The ALIGN attribute may have a value of LEFT, CENTER, RIGHT, BLEEDLEFT, BLEEDRIGHT, or JUSTIFY, the default being CENTER. If the ALIGN attribute is CENTER, the image of the figure is centered on the page with no text flowing around it. If the ALIGN attribute is JUSTIFY, the image is expanded to fill the page to the left and right margin, again with no text flowing around it. The LEFT value aligns the figure image with the left margin of the text. BLEEDLEFT aligns the figure with the left window border. Similarly, RIGHT aligns with the right margin and BLEEDRIGHT with the RIGHT window border.

Text inside the FIG element (before the </FIG> tag) is used in text browsers that can't display the figure. An optional CAPTION element inside the FIG element displays a caption for the figure in a location up to the browser (bottom, top, or sides). Text following the FIG elements may flow around the image of the figure. The following is a simple figure with a CAPTION and text that is displayed if the figure can't be.

```
<FIG SRC="map.gif">
<CAPTION>Map of the Western hemisphere. </CAPTION>

Image of Western hemisphere.

</FIG>
```

Another proposed part of the figure extension is to allow anchors with the SHAPE attribute to be placed into the FIGURE body. After the <FIG> tag and the CAPTION, and anchor is started with the <A> tag. For example the following code places a triangle within the figure caption.

```
<FIG SRC="map.gif">
<CAPTION>Click on triangle to zoom to US. </CAPTION>
Image of Western hemisphere.
<A SHAPE="0.5,0.1&0.1,0.8&0.5,0.8" HREF="usa.htm">triangle</A>
</FIG>
```

Stylesheets

One aspect of the Web that has often been its greatest strength is its ability to define the structure of a document rather than its specific appearance. The browser determines the concrete display of logical and structural aspects of the document. For example, we as Web authors don't define how our first, second, and third level headings appear in the user's document, that is determined by settings of the users browser. We specify that a phrase should be *emphasized* not what fonts, attributes, and sizes achieve that emphasis.

This is a powerful capability: the author can concentrate on the content of their message, the user can specify what appearance conveys the structure relationships best for them. This model has been part of the success of the Web, and no one is proposing wholesale abandonment of it. What is being recognized is that very often, the appearance may in fact contribute and sometimes be part of the message. This is especially true in applications of the Web for disseminating news or advertising. If the Web content is created in parallel or after an effort to design printed material for publication, often much effort has gone into very precise layout of text on the page, a distinct style for fonts, sizes, and positioning.

We have said earlier to concentrate on logical structure when performing Web authoring. By and large, that is still true. However, there may be cases where you may not want to lose the effort invested in creating attractive and readable page layouts. In my opinion, the examples of this are usually restricted to single page displays. As a Web user, if I am going to read a large amount of material, I want to be able to do so in the styles that make the text most understandable and appealing to me. I have that expectation from other Web browsing, and if someone tries to force feed a style on me for reading their content, I will rebel. For example, Web users would start buying browsers that allowed them to override a publisher's style or style sheet if publishers abused any ability to influence browser presentation. Still for one page displays, I think most Web browsers would accept an advertiser or publisher's finely crafted layout.

That being said, going beyond what undoubtedly is a religious war on the horizon as more publishers hit the Web with their information, there is a sensible way to allow people to publish information with some degree of control of the specific appearance. The method first proposed for this is style sheets. A *style sheet* is a set of suggestions outside the information itself that influence the browser's display of the information. The browser can, if it chooses, ignore the suggestions entirely. The purpose of this set of hints to the browser is to make the document appearance closer to the author's intentions, not to prescribe the one true way of viewing it. Style sheets should thus only enhance the effectiveness of Web documents. The biggest reason why stylesheets should really improve Web documents stems from the incredible hacks that some Web authors introduce in order to try to control actual appearance. As we mentioned earlier many, many Web sites have documents which jump around between heading levels just to get specific size fonts, without regard for their structural meaning, thus defeating the original purpose of those tags. With style sheets, suggested appearance can be restricted to the style sheet, leaving the document structure intact. That said, style sheets are quite controversial and will probably not make it into widespread use for a little while yet. You can ignore the issue entirely and still create a great, attractive Web content. You may wish to just skim the following specific methods for achieving style sheets.

Methods for Creating Style Sheets

Style sheets are referenced within the original document with a LINK STYLE tag. There is also the capability defined in HTML 3.0 to incorporate a STYLE element into the document head. The STYLE elements take one attribute called NOTATION which identifies which notation to use to define the style.

Browsers that recognize style sheets retrieve the linked style sheet and apply it to the current document. Successive style sheets in a document supersede the earlier style sheets. There is also a proposal for *cascading style sheets* to allow multiple style sheets to be applied to a document. We present here the basic capabilities rather than syntax down to the individual argument. There are many proposals for style sheets available now.

Here is one method, Robert Raisch's style sheet proposal (**http://gummo.stanford.edu/ html/hypermail/.www-talk-1993q2.messages/443.html**). In this proposal, the following attributes can be defined for an HTML element.

- **FONT.** Has arguments for the font family, spacing (proportional or monospace), size (points), weight, foreground and background colors.
- **JUSTIFY.** Determines how text is justified.
- **COLUMN.** Controls how columns are laid out.
- **BREAK.** Determines the "breakability" of the object. Values include none (can't break), item (break on a complete object), line, or character.
- **MARK.** A facility for associating special marks with an object.
- **VERT.** Describes vertical spacing before and after object.
- **INDENT.** Describes horizontal spacing before and after object.
- **LINK.** Various parameters for linked or selectable objects.

These attributes can be specified to apply to a particular HTML object, or as a default for all HTML objects that do not have that attribute defined.

What exactly are these HTML *objects*? They are various components of a document. The @DEFAULT object applies to the whole HTML document for cases when an attribute has not been associated with a more atomic object. Other objects include:

- @TITLE
- @BODY
- @P (paragraph)
- @H 1 .. @Hn (header levels)
- @A (anchors)
- @UL (begin unordered list)

An example of a defined object from a style sheet is:

```
@TITLE FONT(WEIGHT=BO)
```

This says that titles will have bold fonts.

DSSSL Lite

I used Raisch's proposal as an example of a style sheet notation because I think it's simple and brings up most of the major issues. Another contender for an HTML style notation is the ISO Document Style and Semantics Specification Language (DSSSL), or more specifically a subset of this oriented to HTML style, called DSSSL-Lite. For more information on DSSSL-Lite see **http://www.falch.no/~pepper/DSSSL-Lite/. DSSSL** is probably more rigorous and adaptable than other proposals, perhaps at the cost of immediate understandability to HTML authors Below is an example of defining a "heading 1" style in DSSSL Lite.

```
element h1
(paragraph
font-size: very-large-font-size
font-weight: 'bold
display-alignment: 'center
space-before: big-space-before
space-after: big-space-after
content: (sequence
 (literal
 (format-number (child-number) "1"))
 (literal ". ")
 (process-children))))
```

The important thing is that though specific syntax will probably differ, you will have the capabilities discussed in any final style sheet standard.

Better Forms

Among the new elements proposed in HTML 3.0 are:

- **Range controls.** This include such familiar Windows controls as slider bars and range knobs.

- **File widgets** (for attaching files to forms). This allows Web authors to provide uploadable files in the forms they author.

- **Client side scripts.** This allows more functionality to be associated with authored forms. Many Web browser users are used to a more interactive form authoring environment and are surprised by the passivity of Web forms. For example, you may want to allow other fields to take values based upon what you enter into one field. This will not be solved within HTML itself. Rather, the HTML author may associate a script with a form via the SCRIPT attribute of the form tag. When the user retrieves a form for entry, the specified script will be retrieved as well and interpreted by the Web browser. The script language is not covered by HTML 3.0 so this problem will have to be solved on a per browser basis. As a Web author you will only be able to take advantage of this if you have some idea of what browser the majority of your readers use. This makes this extension of very limited use, but it's a step in the right direction.

Document Backgrounds

Remember when we suggested that you should actually use all the apparently useless keywords such as the *<BODY>* tag. Well they are actually starting to be put to use. You may now give the BODY tag a BACKGROUND attribute specifying an image to be used as a document's background. For example,

```
<BODY BACKGROUND="images/checkers.gif">
```

Better Images

Among the enhancements for images included in HTML 3.0 are HEIGHT and WIDTH attributes for IMG elements. This particular feature was suggested by Netscape Communications as a result of one of their enhancements to the standard deployed in their own server and client. HEIGHT and WIDTH allow the Web author to give a specific size for images. This should eliminate the need to constantly resize images within an image editing tool to adjust Web page layout.

Character Formatting

The following new attributes are available. The *<BIG>* and *<SMALL>* tags were sorely needed. As we have seen, the header tag levels were previously abused to provide this functionality.

- *<S>*   Strikethrough.
- *<BIG>*   Displays in a larger font than current font.
- *<SMALL>*   Displays in a font smaller than the current font.
- *<SUB>*   Subscript.
- *<SUPER>*   Superscript.

References for HTML 3.0

- HTML+ (Hypertext Markup Format) (**http://www.w3.org/hypertext/WWW/ MarkUp/HTMLPlus/htmlplus_1.html.** Early proposal by Dave Raggett about what should be in HTML+).

- HTML 3.0 Specification (**http://www.hpl.hp.co.uk/people/dsr/html3/ Contents.html**) Draft standard.

- Style sheets (**http://gummo.stanford.edu/html/hypermail/.www-talk-1993q2.messages/443.html**). Rob Raisch (of O'Reilly & Associates) early proposal on style sheets. Does not cover cascading stylesheets.

NETSCAPE EXTENSIONS

Netscape Extensions to HTML 2.0

The following are some Netscape extensions made to features in the HTML 2.0 specification. If you use these tags now, they will appear correctly on Netscape but may be ignored by other browsers. Almost all of the extensions stem from legitimate needs, so we think they will all result in changes, if not to HTML 3.0 then to a later standard. However, it is by no means certain that the standard implementation of these features will match Netscape's extension to the letter.

<CENTER>

Centers the surrounded text on the line. This will almost certainly be adopted as part of the standard. It is in very widespread use.

<BLINK>

Displays the characters in blinking mode. This is more questionable as to whether this will be adopted as a standard. Nevertheless, it is becoming common to see it used.

Changes to the <HR> Tag

This tag has been extended with the following attributes:

- **SIZE.** Takes a numeric value which allows the thickness of the <HR> "horizontal rule" to be set.
- **WIDTH.** The horizontal rule now need not take up the entire width of the browser page. The WIDTH attribute can take a value of number of pixels or a percentage of the total width of the page.
- **ALIGN.** Given that horizontal rules can now be partial width, how do we align them? This attribute takes values of left, center, or right.

These extensions to the HR tag were among the first made by Netscape, and use of them has become very common on more crafted Web pages. For example,

```
<HR ALIGN="center" WIDTH="140" SIZE="4">
```

This will create a 140 pixel wide horizontal rule of slightly greater than normal thickness, centered on the page.

PROMPT attribute for <ISINDEX> tag

Currently the ISINDEX tag (described in detail earlier) results in a rather generic, uninformative prompt in most browsers. Netscape introduced an extension to allow this prompt to be configurable.

TYPE attribute for <UL> tag

Nested unordered lists now change the type of bullet as they progress to deeper level. If you wish to specify the type of bullet directly you can use the TYPE attribute with values of:

- disc
- circle
- square

TYPE attribute for <OL> tag

Ordered lists also change types as they nest. If you wish to set the type of numbering directly, you can again use the TYPE attribute with values:

- **1** numbers
- **I** roman numerals
- **i** lowercase roman numerals
- **A** capital letters
- **a** lowercase letters

START attribute for <OL> tag

For ordered lists, this allows you to specify a number to start the list from. I am less convinced this will make it into the standard.

<FONT> Tag

This Netscape extension takes an attribute of SIZE. The valid values are 1 to 7, with a default of 3. Obviously then these are not literal sizes but relative sizes to the normal font of 3. This is a very controversial addition for reasons that we have discuss earlier: a desire to keep HTML away from specificity of presentation. I would not advise utilizing this tag at this time.

Floating Images

Netscape introduced two new ALIGN attribute values to the IMG element to support *floating images* that allow text to be presented and wrapped alongside a browser picture.

- **Left**. Floats the image down to the left margin and allows the text to run alongside it. This might be useful, for example, to have an image in a product catalog with the description and product information appearing to the right of the image. This was not previously possible for multiple lines of text with the existing ALIGN attributes.

- **Right.** A similar feature, but the image floats to the right margin.

There are also new attributes introduced to help in formatting these new floating images. They are the VSPACE and HSPACE attributes of the IMG tag, which space images away from the text above and below and to the left or right of them. These attributes take values as numbers of pixels.

Another change necessary to facilitate floating images was to allow the *
* tag to break text and place it all the way past an image that it might currently be wrapped alongside. The *
* tag now supports (on Netscape browsers) a CLEAR attribute which can take a value of left or right depending on which style of image it is appearing alongside. CLEAR results in the following text being presented below the image as opposed to wrapped beside it.

For example, the following HTML text uses the new floating image related tags.

```
Below is just one of the products one sale this month:
<IMG SRC="widget.gif" ALIGN=left VSPACE=10 HSPACE=15>
<STRONG>Acme Widget #17</STRONG><BR>
Part Number: 132523<BR>
Size: 1" x 5"<BR>
Colors: black, silver (pictured), or gold<BR CLEAR=left>
To order, click on the order button below.
```

Figure 5.5 shows how this HTML results in the following Web browser appearance on Netscape.

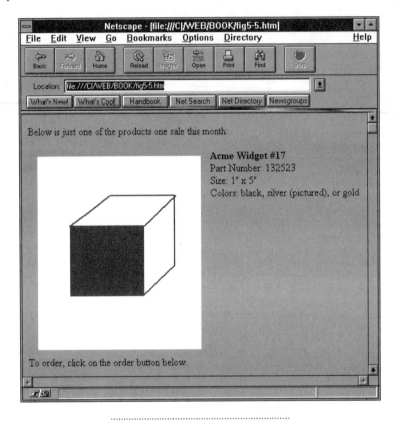

FIGURE 5.5 Demonstration of Floating Images

Other IMG Element Changes

A few other attributes were added to the IMG element unrelated to floating images. Most of these are to improve the level of control over image alignment.

- **absbottom**. Aligns the image with the bottom of the current line (the "bottom" value aligns it with the baseline of the current line).
- **absmiddle.** Aligns the middle of the current line with the middle of the image. "middle" aligned the middle of the image with the bottom of the current line.

• **texttop.** Aligns the top of the image with the highest text on the current line.

There are also new attributes to speed up image download and display. The WIDTH and HEIGHT attributes of the IMG tag allow the HTML author to specify the exact size of the image. This results in the Web browser user not having to wait for the image to be downloaded to calculate the size of the image.

Netscape Extensions to HTML 3.0

HTML 3.0 is not a completed specification yet, but Netscape has found a need for many of the ideas proposed there. So they have often implemented many of the HTML 3.0 features ahead of a firm standard, sometimes with extensions or additions to the proposed standard.

Document Backgrounds

Netscape has implemented the HTML 3.0 BACKGROUND attribute of the BODY tag, and has also implemented some of their own ideas for document backgrounds.

BGCOLOR Attribute

Netscape introduced the BGCOLOR attribute of the BODY tag The idea is that we may not need to have an actual image, and force the download of that image file, but that a background color may suffice. The background color is specified as an RGB triplet (a red, a green, and a blue value), where each value is specified as a two hex digits, allowing a range between 00 and FF (decimal 255).

```
<BODY BGCOLOR="#FF0000">This document will appear all red</BODY>
```

TEXT Attribute

If the background color can be changed, the text color should be able to be changed as well. The TEXT attribute allows the color of foreground text to be set, to allow you to choose a contrasting scheme with your chosen background color.

```
<BODY BGCOLOR="#000000" TEXT="#FFFF00">The foreground text will
appear in yellow, with the background in black.</BODY>
```

Note that this attribute is not relevant, and has no effect, if no background image is loaded and the background color is not specified.

LINK, VLINK, ALINK Attributes

Similarly, we will need some way of setting what colors the links appear in. Netscape allows you to set the color attributes for links in a document (with the LINK attribute), the color for links that the user has already visited (the VLINK attribute), and the color that links display as they are activated (the ALINK attribute). Again these attributes are not active if a background color has not been set and a background image has not been loaded.

One use of this feature would be to disable the "visited link" color attribute in Netscape by setting the color to the same as the active link color: blue. This could be done with:

```
<BODY VLINK="#0000FF">
```

Frames

This is the most recent Netscape extension, introduced with Netscape Navigator 2.0 in October of 1995. Frames allow the display of multiple independently scrollable regions on a browser page, each with its own URL. Frames can be used to provide: banners, parts of content that remain fixed as other parts dynamically change; tables of contents, that allow navigation of large amounts of content from a brief top level summary; and result windows that allow the user to view the detailed results of a query while maintaining the original query display in another panel.

Frames are defined by replacing the BODY element in an HTML page with a FRAMESET element, opened by the *<FRAMESET>* tag and closed by the *</FRAMESET>* tag. The *<FRAMESET>* tag takes two attributes: ROWS and COLS. Both of these attributes takes a comma separated list of values, which define the heights and widths of the various frames in the frameset. These values can be absolute pixel numbers (not recommended), percentages of the total window size (in which case the numbers are suffixed with %), or relative values (suffixed with an asterisk) which partition up space remaining after percentage or fixed values have been allocated.

For example a frameset tag might be specified as follows:

```
<FRAMESET ROWS="50%,2*,*">
```

The values for the ROWS attribute specify that the first frame takes 50% of the available window height, the second frame takes 2/3 of the remaining 50% (or one third of the overall height), and the third frame takes one third of the remaining 50% or one sixth of the overall height. The lack of COLS attribute indicates that all three frames uses the entire available width. Frameset elements can be nested. This is how you would, for example, break a window up into quadrants.

Inside FRAMESET element, individual frames are named and given content with the *<FRAME>* tag. *<FRAME>* takes attributes of:

- **SRC.** Value should specify the URL of the content to be displayed in quotes. Defaults to displaying a blank frame (not very desirable so give it a value).

- **NAME.** Optional attribute that specifies the name of the frame. Defaults to no name.

- **MARGINWIDTH.** Optional attribute that specifies the width of margin in pixels. Default is implementation dependent (its a reasonable value).

- **MARGINHEIGHT.** Optional margin height in pixels.

- **SCROLLING.** "yes" always displays scrollbars. "no" never displays. Default of "auto" displays them when they are needed.

- **NORESIZE.** Attribute with no value that indicates that frame is not resizable by user.

A NOFRAMES element can be nested inside a FRAMESET. It contains HTML to be displayed on non-frame-capable browsers.

Below is simple frame example.

```
<HTML>
<HEAD><TITLE>CyberBooks</FRAME></HEAD>
<FRAMESET ROWS="25%,*">
<FRAME SRC="banner.htm" SCROLLING="no">
<FRAME SRC="detail.htm">
</FRAMESET>
</HTML>
```

This would appear as shown in Figure 5.6. As the user scrolls through the list in the lower frame, the banner in the upper frame remains unchanged.

FIGURE 5.6 SIMPLE FRAME EXAMPLE

References for Netscape Extensions

- Extensions to HTML

  (**http://home.mcom.com/assist/net_sites/html_extensions.html.**) Netscape's HTML 2.0 Extensions, many of which may work their way into the eventual HTML 3.0 standard.

- HTML Page Design

  (**http://ncdesign.kyushu-id.ac.jp/howto/text/html_design.html.**) Examples of Netscape's extensions.

- Frame Basics

  (**http://home.mcom.com/assist/net_sites/frame_syntax.html.**) Documents syntax for frames.

VRML

Just in case you have any doubt that the future of networked information dissemination lies with HTML and the Web, I'd like to talk a little bit about one of the more exciting spinoffs of HTML to appear on the horizon: *VRML*. The Virtual Reality Modeling Language is, in the words of its authors (Mark Pesce of Enterprise Integration Technologies, Anthony Parisi of Labyrinth Group, and Gavin Bell of Silicon Graphics), a "language for describing multi-participant interactive simulations." Basically what VRML tries to do is allow simulated worlds, complete with realistic three dimensional graphics, to be specified in VRML. You can navigate through these worlds just as you might via the World Wide Web. This will provide a Virtual Reality interface to the Web itself and its current content, but even further will allow applications that have not yet been attempted on the Web. VRML is not really an enhancement to HTML. It is not intended to supplant HTML but provides a whole new set of capabilities using the Web as a base to build a new set of capabilities upon. In return, VRML provides a new way of interacting with conventional Web resources with an immersive highly graphical interface to conventional Web resources.

VRML 1.0 is just a language to specify construction of three dimensional scenes built from individual object as well as providing a method to link the component object to other objects: either other scenes, or conventional WWW hyperlinks (later versions of VRML will have more provisions for interactivity than just navigation). The scene description language is based upon Silicon Graphics' Open Inventor ASCII file format. That language has been extended with keywords such as WWWAnchor that allows linking to other scenes or conventional Web resources. There are already experimental VRML browsers available: Web Space from SGI (**http://www.sgi.com/Products/WebFORCE/WebSpace/**) and WorldView from InterVista.

VRML should provide a very intuitive, immersive interface to Web information. As other virtual reality software becomes more common—VR games, output devices such as goggles, input devices such as data gloves—this will become a more popular way of interfacing with the existing Web. My prediction is VRML servers will start off as Web indexes, like Yahoo, that link to all kinds of existing Web resources, but the interface to them will be a virtual reality photorealistic room or scene with objects linking out to various Web sites. More and more of those Web sites will start offering "VRML alternate" home pages (just as in the early days of the Web where alternate text and graphic home pages were offered) for their content. We're not going to try to teach you to author VRML in this book—its a bit early for that, but you should track this closely, because in a few years VRML will be used for at least some Web sites' interface to information.

References on VRML

- VRML (Virtual Reality Modeling Language) (**http://www.w3.org/hypertext/WWW/MarkUp/VRML/**)

## CHAPTER 6

Tools for HTML Creation: HTML Editors

Now that you know HTML thoroughly, you're ready to start creating your content. At this point you have enough knowledge that you could just open up Notepad (or a text editor) and start spewing forth HTML tags. Although this is possible, it's probably not the most productive and effective method of creating initial content. I heartily endorse viewing your generated HTML in a text editor after its initial creation, and even making modifications and doing maintenance in native HTML. But you will want to learn some authoring tools to jump start your authoring efforts and to get a large amount of content written. As this is the first chapter where I begin delving into product evaluations, it is worth noting that in some cases, I will drill pretty deep into the product functionality. For the most part, I do this only when I consider the tool to be very important for your needs. The tools that I review thoroughly are in an essential category for Web development, and among the best of breed in that category. If you don't have the user manual of the product in front of you, you may be tempted to think that this detail is duplicate. It isn't. Most of these Web tools are in their infancy. Even among the better tools, the manuals tend to be minimal and incomplete. So here and in the rest of the tool-oriented chapters, I will exhaustively explore the best-of-the-breed essential tools, making sure that you know everything you need to know about them to use them productively, and avoid false starts and undocumented gotchas.

Authoring HTML: An Overview

Most authoring tools still leave something to be desired, especially to IS professionals used to more polished document creation tools. Word processors such as Word and WordPerfect are much more finely honed over their long history than the recent

HTML authoring tools. For structured documents and document collections, seemingly what HTML is all about, Lotus Notes has much more functionality specific to this need. Indeed, as I discuss in the following, tools are emerging from Microsoft and Novell to allow their word processors to create HTML, and from Lotus to allow Notes to be used as an HTML authoring tool.

Despite the problems with most existing HTML editors, and the increasingly viable option of conversion tools, there will continue to be a place in some environments for the standalone HTML authoring tool. As the state of HTML rapidly advances, many features will not have a good mapping from another environment. If webmasters wish to exploit those features they have two options:

- Write HTML by hand (possible for some, but not sensible for the majority)
- Use an HTML authoring tool

Several HTML authoring tools are presented here: HoTMetaL from SoftQuad, HTML Assistant from Howard Harawitz, Sausage Software's HotDog, and several shareware and freeware tools. Part of the Web authoring process for most current Web servers is creating and editing clickable image maps, so we present a tool (MapEdit from Thomas Boutell) to assist in this process as well.

Bear in mind that these editors are not the only options. In the next chapter I explore add-on packages and utilities that allow Web authoring and conversion using word processors and other existing software packages not tailored to HTML. Also I only present Windows tools here. This is an unabashed bias of this book, as the predominant environment of the corporate desktop. If you are running OS/2, you should be able to run any of these tools in Windows 3.1 mode (since none of these are Win32s apps). If you are running some other platform (e.g., UNIX or Macintosh), bear in mind that, although we don't review UNIX or Macintosh authoring tools, a text editor is a perfectly viable authoring tool for these operating systems.

HTML ASSISTANT

HTML Assistant is one of the earlier Windows-based HTML authoring tools to come on the market. At first glance it appears somewhat spare—there are just three options on the main menu. When you first execute it, it looks like Notepad (the old Windows text editor), but instead of File, Edit, Search, and Help on the menu there are File, Options, URL, and Help. But there's a big feature that distinguishes this tool over Notepad, especially for HTML authoring: there are buttons below the menu for all common HTML tags.

HTML Assistant also includes a variety of commands for managing URLs. You may insert links to other Internet resources from a list of URLs. This list of URLs is stored as just a flat file list of linking HTML. For example (from one of their supplied URL files):

```
<A HREF="http://info.cern.ch/hypertext/WWW/MarkUp/Tags.html">HTML
Info for programming</A><P>
<A
HREF="http://info.cern.ch/hypertext/WWW/MarkUp/MarkUp.html">HTML
specs</A><P>
<A
HREF="file://localhost/c:\hhstuff\internet\html\howard1.htm">Howar
d's Current Hotlist of URLs</A><P>
<A
HREF="http://info.cern.ch./hypertext/WWW/Markup/SGML.html">SGML:
the standard markup language</A><P>
<A HREF="http://www.cs.dal.ca/home.html"">Dalhousie's Home
Page</A><P>
<A
HREF="http://www.ncsa.uiuc.edu/SDG/Software/Mosaic/StartingPoints/
NetworkStartingPoints.html">WWW Network Starting Points</A><P>
<A
HREF="http://www.ncsa.uiuc.edu/General/Internet/WWW/HTMLQuickRef.h
tml">HTML Quick Reference</A><P>
<A
HREF="http://www.ncsa.uiuc.edu/SDG/Software/Mosaic/NCSAMosaicHome.
html">NSCA Mosaic Home Page</A><P>
<A
HREF="http://www.ncsa.uiuc.edu/SDG/Software/Mosaic/Demo/metamap.ht
ml">WWW Meta-Map Demo</A><P>
```

These files can be written from scratch with a convenient dialog box they provide or imported from many browser bookmark file formats.

Assistant provides a single command to insert a standard document template:

```
<HTML>
<HEAD>
</HEAD>
<BODY>
</BODY>
</HTML>
```

This is great, but I wish they had taken it a bit further and included an empty title element, an empty *<H1>* element, and a "signature" block at the bottom of the page. They also have commands to mark blocks as BODY, HEAD, or HTML. I think all of these commands, but especially the Document Template command, should appear on the button bar (see Figure 6.1).

FIGURE 6.1 HTML ASSISTANT

HTML Assistant could certainly be more aggressive about incorporating more features, and making it closer to a document authoring environment, à la Word. But it does what it sets out to do very well, and has met the challenges of providing a good interface to HTML. It is probably the best native HTML authoring environment for Windows. However, let's look at another tool that takes a more ambitious approach to

HTML editing functionality: SoftQuad's HoTMetaL. You can decide whether the additional functionality results in benefits to the HTML author.

SoftQuad HoTMetaL

SoftQuad's product has garnered a lot of attention as one of the earlier Windows-based HTML-specific editing tools. HoTMetaL comes in two versions: HoTMetaL and HoTMetaL Pro. For many Web authors, HotMetaL can be quite a frustrating tool. When starting to work with a tool, it is likely that an author already has some Web content: either some of their own making or fragments downloaded from other webs. Before loading a file, HotMetaL makes aggressive attempts to parse the input for "correctness". The problem is that their parser has quite a few problems of its own, and it has rejected many a flawless Web page that I have tried to load into it. Even when HotMetaL loads the file, it has its own ideas about how to present raw HTML input. For example, in your original HTML you may have carefully laid out spacing to make your HTML input understandable to you and future maintainers of your source. HotMetaL ignores this and spaces the original tags for editing as it sees fit. It doesn't actually change your HTML source. It just has its own way of viewing that source that is somewhat removed from its actual appearance in the file. For those starting their efforts in HotMetal itself, and committed to using just one tool, these drawbacks are less severe.

But other problems remain. As a Windows application, HoTMetaL is rather primitive and idiosyncratic. There are no button bars. HTML cries out for display of the available tags. Instead they provide an Insert Element menu option that brings up an ungainly dialog box, which gets in the way of the text that you are supposedly editing at the time. The main menu is ordered wrong—the last command on the menu is Window not Help! Its options (such as the reference to a Web browser that it uses for many functions including Help and Preview) are not configurable with HoTMetaL itself. Due to its ambitious display philosophy for editing HTML (described below), it is quite slow in loading HTML for editing.

On the positive side, HoTMetaL, probably more than any other editor reviewed here, uses the capabilities of a graphical environment to clearly differentiate between tags and content when in editing mode, and more generally to provide graphical representation of the structure of your content (see Figure 6.2). They go to quite a bit of effort to make the text seemingly attractive with elaborate graphical surrounding of tags, colored representation of links, and font size changes. There are options to hide or show markup tags, to hide or show URLs, and to hide or show inline images. With tags and URLs hidden and images shown, it looks a lot like a Web browser (but a very slow one given that it's editing local text).

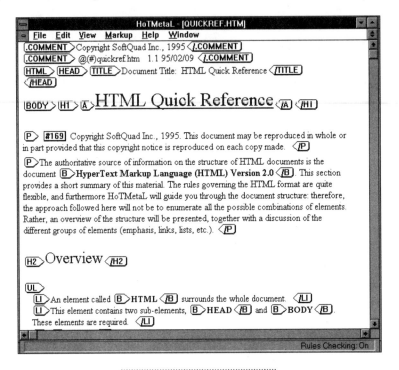

FIGURE 6.2 SoftQuad HoTMetaL screen

There are some other nice features of HoTMetaL: it will publish your content by converting your URLs to full Internet URLs at your command. In other words, it will take the URLs that refer to local files and replace them with URLs that include your hostname (e.g., prefixing the file name with **http://ourstore.com**). It has planned the integrated use of Web browsers and the WWW itself to document and supplement the program well (though again you can't configure your browser selection within the program). It has some very useful local HTML files that ship with the product: Good examples of these are HTML Quick Reference and a tutorial on writing HTML with HoTMetaL. In general, HoTMetaL seems like an attempt to create an environment for HTML creation rather than a tool (though this distinction is admittedly vague and imperfect). Suffice it to say that many beginning Web authors will like this, especially those oriented to content creation from scratch. If you want to evaluate HotMetal for yourself, check them out at **http://www.sq.com**.

HTML WRITER

This is an extremely minimalist HTML authoring tool (see Figure 6.3). The value of HTML Writer above what is offered by a text editor is pretty much just a set of menus for inserting HTML tags. There are no buttons provided for inserting tags as in HTML Assistant. In other words, its an MDI (Multiple Document Interface) Notepad with an HTML menu option. There are no URL management facilities, test viewing facilities, or URL conversion facilities. HTML Writer is also actual *freeware* (no payment or contribution is required). This may be useful in a situation where you wish to leave the client with software that they can maintain their content with, but you don't want to leave them with unregistered shareware. To retrieve a current copy of HTML Writer, go to **http://lal.cs.byu.edu/people/nosack/get_copy.html**.

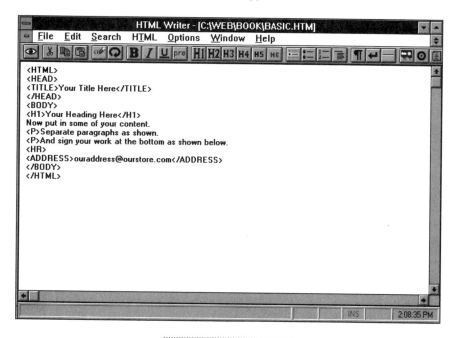

FIGURE 6.3 HTML WRITER SCREEN

HTMLEd

This is another more minimalist authoring tool, but it has some nice features. It includes a reasonable subset of HTML tags on the button bar (though not as many as HTML Assistant). It includes major areas of HTML functionality at the top level of the main menu: Elements, List, Link, Style, and Entity (see Figure 6.4). The Elements menu includes commands to mark headings, titles, addresses, paragraphs, and as with HTML Assistant, to insert a standard document template. The List menu has commands for creating lists and menus. Style allows text to be marked as bold, italic, underline, and HTML-specific tags such as STRONG, EM, and CODE. The Entity menu inserts the escape sequences for various special characters such as <, .>, and &. HTMLEd can be ftp'ed from **ftp://tenb.mta.ca/pub/HTMLed/**.

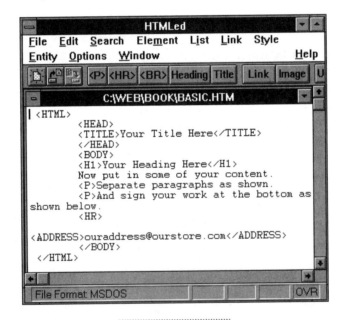

FIGURE 6.4 HTMLED SCREEN

HTML HYPEREDIT

This is another freeware authoring tool (it modestly states that it was "thrown together by Steve Hancock.") It is an acknowledged quick hack in Asymetrix' Toolbook, but it actually has some nice features, including buttons to place signatures and images, several buttons to perform various types of linking, and a Custom button to add tags to a pick list (see Figure 6.5). It's available by ftp from **ftp://info.curtin.edu.au/ pub/internet/windows/hyperedit/htmledit.zip**.

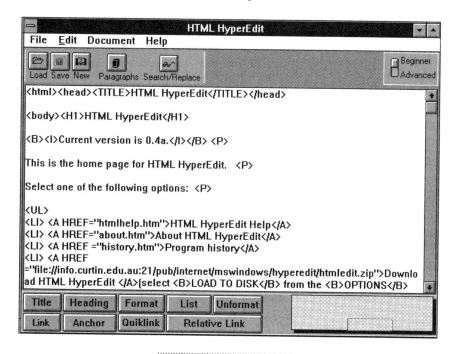

FIGURE 6.5 HTML HYPEREDIT SCREEN

MAPEDIT

I discussed the generation of image maps earlier and art of that process is to create image map files in the formats that I mentioned. This can certainly be done manually with a text editor, just as raw HTML can be created manually. But in the case of image map files, it is much more painful. It would be very difficult to determine the coordinates of clickable objects in the image file without a tool. One such tool is MapEdit.

MapEdit lets you load the GIF file that you wish to turn into an image map and to mark circles, rectangles, and polygons as clickable objects on the image, as well as to identify the URLs that those objects link to (see Figure 6.6).

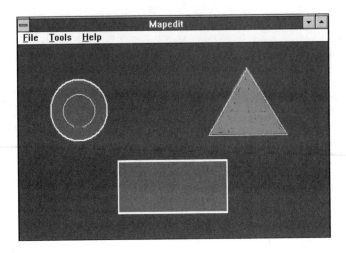

FIGURE 6.6 MapEdit Image Map Editor

Note that you may only use GIF files here, not JPEG files. That, and the fact that most browsers provide support for incremental downloading of interlaced GIF files makes GIF files a better choice. MapEdit will generate map files that can be used directly by the CERN and NCSA Web servers, and derivatives thereof (which include Netscape). These map files are text files which list the coordinates of the clickable region followed by the URL to which the region links. These files are very readable within a standard text editor. This is good news since MapEdit will not create map files for https. This means that you will need to create the map file within MapEdit, and save it as CERN format—the closest approximation of https format that MapEdit supports. Then you will need to edit the resulting to text file to convert the CERN style region definitions to https style. This is not too bad the first time, but it makes the ongoing development and maintenance process somewhat awkward. Every time you decide to add or edit an object to the image map, you must reedit the map file for the *entire* file.

Creating a Clickable Image Map

Let's walk through the process of creating a clickable image map using the MapEdit tool.

Acquire the image

First create your diagram, or acquire the image you wish to use as the background of your image map. This will usually be in Windows bitmap (.BMP) or some other common PC format—not usually in GIF format. You will normally keep your images in a separate subdirectory (often called IMAGES). This makes your collection of images much easier to manage.

Convert to .GIF file

Convert the BMP (or whatever format) file to a GIF file. You can use a tool such as LView Pro (supplied in this book and discussed in the Chapter 7 in the section on conversion tools). You can also use Corel or some other high-end drawing package to do the conversion. Alternatives to LView Pro include other dedicated conversion tools such as HiJaak.

Load into MapEdit

Run **MapEdit**. Choose **Create** from the Open menu and select the correct GIF file. You will be prompted at the same time for the name of the map file. A reasonable convention is to use the sample directory and name as the image, but substitute .MAP as the extension.

Identify the clickable objects

Use the Tools menu option to identify the areas that you want to be clickable and the URLs that they link to. You can select Circle, Rectangle, or Polygon. After positioning and sizing the shape, click the right mouse button. You will then be prompted for the URL to link to as shown in Figure 6.7. Enter the **full resource type**, **host name**, and **path**. Do not enter a relative reference such as another HTML file name alone. Also, do not enter the URL in quotes, just supply the full URL as a plain text string.

Choose **Edit Default URL** from the File menu to set a URL to be used if the user clicks outside any other identified region. You can list the default URL the URL of the containing document, or you may list the URL of a document that contains an error message indicating that the user's click was not on a valid region. If you use this technique, you will want to include a link on the "error document" back to the containing document of the image map.

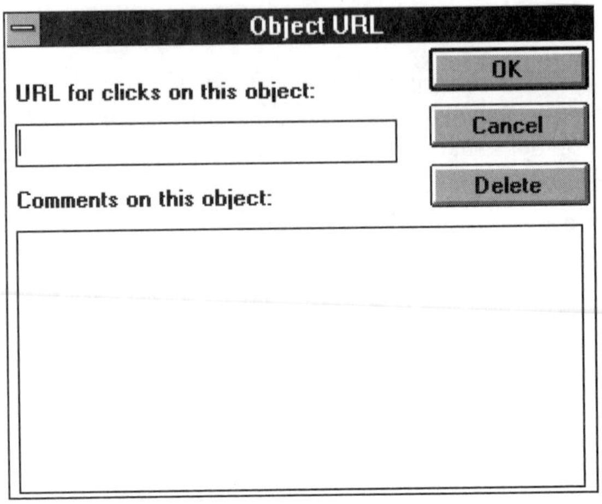

FIGURE 6.7 MapEdit Prompt for URL

Save the image map

If you are using a CERN-based server, save the image map in **CERN** format. If you are using an NCSA-based server (e.g., WebSite, Denny's httpd for Windows) save it in **NCSA** format. If using Emwac's *https* or Process Software's Purveyor, save it in **CERN** format, but you will need to edit it by hand to make the map file usable. The following is the native output when saving from MapEdit as CERN format.

```
#Mark the region, then click on the right mouse
#button to bring up this modal dialog box prompting
#you for the URL to link the identified object to.
circle (94,99) 25 http://ourstore.com/circ.htm
# rectangle marking requires just a single click and drag
rect (154,175) (319,250) http://ourstore.com/rect.htm
#a triangle region can be made with the Polygon tool
poly (350,39) (291,137) (412,137) (349,37)
http://ourstore.com/poly.htm
```

Use the text editor to convert files

Use NotePad or another text editor to view the image map text file and insure that it meets the format of your server. If not, *carefully* edit the map specification. The following is the output converted to https usable format.

```
#Mark the region, then click on the right mouse
#button to bring up this modal dialog box prompting
#you for the URL to link the identified object to.
circle 94 99 45 http://ourstore.com/circle.htm
# rectangle marking requires just a single click and drag
rectangle 154 175 319 250 http://ourstore.com/rect.htm
#a triangle region can be made with the Polygon tool
polygon 350 39 291 137 412 137 349 37
http://ourstore.com/poly.htm
```

Embed references to the image map in a larger HTML document

In the document where you would like the image map to appear, embed the *<IMG>* reference to the image file itself inside an anchor linked to the map file specification. This may be in a containing document devoted only to holding this image map (not required but in very common practice), or the image map may be displayed as part of a larger document containing other information.

For example:

```
Click on the item you wish to see more information on.
<P>
<A HREF="map.map"><IMG SRC="map.gif" ISMAP></A>
```

Test your working clickable image map

Load the containing document, and attempt to click into each region of the image map. This will make sure that links from all objects are working and that the URLs that they link to are valid.

MapEdit Evaluation

MapEdit is a very useful tool. It's difficult to imagine creating image maps without it or a similar tool. However, the amount of effort necessary to create files in non-supported formats is quite a drag on productivity (for example to be used by EMWAC https or Purveyor). It also creates a built-in maintenance problem. There is a large incentive not to make minor modifications to optimize the image map's appearance since just editing one object will require reediting the image map file completely to convert it for https. Just adding support for https-format image maps will make a huge difference.

Beyond that major usability issue (which should actually be a minor software modification), there are several minor enhancements that would improve its usability. One should not have to identify the destination map file when loading the GIF file that serves as its input. The map file should default to the directory and base file name of the GIF file that it is based upon. This is a natural user expectation anyway. Button bars would also be useful: a button with a circle to mark circle, a button with a rectange to mark rectangles, a button with a triangle to mark polygons.

For more information on MapEdit and a link to its ftp site, go to **http://sunsite.unc.edu/boutell/mapedit/mapedit.html**. MapEdit is not freeware. For commercial users, Thomas Boutell, the author of MapEdit, requests a contribution to the address supplied in the Help About box.

InContext Spider

InContext's Spider HTML authoring environment takes a very idiosyncratic approach to the HTML authoring process. Briefly, it works similarly to HoTMetaL by attempting to provide both an environment for HTML creation, and be close to WYSIWYG during the editing process. But the software really takes the level of abstraction offered by HoTMetaL to a new level. Beyond just attempting to show all of the structural elements of an HTML documents visually, it creates a "structure pane" on the left hand side that attempts to identify the HTML element that each portion of text in right hand windows lies in. Spider shows a few more of the actual HTML tags in editing mode than HoTMetaL does, which I find useful.

No tooltips are provided for any of Spider's button bar entries, so a tour of the product enumerating the available buttons is useful. Spider creates new document from existing template files. Templates for several common types of Web pages are supplied: the corporate Web page, a welcome page, a personal page, and other types of pages. Its a great idea but somewhat flawed in execution. The examples are not too compelling, and I really don't think a template should actually be *required*. Spider also lets you load documents, including existing HTML files that you may have created earlier. It provides a preview mode which lets you look at the true display of your content.

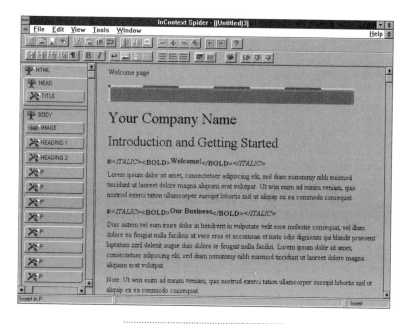

FIGURE 6.8 INCONTEXT SPIDER MAIN SCREEN

Spider attempts to display embedded GIF files inline within the editor, even in authoring mode. This is an innovative and nice feature, but has two problems. First, the GIF files are often just approximations of the actual image (probably due to rendering it in 16 colors and low resolution for efficiency). Also now that the editor is a graphics viewer as well, you can forget any pretense of performance. The process of loading a document into Spider is painfully slow, and once the document is loaded the editor is still no speed demon. Even on very fast machines redraws crawl along as you edit. The images in your document can be collapsed which helps performance somewhat, but the problem remains: this is a very slow editor.

The collapse capability applies to all of your HTML content. Spider sees your HTML document as one big hierarchy. The minus and plus sign buttons allow you to collapse individual elements to just the name of the element displayed and no text, and expand to display the text or subelements of a selected element. The double minus and double plus buttons collapse and expand the entire document. This collapse and expand metaphor is potentially useful for large highly structured single documents, but feels very unintuitive for most HTML pages.

The left pane button moves you into the structure pane of the document. Changing the structure of your document, i.e. adding HTML elements, is limited in many ways to this pane, making the software more modal than really necessary. The right pane buttons move you into the document pane where the text of an element is edited. Again, this approach certainly allows the structure of an HTML document to be clearly understood, and allows larger, more complex single HTML documents to be more easily navigated; however, it is clumsy for smaller simpler HTML pages. Since good HTML content should really be composed of smaller pages, with links where necessary to supplementary material, this metaphor really seems to be the wrong one for the job at hand.

Further buttons are available for creating headings, of level one through four (why not six which HTML supports)? Again these buttons are only functional from the structure pane. The anchor button lets you to create links to arbitrary URLs. Spider requires you to invoke Anchor and then supply the URL to link to in a dialog box. It then creates a link, but with the URL itself as the original linking phrase. You must then replace the URL with the actual phrase that will appear to the Web user. This happens even if you start the linking process by highlighting the desired linking phrase in your text. Almost all of the higher level tools that attempt to insulate the author from HTML (a category in which I would place Spider) allow you to create links by highlighting the linking phrase and then invoking the linking operation. The way that Spider performs this essential task of linking to other HTML content is very unintuitive, belying its tantalizing name.

Overall, I found the user interface metaphor of Spider inappropriate for most HTML content, and many details of its operation somewhat awkward (including positively atrocious performance). Still, Spider is putting forth some innovative approaches to the HTML authoring interface, and its early enough in their history to forgive some of the clumsiness of the details of operating it. Spider retails for $99. Evaluation versions of Spider can be downloaded from **http://www.incontext.ca**.

HotDog

Though you've seen several tools mentioned earlier reviewed favorably, I've saved the best for last. HotDog, from Sausage Software, is one of the more advanced tools in the area of support for HTML 3.0 and Netscape extensions. Sausage is careful to point out the difference between these two concepts, as we have done repeatedly in this book. Many other tools only have support for authoring Netscape extensions and not elements of HTML 3.0. Also, HotDog takes an approach similar to HTML Assistant (reviewed favorably earlier in this chapter), and different from Spider, HoTMetaL, or Word Internet Assistant: it shows you the raw, native HTML in all its unadorned glory. I find that this approach gives you a much better chance at keeping your HTML usage current, and tailoring it very specifically to just what your needs. HotDog takes the philosophy of providing a great user interface and many easily invoked assistant dialogs to aid in creating correct HTML tailored to your exact intention; however, it makes the display of the document show the native HTML and not some supposedly friendly graphic interpretation. Sausage recognizes that users want assistance with creating functionally exact, correctly formatted HTML, and that a good tool with a great interface can assist in this generation process. But they also understand that the author needs to be in close contact with the resultant HTML output. And the only way to do that is to show the output to the author in native form, as opposed to some half-baked idea that the graphic representation of the HTML tags and elements will convey the meaning of those tags indirectly. This product is a tour de force: every webmaster owes it to themselves to evaluate it before settling on one native HTML authoring tool. You may decide after reading the next chapter on HTML converters to do the majority of your content creation in Word or other familiar desktop software such as Notes. But even if you choose this path, there is a place in most HTML authoring projects for a tool dedicated to HTML authoring specifically, if only for content revision and fine tuning.

Another major aspect that distinguishes HotDog from the other HTML authoring tools (as opposed to the Word-based tools presented in the next chapter which get Word's modern interface for free) includes the relatively modern Windows GUI. A very intuitive button bar with large size buttons (that *do* have tooltips unlike some other products reviewed) appears just below the menu. This button bar exposes all the major areas of functionality of the HotDog editor. Below that, an element bar supports file and clipboard management functions, character formatting, creation of header elements, image alignment options and image breaks, creation of various types of list items, paragraph markers, and horizontal rules. A document bar at the bottom of the screen allows multiple files to be edited and selected from using tabs labeled with document titles. The status bar shows date and time as it does in Microsoft Word. The location and presence or absence of all of these bars is configurable.

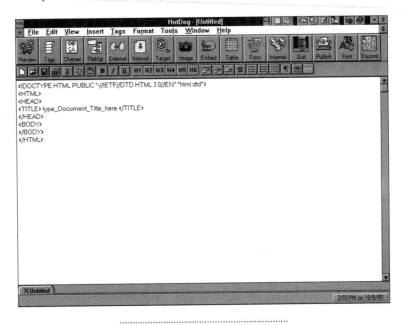

FIGURE 6.9 HotDog HTML Authoring Tool

HotDog allows you to configure any Web browser you wish for the Preview function, and the program icon of the browser appears on the button. The tags button brings up a window displaying almost all of the available HTML tags. Three columns are presented: the descriptive name of the tag, the begin tag, and the end tag (if relevant). All authoring tools make some sort of selection list available for HTML tags, but HotDog is the only tool that is remotely close to being complete. The tag list appears in Figure 6.10. Note the Windows 95 minimize, maximize and close buttons on the dialog despite the fact that this software was running on Windows NT 3.51 without the Windows 95 shell. If you find this flat alphabetical list somewhat overwhelming, the Tags submenu available from the HotDog main menu is much more hierarchically organized: twelve categories, each with no more than twenty menu items, expose the full set of tags that can be generated from HotDog.

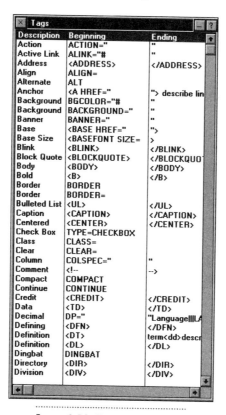

FIGURE 6.10 HotDog HTML Tags List

The CharSet button presents a list of entity codes for reserved characters such as ampersand (&), less than (<), and greater than (>). The FileMgr button allows files to be selected for HTML linking via a Windows 95 Explorer-like file selection dialog. The External button brings up the External Hypertext Link dialog, which allows you to build HTML links to external Internet resources. Fields are presented for all of the possible components of such a link, as shown in Figure 6.11. You are also presented with a list of all possible Internet resource types, including port numbers, directory locations, and named anchors within a specified document. My only quibble with this very useful feature is that the named anchor field (labeled "#") is not relevant if the field type is anything other than http, and should be grayed out in those cases, but it is not. The Internal buttons builds HTML links to named locations in local content.

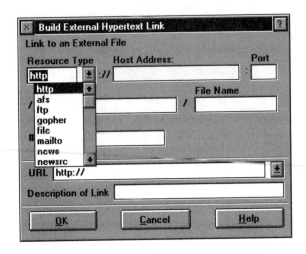

FIGURE 6.11 HotDog External Hypertext Link dialog

The support for HTML table creation is among the best I've seen. A dialog, shown in Figure 6.12, lets you create the number of rows, number of columns, number of heading rows and columns, width and height of cells, spacing and padding between cells, alignment of content in cells, and table border width. I haven't seen any other tool with this level of control. This is not totally surprising since support for tables is still emerging among popular browsers. Netscape has it now, but Microsoft's Internet Explorer 1.0 and many other popular browsers do not have support for tables. However, Internet Explorer 2.0 which is now in beta, does have table support, and many other browsers have this feature in the pipeline. As discussed in Chapters 4 and 5 on HTML, by the time you read this, it will probably be safe to use HTML 3.0 tables in your authoring efforts. A tool that supports this feature will be quite useful, especially since fine tuning the appearance of HTML tables in the native HTML can be quite a lot of work.

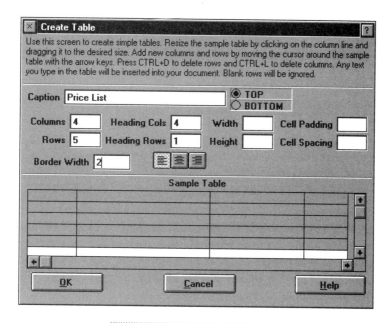

FIGURE 6.12 HOTDOG TABLE CREATION DIALOG

The Form button brings up the Define Form Elements dialog, which lists all of the available form field types. Once the first form field is inserted into your document, you will be prompted for the ACTION which is associated with the form (typically a CGI script that processes your form data). Note that the field types listed do not include specifying the type of field to input, such as the capability in HTML of stating that a particular field only accept integer input. Also note that there is no explicit support for grouping of radio buttons or checkboxes. Finally, and most egregiously, if you add a form field outside an existing FORM element but in the same document, you are not prompted a second time for the FORM tag attributes of this presumed second form.

Since there is no reason why one document could not have more than one form, this is a serious limitation. The form support is simplistic and flawed in some serious way. It should be enhanced with the same type of creative ideas and attention to detail that the product shows in other areas.

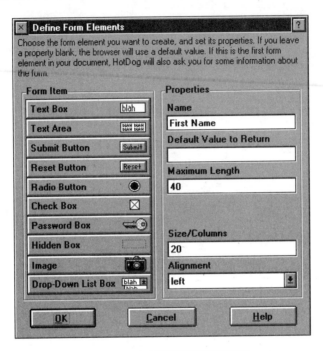

FIGURE 6.13 HotDog Form Creation dialog

The Publish button potentially performs a variety of processing tags on your HTML content in preparation for placing it onto your Web host. Many of the transformations available are due to moving the content to a UNIX machine for hosting. These include include removing carriage returns from the text, and replacing backslashes in URLs with slashes. Other replacements are more generically useful even when hosting on an NT-based Web server. For example, URLs referring to local files can be changed to URLs containing the local host name. The Publish concept, with options set as appropriate, is quite valuable and should probably be available in any full-featured HTML authoring environment.

Overall, HotDog is an excellent standalone HTML content creation tool, probably the strongest of those reviewed. HotDog sells for $29.95, and evaluation copies are available from Sausage Software's Web site: **http://www.sausage.com**.

CHAPTER 7

HTML CONVERTERS: CREATING HTML FROM EXISTING SOURCES

This chapter presents a variety of tools to assist in creating Web content from existing data or with familiar desktop software. Native HTML editors are useful for creating a single home page or a few supplementary pages of content, and for learning the basics of HTML. Currently however, the best way for most businesses to get existing data of interest up on their Web servers is to use an HTML converter.

Some of the converters I discussed are word processor add-ons. Since these can also be used as original authoring tools for HTML, it may seem strange to include them in conversion tools. Conversion tools share the common problem of translating from a format that does not always have direct analogs for component elements in HTML. HTML, with its emphasis on structure over appearance and its incorporation of hypertext linking to disparate objects, is quite different from each of the formats that we will convert from, in the tools below. This is just as true for creating HTML from word processing documents, as it is in converting from database formats.

The emphasis of this chapter is on *static conversion*: taking your data and converting it to HTML before making it available on your web. Many of the formats you may need to convert from may be done dynamically via gateways. Gateways will be discussed separately in a later chapter. Just be aware that your options for getting data onto the Web are by no means limited to the conversion tools I present in this chapter. By the time you learn about both conversion tools and gateways you should have a good idea from which data formats you can get your HTML content.

WORD INTERNET ASSISTANT

One tool of particular interest is Microsoft Word Internet Assistant now available free on Microsoft's Web server (**http://www.microsoft.com**). This tool creates HTML content from Microsoft Word documents. It requires Microsoft Word 6.0 or greater to run. The idea of enabling HTML authoring from a conventional word processor is certainly not new Several other Word macro-based packages for HTML authoring appeared prior to the introduction of WordIA. CU_IITML, a set of macros for Word 2.0 from Chinese University of Hong Kong, was the first to appear. This was followed by ANT HTML a set of macros for Word 6.0 from Jill Swift (**jswift@freenet.fsu.edu**). These packages invented the category, but I don't review these here because Word Internet Assistant has provided more functionality, in freely downloadable form.

Word Internet Assistant also raises the bar higher for functionality than its predecessors by actually allowing Web *browsing* from within Word. The browser is InternetWorks from BookLink technologies, now a subsidiary of America Online. Invoking Browser Web from the File menu will allow you to view Web pages from within Word. You may not find this to be the ultimate Web browser, but it will let you capture the HTML content and structure you wish to view, right into the comfort of your HTML authoring environment. The HTML authoring portion of the package (what we're interested in here) was developed for Microsoft by Charles View, Inc.

WordIA installs with a conventional Windows SETUP program as an add-on to Word. Once installed, you can create a new HTML document from the File New command by choosing the "Html" template that WordIA creates. You can also create HTML from an existing Word document, by selecting **Save As** and choosing **HTML 1.0 Converter** as the document type.

A note regarding versions of Word Internet Assistant: The text of this review is based on Word Internet Assistant 1.0, for two reasons. First, Word Internet Assistant 2.0 may not be available by the time you read this. Second, Word Internet Assistant 2.0 requires Word 95 (also known as Word 7.0 for Windows 95), or Word 6 for Windows NT. Not all users have this configuration, so it's reasonable to assume capability to run WordIA 1.0 as the base level of functionality. The perceptive reader familiar with these tools may notice that the screen figures are from Word Internet Assistant 2.0 (see Figure 7.1). WordIA 2.0 is one of my primary authoring tools, and it is what I have installed on the machine used to write this review. Nevertheless I have tried to restrict discussion of the functionality to version 1.0. There are actually relatively few functionality differences between the two versions. WordIA 2.0 is much faster, but much of that benefit was expected now that it is a true 32 bit application. The HTML viewing capability is somewhat improved in version 2.0, but not enough to remove some of the reservations we express later about full access to native HTML. Finally, WordIA 2.0 has added support for some HTML extensions, but nothing close to all of them.

The Button Bar

Once you begin working with an HTML document, a button bar appears presenting the various Internet Assistant-related commands.

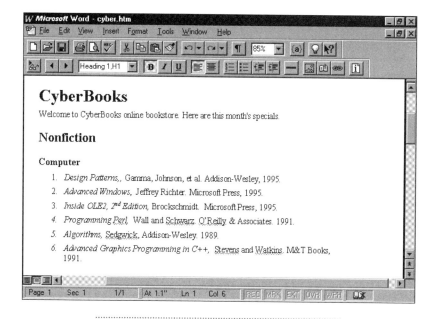

FIGURE 7.1 WORD INTERNET ASSISTANT EDITING AN HTML DOCUMENT

The first button bar switches between Internet browsing mode and HTML authoring mode. In authoring mode, which it calls "Edit View", the various heading levels can be set on a phrase by marking the phrase and invoking the style dropdown box. All other block attributes can be set from this style box. The font style dropdown box does not appear on HTML documents, but the bold, italic, and underline buttons do.

Ordered and unordered lists are created using the familiar mechanisms for numbered and unnumbered bullets that have always been on the Word toolbar. This mechanism is easy and familiar to Word users and an improvement on the amount of steps necessary to create lists in HTML. The next two buttons for Increase Indent and Decrease Indent on the Edit View button bar are only relevant to list items when used in an HTML document. Don't be tempted to use them elsewhere as you might be used to with Word. They will display the results of your indenting or backdenting but not affect the HTML at all.

A button is present to create horizontal rules, although this can also be down from the style box. Another button is provided to allow insertion of images (via the *<IMG>* tag). Using the advanced options dialog box, you may control the alignment of text next to the image as "TOP", "BOTTOM", or "MIDDLE", and specify whether the image is a clickable map or not. But that's it: none of the other plethora of image control options are available from within WordIA. Also the embedded image map functionality is limited to placing an ISMAP attribute within the IMG element. No surrounding anchor linking to the map file is generated. Even better would be to provide this link as well as the ability to launch an image map editor such as MapEdit. Indeed this is where WordIA could add a lot of value over existing tools: as an integrated authoring environment for the less HTML-savvy. Experienced webmasters know how to multitask between the various necessary authoring tools. Novice ones (except those of you reading this book) are less familiar with the sequence of steps. WordIA, despite the fact that it may never be as rich in HTML options as a dedicated environment, is the leading contender for acting as a simplified integration environment for disparate HTML creation utilities.

The next button available is for "bookmark creation". Don't let this throw you off. It does not refer to conventional Word document bookmarks to hold your place. It refers to HTML named locations within your document, or the named anchors that were discussed in Chapter Four. In other words, it encompasses the highlighted phrase with *<A NAME="bookmark name">* and *</A>*. For example (to recycle the earlier instance):

```
<A NAME="Conclusions">Conclusions<./A>
```

Once the bookmark labeling a location or section has been created, it can be linked to from within the same document or from another document using the Link button, just as one might link to an URL of a resource remote to our site, or the file location of another document or image on our own site.

Linking

In general hypertext linking is invoked with the Link button, which invokes a tabbed dialog box allowing various types of linking (see Figure 7.2).

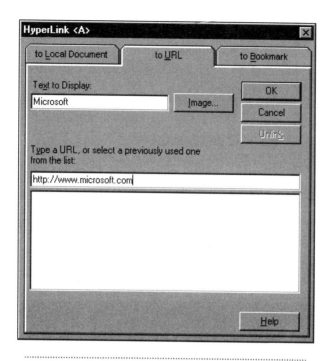

FIGURE 7.2 WORD INTERNET ASSISTANT HYPERTEXT LINKING TABBED DIALOG BOX

Links can be built to local documents, which are selected from the **to Local Document** tab of the HyperLink dialog. This tab is very similar to the standard File Open dialog, except with an area to specify a phrase to link to the document with. The tab also provides an Image button allowing you to select a JPEG or GIF image to use as the linking mechanism.

The HyperLink dialog's To URL tab lets you specify a URL from a presented list of Internet URLs or build a new URL which is then maintained in this list for future use. It would be useful if this list could be imported from Mosaic or Netscape bookmark files, especially if the import were to allow appending of information to the existing list. This feature could be implemented as another Advanced button on the URL tab. It should not be a separately invoked menu option or utility, especially since bookmark files of browsers change often. Also, though the URL tab does allow the author to specify a linking phrase (as with the Local Document tab), it doesn't provide a method of storing it. Indeed there is no way to mnemonically label the URLs that you store for future reference. This means that you can maintain a list of frequently-used URLs to link to, but you can't associate text with it that tells you what that resource is. Browsers such as Netscape and Mosaic store the titles along with the URLs in their bookmark files, so mnemonic information is available. HTML Assistant allows importing of browser bookmark files into URL list. If WordIA did the same, it would have a ready source of labeling information for the URLs. As with the previous tab, you may specify an image that the user will click on to activate the link.

Finally the To Bookmark tab allows linking to the bookmarks that have been stored as described in the last section. It creates the *<A HREF="#bookmark>* HTML code to allow linking to a named location in the document. The way that Word handles linking to bookmarks, and linking to resources in general, is a tour de force—much easier and more intuitive than any other authoring tool reviewed here.

Forms

This is another area that sets Word IA apart from other HTML authoring tools. Notice that even our favorite thus far, HTML Assistant, had no special support for forms. They don't even list the *<FORM>* tag on the button bar. By contrast, WordIA has very robust form support (though perhaps not as robust as QuarterDeck WebAuthor), with one caveat: Nothing is as robust as knowing HTML thoroughly and viewing and finetuning the HTML code natively, especially since forms functionality in the HTML specification is rapidly changing. As noted in the following, despite WordIA's strength in dealing with forms, it may be necessary to supplement it with a tool that allows direct editing of the HTML.

To create an HTML form in an HTML document with Internet Assistant, choose **Form Field** from the Insert menu. You will be informed that you are creating a new form, and asked to confirm it. Top of Form and Bottom of Form bars are placed in your document, and a new field of the type you specify is placed between these markers. Once the form has been created, the Forms toolbar appears. The toolbar has buttons for inserting fields and Submit or Reset buttons. The types of fields available are text box, check box, and dropdown lists. Each of the field types can have options set for them by double clicking on the field or by invoking the Field Options button on the Forms toolbar (see Figure 7.3).

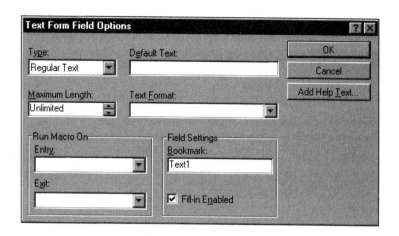

FIGURE 7.3 WORD INTERNET ASSISTANT TEXT FORM FIELD OPTIONS DIALOG BOX

A text field may have a maximum length (the MAXLENGTH attribute) and default text contents (the VALUE attribute) specified. It may also be specified to take numeric input only (which will set the INPUT type to INT). It may *not* have the SIZE attribute, the attribute specifying the width of the editing box, specified from Internet Assistant. This is a crucial omission. It means that you will need to use a text editor to add this attribute to your authored forms. Also several form text field options, that are apparently included to author non-HTML based forms (Word forms) are not relevant to HTML and some have strange consequences on the generated HTML. For example, the help text option causes the Help Text to become the HTML field name. Field names are not visible but are used to transmit the form data to a form processing application, and are used by the form processing program to process the information. If you know that the Help Text option sets the generated field name, you can exploit it to set the field names. If you don't know this, you may invest time in writing help text that is never used, and generating strange field names along the way that may give problems to CGI form processing programs. The status bar text option causes the supplied text to be placed inside the generated HTML INPUT tag, but does not affect what a Web browser can see when displaying the form.

Besides the options that have strange or incorrect results in the generated HTML, many of the options are just irrelevant to HTML documents and have no effect. These options should be grayed out or disabled in some other way when working with HTML documents, but they aren't. You should be careful then about investing time in setting these options, and assuming functionality that won't take place. We solve part of the problem here by enumerating the nonfunctional options, but you will need to refer back to your own understanding of HTML to not set options that you suspect will not have an effect. The other check is, again, to always view the WordIA-generated HTML in a text editor to check if your option affected the generated INPUT tag.

The nonfunctional options related to form fields include:

- the text format options to set the format as uppercase, lowercase, or first caps. These might be nice features in HTML but they don't exist. If you set them they will not affect the HTML, and will thus not affect what the user can do in the browser.
- the run macro on entry and exit options.
- the help text and status bar options do not have the intended effect (but as mentioned the help text option can be used to set field names).

WordIA lets you generate what it refers to as "drop-down form fields", which are really just HTML SELECT fields. It allows you to construct the list of OPTION tags for the SELECT element, using the Item Add capability on the drop-down form field dialog (see Figure 7.4). Unfortunately you cannot set whether the SELECT option will allow multiple selects (the MULTIPLE attribute), or whether or not an option is enabled by default. In other words, for dropdowns that allow multiple selections you will have to edit the code manually. As with text fields, you may use the help text option to set the field name.

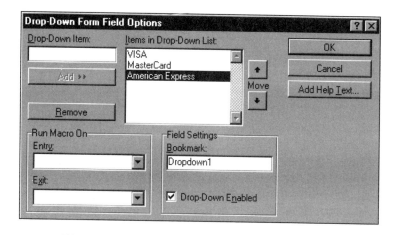

FIGURE 7.4 WORD INTERNET ASSISTANT DROPDOWN FORM FIELD DIALOG BOX

Another field type that can be generated with WordIA is the checkbox field. Unlike the case of drop-down field items, WordIA *will* let you specify whether checkboxes are enabled or disabled (checked or not checked) by default.

The types of HTML form fields that *cannot* be generated from WordIA (except by inserting HTML markup manually) include:

- The "radio" field type for INPUT elements. These create radio button fields.
- The "image" field type for INPUT elements. These allow form submission to be invoked by clicking on the specified image.
- The "password" field type for INPUT elements. This a text field where the user's characters are not entered to the screen)
- The TEXTAREA element. This allows entry of multiple line text fields.

These are reasonably common field elements, so, again, keep your text editor at the ready to make the final cut of your HTML forms. You can still go back and use WordIA for editing your content, but the display of unsupported field types will be unpredictable and if you work with those particular elements within WordIA you are not likely to get the result you seek. If you make a change to an unsupported field type within WordIA, you will again want to check the output within your text editor.

Tables

When using WordIA, it is not possible to insert tables while in HTML authoring mode in an HTML document. The Table menu option and table-related buttons do not appear in Word menu system when working on an HTML document. However, WordIA *does* convert existing tables from Word documents into HTML tables when performing a Save As to an HTML file type.

One might think the lack of exposure of this feature was due to an incomplete or early implementation of the table conversion feature, and that might be true. But in fact, this feature works quite nicely. Word tables are converted, as far as possible, into reasonable HTML table tags. The generated tags are a bit on the wordy (sorry) side. For example, all *<TH>* and *<TD>* elements are always closed by WordIA (with *</TH>* and *</TD>* at the end of the element, when in fact such fastidiousness isn't really necessary and certainly isn't practiced by most current HTML authors.

Since the functionality to do the conversion of Word tables to HTML tables is all there, I assume that the ability to actually insert a new HTML table into an HTML document will be available shortly.

The Document Head

Word Internet Assistant lets you set various parts of the HTML document head, by clicking on the **I** button or choosing **File/HTML Document Info**. Within the main dialog the option available to set is just the document title, but clicking on the Advanced button exposes other options including setting the base URL (the BASE element in HTML) of the document (see Figure 7.5).

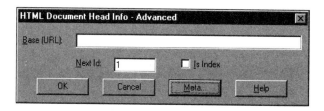

FIGURE 7.5 HTML DOCUMENT HEAD INFO-ADVANCED

The base URL can be used to make relative references that occur in a document unambiguous it makes it very clear the full URL to which those relative URLs correspond. This can be useful if a document is moved to another Web site. Without the BASE element, the relative URLs in the document would become useless if the referring document was moved by itself.

The advanced option dialog also contains a checkbox that lets you add an ISINDEX element to the HEAD. This is somewhat strange since typically ISINDEX elements appear in documents generated by CGI search programs as front-ends to those programs. ISINDEX indicates that the same URL used to retrieve the document (usually a URL of an executable program) may have a query string appended to it with the various search terms and that a search will be executed that will return another document listing the search results. This will be discussed this in greater detail in Chapter 10 on gateways. For now, this is not a likely element to want to place in a statically authored document. Again, be wary of assuming that all options available to you in WordIA are really relevant.

HTML Extensions

WordIA has so far not been overly aggressive about incorporating HTML extensions. It is doubtful whether the tool could keep up in the short term with the rapid pace of change in the HTML specification. This means that there is an occasional need to use HTML directly. WordIA has some support for this but it is not sufficient, so until this is remedied you will probably need to supplement WordIA with another tool—a text editor should serve the purpose fine.

Word IA provides a menu option that allows you enter HTML markup directly. From the Insert menu, you choose **HTML Markup.** You will be prompted for a single HTML tag. Unfortunately, WordIA does not provide the ability to view all of your HTML content in native HTML text form. This means that to take advantage of HTML extensions to the WordIA generated tags or to fine tune the HTML content, you will need to use a text editor.

What Is Not Translated

Most important to remember when converting *existing* Word documents is what will *not* translate to HTML. Many elements either have no valid translation to HTML or the implementors chose not to invest the effort in whatever indirect translation might be available. The problem is usually the former. This also explains why your documents may appear differently after they have been reloaded into WordIA.

As discussed in the WordIA help guide, the elements include:

- annotations
- borders and shading
- captions
- character formatting (e.g. font, superscript)
- drawing layer elements
- embedded objects, or "cut and pasted" objects, such as equations, clip art, Word Art, and MS
- Draw objects
- fields—only the field result is converted
- footnotes and endnotes
- frames
- graphics embedded via the Clipboard
- headers and footers
- indented paragraphs in any paragraph style other than OL or UL
- index entries
- page breaks and section breaks

- revision marks
- tabs in any paragraph style other than PRE and DL
- TOC entries

Evaluation Summary

Word Internet Assistant is an extremely valuable tool for Web authors. It raises HTML writing to a level of abstraction it had not enjoyed before allowing the author to remain in the familiar environment of Microsoft Word for most of the work required to generate Web pages. To its credit, it is not just a vanilla, unambitious Word document conversion program. It actually attempts to automate features, such as forms, that were not addressed by any previous tool. In WordIA vast majority of your content can be created with blissful ignorance of the HTML tags generated.

Nevertheless, you will need to supplement WordIA with a text editor to take advantage of new tags, extensions to current HTML tags, and default tag generation that WordIA performs that doesn't quite match your intended output. In particular though it is one of the few tools with support for HTML form creation, its support is limited, and there is a good chance you may have to use a text editor to get precisely the form you wish. Future versions of Internet Assistant should (I hope) address the issues of extension support, full support for all form elements, and allowing easy viewing and editing of HTML tags. In the meantime it is still quite a useful tool for a large set of common tasks. You can download Word Internet Assistant freely from Microsoft's home page **http://www.microsoft.com**.

QUARTERDECK WEBAUTHOR

Another tool used to allow authoring HTML content from Microsoft Word 6.0 is QuarterDeck's WebAuthor. WebAuthor is similar to WordIA in that it works entirely from within Word 6.0. Once installed, the main method of starting up WebAuthor is to choose **New** from the File menu and choose **HTML 6.0** as the document type. A dialog appears allowing you to either create a new HTML document, open an existing HTML document, or open an HTML authored Word document (see Figure 7.6). This, in effect, is what starts up Web Author. In addition new menu options are available on the File menu: New HTML, Open HTML, and Save as HTML.

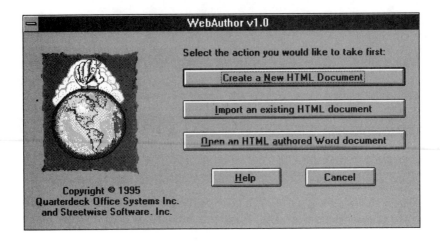

FIGURE 7.6 WEBAUTHOR'S NEW DOCUMENT DIALOG BOX

This is a different approach than Word IA, which used the same menu commands for loading, creating documents, and saving, but had a different type for HTML. QuarterDeck's approach allows it to coexist well in a Word installation where Word Internet Assistant has already been installed.

If you choose Create a New HTML document, you are prompted for the title of the page—unlike WordIA where you must remember to enter the title of the page yourself. Once supplied, the title appears at the top of your Word document. Again this contrasts to WordIA where the title appears only in the document information which is not normally displayed during editing. WebAuthor's approach is probably a bit better since titles certainly are viewable to the Web reader (generally on the browser window title bar), and you would like to always be viewing something close to what your readers will see.

When a new document is created, a Heading 1 and Normal text area are created as the basis of the page. WebAuthor tries to provide more information about the HTML content than WordIA—which generally shows something resembling the viewable output of your Web information, and hides the HTML generated by the various Word commands. WebAuthor displays the paragraph style of a block of text (e.g., Heading 1, Heading 2, Normal, List, Form) in the left margin of your Word document. The style view can be toggled on and off from the View/Style command; although, again, WebAuthor displays its own idiosyncrasies by not placing a checkbox or some other visual indication of whether view style is on or off.

This is not quite as informative as displaying the actual HTML, but the text is more readable in this form while still conveying to you some information about the generated HTML. This tradeoff between "readability" and "knowledge of the guts" is a common one among HTML tools, but WebAuthor's compromise seems among the best. Still, they don't provide a native HTML viewing mode, as was the problem with all HTML authoring tools that attempted to provide some form of WYSIWYG facility.

WEBAUTHOR CONTENT CREATION

When editing documents with WebAuthor, it installs its own toolbar, HTML Authoring–Small onto the Word desktop. The toolbar contains the inevitable buttons for general file functions like new, open, and save, in both their HTML and Word document flavors. Remember WordIA operates common functions like new, save, and load of HTML documents from the same menu commands but uses the file type field in the common dialogs to distinguish what kind of document it is.

To the right of the six file-oriented buttons appears an eye that toggles the document into viewing mode, enabling an approximation of what a Web browser would display for the given content. The next button, labeled Style, presents a list of available HTML styles that can be used to format blocks of text. The list can be restricted to character styles (including physical styles such as bold and italic, and logical styles such as "emphasis" or "strong"), paragraph styles, or both. This is an improvement over WordIA—just including the available HTML style amongst the Word styles. However, since the next button on the toolbar provides only character formatting styles, the Style button should be restricted to paragraph styles by default, instead of presenting all HTML styles by default as it does now.

The next group of buttons provide the ability to create links, images, or forms. The link button, labeled Anchor Manager, invokes a dialog (see Figure 7.7) allowing you to specify a *jump* (a jumping off point for a pointer link), a *destination* (a named target of another link), or an anchor that serves both purposes. The anchor manager is also available by choosing **Hypertext Link** from the Insert menu item.

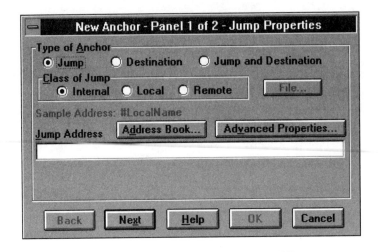

FIGURE 7.7 WEBAUTHOR ANCHOR MANAGER DIALOG BOX

If the anchor is a jump, then three options are available for linking:

- **Internal.** Allows linking to named anchor within current document
- **Local.** Link to another document on local server
- **Remote.** Link to resource on another server

The meaning of each of these link descriptions is indicated by the sample text below the set of radio buttons. However this explanatory text appears in gray, which means something more like "option not available now" to most Windows users than suggesting "this text for information only."

If the option chosen is Local, a File button is ungrayed to allow choosing the local file from the Windows File Open common dialog. This dialog can be used to fill in the Jump Address field. This field can also be filled in from a pick list of stored URLs, or you may just enter the text manually. There is an Advanced Properties button on the dialog that allows link attributes that are rarely used to be set (these include TITLE, REL, REV, METHODS, and URN). The relevant attributes are discussed earlier in chapters on HTML. Though these are not commonly used attributes, the philosophy of making even advanced options available from the tool is commendable.

The image manager, also available on the Insert menu, lets you insert pictures into your HTML. To insert pictures, Image Manager asks you to select a file from an Insert

Picture dialog, specify alternate text for readers with text-only browsers, and specify an alignment of the image. Unfortunately the alignment can only be top, middle, or bottom: No Netscape extensions, such as left or right are provided. This is unfortunate as it reduces the author to editing text from a text editor again to get the desired effect. An approach that QuarterDeck may want to consider is to allow additional options to be added to the dropdown list. Whatever text was placed in the list would be placed as the attribute value for the ALIGN attribute of the IMG tag. In general, HTML authoring packages should consider this approach for functions that create tags that are likely to have extensions added.

The Form Manager, is also available as the Form command from the Insert menu. When a form does not yet exist, invoking Form Manager places an HTML form element into the current document, complete with Reset and Submit buttons. Unfortunately the Submit and Reset buttons created are not renamable (e.g., labeling the Submit button as "Place Order") as they are with WordIA. Subsequent clicks on the Form Manager present a list of available field types (see Figure 7.8) which may be placed into the form. The list of fields is quite complete.

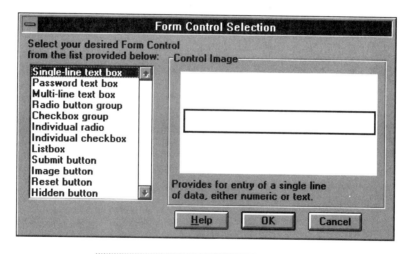

FIGURE 7.8 WEB AUTHOR FORM FIELD INSERTION DIALOG BOX

The next button lets you create items for each HTML list type: ordered lists, unordered lists, menu lists, definition lists, and directory lists. The final button lets you insert special characters and symbols: such as copyright © symbols, registered ® symbols, trademark symbols, ellipsis (...), and quotation marks.

WebAuthor Options

On the tools menu are several other WebAuthor functions. WebAuthor options lets you set default directories for files and images and display options for HTML authoring. The URL Address Book lets you build up a directory of URLs to be inserted as destination links with the link manager. Choosing **Verify HTML** checks the syntax of an external HTML file (not the current file) against the HTML 2.0 specification. The current document can be checked by invoking the Save HTML function. Unfortunately the syntax checker's operation leaves quite a bit to be desired. There are many extensions to the HTML 2.0 specification that are in common use, as we discussed at length in earlier chapters. The checker should just report the errors with the option of leaving them intact and going on to report the next error.

WebAuthor does provide the ability to mark a particular tag as a custom tag and therefore be accepted by the syntax checker, but this is time consuming to do on a regular basis as one might do with many HTML extensions such as *<CENTER>*, *<BLINK>*, or extended IMG ALIGN attributes. The method that Web Author uses hide the custom tag from the syntax checker is to prepend the tag with the *<QIGNORE>* tag and append the tag with a *</QIGNORE>* tag.

Though Web Author does provide the capability of inserting a custom tag, it doesn't provide Internet Assistant's command to insert an arbitrary HTML tag directly. You effectively have the same capability with custom tag but then of course you lose the syntax checking on what might be a perfectly ordinary tag that wouldn't require disabling the syntax checker. An even more ambitious approach would be to allow Custom Tags, but to "teach" the syntax checker about them so the custom tags get the same level of checking. As pointed out earlier, you will still need to use a text editor for some tasks.

Web Author also has the ability to insert HTML comments (i.e., the *<!—- >* tag). This is missing as an explicit feature from WordIA, though it can be done indirectly with the Insert/HTML Markup command.

One of the features that is glaringly missing from Web Author is HTML table creation. In WordIA, table creation is undocumented and there is no way to invoke table creation when editing an HTML document. Still you can use WordIA to convert Word documents that contain tables, and it will generate HTML table tags. Web Author doesn't have any table creation facility. It's just not there at all. If you attempt to convert a Word document that has a table you will get several convert errors and the resulting file will contain paragraph tags (*<P>*) for each cell.

Evaluation

WebAuthor is a very full-featured Word-based HTML authoring environment. It is missing some crucial features, such as table creation, and syntax checking of entire documents without performing changes. If you can accept the lack of table support and you need an environment with a bit more full-featured support for other HTML tags and attributes than Word Internet Assistant provides, you will want to consider WebAuthor as your HTML creation tool. WebAuthor can be ordered from QuarterDeck's home page (**http://www.qdeck.com**).

TILE

Lotus Notes is a groupware package combining database and messaging features to facilitate collaborative work. It allows rapid prototyping and creation of ad hoc databases by the corporate end user. For this reason, a lot of valuable corporate data is now stored in Notes databases. The data that tends to be stored there is often very current (since Notes databases are so easy to create), and applicable to a large group of people (the reason to put it into a Notes database in the first place). A way to make this data available to an even wider audience is to make it accessible from Web browsers. The Notes database paradigm of providing several views (or ways of organizing information) of the same data, and the ease of creating those views, makes Notes a compelling authoring environment for Web content in general. Web content often has less hierarchical structure than that provided by Notes views. Web sites are often just a tangled mess of links where it is difficult to determine just how to navigate to areas of interest, and to make sense of the whole. The Notes view mechanism is a good solution to this problem. The site is then structured hierarchically, but with several different hierarchies. In short, the idea of using Notes databases to author Web content, and to provide access to Notes data from Web browsers, is a compelling one. One such Lotus Notes-to-HTML converter is *TILE*, The Internet-Lotus Exchange from the Walter Shelby Group of Bethesda, Maryland.

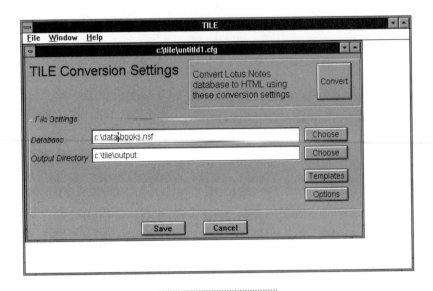

FIGURE 7.9 TILE MAIN SCREEN

TILE is a Multiple Document Interface (MDI) Windows application. Each document in this MDI interface is a two-field mapping between a source Lotus Notes database and a destination directory for converted files. Once you specify the source database and where you wish the converted HTML files to be generated, you click on the **Convert** button and the HTML is generated. Each of these mappings is saved in a config (.CFG) file for later use.

The generated HTML is a top-level page listing each of the available views in the Notes database (see Figure 7.10). There are then pages generated for each of the views, linked to from the database top-level page. There are also pages generated for each document in the database, linked to from the view pages. TILE also generates help and about pages from the Notes Help and About documents. By default, these help and about pages are linked to from every HTML document generated. In summary generated document types are:

- the view list
- views
- documents
- help
- about

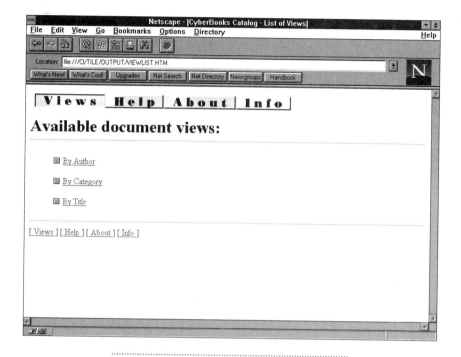

FIGURE 7.10 TOP LEVEL HTML PAGE TILE-CONVERTED DATA BASE

Thus TILE creates a very structured Web site, taking advantage of the Notes view mechanism and the inherent structure of the original Notes database. The structure is created automatically. When you author HTML from Word documents, you must build the links to the individual documents from top level pages that you author yourself. Sites created from Notes databases are not just easier to structure, they have more and better structure. Notes databases tend to have many views that organize the data in various ways. For example, a product database might have views By Product Name, By Manufacturer, and By Category. These various ways of viewing the database make the database more navigable and understandable to the reader. It's not that Web sites can't have the same "multiple views of the data" approach. The best Web sites can and do allow multiple ways of organizing the information. The hypertext nature of HTML makes this quite feasible. It's just that most Web authors don't take the time to do the inevitable amount of work necessary to create the organizing pages that list the documents in various ways. In Notes, the organizing is done automatically (once a view is defined).

Also, Notes doclinks are converted into HTML hyperlinks. Most authors should find the Notes doclink creation mechanism a bit more intuitive (since it just involves navigating between the two documents within Notes) than writing the HTML directly.

TILE lets you specify definable templates (in HTML) for the headers and footers of each of the types of generated documents: view lists, views, documents, and the help and about documents. The default footers supplied provide the links from each page to the help and about documents and the view list mentioned earlier. You can supply your own templates, or modify the HTML templates supplied by TILE to add more links, remove the ones listed, or add graphics to give your own style to the generated HTML documents.

TILE does have some limitations. Embedded bitmaps in Notes richtext field (the way to create visible images in Notes) were *not* converted into *<IMG>* tags and GIF files. Also HTML headers (*<H1>* through *<H3>* tags) are created with some arbitrary mapping rules. First-level headings are typefaces 16 points or larger. Second-level headings are 14 points or larger. Third-level headings are 12 points or greater. Any smaller type is normal. This logic may may result in unanticipated header creation for many Notes documents where the larger type is just some emphasized normal text. Figure 7.11 shows an original notes document and its converted HTML equivalent.

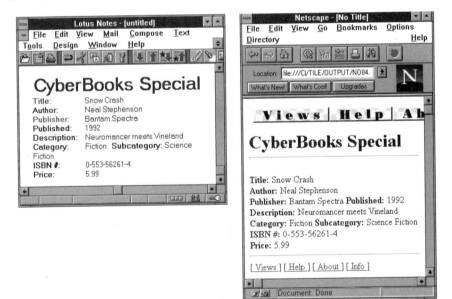

FIGURE 7.11 NOTES DOCUMENT BEFORE AND AFTER CONVERSION TO HTML

Overall, TILE is quite a useful tool, that will doubtless improve over time. If you have a large amount of Notes data which you wish to make available via the Web, this is a good alternative.

WEB BUILDER

This tool from Information Analytics, Inc. allows creation of Web content from a Microsoft Access database specially designed for authoring Web-based product catalogs (**http://www.infoanalytic.com/webbldr/index.html**). Web Builder is a stand-alone Visual Basic application that uses Microsoft Access as the database store for its product catalog approach to HTML content authoring. It is *not* a package designed to convert any arbitrary Access database to a set of HTML documents. It would be easy to imagine such a tool, and that tool would be quite useful for many purposes, but it will have to come from elsewhere. However, you should be able to import your data from other Access databases, or other sources, into the Access database that Web Builder uses.

The idea behind Web Builder is that many Web sites, especially Web sites for electronic commerce can benefit from a "catalog" structure to their content. Web Builder asks you to build a database of catalog items, and then specify how catalog items are placed onto HTML pages by designing *page components*—headers, footers, and navigation components assembled with data for each document into HTML pages. Bear with me if this isn't completely clear yet. This product is different from all of the other off-the-shelf products reviewed here, because it takes a higher-level view of Web site authoring than just creating HTML documents. This higher-level view is that you are working from a database of products, and that there are common elements across all product pages that need to be captured in page component definitions. There is also a page type known as *index* or *main index* that lists all the documents and provides links to those documents. Finally there is a page type known as the *keyword index* that provides functionality similar to a book index, where keywords are listed along with the places in the book that refer to that keyword. As various parts of this product are presented, these special constructs and unique terminology (none of which are really related to HTML itself) will become clearer.

The basis of the Web Builder interface is a tabbed dialog with each major area of operation assigned to a single tab of the dialog. The best place to start the discussion is with the Page Layout tab. It is here where options are set and the components are listed of each page type created by Web Builder: the document page type, the main index page type, and the keyword index page type. On the left side of the page is a spreadsheet control that lists information on each of the three page types. This includes the file name, the page title, and the header, navigation, body, and footer document components associated with the page type. The document page type has no file name, because it will vary for each document in the database. The page title is the special value Page Title because that will vary per actual document as well.

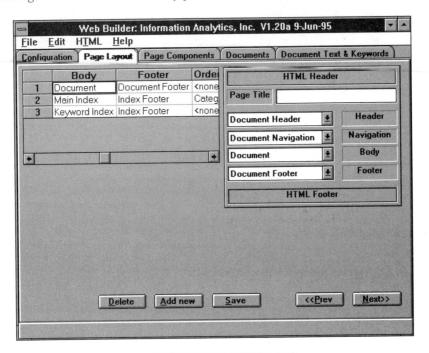

FIGURE 7.12 WEBBUILDER PAGE LAYOUT TAB

The Header for the document page type refers to a page component that contains HTML text to be placed in the top portion of every document. This will not just be a title and other HTML head information, but potentially a top-level heading and other literal text normally associated with an HTML body. This highlights one of the problem's with Web Builder's terminology: an HTML head has a specific literal meaning that is more narrow than a WB Header. A WB Header is just any HTML at the top of a document that will remain constant across all documents. The specific contents of the named document Header are defined on the next dialog tab entitled Page Components.

The next column for each page type is Navigation which is where a consistent set of link references, along with link phrase text, is presented that will allow linking from each document to various parts of the Web site, including the main index home page and the keyword index reference page. The Footer column specifies the Footer Page Component that sets text appearing at the bottom of documents that doesn't vary per document.

It turns out that the Page Layout tab settings of Page Components for various page types are already defined in the sample database and can be left at the same settings in your authoring effort with good results. In fact, if you choose **New Database** from the main menu of Web Builder rather than using the sample database (called DEMO.MDB) you will want to imitate the settings they have for DEMO on the Page Layout tab.

Once you have specified the Page Components that each page type will use, you will need to define the Page Components on the next dialog tab (see Figure 7.13). The Page Component definitions will need to be changed from what is in the sample database to have, for example, Document Headers and Footers written which apply to the database you are working on. The Page Components defined in the DEMO database will not be appropriate to use in your own efforts.

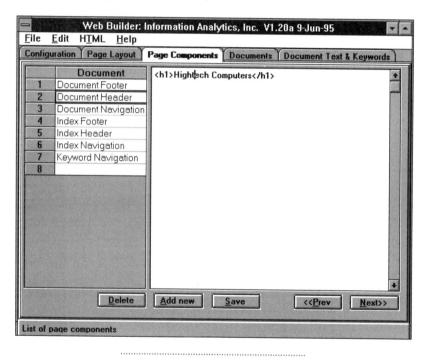

FIGURE 7.13 WEB BUILDER PAGE COMPONENTS TAB

The Page Components tab lets you define the HTML content for the Document Header, Document Footer, and Document Navigation (a portion of the document which contains links to other parts of the Web site, such as back to the home or main index page). It also lets you set the HTML for the Index Header, Index Footer, and Index Navigation page components. Remember that the Index or main index is essentially the home page of the database with links to each of the database's documents, so these options essentially control the home page top and bottom text and the navigation text used to link from the home page elsewhere within the Web site (such as to the keyword index page) or to other sites. The Keyword Navigation page component lets you specify hypertext links away from the keyword index page, similar in function to the index of a book.

Once the Page Layout and Page Components have been defined, you are ready to create the actual documents that make up the product database. This is performed from the Documents tab (see Figure 7.14).

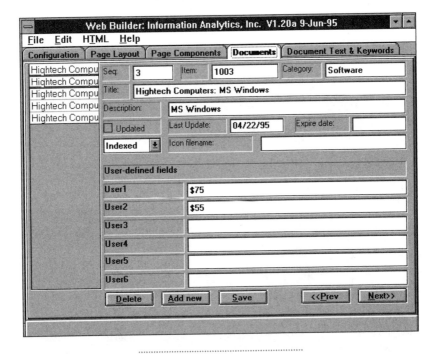

FIGURE 7.14 WEB BUILDER DOCUMENTS TAB

The Documents tab allows you to create records, one per product, with a set of fields which you may define. From the Documents tab, you specify the raw data, just the fields, not their positioning on the HTML pages. There is a built-in set of fields for each record chosen to be useful for product databases. These fields are:

- **Seq**—the record number
- **Item**—inventory number
- **Category**—product category
- **Title**—the product name
- **Last Update**—last time record was updated
- **Expire date**—when this record becomes obsolete

There are six fields available, entitled User1 through User6, for data that needs to be tracked for each product yet doesn't fit into any of the fields mentioned above. Be sure to be consistent between different records in how you use the user-defined fields. The Documents tab allows you to create new records with the Add New button and scroll through the records with the Next and Prev buttons. The Save button stores your recordset.

Once you have created all of your records, you will still need to specify how the field data appears on individual HTML pages. This is done on a per document basis using the Document Text & Keywords tab (see Figure 7.15). As you look at the HTML in this tab, notice that it is just the raw unvarnished native tags. The approach is much more similar to the HTML editors discussed in the last chapter than it is to the Word-based tools that attempt to shield you from the HTML. This approach would be fine, as we have seen hiding the HTML often necessitates going to a text editor to finetune the content, except that the support for inserting HTML tags is somewhat limited. Its just a brief menu with fewer than 20 tags appearing on it. For the HTML novice the approach taken by other tools such as HTML Assistant of listing almost all the frequently used tags works much better.

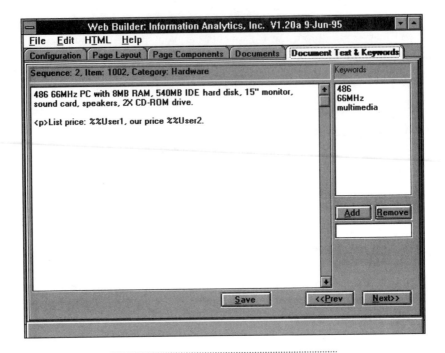

FIGURE 7.15 WEB BUILDER DOCUMENT TEXT & KEYWORDS TAB

When you are ready to create HTML files from your database, choose **Create all HTML Files** from the File menu. This creates a set of HTML files in the directory specified on the Configuration tab (see Figure 7.16). You may change this directory as you see fit from this tab, or change other options such as the location of navigation menus.

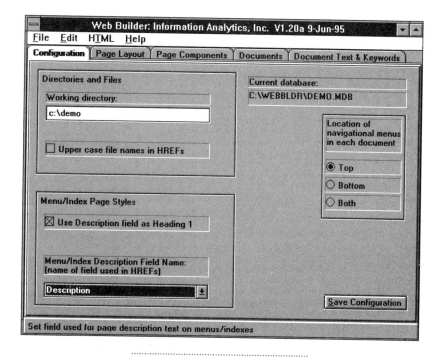

FIGURE 7.16 WEB BUILDER CONFIGURATION TAB

The generated HTML files include a main index page with links to all document pages (see Figure 7.17). Note the "Created by Web Builder" at the bottom of the generated HTML. This phrase should have a toggle so that it can be turned off. As a webmaster with a commerce site in a competitive marketplace, my choice of authoring tool should be my business alone. Notice too, that the categories were created automatically since the Order By column of the index page type was made into the top level category.

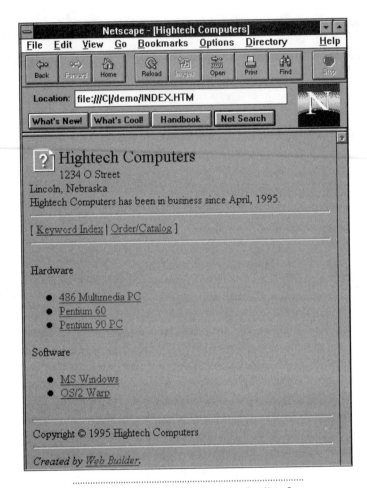

FIGURE 7.17 WEB BUILDER GENERATED "INDEX" OR HOME PAGE

Unfortunately, there are still some problems with this functionality. Note the "?" image in Figure 7.17. It is due to Web Builder creating a reference to an image called logo.gif from the home page. To its credit, Web Builder lets you specify an image to appear on a page, and then inserts a reference to that image. But if no image is specified, it shouldn't create the reference. Another problem is that when you choose **Create all HTML Files** with v.1.20a, if you specify a directory that does not exist, it reports successful file creation but doesn't create any HTML files. Either an error message or creating the directory and then creating the HTML files would be acceptable.

Web Builder Evaluation

Web Builder is an innovative tool that recognizes a real need in the marketplace. Much HTML writing within a Web site, especially a Web site for commerce, is quite repetitive. A tool that lets the user define the common elements appearing on all Web pages eliminates a large amount of work for the Web author. Web Builder also recognizes that most Web sites for commerce consist of product databases. So it is logical to use Access to store product documents—each document's data is stored as a record in the database. The default database definition contains several fields relevant to storing product information, and a set of user-definable fields. The product database resulting from a Web authoring effort is then viewable and manageable from Microsoft Access. This is a huge improvement over having the master database of products being nothing more than a group of HTML files lying around in a directory.

Despite Web Builder's innovativeness and perception of the true needs of the Web authoring marketplace, it still falls short in several ways:

- The interface is quite awkward, especially the Page Layout tab with its mostly obscured spreadsheet control for setting options on page types.

- There is no online help local to the system. Access to the Internet during HTML authoring cannot always be assumed and help and documentation for Web Builder is provided via InfoAnalytics' Web server.

- HTML support is somewhat barebones. It assumes good knowledge on the part of the user of what tags to use, despite the fact that in other ways it insulates the Web author from many HTML details.

IMAGE CONVERSION TOOLS

Although strictly speaking, image conversion is not part of creating HTML, in fact creating images is very much a part of the Web authoring process. Most drawing tools do not work with GIF files natively, nor are stock images usually distributed that way. This means that the image creation portion of a Web authoring effort is almost always a conversion task.

Notice that I mentioned that you will want to create GIF files. Web browsers typically display JPEG files as well but without all of the capabilities of GIF files. The GIF format was developed by CompuServe for downloadable graphics and thus has very good compression (i.e., the files are quite small). They do this via Lev-Zimpel-Welch (LZW) compression. LZW was invented by Unisys who have since claimed patent rights on the algorithm, though in cooperation with CompuServe who of course would have been the largest original violator of the patent. GIF is now probably the largest standard in the world for image formats, especially for free distribution, so it seems doubtful that this could ever be enforced. Do not let this dissuade you from creating GIF images (not that you have many other alternatives on the Web anyway). Any required licensing fees will have been paid by the vendors of the tools you use to create or convert your images.

The major advantages over GIF files over JPEG are:

- Browsers often have support for *interlaced GIFs*, images that gradually resolve to finer and finer detail. If you have a large image that your Web readers must wait to see, interlaced GIFs are the way to do it.
- Clickable image maps work with GIFs. For example, the tool reviewed above, MapEdit, only allows GIFs to be used to create image maps.

The disadvantages to GIFs include the fact that JPEG often has better compression. However, in my opinion this is offset by the lack of support for interlaced JPEGs, but for some purposes you may want to consider using JPEG images.

Most full-featured drawing tools should be able to export images to both GIF and JPEG formats. For example, Corel Draw! has had GIF and JPEG export for several versions now. Effectively this gives you the ability to convert from every format the drawing package can import.

Still you will often be converting from images not necessarily created in your drawing package, and for large scale efforts the overhead of invoking your full-fledged graphics application to perform a simple conversion can be tedious. There is a place for dedicated, single purposes, lean and fast conversion tools for creating GIF and JPEG files. One such package is LView Pro.

LView Pro

Leonardo Loureiro's excellent image conversion software, at this writing entitled LView Pro 1B, allows conversion of images from a variety of formats to the GIF, interlaced GIF, and JPEG formats required for inline image display by most Web browsers. The first step in conversion is to load up your source image with the File/Open command. LView accepts files in Windows bitmap (.BMP is a very common format used by Windows Paint and many other Windows utilities and system components), OS/2 bitmap (.BMP) format, GIF files (which is useful to convert back from GIF files to an original format for editing), Targa, and PCX (the format used by PaintBrush).

All that is necessary to convert the image to a GIF file is to choose **Save As** from the File menu and the save the file as a **GIF** and a file name with extension of .GIF. If you wish to convert the image to an interlaced GIF make sure that the **Save GIFs Interlaced** is checked in the Options menu. An interlaced GIF, as you probably already know from your Web surfing experience, is an image which is downloaded with successively greater resolution, allowing your users to instantly get some sense of what the image is. My opinion is that most large images should be presented as interlaced GIFs.

LView Pro remembers this file type and even the extension used to save the image with. On second and subsequent conversions, the Save As file name and type defaults are set automatically. That is, the file name for Save As is the base name of the source file with an extension of GIF and the type to Save As is GIF. So converting large batches of files to GIF files is very easy. It's a great tool to have available and vastly more efficient than most full-fledged graphics programs for this special purpose task.

LView can resize images to four pre-defined sizes corresponding to common screen sizes. These are 640 x 480 pixels, 800 x 600, 1024 x 768, and 1280 x 1024. It can also convert to a selectable image size (specified in pixels), either maintaining aspect ratio (the height to width proportion) or changing it. Creating "thumbnail" images requires this functionality. For example, a thumbnail image, might be 160 x 120 and linked to a 640 x 480 image via HTML. You will need to be able to resize the image to be able to create thumbnails of larger images (a highly recommended practice). Also you should restrict your larger images to 640 x 480 to handle the worst case screen resolution of people running Windows-based Web browsers.

Usually you will want to maintain the aspect ratio (click on the **Maintain Aspect Ratio** checkbox) when using the tool. Be careful to save any resized smaller images with a different file name than the original file. The name should be some naming convention based on the original file name. For example, I usually prepend a smaller image file name with an underscore (e.g., _logo.gif). This naming convention extends nicely to multiple levels of "shrinkage." One reason saving the original large image is particularly crucial, is that you can't really restore the larger image by resizing it back up. The original information has been "averaged down" to a smaller image summary. Reexpansion results in large splotchy areas where fine detail once stood.

Also among the most essential functions is the easily invoked Crop! facility on the Edit menu. Just click and drag to mark a region which is shown with red and white "barber pole" emphasis. Choosing **Crop!** then cuts the image down to the marked region. Again, it is prudent to save the changed image to a different file name than the original.

These four functions, opening files, resizing, and cropping them, and saving the resulting images as GIFs will accomplish most of what you should need in an image converter program, but LView carries some other useful features as well. The Multiple Open dialog in the File menu allows you to place multiple images on a contact sheet, or "art gallery" to display all of them (which itself can be made into a GIF image).

Other Edit menu features include the ability to flip or rotate an image (rarely used), or annotate an image with text. Image annotation is very useful in Web authoring. You may have photos that you wish to use as image maps and adding text can help clarify just how regions in the image are used for navigation.

Many image enhancement features are available in LView from the Retouch menu. Most of the time you shouldn't need to use them. But sometimes they can overcome quality problems in your images. The major options are Gamma Correction and Contrast Enhance. In effect, these are options for brightness and contrast and can often make your images more attractive. Test any adjustments you make at different brightness and contrast settings on your monitor and on other monitors as well to insure you aren't optimizing for your own monitor. Other options can affect the depth of color (saturation) in your images and the bias toward red, green, and blue in the image. The Retouch capabilities are great to have, but you should generally try to avoid them in the conversion phase as it just makes the effort more complicated. However, LView's Retouch facilities may not exist in the original graphics package or in the software that captured the image from a scanner, so they may often prove useful.

Leonardo Haddad Loureiro can be reached at **mmedia@world.std.com**. A Web page is devoted to LView at **http://mirror.wwa.com/mirror/busdir/lview/lview.htm**. The software can be both registered and downloaded from this page.

Creating Transparent Background Images with LView

This tool can also be used to created transparent background images. Netscape, and presumably other browsers eventually, lets you specify a background image for your HTML page. For those images, it may be useful to have the background color of them be "transparent" and thus show the background color specified for the Web page. Choose **Background Color** from the Options menu to set the background color for the image. Then select the color which you wish to have become transparent. Then save the image as a GIF file.

Image Libraries

While still on the subject of content creation and discussing image conversion, we should mention some icon and images libraries that are available that may make your authoring task easier. However, bear in mind that you do want to create a distinctive look for your Web site. Overuse of everyone else's blue spheres for your buttons just makes you look like every other site.

- Icons for Building Web Pages contains a very good collection of useful images (**http://www.jsc.nasa.gov/~mccoy/Icons/index.html**).

- The Bitmap Vault (**http://www.cs.uwm.edu:2010/**)

  This service, by Guy Hussussian and Naveen Jamal, takes an interesting approach to the problem of acquiring reusable image content. The software consists of three components: a bitmap worm which collects bitmaps from various places, a bitmap server which allows search for appropriate images, and a social worker which assists in cataloging bitmaps.

- W3 Org Icon Collection (**http://www.w3.org/hypertext/WWW/Icons**)

- Images, Icons, and Sounds (**http://melmac.corp.harris.com/images.html**)

- Yahoo: Computers: World Wide Web: Programming: Icons (**http://www.yahoo.com/ Computers/World_Wide_Web/Programming/Icons/**)

  Use Yahoo to get the complete up-to-date listing of available resources. Yahoo also has links to several clip art sites. But beware, there are a lot of mediocre, sites out there in this category.

PART 3

SETTING UP YOUR
WEB SERVER

## CHAPTER 8

SETTING UP YOUR INTERNET SERVER

Once you have your content put together, you need to provide a method that will allow readers to reach it over the Internet. This involves establishing a server platform with an Internet connection, then putting up a Web server to make your Web content available to the public.

The first step is to get your server platform machine up and running with access to the Internet. This may seem like a mundane task, and indeed there isn't too much complexity to it, nevertheless, it is an important step in the planning process. So I'll begin with that and then I'll go on to discuss the various Web server platforms available to you.

HOSTING SERVICES: THE "WEB SERVICE BUREAU" OPTION

Your Web server doesn't have to be located on your own Web server hardware. Once you have created the content, you can declare victory and put your content up on a third party Web site. If you plan to use a third party web site, you can dispense with the next chapter on Web server software, and, potentially, later chapters on gateways. Why not cover gateways, especially if you have data stored in other forms than HTML such as SQL? Because typically you will provide the hosting service with your set of HTML pages, which they will place on their Web server. Even if you aren't providing the hosting service with HTML pages, you will likely be providing them with some form of static content: Word documents, Lotus Notes databases, text files, or the like. You may want to have the data be dynamic and integrated into the rest of your business. This is not likely to be an option that is available with a hosting service. If your goal is to integrate your Web site into the rest of your information systems (probably applicable if you are reading this book), there is a good chance that using a hosting service may not be appropriate.

Hosting services can generally be divided into two categories, with perhaps some blurred lines between the two. The first category is the strict *home page vendor.* You give your content to the service. They put it on their Web server and they give you an URL, such as **http://www.rent-a-site.com/ourstore/ourstore.html.** This type of URL, an HTML file in a directory below the hosting service host name, was typical for early hosting services. Now, many Web server software packages, such as WebSite, discussed in Chapter 9, allow one server to "multi-host" several different base URLs. So you should now be able to get **http://www.ourstore.com** from a hosting service. In fact, if you go this route insist on it. Most home page vendors have evolved to a fixed price per month pricing model. Some vendors charge more for additional pages and volume of data contained, but this is infrequent. Yet other vendors charge per user access, but this is rarer still.

The other category of hosting service is the *web mall*. The service hosts your content, and gives you a URL directly to your home page, but you also appear as an entry in their directory. Typically your URL in a web mall will be something like **http://www.mall.com/directory/ourstore.html**, rather than your own **http://www.ourstore.com**. Web malls will often try to add value by assisting in the authoring process, sometimes doing most of the authoring based on your initial plain content, in order to give a consistent look and feel across the mall. If the mall is well trafficked and has other sites with good content, perhaps in a related but complementary area to your own line of business, the mall model may provide some benefit over a straight hosting service. Most importantly a web mall can provide all of the commerce-related infrastructure for a store: the catalog system for product display and searches, the ordering system, credit card secure transmission, credit card verifications, and so on. I spent a lot of space (and will devote more space) in this book giving you the knowledge to build such systems. But for many businesses, having someone else worry about the details of building links to product catalog databases, allowing searching and display from those databases, putting together a secure http server for credit card number acceptance, automating credit card verification, is very compelling. Being able to amortize that effort over all of the mall's vendors makes this even more attractive.

When evaluating pricing for the service, since web malls are generally interested in stores with good content, you may be able to cut better deals with a web mall than with a hosting service. In general, you will encounter the following pricing models from web malls. In the hosting model: just like the previous discussion of home page vendors, you are charged for your presence on the site. This actually occurs fairly often, but doesn't seem to take care of the opportunities for creative synergy that occurs with a mall. Probably a better model for those businesses selling something tangible (including a discrete service) is the *merchant model*, that charges a percentage of generated sales. This creates a partnership between the "store" (we use the term store here loosely—it's really just any business) and the mall. The mall adds value in terms of presentation of store content and attracting customers to the store. The mall shares in the store's success, and thus can price the basic rate for presence (if one even exists) much lower. The store then has a lower risk proposition in deciding to vend their wares over the mall. Even if you put up your own site, you should at least be aware of the web mall concept, and take note of the good players, since having links to your site from these places, especially if they cater to your business segment, can increase your traffic.

Regardless of which model you choose, here are some things to look for in a hosting service:

- **Bandwidth.** What's their connectivity level? Is it V.34 dialup, 56kb frame relay, full T1, 64kb ISDN, 128kb ISDN. These terms are defined in later sections in this chapter, but what you want to find out is the resulting speed of sites they host.
- **Cost**. Kind of obvious, but the pricing models for hosting services haven't jelled too well yet. You will find wide fluctuation in pricing and the pricing models offered, so this bears careful analysis.
- **Venue.** If it's a mall, the attractiveness, popularity, and whether the neighbor businesses in the mall that complement your business are important factors in deciding to place your content there.
- **Commerce software.** If it's a mall, you may be interested in those sites with catalog software for searching among your product base (this may not always be relevant to your business) and ordering software to accept product orders from customers and transmit the results to you. Ordering software is almost always relevant in a web mall environment, and the ability to electronically integrate in some way, even if it's just emailed batches of orders, is very important.

In Appendix B, I list several Web service bureaus and electronic malls devoted to putting up Web content.

CONNECTING YOUR OWN SERVER

Web hosting services can be an attractive option for many small to mid-size businesses that want to stay focused on their primary work. Nevertheless, many of the readers in this audience will want and need to create their own Web servers. One crucial determining factor in deciding whether to have a service host your content is what level of integration is needed to the rest of your business' information systems. If that level is very high and potentially complex, you will want to read the rest of this chapter (and the later chapters in the book for that matter) to learn how to build your own Web server.

Choosing an Internet Access Provider

If you do not currently have Internet connectivity, the first step is to get it. If you are in a large company, government agency, or university, there is probably an Internet link somewhere on your organizational network, and you may be able to connect to that link from your server using TCP/IP, in which case skip to the next section on Windows NT Internet connectivity. Otherwise, you will need to choose an Internet Access Provider (IAP). Those of you with part time Internet connectivity for Web browsing are already familiar with the term (and after all, I do assume that you have done Web browsing before reading this book). It's a company that exists to provide individuals and organizations with part time and full time connectivity to the Internet.

Part time Internet connectivity for individuals is provided by many companies: Netcom, PSI, Delphi, and a few others at the national level and hundreds of small local IAPs. If the net is widened to include the quasi-connectivity provided by the online services such as AOL, MSN, Prodigy, and CompuServe, you can see that there are many options for the end user and it is a very competitive business.

For full-time dedicated Internet connectivity for organizations wishing to establish Internet hosts, the business is more narrow, but still competitive and you still have many companies to choose from. At the national level, the largest players for providing full-time access include Performance Systems International, the Uunet (the provider for the Microsoft Network's Internet connectivity and local points of presence) AlterNet service, Evergreen Internet, SprintLink, and a few others. Once you include local IAPs, there are many companies to choose from. For a reasonably complete list, see **http://www.yahoo.com/Business_and_Economy/Companies/Internet_Access_Providers**.

To start the process, you pay the IAP a setup fee, which sometimes requires purchasing a dedicated modem for your use at the IAP's site. The setup fee may or may not include registering your domain name. Registration of domain names is now a fee-based service (as of September 1995) even when dealing directly with the registration body (InterNIC). So it's now particularly useful to go through your IAP to have this done. In earlier times, you could try to save the fee to the IAP for domain registration (typically $50 or less) by dealing with InterNIC directly. Of course this introduces one more coordination issue: making sure that the IP addresses are identical between the address that the IAP service allots to you and what you register with InterNIC. You are better off letting your IAP perform this service for you, and doubly so now that the process is no longer free if you go direct to InterNIC.

You will need to decide what data rate option you need. If you are a small business, I make the somewhat controversial recommendation of starting out with V.34 (28.8 kbps) dialup. You can always upgrade to frame relay or T1 later if the network traffic onto your site justifies it. If you are using your Web site to sell or promote your business, the heavy volume is a good problem to have and you will probably be more than willing to upgrade your connectivity at that time. One of the things you will want to check with prospective providers is if you have to invest in new setup fees to upgrade, or if your original setup fee for V.34 dialup access can be applied to the setup fee for higher speed access.

The next step above V.34 dialup is 56 kbps (56 kilobaud frame relay).Here you share a 56 kbps line—the resultant speed is somewhat less than 56kbps, but is burstable close to that speed. You can get 56kbps leased line usually for a little more than frame relay. You will have to add the phone charges for the line to these estimates. As part of your survey, you will want to check into the availability of reasonably priced ISDN in your area, and if available from your telephone company, ask your prospective provider about rates and availability of ISDN access. Most providers still do not offer ISDN access, but many of the larger providers do. Be prepared to spend more on modem hardware, however, if you choose this option. Total cost between the ISDN modem and a compatible router should be less than $2,000. Also in most areas of the country right now, ISDN tariffs are very expensive. Plan for at least $400 per month for full time use. As part of your evaluation of alternatives, you should at least find out the costs of ISDN if it is available. Contact your local telephone company business office and ask for a quote on *fulltime* ISDN. You might have to do some computation, because most ISDN packages currently offer a certain amount of time for a fixed price, and beyond that per minute charges. ISDN provides one voice and two data lines, and the data lines can be combined to offer 128 kbps speed. If you want to use the two data lines, you will get 64 kbps speed on each, and your provider may offer a lower price for 64 kbps access.

The next step above this is fractional T1. This should give you at least 128 kbps speed. A T1 leased line should give you close to 1.5Mbps. If you are a medium- to large-sized business, it may be appropriate to start out with a fractional T1. The cost of fractional T1 is now generally close enough to that of 56 kb lines. If performance of dialup is insufficient, then it makes sense to go to fractional T1. Plan on spending about $3,000 for communications hardware to support this connection. A T1 channel service unit to get you your connection should be about $1,500 at street price. ADC Telecommunications' Kentrox subsidiary makes one. Information on this product is at **http://www.kentrox.com/tserv.html**. A router suitable for 56 kb or T1 should cost about $1500 street price. A popular alternative is the CISCO 2501. Your IAP should be able to offer you very good deals on hardware.

How should you go about choosing your provider? If you are currently using an Internet access provider for part time individual use, ask them what they would charge for the connectivity rate that you have in mind. For good measure, ask them to fill out the information in Table 8.1. Check out the Yahoo IAP list mentioned above for providers in your area. Ask them to complete the rate table below at least for the rate options you are considering. If you are pricing V.34 dialup or 56 kbps service, find out if your original setup fee can be applied to the setup fee for fractional T1.

Table 8.1 shows the costs for various connectivity options from a major national IAP and a low cost competitor. These figures are valid as of October 1995. The numbers are meant merely to give you a rough sense of how the costs scale with higher speed, and the cost differences between the "guys with a bank of modems in their basement" and a top tier player. Inevitably the actual quotes will be slightly lower (but not that much lower) by the time you read this.

TABLE 8.1 INTERNET CONNECTIVITY OPTIONS AND PRICING.

Connectivity Option-	Speed	Setup Cost - Major Vendor	Monthly Fee - Major Vendor	Setup Fee - Lowest Cost Local Competitor	Monthly Fee - Lowest Cost Local Competitor
V.34 dialup	28.8 kbps	$750	$250	$300 ($100 setup, $200 for V.34 modem)	$100
56 kbps frame relay	<56 kbps	$495	$545 w/ 1 year commit	$400	$500
56 kbps leased line	56 kbps	$795	$645 with yearly commit	$600	$600
ISDN - 1B channel	64 kbps	$395	$295 (+ ISDN tariffs!)	$250	$250
ISDN - 2B channels	128 kbps	$495	$495 (+ ISDN tariffs!)	N/A	N/A

Connectivity Option-	Speed	Setup Cost - Major Vendor	Monthly Fee - Major Vendor	Setup Fee - Lowest Cost Local Competitor	Monthly Fee - Lowest Cost Local Competitor
fractional T1	128 kbps	$3000	$895 w/ 1 year commit	$2500	$800
full T1 leased line	512 kbps (example rate)	$5000	approx. $2500	$4000	$2000
tiered T3	3 Mbps (example rate)	$6000	$5000	N/A	N/A

Information from Your Provider

Once you have selected a provider, the first thing you should have them do is register your domain name. This can take some time, so you want to have them start on it right away. The good news is that you can get all of the rest of your connectivity configured and tested before the domain name is returned. Your domain name is a convenience to your users so they do not have to type out your TCP/IP addresses to reach you.

You need the following information from your provider:

- The access phone number.
- The PPP logon name and password (there is no current reason to still use SLIP access, so we assume PPP in this entire treatment).
- Your IP address.
- Your subnet mask (usually 255.255.255.0).
- DNS server and backup server address (generally on your provider's system).
- Whether or not VJ header compression is used.
- Whether or not to use default gateway on their network.

Windows NT Internet Connectivity

The next step is to get your Internet server set up. If you haven't noticed by now, I take a currently, somewhat controversial view that Microsoft Windows NT is the best

Internet server platform for price, performance, ease of administration, compatibility with most businesses MIS staff knowledge base, and other factors. So I will describe Internet connectivity set up for NT in some detail. Currently many of you may have your Internet connectivity with a UNIX server connected to your Internet provider. You can network Windows NT to that UNIX box with TCP/IP, and use all of the great NT-based Web servers presented in the next chapter. Or you can host your Web server directly on that UNIX box, using the CERN server or NCSA's httpd. All of the authoring tools and HTML techniques discussed so far can be used to create content for these servers.

However, it is likely that if you use an existing UNIX server for your content you already have Internet connectivity. We'd like to show you how to get Internet connectivity if you don't already have it. For this we'd like to use Windows NT to demonstrate that process, and concentrate on PPP access though other NT connectivity options are available.

Before describing the specifics of NT TCP/IP configuration, a brief note about hardware and operating system platforms is in order. If you plan to have a high-quality, commercial-class Web server hosted on a Windows NT server, you should not push the lower limits of NT's requirements. I recommend using Windows NT Server versus using Windows NT Workstation. NT Server is much more tuned for throughput and other considerations important to running a high performance Web server. My experience is that for NT Server to really perform well you should install it with 32 megabytes of RAM. If you must run NT Workstation (and I don't recommend it), you can probably get away with 16 megabytes of RAM. To install all of the services that I discuss in this book, you will want to have at least a 500 megabyte hard disk, with most of it available to the Web server, Web server related software, other Internet services, and your HTML content. Many of my gateway examples show connectivity to SQL backends. Microsoft SQL Server 6.0 is a good fit in this environment for these purposes, but if you install this as well on the same platform, don't even consider having less than 32 megabytes of RAM available. If you choose to use Microsoft Exchange Server to provide your SMTP Internet mail capability, and you have the Web server running on the same machine, you should provide at least 48 megabytes of RAM, but 64 megabytes is more appropriate. The processor you use for all of these services should at least be a low-end Pentium if you are running NT Server. You may be able to squeak by with a 66 megahertz 486 DX2 if you are running NT Workstation. Optimal configuration is a 90 megahertz Pentium or better. Sufficient memory is more important here than the fastest CPU. If you are planning to serve a very active user base, you may want to take advantage of NT's capability of running on other platforms. However, currently the NT-based Web server software that I review in the Chapter 9 is only available for Intel and Digital's Alpha platforms, with the exception of WebSite which is only available for Intel. However, an Alpha-based NT platform (especially with the recent 233 megahertz Alphas) will compete head to head with the most powerful UNIX Web servers. This means that even for the most demanding Web site needs, NT cannot be dismissed. I am not advocating starting your Web site with an Alpha (although I use an Alpha as my Internet host and it does a great job), but its reassuring to know that such a growth path exists, and you won't need to change software platforms as your needs grow.

NT RAS PPP TCP/IP Setup

If you do not have the Remote Access Service already installed on your NT box, you will need to install it first. In the Network applet in Control Panel, invoke **Add Software** and choose **Remote Access Service**. It may already be available if you have been using this NT machine for RAS access. Before allowing automatic detection of your modem, check that the modem is on and is connected to the COM port of the machine. If it fails to detect your modem, check that the modem is on the NT Hardware Compatibility List supplied with your Windows NT 3.5 software.

NOTE   These instructions all apply to Windows NT Version 3.5 or greater. The dialogs shown in the presentation are actually from Windows NT Server Version 3.51.

Invoke **Configure**, and select **Dial out only** (which is *not* the default though it should be for security reasons). Then invoke Network and configure the modem for TCP/IP only. When prompted for TCP/IP options be sure to include the ftp service among the options you select. Do not worry about configuring the ftp server properly right now. You can go back and configure ftp to your exact specifications later, and I will show you how to do so in the next section. Just accept the defaults. SNMP and TCP/IP printing are not necessary for anything I discuss here, but you can include them if you wish.

Restart the system to complete the installation of RAS and TCP/IP. If you are planning to use SLIP connectivity, the TCP/IP configuration is more involved than what I document here. See your Windows NT documentation, the Windows NT 3.5 Resource Kit, and the TCP/IP related help pages. However, there is little reason to use SLIP nowadays. The modern equivalent of *SLIP* (which stands for Serial Link Interface Protocol) is *PPP* (Point to Point Protocol). PPP is more advanced allowing automated logon and scripting for more advanced needs. It also allows much easier configuration under Windows NT.

Once restarted, select the **Remote Access** icon in the Remote Access Service program group. Choose **Add** to create a new entry. Give the entry a name (usually the name of your provider service) and the access phone number you were supplied. Click on the **Network** icon, and then click on **TCP/IP Settings**. You will see a dialog box such as that shown in Figure 8.1.

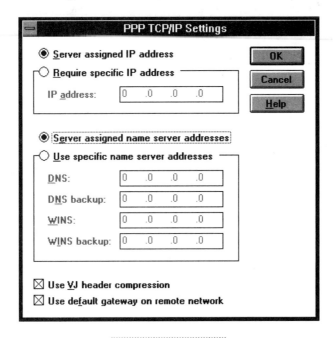

FIGURE 8.1 TCP/IP SETTINGS

Since you are setting this up to be a fixed address Web site, and not just for your own Internet browsing, you will need to change the option from **Server assigned IP address** to **Require specific IP address**, and supply the IP address that your provider gave you. You will also most likely need to change the **Server assigned name server address** to **Use specific name server address** and supply the DNS and DNS backup addresses given to you by your provider. Your provider should have also given you information about whether VJ header compression is appropriate and whether to use the default gateway. If not, try both settings initially deselected. Figure 8.2 is an example entry:

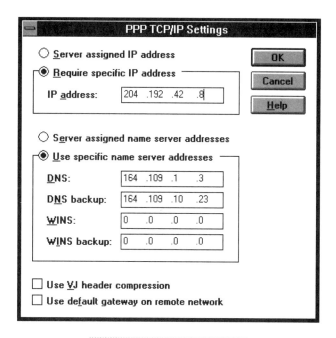

FIGURE 8.2 CONFIGURED TCP/IP SETTINGS

Now you are ready to dial up your provider. Invoke the **entry** in the RAS phonebook and you will be prompted for your logon ID and password. Supply the values given to you by your provider and PPP will handle the logon process for you. Should you have logon problems, choose **Security** button on the RAS entry to logon manually, by selecting **Terminal** as the After Dialing option. With PPP however this should not be necessary as the default, and should only be used to troubleshoot your connection if the automated connection is unsuccessful.

You now have your server on the Internet! It's not doing much at this point but you are a site on the information superhighway. If your friends and colleagues ping your TCP/IP address, it will report back successfully. If your domain name registration has gone through, your domain name (for example, ourstore.com) can also be pinged. Now let's go on give your site some services that will be useful supplements to your Web server, and also assist in the Web server content creation process.

WHAT YOUR SERVER WILL NEED

At this point you could just set up your http server as shown in the next chapter on Web servers, and you would have your basic presence on the World Wide Web. To have a really good Internet host that will allow optimal maintenance of your Web content, and provide other capabilities expected from a company with Internet presence you will need more than the Web server. For example, you should have some way for your customers to reach you via Internet SMTP mail. You should have the option of allowing selected individuals to place content onto your Web server in designated places, via the Internet. For this you will want to enable NT's built-in ftp server capability.

ftp Server

Windows NT has a built in ftp server service. It is useful to allow your clients to download information in a more ad hoc fashion than is possible via your Web server. You don't have to author a page to allow someone to download a file. If you used the Internet before the advent of the Web, you likely used ftp yourself often. You can make files available via anonymous ftp. Any user with an ftp client program just applies your host name as an argument to ftp, or types **open yourhostname.com**. They supply a username of **anonymous** and their email address as a password. They can then access a directory that you have set up for anonymous ftp access.

You can also give users their own accounts on your server (using NT's User Manager program), and a home directory that is ftp accessible. When they log onto your host via ftp and supply their own username and password, they will be deposited into their directory where they can download and upload files. It is this last capability that is most exciting and labor-saving for the webmaster. You can allow responsible individuals to upload their own content to your NT server. Even more exciting is that you can allow selected individuals direct access to the directories containing their live HTML content. Typically if you do so you will want to place these directories as subdirectories of your main HTML directory. You want to make it difficult for people to affect the HTML content that you are responsible for, such as the home page. If you are going to allow ftp access to the directories or subdirectories of HTML content, you will only want to do this on an NT File System (NTFS) volume. NTFS allows you to set permissions for users on a file by file basis, securing you against the possibility that one of the ftp accounts you created will be able to delete or retrieve content they do not have permissions to. Granting ftp access to individuals for their own content is a great way to devolve some of the work in HTML file maintenance to the responsible individuals.

So, here's how to set up ftp. Ensure that when you first install TCP/IP, you check the boxes necessary to get the ftp service. If you didn't remember to do that, use the **Add Software** command in the Network Control Panel applet to add the FTP software later. Choose **TCP/IP Protocol** and related components option. Either way, once FTP is installed, there will be an FTP server applet in Control Panel. Invoke the **FTP Server** applet and click on the **Security** button. Choose a partition (**C:**, **D:**, or **E:**) for your ftp server. If this partition is the same as one where you will have working HTML content for your Web server, you should be sure the partition is an NTFS partition. If not, exit from the applet and run **Disk Administrator** located in the Administrative Tools group, attempt to create such a partition, and come back to the ftp server configuration. Configure the selected partition for both **Read** and **Write** by enabling the checkboxes. If you are very concerned about security, and you really won't ever want users and HTML contributors to deposit files on your server, you can leave the **Write** checkbox disabled, but this may be an unnecessary restriction. Note that ftp access to all partitions is initially disabled.

Now click on the **Networks** applet in the Control panel. Invoke **Configure** on the FTP Server software. Choose a directory on the partition you just selected. For example, if you selected partition **D:**, you might supply directory **D:\PUB** (you can create the PUB directory after this step, but before starting up the service). You may decide to allow anonymous connections or not. Since you are doing this on an NTFS volume, it is reasonably safe for you to do so, since you can assign all of your sensitive directories as available only to specified individuals (for example, those in the Administrators group). If you do select anonymous connections, fill out the username for this as **anonymous** and leave the password empty. This is how users expect to work with an ftp server that allows anonymous connections, so if you aren't going to configure it this way, don't even bother allowing anonymous. For the purposes that you will probably have for setting up the ftp server, you should probably *not* restrict access only to anonymous connections. You will probably set up accounts for individual users and allow them access to subdirectories of the *pub* directory. The result of this configuration is the dialog box in Figure 8.3.

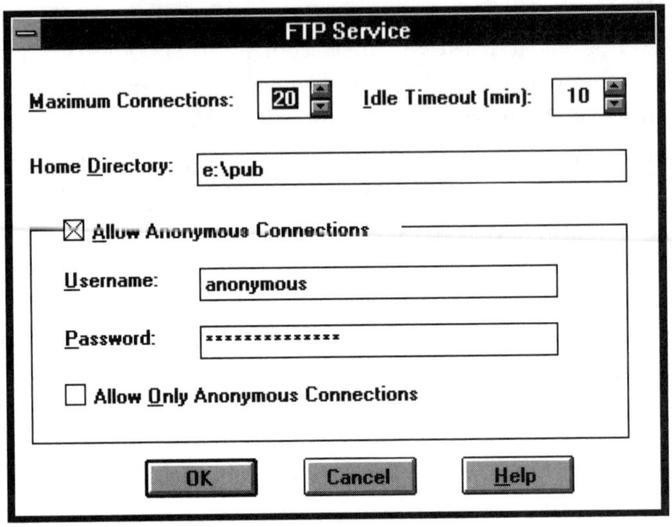

FIGURE 8.3 FTP SERVER CONFIGURATION

Now invoke the **Services** applet in Control Panel. You should see the ftp service available if you installed TCP/IP properly. If not, you will need to reinstall TCP/IP to include the ftp service utility. Once you see the ftp service in your Services applet, change the **Startup** property to **automatic**. Click on **Start** as well to start the service. Ftp is now running on your machine, but no users (except anonymous) are allowed access yet. Go into **File Manager** and use **Security/Permissions** to insure that **Everyone** is allowed **Add&Read** access to the **D:\PUB** directory. You can now place files you wish users to have access to in the D:\PUB directory (or whatever directory you configured) and they can retrieve them via familiar anonymous ftp. They can also deposit files in this directory, assuming you have enabled ftp server Write on this partition.

You should get an immediate benefit from just going this far. Users can use anonymous ftp (supplying your host name or TCP/IP address to ftp) to download files you make available. HTML authors you are working with can send you files. But this one big dropbox of files is probably not secure enough for most company's

Webmasters. You want each contributor and participant in your Web server effort to have their own area to drop off and retrieve files from. Go to the **User Manager** program in the Administrative Tools program group. Invoke **User/New User** to give each individual an account. Be sure to disable the **User must change password** checkbox, and enable the **Password never expires** checkbox, as shown in Figure 8.4.

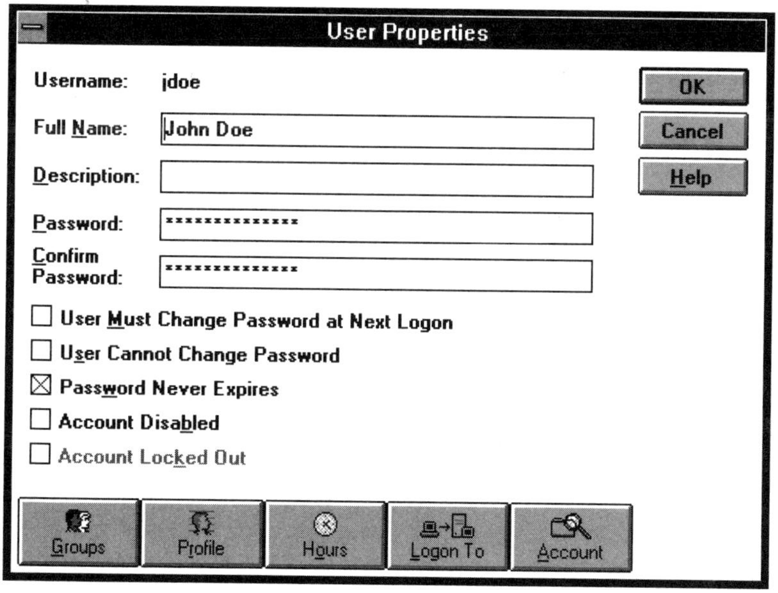

FIGURE 8.4 USER MANAGER ACCOUNT CREATION

Then create directories for each user *under* the configured ftp directory D:\PUB (or whatever directory you configured when configuring the FTP Server software in the Networks applet). Using File Manager's **Security/Permissions** command, configure the user's subdirectory to only allow the user and Administrators to have **Full Control** (remove the permission for **Everyone** and add the **Full Control** permission for the user). The resulting permission set should appear as shown in Figure 8.5.

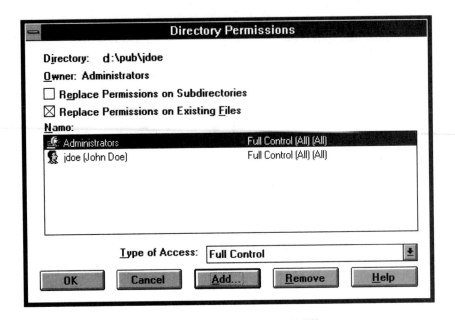

FIGURE 8.5 FILE MANAGER SECURITY PERMISSIONS

Interestingly enough, due to the behavior of NT ftp, you do *not* have to go to the Profile button on the User Properties dialog in User Manager to set the user's home directory for ftp. In fact, setting the home directory won't even have any effect. When a user logs into an NT ftp server with a user ID (non-anonymously), ftp deposits the user into a subdirectory of the ftp server directory with the same name as the user ID (D:\PUB\JDOE), if it exists. If it doesn't exist, the user is placed in the general anonymous ftp directory (D:\PUB). This behavior is not documented, and is somewhat strange and unintuitive for the experienced UNIX administrator. The good news, is that if you know it (you've read this book or discovered it yourself) it actually does save some time in setting up new ftp accounts.

You may also want to allow selected users to have permissions to directly replace their content on the Web server via ftp. You can do this in the following way. Create a directory on the partition that allows ftp reads and writes, for example **D:\HTDOCS**. Give this directory access *only* to Administrators. Create subdirectories of that directory with access for specific users or groups of users. For example: **D:\HTDOCS\MKTG**, **D:\HTDOCS\ENGRG**, **D:\HTDOCS\HR**. Using File Manager's **Security/Permissions** command, assign rights to these directories to the appropriate users. These users can then change directories into the areas for which they have rights. For example, HR personnel might ftp onto your server, and then enter **cd\htdocs\hr** and perform an FTP **put** command to update their content.

When you set up your Web server, which I describe in Chapter 9, you will configure it to find its home page in D:\HTDOCS (or whatever else you configured). The home page and supporting pages will have references to HTML content in these departmental directories with a relative directory reference followed by the file name. For example, to access Human Resource's recruiting page, the HTML reference might be **<A HREF=HR/RECRUIT.HTML>**.

You now have an ftp server that your users can retrieve files from or make submissions to. I've also given you the steps to follow to allow your HTML authoring collaborators to administer their own content, without physical, or even same network, access to your server. The next step in creating a full featured Internet server for supporting a Web site is to introduce email to allow your future Web browser users to communicate with you.

SMTP Server

Remember all of the "**mailto:webmaster@ourstore.com**" references in the earlier chapters on HTML? Well, users will be quite disappointed if they send email by clicking on these links and the messages are bounced back to them. To be a complete Web site, you really must have an SMTP mail server as well.

This particular topic may be the chink in Windows NT's armor in terms of NT's strength as an Internet server. It does not ship with an SMTP server, nor is one available on any of the NT 3.5 Resource Kits. The official Microsoft solution for this is the SMTP Connector that ships with Microsoft Exchange. By the time you read this, Microsoft Exchange will be shipping, but it requires 48 megabytes of RAM, and could be considered overkill by some to just allow email to be sent to the webmaster.

There are a few third party SMTP servers for NT. I will examine a particularly good one known as NT Mail from Internet Shopper. Evaluation copies of this software can be retrieved from **http://www.net-shopper.co.uk/** The distribution is downloadable as NTMAIL10.ZIP. Extracting the file into a chosen directory yields the three main executables: SMTP.EXE, POP.EXE, POST.EXE. Run each of these programs with the **-I** option to install them as services.

To run the evaluation version, you will need to retrieve a key from them at **http://www.net-shopper.co.uk/software/ntmail/key.htm**. This key will need to be placed into the registry using the REGEDT32.EXE program. Run **REGEDT32** and select the **HKEY_LOCAL_MACHINE** window. Under the **Software/Internet**

Shopper/Mail hive, double click on the **Key** key. Insert the key you retrieved from Internet Shopper.

Now you just need to create user mailboxes. You will want to create a text file. The format is:

```
mailboxname username password alias1 alias2 ...
```

For example, name the following file mail.txt:

```
MB0000 root password root administrator webmaster
MB0001 jdoe password jdoe john_doe john
```

Now invoke:

```
mail -lmail.txt
```

Two SMTP users are now created, and a total of six email names are now reachable: jdoe, john_doe, john, root, administrator, and webmaster.

Now let's get the services running. Click on the **Services Control Panel** applet and start up the **SMTP**, **POP**, and **POST** services. Make sure that the **Startup** properties are set to **Automatic**. Now all your HTML references to **"mailto:webmaster@ourstore.com"** will work.

Perl

A working installation of Perl is an essential tool to a full-featured Web site. There are many Perl scripts for common Web tasks such as log analysis, data format conversion, and HTML content analysis. In Chapter 11, I present a summary of how to program Perl for various Web tasks. I also present several useful sample Perl scripts. Even if you don't plan on programming your own Web tools however, there are so many Web tools written in Perl that you should plan on installing a copy of Perl as part of your Web server..

There are several ports of Perl to NT available on the Internet: one from Intergraph, one from Digital Equipment Corporation, and one from Bob Denny, the developer of WebSite. An excellent implementation of Perl 5 is available with the Microsoft Windows NT 3.51 Resource Kit. This Perl 5 port was developed by Hip Communications and is also available via their ftp server.

SECURE PAYMENT METHOD

If you want to accept orders online with your Web site, you will need to have some way of accepting payment securely from your customers. There are a number of ways of doing this. If you choose to run a secure http server that uses Secure HTTP or Netscape's Secure Sockets Library (such as the Netscape Commerce Server or a future version of Web Site), you can implement your own secure payment service by accepting credit card information in the HTML order forms you create. Chapter 11 on gateways presents the techniques for developing CGI programs that will store this information and communicate it to other information systems in your organization. In fact, I have developed some programs for this purpose that I present in Chapter 11.

However, you may not be running a secure server, and you also may not wish to restrict electronic ordering to users running secure browsers that interoperate with your server. Fortunately there are other options. These fall under the general categories of electronic cash schemes and secure payment transmission schemes. With electronic cash, an electronic cash bank allows ecash users to purchase serial numbered "bills". The user may then spend those bills at any Internet merchant that accepts that particular electronic cash type. The merchant may then submit the numbers to the electronic cash bank for payment in real currency. Alternatively, the merchant may choose to keep a reserve of electronic cash bills for making change or spending at other merchants.

Electronic cash schemes are still an emerging technology. DigiCash, founded by David Chaum, has a technology known as eCash. DigiCash (**http://www.digicash.com**) sponsored a limited eCash trial, but this technology has not been released as a general availability product, and thus eCash is not widely accepted on the Internet. Microsoft is known to be working on a form of electronic cash. CyberCash is working on an electronic cash system, known as *Money Payment Service,* which should operate very similar to their secure payment service that I describe in this section.

Secure payment schemes are not nearly as ambitious as electronic cash schemes. They attempt merely to solve the problem of transmitting credit card information securely, without assuming a Web browser to server secure protocol such as Netscape's SSL or Microsoft's Secure Transaction Technology (STT).

CyberCash

One such secure payment scheme is CyberCash's *Secure Internet Payment Service (SIPS).* CyberCash was founded in 1994 by Bill Melton, also the founder of VeriFone, the leading credit card verification automation system; they certainly are well positioned to be leading provider of secure credit card transmission systems. CyberCash is also interested in delivering an electronic cash system, and their forthcoming *Money Payment Service* is intended to do that. However, their current product offering is SIPS.

First let's describe how SIPS appears to the end user Web shopper. A user browses the Web and sees a site where he wants to buy a product. The potential customer may not be using a secure browser such as Netscape, or the site may have chosen not to run the Netscape Commerce Server or another secure server. However, the site says that they use CyberCash's Secure Internet Payment Service, and includes a link to CyberCash's home page (**http://www.cybercash.com**), or preferably to the URL where the client software can be downloaded (**http://www.cybercash.com/cgi-bin/download**).

The customer downloads the software for his platform (Windows or Macintosh only now available) and runs the self-extracting file to unpack the SETUP program. All Web browsers should be shut down before running the SETUP program. The user then runs the SETUP program, which detects a number of supported Web browsers during the installation process and registers new MIME types (*x-cybercash* and *cybercash*) with the selected browsers. This will result in the CyberCash being launched whenever the browser detects that type. Unfortunately the SETUP program only searches the C: drive, but the MIME type can be registered manually with most Web browsers for users with their browsers installed on other drivers (or using unsupported browsers).

SETUP will prompt the customer for a CyberCash ID and password to be used. It will then communicate with CyberCash via TCP/IP to register the ID and password. The ID may be changed by CyberCash (usually a suffix will be added) to ensure uniqueness. The SETUP program will then prompt the user to link a credit card to their ID as shown in Figure 8.6.

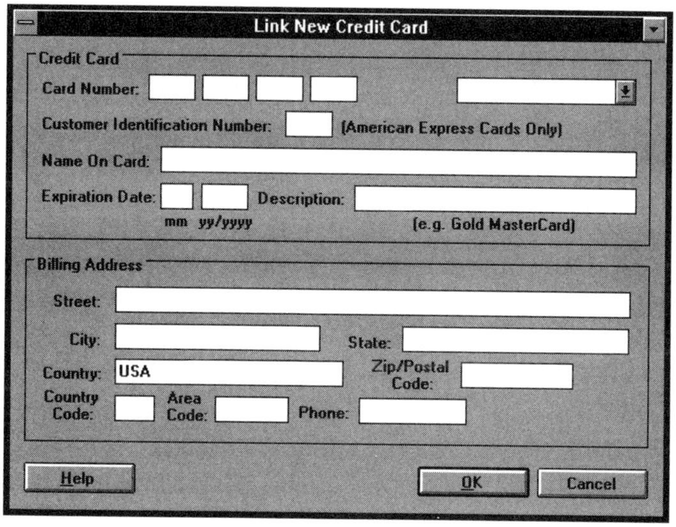

FIGURE 8.6 CYBERCASH LINK NEW CREDIT CARD DIALOG

Once the CyberCash client is set up, the customer can pay the CyberCash merchant by using his CyberCash client. Typically this will be done by the Web merchant by embedding a button in the HTML that invokes a script that processes the transaction. The merchant software will return a CyberCash transaction as a MIME object of type *cybercash* or *x-cybercash*. If the CyberCash client SETUP program did not create a MIME mapping for the object, many browsers (such as Netscape 1.2) will prompt the user to create a viewer for the MIME object on the fly, as shown in Figure 8.7.

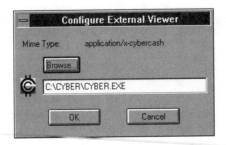

FIGURE 8.7 CONFIGURATION FOR CYBERCASH MIME OBJECT

Once a mapping is established for the object, the CyberCash client will be invoked any time a *cybercash* MIME object is received by the browser. First the customer will be asked to login with his CyberCash ID and password. The userid and password will be verified via encrypted transmission over the Internet to CyberCash. Then the customer will see a dialog such as that shown in Figure 8.8 asking him to confirm the transaction.

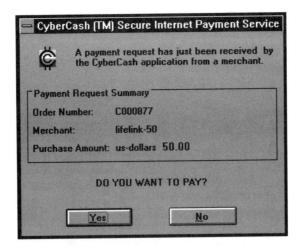

FIGURE 8.8 CYBERCASH TRANSACTION CONFIRMATION

After confirming, the user will see a dialog similar to Figure 8.9 which asks him to choose from his registered CyberCash credit cards. Once the credit card is selected, the customer clicks Pay, and the payment information is sent in encrypted form over the Internet to CyberCash, and the transaction is confirmed. Note that this mechanism can easily extend to supporting electronic cash or *Money Payment Services*, and the Available CyberCash label in Figure 8.9 implies that such support is coming. So the customer will be able to make electronic cash payments with presumably the same set of steps that have been shown here.

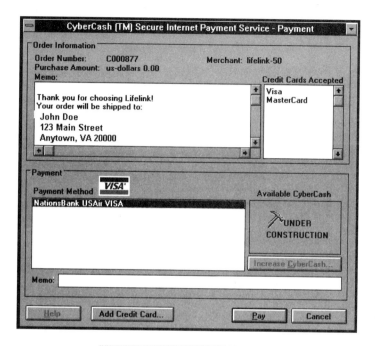

FIGURE 8.9 CYBERCASH CREDIT CARD SELECTION

How do you, the prospective Web merchant, get this set up? First you need to be a credit card authorizer. Second, your bank needs to execute a service agreement with CyberCash (CyberCash supplies a list of financial institutions that have already done so). You can also choose to use a bank for your credit card that has already executed an agreement. A list of these can be found at **http://www.cybercash.com/merchants/ merch_banks.html**. Third, you need to have a Web-based store and the SIPS server software. If you have met the first two requirements, you can apply to be a CyberCash merchant at **http://www.cybercash.com/merchants/merchantapplform.html**.

First Virtual

Another payment service that you may wish to evaluate if you are selling information is First Virtual (**http://www.fv.com**). First Virtual is oriented to providing a method for information providers to charge for their content. As you will see from the following description, it is not particularly suited to selling tangible goods.

Both the merchant and the potential customer must both have First Virtual accounts for the scheme to work. Users set up accounts with First Virtual by filling out an application without credit card information (at **http://www.fv.com**). They will then receive email instructing them to call an 800 number and supply their credit card number, bypassing the Internet insecure transmission issue.

As a business, you can establish yourself as First Virtual merchant by filling out an application on the same page, and sending First Virtual a check for $10. The check will have the necessary information to allow First Virtual to deposit funds to your account. Once your merchant account is established, you can advertise on your Web site that you are a First Virtual merchant, and identify the information that is available for sale (via download) with a First Virtual account.

First Virtual strongly encourages you to let customers "try before they buy" but it isn't required. One thing you may decide to do before allowing the trial is to at least verify their First Virtual account status. You can do this via telnet, finger, and a custom application they make available called *FV*. Account verification is also available via email but turnaround is not likely to be quick enough to be practical. If you do not allow trials, this step is likely to be optional, and you will only need to automate initiating transactions.

Once the user has requested to make a purchase, you will need to initiate a transaction. To do so, you will need to supply to First Virtual the customer's First Virtual account, your First Virtual account, the amount of the sale, the currency and a description of the transaction. You can submit this via email, telnetting to the Fist Virtual host, or using a proprietary Internet protocol First Virtual makes available. After the transaction has been submitted, First Virtual will attempt to confirm the transaction with the purchaser via email.

Since there is a long potential delay between when the transaction is initiated and when you receive confirmation back from First Virtual, it is generally intended that the "purchase" take place at the time the transaction is initiated. This implies a risk factor, but its usually acceptable for the markets that First Virtual is targeted to (selling information). If and when the buyer replies and confirms the purchase, a confirmation message is sent to you confirming their purchase. The amount of the purchase will then be direct deposited by First Virtual into your checking account, less First Virtual's transaction fee. This fee is 29 cents plus 2 percent of the amount of the sale.

First Virtual is an attractive option if you are selling low cost information, with little or no unit cost to yourself. First Virtual also has the advantage of allowing you to accept credit card transactions without being a credit card merchant. It is not a good option for selling tangible goods. It is here where CyberCash or one of the other emerging schemes may be necessary if you wish to allow credit card purchases via your Web site.

Rolling Your Own

You may decide that none of the available third party mechanisms for secure payment are acceptable. For example, you may be using Netscape's Commerce Server but decide that you need to allow other browsers to submit sensitive information as well. You may decide that having the user establish a CyberCash account and download and setup the CyberCash client is too burdensome for the impulse purchases you want to encourage. Finally you may decide that First Virtual's scheme is inappropriate for the wares that you are vending on your site.

Do not despair! What you really want to do is just provide some way for your customers to get their credit card number to you securely. There are a number of ways you can do this without necessarily having a secure Internet protocol such as SSL or using a third party intermediary. The methods include setting up a voice mail system to accept credit card information only after the rest of the order is placed electronically, gathering credit card information with callbacks, or allowing your customers to send you the credit card information via encrypted email.

Let's first discuss the phone-based methods. You can have your customers fill out HTML-based order forms for all of the product purchase information *except* the actual credit card number (Chapter 5 discusses HTML form syntax in detail, and Chapter 11 shows you how to process these forms with CGI programs). Your form processing program can return a transaction number to the user and request that she call an 800 number and leave her credit card number with a human operator, a voice mail system, or a touch tone response system. Alternatively, you can have your human staff call back the user to confirm the order and solicit the credit card information at that time. In either case, your human operator or voice mail system can also ask whether the customer would like her credit card number saved for future purchases. If the answer is yes, the credit card number is saved along with other customer information, The next time that customer purchases a product on the Web site, the CGI gateway program that processes her order form can retrieve the stored credit card number, and ask the customer if she would like to use the stored credit card number for the purchase. In this case, the user will not be asked to call into the 800 number to supply the credit card information.

Another alternative is to allow your customers to send in their credit card information via encrypted Internet mail. One freely available encryption is Phil Zimmerman's PGP (an acronym standing for Pretty Good Privacy). PGP was under a legal cloud for a while when RSA was alleging infringement of the patents that it holds on public/private key encryption methods. Zimmerman reimplemented PGP using RSA's publicly available API, and that challenge has now been removed. PGP is still under export restrictions. But luckily you don't need to concern yourself with this issue. You should generally include a link to a site for customers to retrieve PGP if they don't already have it, but it won't be your job to police access to the PGP software.

What you will do with PGP is to publish your public key (or the text representation of it) directly on your Web site. You should include brief instructions on how users can add this public key to their PGP "keyring". This involves them saving the HTML page to a text file, such as PGPKEY.HTM, and then issuing the PGP -KA command, as in the following:

```
PGP -KA PGPKEY.HTM
```

This will add your public key to their keyring. You should also describe how to encrypt the information they will send. The command is the PGP -E command. An example command is:

```
PGP -E APPLIC.TXT "CyberBooks"
```

Documenting this sequence of steps and making such a page available linked from your account application or product order form will allow your customers that do not have secure access to your server to establish an account or order a product from you via encrypted email. Figure 8.10 shows an example page illustrating how you might describe to your users how to establish an account with you using PGP encrypted mail.

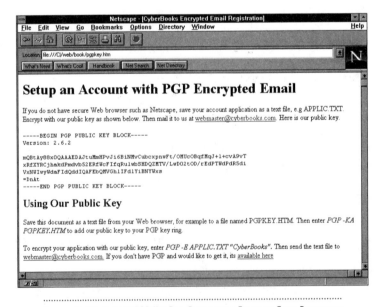

FIGURE 8.10 EXAMPLE PGP KEY PAGE DOCUMENTING ENCRYPTED EMAIL PROCEDURES

If you are a United States and Canadian citizen or permanent resident of the U.S. you can legally retrieve the latest version of PGP (2.6.2 at this writing) by following instructions located at **ftp://ftp.csn.net/mpj/README.MPJ** (due to export restrictions we have not included PGP on the accompanying CD-ROM). You should also include a link to this or another PGP site from your page that describes the PGP encrypted email process.

This obviously requires some effort, though only one time, from your customers. However, if the majority of your users are accessing your Web server securely, and you want to have some method to offer your non-secure Web browser customers of making secure purchases as well, this could be a good low-cost alternative to human operators or elaborate voice mail systems.

HTTP SERVER

For completeness we mention that (surprise!) you will need to install an http server to run an effective Web site. The next chapter covers a slew of excellent Windows NT-based Web servers.

CHAPTER 9

WEB SERVER SOFTWARE

Once you have your server operational and connected to the Internet, you are ready to deploy your http server. Of course, as mentioned earlier, if you are going to host your content on someone else's server, you do not need to read this chapter. But that is not likely to be the case if you've made it this far.

In many of the earlier chapters, the information presented such as reference material on HTML, the CGI standard, and authoring tools applied to whatever platform (UNIX, Macintosh, OS/2, NT) you might be using for your Web server. Even the Windows authoring tools generate portable HTML that you can host on any platform. In this chapter however, I will be focusing on Windows NT-based Web servers only. Why? I believe that NT represents the most cost-effective, powerful, and easily managed platform for hosting Web servers. A Windows-based Web server, such as the freeware SerWeb might be acceptable to put up a true home page (meaning a single page) that is accessed by a limited few. But it's not appropriate for the applications I have in mind. If you've read this far, you are serious about your Web server application. My recommendation is that if you don't have Windows NT now, get it and use it for your Web server. Or place it on a hosting service if that's not a viable option.

The NT-based Web servers I present here are all relatively new, and in some cases not well-documented. I will see supplement their manuals with discussions of installation, configuration, and maintenance. There is much commonality in how these products are configured and administered, so discussing them all at the same time makes sense. Part of the reason for the similarities is that in some cases the common heritage that some products (such as EMWAC https and Purveyor) have. But most of the similarity stems from NT's philosophy and recommendations of how to manage server software. These include guidelines on when to use Control Panel applets, using the Event Viewer log for logging, implementing programs as services when that's what they are, and using the registry for configuration. All of these programs are exemplary in their use of NT, and it makes them much easier to administer. Nevertheless, many of you, even those of you using Windows NT as your desktop operating system, may not have detailed knowledge of how well-constructed NT services are administered. In the discussion here, you will see a lot about how this is done that will apply to whatever NT-based server you will use, be it one of these products or a future NT-based Web server.

Finally, and perhaps most importantly, you can use this survey to make a decision about which Web server you will use in your own environment. You will learn a lot about the configuration and administration of these products without having to purchase each one separately or obtain an evaluation copy. I won't be recommending a specific product explicitly. But you will learn enough about the strengths, weaknesses, and idiosyncrasies of each product to make an informed decision about which product to choose.

Note that I restrict my review to Web servers for NT that cost $3,000 or less. Where did that number come from? Well, the Netscape Commerce Server, a very powerful, high-end product, sells for $2995. Netscape's product is the first to introduce a secure HTTP protocol (specifically Secure Sockets Layer or SSL), so it's difficult to see the rationale behind products costing much more that don't have that functionality. Also, another rule of thumb in software pricing is that consumers do not expect to pay more for software than they do for the underlying hardware. Since Windows NT platforms can be purchased for around $3,000 (at this writing a 90 megahertz Pentium with 32 megabytes of RAM and 2 gigabytes of hard disk can be purchased for around that amount from several vendors), I think products costing much more than that are not likely to be successful in the marketplace.

I will evaluate all of the products meeting these criteria, starting with the simplest and cheapest and working my way up. Fortunately, this works since there is a correlation between the two factors: the more expensive Web servers do provide more features. Note that all of the products reviewed below will work with what I have recommended as the minimum appropriate Windows NT configuration for a Web server:

- Windows NT 3.5 or greater
- 16MB RAM or greater
- 10MB free disk space or greater

Since all of the Web servers reviewed below will work well on such machines, I will dispense with listing these requirements individually.

HTTPS FOR WINDOWS NT

The first HTTPS server we examine is https from the European Microsoft Windows Academic Centre. This server is freeware available directly from EMWAC at **http://emwac.ed.ac.uk.** It is also available on the Microsoft Windows NT 3.51 Resource Kit. HTTPS was the first http server available for Windows NT. Several Windows-based Web servers had appeared earlier that of course could run on NT. But HTTPS truly leverages the strengths of NT, including installing as an NT service and logging to the NT Event Log.

Where does the name https come from? As discussed earlier, *http* stands for HyperText Transfer Protocol, the protocol for transmitting HTML content over the Internet, first specified by Tim Berners-Lee. The first http servers were CERN's HTTP server and NCSA's httpd, standing for "http daemon". A daemon is a background process on UNIX, and the closest equivalent on NT is the "service". Hence the name *https*: hypertext transport protocol service.

Installation

Here's an accelerated set of steps for getting HTTPS installed on your NT server. This should save you wading through the documentation HTTPS.doc that comes with the distribution, at least for getting the server up and running initially.

- Log on to NT with administrator rights.
- Copy the **HTTPS.EXE, HTTPS.CPL** and **HTTPS.HLP** files to the \WINNT\SYSTEM32 directory.
- Run **HTTPS-install** to install the HTTPS as a service. It should then show up in the NT services list. Click on the **Services Control Panel** icon to check that it has been installed. Do not actually start the service yet.
- Run the **HTTP Server Control Panel** applet to configure the directory for the service, as shown in Figure 9.1. Set the data directory to be the directory containing your HTML (for example, **D:\HTTP**). If you wish users to be able to access your page with only a server URL (for example, http://ourstore.com) make sure that your top level page is contained in file DEFAULT.HTM. Other options in the Control Panel are documented in the Configuration section.
- Test that your server is running by accessing it from your Web browser.

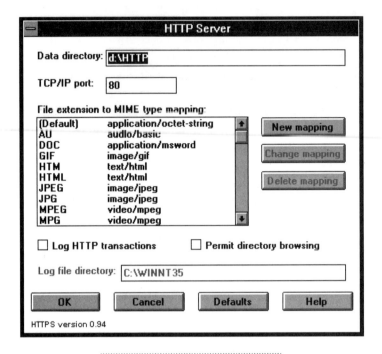

FIGURE 9.1 HTTP SERVER CONTROL PANEL APPLET

Configuration

Though https is a simple product, it does have the capability to change several options. These include the port used, whether or not logging of user accesses is enabled, directory browsing, and MIME mapping. The following options appear in the HTTP Server Control Panel applet depicted in Figure 9.1.

- The TCP/IP port should typically be left at 80. However, it is useful to have the capability to change this, to, for example, run another Web server on another port.

- If you wish to log accesses to your data, click the checkbox for **log transactions** on. Note that HTTPS does *not* perform DNS resolution for logging. That is, what you will see in the logs is a bunch of IP addresses, not domain names, and what files they accessed. Depending on what you need to track, this may be sufficient, and is actually much higher performance than doing lookup in a DNS server.

NOTE   DNS stands for Domain Name System and is a method of translating friendly text names such as ourstore.com into their actual Internet Protocol addresses (in the form nnn.nnn.nn.n).

- Enabling directory browsing allows users to browse through files in a directory by just giving the URL to that directory. For example, if you wish to let users download files in the directory **\products** off of your root directory, enable this option, and then include the URL for the directory in your HTML. Users that click on the reference to the directory then get directory browsing.

- MIME mapping allows the Web server to deliver files with given extensions as specified MIME types. A number of mappings are built-in, but you can add more with the specified dialog.

Evaluation

https is a good solid Web server that will meet the needs of many companies. The price is right (it's free). It's readily available at a moment's notice (via the Web or on the NT 3.51 Resource Kit). Missing features that are available on other platforms include domain name logging, user by user permissions for files, and of course any form of secure transmission.

Strengths

- Cost. It's free.

- Availability. Via the Internet or on the Microsoft Windows NT 3.51 Resource Kit.

- Setup. Simple installation.

- Integration with EMWAC WAIS Server for text searching. See Chapter 10 on CGI gateways for details on how this works. The EMWAC https integration with EMWAC WAIS is simpler than other Web-WAIS cooperation schemes currently available.

Weaknesses

- Security administration. No user-level file and directory permissions recognized by the server.

- Secure protocol. https does not now have, nor will it have support for any secure HTTP protocol.

- Future maintenance. Since Process Software is now marketing the commercial release of this software new enhancements are not likely to be appearing.

Please note that I do need to cover the gateway interface for EMWAC, but details on the CGI interfaces for all of the server products in this chapter are presented in Chapter 11 on gateway programming. Since this is an avowedly simple product, we will not belabor the evaluation any further, before covering the commercial incarnation of https: Process Software's *Purveyor*.

PURVEYOR WEBSERVER FOR WINDOWS NT, VERSION 1.1

Process Software sells a commercial version of the EMWAC https server with several additional features, likely to be interesting to the readers of this book. The major new features of the Purveyor Web Server over and above EMWAC version are:

- Authentication
- Access Control
- Virtual Paths
- Proxy Servers
- "Common" Log File Format
- Icons for File Types
- Redirection

New features with Purveyor 1.1, which you should be able to purchase by the time you read this book, include:

- Multiple site hosting
- Database integration
- An API (beyond CGI)
- Enhanced log viewing

Installation

Installation is performed from a fairly minimalist graphical installation program. It just installs the program files and sets up the program group, and doesn't ask questions about how you want your site configured. When SETUP is complete it creates a program with the Purveyor configuration applet, a log viewer, an HTML Link browser, ODBC driver setup including ODBC drivers for Microsoft SQL Server and Microsoft Access, and a "data wizard" for setting up connectivity to ODBC data sources. The program group generated is shown in Figure 9.2.

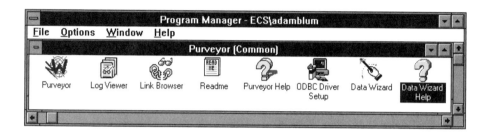

FIGURE 9.2 PURVEYOR PROGRAM GROUP

Once installed, Purveyor is administered from the Purveyor configuration property sheet, which is installed as a Control Panel applet, and appears as shown in the first icon in Figure 9.2. We will need to use the Purveyor applet to finish setting up the Purveyor server for use. The tab you will want to use first is labeled **Virtual Servers** as shown in Figure 9.3. Fill in the name of your host. Set the data directory to the location of your HTML files. Notice that Purveyor allows changing the default HTML file (the one that appears when the user just enters the URL of your server) to whatever name you wish: **default.htm**, **index.htm**, or some other file name perhaps derived from your site name.

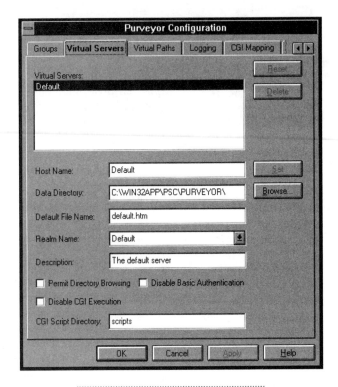

FIGURE 9.3 PURVEYOR APPLET VIRTUAL SERVERS TAB

Once these options are set, you are ready to start up the Purveyor service. There are two ways to do this. Since it is a service, you can click on the **Services** applet in **Control Panel**, find the **Purveyor Server** service, and **Start**. At this time, you will also probably want to change the Startup property of the service to automatic. Alternatively, you can use the Purveyor applet to start up the Purveyor Server service by clicking on the **Main** program tab, and clicking the **Start** button there. You will still eventually want to change the service Startup property to Automatic, so the first method is probably better.

Configuration

The Purveyor environment is rich with configuration options, especially compared to its minimalist forefather https. Purveyor 1.1 is robust even compared to version 1.0.

The Realms, Users, and Groups tabs let you establish users and groups, and "realms" where those particular users and groups apply to provide fine-tuned access control to your HTML content and CGI gateway programs. For use within one Web site, the Realms feature might seem like overkill. But this is particularly valuable if you are using Purveyor as the server for more than one Web site.

How can this be done? The Virtual Servers tab lets you configure Purveyor to support more than one domain name. For example, if you are hosting several companies on one Web server machine, this might have been done on HTTPS or other earlier http servers, by putting each company's content into a separate directory. Alpha, Inc. might have an URL of **http://www.stores.com/alpha**. Beta Company would have an URL of **http://www.stores.com/beta**. The Virtual Server feature lets Purveyor give each company their own server address. The URLs would become **http://www.alpha.com** and **http://www.beta.com**. Even if you are not acting as a Web hosting, such as the **www.stores.com** business implied by this example, this feature is very useful if you are supplying a server for several departments in an organization.

The Virtual Paths tab lets you define a logical path name to the physical path name mappings. This is very useful if you have several hard drives you wish to place HTML content on, or if you want to allow use of network drives for some content, and allow content contributors to place their HTML onto particular shares.

Transaction logging is configured from the Logging tab. Logging is enabled with the **Log HTTP Transactions** checkbox. This is clicked off by default so you will want to remember to enable this feature if you wish track user access to your content. The log directory can be set to any directory, and you will probably want to change to a directory associated with your content, such as a **log** subdirectory below your directory of HTML files.

The log file is by default in the "common log file format" initiated by HTTPD and CERN, and used by many log analysis tools, but can be configured to a very fine degree of detail with an Add/Remove dialog that allow fields to be inserted and removed from the log file line. Below is an example line from the a default style log.

```
www.stores.com - -[10/Sep/1995:02:39:46 -0400]"GET / HTTP/1.0"304
```

Purveyor maintains its logs in files in the logging directory named for the particular day, each day's accesses stored in a separate file. For example, the log for October 1, 1995 would be stored in file HS951001.LOG.

The CGI mapping tab lets you associate programs with file extensions for embedded references to gateway programs. For example, a mapping is provided with Purveyor so that when a link to a .PL file is given, the Perl interpreter is invoked with the specified .PL script.

Two more tabs, MIME Types and MIME Icons, allow mapping of file extensions to server functionality. MIME Types lets you associate a MIME type that the server will broadcast to a Web browser when the browser attempts to access a file of a particular extension. The MIME Icons tab associates icons with specific file types, this is particularly useful if you have enabled **Directory Browsing** on your Web server. Directory browsing is functionality where the server generates HTML to be displayed to a Web browser that corresponds to the contents of a directory, if the Web browser supplies an URL that corresponds to a directory name.

Tools

The Log Viewer provides the capability of loading logs into a spreadsheet-like environment and performing sorting, querying and reporting on various criteria. The Log Viewer lets you load log files of successive days into the same viewer. You must point the viewer at the right directory, which is disappointing. The log viewer should know where the logs are stored, from the configured Purveyor Server option.

The loaded logs can be sorted by remote host name, date and time, type of request, and other criteria. The same factors can be used for searching for individual log records. Reports can be created to generate summary statistics for number of hits, number of distinct remote hosts, number of distinct logon IDs, and so on. The reporting module was not functional at the time of this review (that is every attempt to execute it on even the smallest logs failed), but a review of the available menus and help documentation suggests it will not be as flexible as some of the third party log analysis tools. However, its very existence is at this time unique among available NT Web servers.

The Link Browser is an HTML content manager/hierarchical viewer. It's very similar in spirit to WebView, the tool bundled with O'Reilly's WebSite, that is reviewed in the next section. Point the **Link Browser** at your home page, and it generates a tree hierarchy of all of the pages on your site. Unlike WebView, Link Browser shows you its progress in pulling in the links made from a page in realtime. That is, it displays the changes to the hierarchy (subdocuments found, changes of icons from red closed books to gray open books for completed nodes) as it is performing the analysis. It takes a long time for this process to be completed on even some modest amount of content. Link Browser takes a similar approach to WebView in that once the tree is created, the HTML author can navigate amongst the nodes and then invoke an "editor" on whatever node is selected. However the details of this operation are still very rough and fall far short of what WebSite has provided. For example, instead of just clicking on the node to invoke the editor, you must select the Invoke submenu from the main menu. The **Invoke** submenu has one command, called Mapped Editor. Besides being poor menu design in the first place, this command should be available to the author as a simple single or double click on the node representing the HTML content.

But wait, it gets worse. The Invoke Mapped Editor command will invoke a program associated with the object's file extension whenever you click on an object in the hierarchy. There are some mappings supplied for objects that should *never* appear in your HTML content, such as Word .DOC files and Windows .BMP files, but there are no mappings for such basic object types, such as, say, HTML files (which should really be the majority of the nodes in the tree).

Other details of poor design abound. When at the first step of choosing an HTML hierarchy to analyze and display, instead of taking you directly to your home page as configured in the Web server setup (as WebView does), it gives you a selection of all HTML files in the directory where your home page is. You must then identify the HTML page that is your actual top level page (even though the tool could certainly get it from your Purveyor configuration). The Preferences dialog is invoked off of the Edit menu. Top level menus have an average of two submenu items. There are no toolbars. The Help About command doesn't show name and version but takes you into the Help system into an apparently arbitrary topic. Purveyor has many innovative useful features, but this tool should simply be scrapped. It may be improved by final release of Purveyor 1.1, but it is such a poor foundation that it's doubtful this particular tool will be worthwhile. It warrants a complete rewrite.

The final tool available in Purveyor is an ODBC interface. This is a great move I will emphasize in the next chapter: access to corporate data is critical to a successful Web site for an organization. The essence of the tool is the "Data Wizard." Data Wizard's interface is a six tab dialog. The first tab, labeled DataSource, lets you pick an ODBC data source and database. When you move to the second tab, labeled Tables, the list of tables available in the specified database appears. When you select a table and move to the Fields tab you can choose the fields which you want to use. Once the fields are selected, click on the **Action** table to select whether you wish to use these fields to **Add** a record or **Search** for a record based on this information. The final Layout tab lets you position the fields on the HTML page that will be generated. When you've finished this last step, click on the **Disk** icon to save your form to an HTML file. You will be presented with a File Save dialog to name your HTML output. A file will be generated similar to the output below, which was generated from the sample Pubs database, Authors table supplied with Microsoft SQL 6.0.

Purveyor Data Wizard Output

```
<HTML>
<FORM METHOD=POST ACTION="Process.exe?Backend.exe">
<HEAD>
<TITLE></TITLE>
</HEAD>
<INPUT TYPE="HIDDEN" NAME="FORMNAME"VALUE="TEST.HTM">
<CENTER>
<H1></H1>
<H2></H2>
<HR>
</CENTER>
<P>
au_id: <INPUT TYPE="TEXT" NAME="au_id" MAXLENGTH=11 SIZE=11 >
<P>au_lname: <INPUT TYPE="TEXT" NAME="au_lname" MAXLENGTH=40
SIZE=40 >
<P>au_fname: <INPUT TYPE="TEXT" NAME="au_fname" MAXLENGTH=20
SIZE=20 >
<P>phone: <INPUT TYPE="TEXT" NAME="phone" MAXLENGTH=12 SIZE=12 >
<P>address: <INPUT TYPE="TEXT" NAME="address" MAXLENGTH=40 SIZE=40
>
<P>city: <INPUT TYPE="TEXT" NAME="city" MAXLENGTH=20 SIZE=20 >
<P>state: <INPUT TYPE="TEXT" NAME="state" MAXLENGTH=2 SIZE=2 >
<P>zip: <INPUT TYPE="TEXT" NAME="zip" MAXLENGTH=5 SIZE=5 > <P>
<CENTER>
<P><INPUT TYPE="submit" VALUE=" Add ">
</CENTER>
</FORM>
</HTML>
```

Once again, this tool is not implemented particularly well. You cannot move back to previous tabs when making selections, but must reopen a database and start over if you make a wrong decision. For example, you cannot go back and change what table you are working off of. This makes the whole tabbed dialog interface misleading and inappropriate. Actually there are Windows controls for this kind of sequential, linear task. They're called, fittingly, *wizards*, but they involve multiple dialogs to be presented, each using the wizard style. The Data Wizard should be rewritten to be a true wizard. Also, note in my review of similar products such as WebDBC and Cold Fusion, that this functionality is not as robust as its competitors.

Evaluation

Purveyor provides many new areas of functionality over its parent https. The authentication features allow fine tuned control of user access to information. Virtual servers allow one copy of Purveyor on one machine to serve as the host for several logical Web sites. Virtual paths allow building of larger webs spread over drives, networks, and CD-ROMs. The revised log file format allows the host of new log analysis tools written for CERN and NCSA servers to be deployed on Purveyor servers. The Log Viewer provides a level of reporting and analysis not found in other Web server packages, though still short of standalone log analysis programs. The new features in version 1.1 of built-in access to ODBC database drivers, combined with the new API, provide new options for Web-integrating application developers: no separate ODBC gateways needed and no CGI interface to learn.

Purveyor's 1.1 release still does not include any form of secure HTTP protocol, though this is promised for a future release. This is probably the biggest advantage of Netscape's server over their competitors. Also the API for the server might not be much of an advantage. The API is hardly a standard (as compared to the Common Gateway Interface) and Purveyor cannot claim overwhelming market share, so the API might really not see much use. Though aggressive about bundling utilities, the merit of some of the bundled utilities is questionable. The Link Browser is almost worthless without major changes to its interface. The Log Viewer is a good idea, but needs some improvements in flexibility of its reporting options to really compete with similar standalone utilities, some of which may become part of Purveyor's competitors' products.

Purveyor recently reduced their price to $495, making it and WebSite very compelling choices for the budget-conscious webmaster. Fully functional evaluation copies of the software, and further information for purchase, can be accessed at **http://www.process.com**.

WEBSITE

I cover WebSite next because it has some features over and above Purveyor, but not quite all the functionality present in Netscape. WebSite was developed by independent developer Bob Denny, and founder of the messaging company Alisa Systems. It stemmed from his original effort to port NCSA's UNIX httpd server to Windows, which was made available freely over the Internet. The Windows httpd was a good product, about as good as could be expected from a first effort on a Windows-based server. Luckily for the Web community, Bob also realized that the server should be NT-based.

Installation

The installation works from a simple straightforward setup program. You will be prompted for the name of your host and the email address of your webmaster. If you are starting your content from scratch and can live with their directory conventions, this is all there is to the installation. The Install program will create a program group that appears as shown in Figure 9.4.

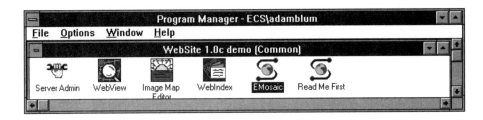

FIGURE 9.4 WebSite Program Group

The WebSite executables include:

- The Web Server itself, which can be run as a service or as a normal program.
- The Server Admin program which configures the operation of the Web server.
- The WebView program which allows you to manage your HTML content.
- Image Map, for creating clickable image maps.
- WebIndex, which makes the text content of your web searchable.
- O'Reilly Enhanced Mosaic, configured to initially point to the WebSite documentation.

I will discuss these components in detail later. Before executing the Web Server, let's look at what options were installed as a result of the SETUP program. If you invoke **Server Admin**, a tabbed dialog will appear as shown in Figure 9.5. Note that our server and email names appear on the general tab. The only option that you are likely to want to change is the Run Mode. You have a choice of running as a Desktop application, as an NT Service, or as an NT Service with an icon appearing on the desktop. For the first run, you may wish to leave it as a desktop application.

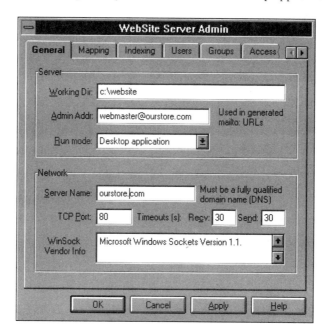

FIGURE 9.5 WEBSITE SERVER ADMIN DIALOG

Now let's get your server running. If you are willing to move your HTML content into the \htdocs subdirectory of the WebSite installation directory, you can copy your content there, and then invoke Web Server program. Make sure that you title your top level page **index.html**. That is the default document that WebSite will use. If you were using Purveyor or another Web server earlier, you may have titled your document something more descriptive since Purveyor and some other servers let you directly specify a default document name.

However, I prefer to have my content in a fixed location, and potentially switch between Web servers, configuring them as needed to point to a set of documents that exists *independently of a specific Web server*. The content should live on, and you should be able to use whatever Web server that comes along that meets your needs. That's the theory. In practice, differences between CGI interfaces (see the Chapter 10) mean that if you have gateways deployed you will need to make changes to use another Web server. But since your home and support pages are usually what you start with, this is a reasonable goal.

So in installing these Web servers, don't consider yourself done until you've pointed the server to your content. With WebSite you do that by invoking the **Server Admin** program, and clicking on the **Mapping** tab. The Mapping tab controls mapping of URLs supplied by users to physical directories. By default the Mapping tab is set to map the root directory of the Web server (/) to the \HTDOCS directory of the WebSite install directory, and the \WSDOCS subdirectory to the \WSDOCS subdirectory of the WebSite install directory. You may wish to change this to have the root directory of the Web server, the directory resulting from the user just entering your server name, point to your content in another directory. For example, Figure 9.6 shows the result of reconfiguring the server to point to the D:\OURDATA directory. The mapping to the root directory was changed, and the mapping to the \WSDOCS directory was removed.

FIGURE 9.6 WEBSITE SERVER ADMIN MAPPING TAB

At this point you are ready to start the Web Server program. Once it's up and running distributing your content, you'll want to learn more about how to use and configure this very powerful suite of programs.

Configuration

The configuration options for the WebSite Server are all controlled from the Server Admin program, a many-tabbed dialog box. You have seen the General and Mapping tabs in Figures 9.5 and 9.6. The General tab is self-explanatory. The Mapping tab can be used to map specific directory URLs to other physical directories on the local machine or the network, facilitating the creation of large enterprise-wide webs. Also helping this is the ability to map URLs supplied by users or referenced in our HTML content to other URLs anywhere on the Internet. The mapping facility allows CGI program references to be redirected to the specific location on the hard drive where they reside. This is particularly useful while testing gateway programs during development, when the executable is invariably nested inside some tortuous directory hierarchy.

The Indexing tab lets you control the directory indexing process. If directory indexing is enabled and there is no index.html document in the directory specified by an URL, an HTML document will be created containing information about the contents of the directory. The first checkbox controls whether or not directory indexing is performed at all. If it's enabled, a list of the files in a directory is displayed to the Web user if an URL to a directory is supplied and no index.html document is present. For example http://ourstore.com/products might refer to a products subdirectory containing descriptions of various products a company sells. If you assume a knowledgeable user, they may be able to tell what to download based on the file name (especially if you use the NT File System's capability of displaying long filenames). This certainly saves time over authoring HTML pages that list filenames for ftp retrieval. However, it should really be restricted to cases where a set of files needs to be made available and is frequently updated. It is not a particularly user-friendly experience, and it should be used rarely on sites where accessibility to the user is important (as most commercial sites will be). The extended indexing feature allows the display of icons for file types, show the dates and file sizes, and other information about the files in the directory. Since this feature is not particularly relevant for carefully crafted sites, I won't discuss all the potential customizations, but they are extensive.

FIGURE 9.7 WEBSITE SERVER ADMIN INDEXING TAB

The next three tabs let you establish users, groups, and access control. The users and groups tabs let you establish users and groups that can then be used for access control of an URL to a directory. Access control cannot be specified on specific documents, just on the directory that contains the document. The lowest level directory's access control overrides the access control of parent directories.

You can actually have multiple sets of users and groups, each collected into a named *realm*. For example the Administrators group might be different in one realm than another. If you have a very large hierarchical web with distinct areas, the Administrators group might be allowed access to a particular subdirectory in one part of your web, but in another part of the web, you wish the Administrators group to be a different set of users. I am not really convinced of the absolute necessity of this feature (why not just more groups), and it does make the user authentication part of WebSite's access control scheme more difficult to learn. Nevertheless, once understood, it doesn't really get in the way, and you can choose to use just one realm, such as the Web Server realm that they supply.

Once your users and groups are established, you can apply access control to specific URLs of directories in your web. For example, you may decide that a particular subdirectory, call it **\admin**, is only available to the Administrators group. To do this, click on the **New** button next to the Access Control tab URL Path field, and create **\admin** directory. Then select the Administrators group from the Web Server realm as one of the Authorized Groups & Users. Figure 9.8 shows this restriction applied. If no Authorized Groups & Users are selected for an URL, then the directory is assumed to be available unrestrictedly.

FIGURE 9.8 WEBSITE SERVER ADMIN ACCESS CONTROL TAB

WebSite also lets you perform IP address and domain name restriction. For example to restrict access to the directory just mentioned to all users within a particular IP subdomain, click on the **Deny then Allow** radio button in the **Access Control** tab, then click on the **New** button of the class restrictions, and supply as much of the IP address as you wish (partial IP addresses match all IP addresses beginning with the same numbers). Figure 9.8 shows that in addition to restricting access to the \admin directory to administrators, you can restrict them to accessing it from IP addresses beginning with 204.192. You can also restrict access using domain names, but since this requires a potentially time-consuming DNS lookup (to find the corresponding IP address) it should be avoided if possible.

The next tab controls the server's logging. WebSite maintains three logs: an access log (the most common one to want to view and analyze) tracking all user accesses to your content, an error log with all failed http requests, and a server log with all severe server errors and tracing. Several kinds of tracing can be performed. The log format is the same as presented earlier for Purveyor: the common log file format. Also note that the directory set for placing the logs in must be a *relative* directory name (no leading drive letter or slash). The result is that the logging directory is always a subdirectory of the WebSite *working directory*. This limitation is mildly irritating since many other Web servers (all of the ones reviewed here) have no such restrictions on placement of their logs. Given how large log files can get, flexibility in deciding where to put these files is not always a trivial issue.

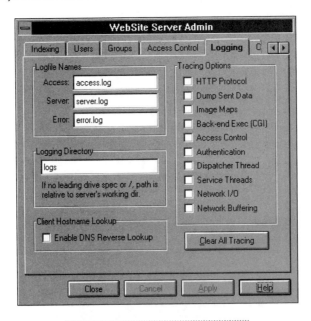

FIGURE 9.9 WebSite Server Admin Logging Tab

The last tab allows customization of WebSite's CGI interface, a discussion I will defer since WebSite's CGI interface is presented in Chapter 11 on gateway programming.

Tools

The WebView program lets you visually understand and manage large amounts of highly nested and interlinked HTML content. It displays the HTML pages present at the specified URL, and the pages and objects that they link to, in hierarchical "tree diagram" form. Figure 9.10 shows the hierarchy of the O'Reilly site, including a subtree devoted to WebSite. Clicking on any of the individual pages loads the HTML documents into an HTML editor of your choice (by default it's configured to be Notepad). Clicking on a plus sign (+) next to the page, shows the "child" pages. The tree navigation interface is very similar to Explorer, the file manager in Windows 95, so you should find it easy to use.

A tree is not the only diagram metaphor that could have been used. It doesn't depict all the various crosslinks among documents. If a page is referred to on another page, it appears as a child node on the tree, even if it was already the parent node. Still it works well enough to organize large amounts of material, especially if the material is mostly hierarchically structured. Including it free with the package really sets WebSite as the leading contender for providing comprehensive tools for Web development. They may be missing some features in their server that Netscape has, but Netscape has not made quite the level of commitment to authoring and management tools that WebSite had evidenced.

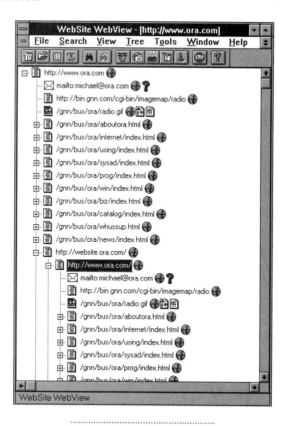

FIGURE 9.10 WEBSITE WEBVIEW TOOL

Another useful tool that can be accessed from within WebView for your site is WebIndex. A dialog box lets you select subdirectories on your site to be indexed for text searches. Once the index is created, you can allow your users to search for documents containing keywords with the supplied **webfind.exe** program, just by including the **webfind** program as an embedded URL.

WebView has a feature known as the Wizard which will create a start at a home page, a What's New page, and an About page for you. The Wizard actually embeds a search capability, **webfind**, into the skeleton home page, as shown in the following:

```
<title>Our Store Home Page</title>
<h1>An Example Web Store Home Page</h1>
<ul>
<li> <a href=whatsnew.html>What's new at Our Store</a>
<li> <a href=/cgi-bin/webfind.exe>Search this site</a>
<li> <a href=about.html>About this site</a>
<!- put links here ->
</ul>
<hr>
```

The Image Map Editor that WebSite provides creates clickable image maps that are "registered" with the WebSite server. You cannot use MapEdit to create WebSite image maps, but the process of creating image maps is very similar to that described earlier. One nice feature of WebSite's Image Map Editor is the ability to mark an elliptical area as opposed to just a circle.

Evaluation

WebSite is a very full-featured set of Web server and server management software. It actually has more components, and attempts to solve a broader range of Web server management issues than any other package reviewed. *And* it sells for $495, tied for cheapest among the commercial packages reviewed. As you will see in Chapter 11 on gateway programming, WebSite also has incredibly rich and flexible gateway interface capabilities, leaving many options for languages used to develop CGI programs, and providing a lot of supporting tools and examples to do so.

However, it does not currently support any secure HTTP protocol (either Secure HTTP or SSL). For those attempting to do true electronic commerce, this is a major drawback. As you will see later when evaluating Netscape's server, the support for remote administration is stronger with Netscape.

In summary WebSite may be a good choice for many organizations, especially those concerned with cost, those that plan to do extensive CGI development, and those for whom the integrated content management tools provide particular benefit. Be sure to continue on to the review of Netscape's offerings before making a final decision. Fully functional 60 day evaluation copies of WebSite are available at **http://website.ora.com**.

NETSCAPE COMMUNICATIONS' NETSCAPE COMMERCE AND COMMUNICATIONS SERVERS FOR WINDOWS NT

In 1994, Jim Clark, founder of Silicon Graphics, lured Marc Andreessen and several other developers of the original NCSA Mosaic from NCSA to form Mosaic Communications. Now called Netscape Communications, they are renowned for their excellent Web browser and useful innovations to the HTML standard, several of which were discussed earlier.

Since Netscape's free browser has approximately 50 percent of the installed base of Web surfers, using their servers to leverage the extended features they introduce becomes very attractive. The most significant feature here is security, or more specifically, use of the Netscape-developed Secure Sockets Layer (SSL) to transmit data back between browser and server in encrypted form. This feature is only available in the Netscape Commerce Server. As you will see, although the Communications Server is a good product, and very similar to the Commerce Server, it doesn't provide special features to the Netscape browser, so it must be evaluated on its own merits as a standard http server.

Much of the setup and configuration of the two products is identical so I will discuss them at the same time, veering off only to discuss the Commerce Server's public/private key setup aspects.

Installation

The Netscape for Commerce Server for NT starts up as a conventional Windows-based Setup program. It first asks you for information about your host address. You will need to know the mnemonic name of your host (ourstore.com) and whether or not the DNS server that you use already has that host listed (see Chapter 8 for details about DNS servers).

After that step it becomes a Web-browser (Netscape that is) based setup process. This is one of its more innovative features: everything in the program is administered from HTML forms. In fact a separate NT HTTP service is created just to perform administration of the main HTTP server. The installation process (and the follow on configuration procedures) involve filling out three forms accessible from the main administration server page, shown in Figure 9.11.

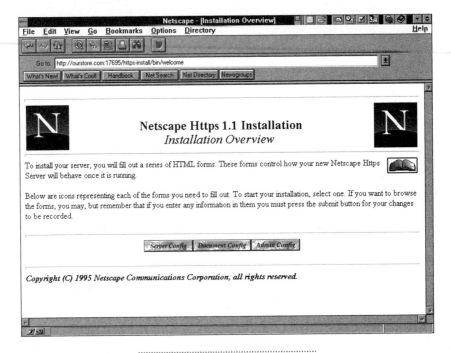

FIGURE 9.11 NETSCAPE INSTALLATION OVERVIEW

The server configuration page (shown in Figure 9.12) allows you to set the server name, port number, and location, but all fields should be successfully filled out as a result of the Setup program. Just verify that these values are correct.

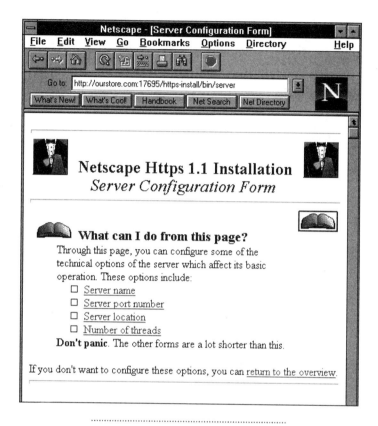

FIGURE 9.12 NETSCAPE SERVER CONFIGURATION FORM

The document configuration page shown in Figure 9.13 lets you set where your HTML content is located, what the name of your home page is, whether directory browsing is enabled, and if so, what the document name is for generated directory indices. Directory browsing is discussed in the earlier sections on other Web servers.

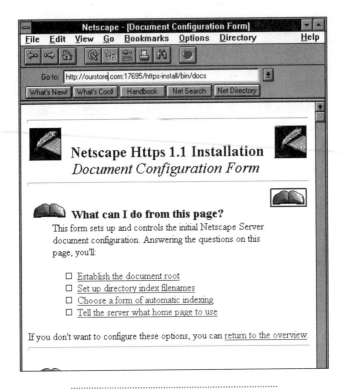

FIGURE 9.13 NETSCAPE DOCUMENT CONFIGURATION FORM

The final page to fill out is the Administration Configuration form shown in Figure 9.14. Here you fill in an administrator user ID and password to access the administrative HTTP server, and a port number that the server will use. Since the secure HTTP server uses port 443 by default, I like to configure the admin HTTP server to use 444: it's easy to remember.

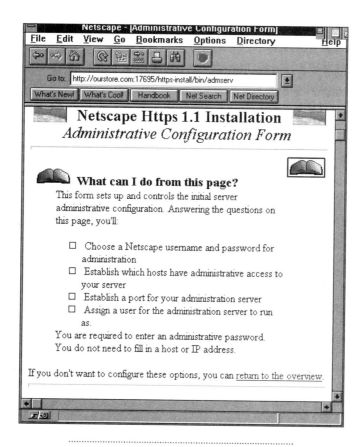

FIGURE 9.14 NETSCAPE ADMINISTRATIVE CONFIGURATION FORM

Once all of these pages are completed, a configuration summary shown in Figure 9.15 is presented, and if the options look good, you can click on the **Go For It!** button.

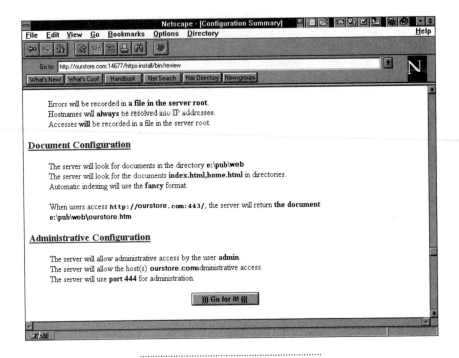

FIGURE 9.15 NETSCAPE CONFIGURATION SUMMARY

Check that the server is operational by loading your home page into your browser.

CONFIGURATION

Once the Web server is installed, you administer its options by giving the port number of the admin server in your Web browser. For example, if you configured your port number for the admin server as **81** (be sure not to use 80 or 443 as the number), you would enter **http://ourstore.com:81** into your browser. The great aspect of this approach is that if you are remote from the server console, you can still administer the server over the Internet. When you enter the URL of the admin server, a page will appear allowing you to control various options of your Web server, as shown in Figure 9.16.

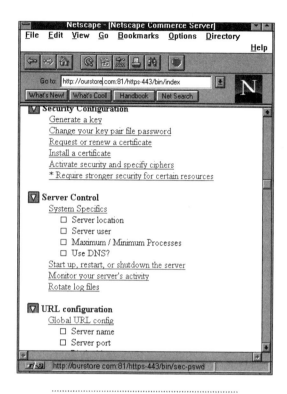

FIGURE 9.16 NETSCAPE ADMIN SERVER HOME PAGE

Security

If you are using the Netscape Commerce Server, and have shelled out the extra $1,500 or so for a secure server, you will presumably want to configure your server to run securely. The first step is to generate a key file, the first option under Security Configuration on the admin server page. Record the password you supply in a safe place.

The next step is to request a certificate. In theory, there are several "certificate authorities" you can request certificates from. In practice, right now there is only the certificate management subsidiary of RSA. RSA is the patent holder of public/private key encryption that is crucial to the Netscape security scheme. You are requesting a server certificate from them, that is really a public/private key pair. Your public key is then registered with RSA. See VeriSign's home page at **http://www.microsoft.com**, for more information.

The certificate request involves supplying information about your company to create what VeriSign calls a *server distinguished name*. An example of supplying this information is shown in Figure 9.17. This process is not documented too well in the Netscape product itself. They refer you to RSA for details, but not to the correct page. The relevant documentation is on VeriSign's server at **http://www.verisign.com/ netscape/naming/index.html**. The important thing to remember is that the distinguished name must really apply to your server (not just your organization), and be unique within your organization. So you may need to use the organizational unit fields.

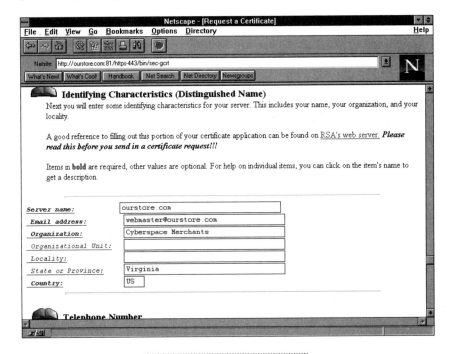

FIGURE 9.17 NETSCAPE CERTIFICATE REQUEST

Once you are assured that your name is correct, click the **Make these changes** button to complete the request. You will see the following text generated:

Certificate Request Text

Creating certificate request

Creating certificate request...

```
Done. The certificate request contains:

Certificate Request:
    Data:
        Version: 0 (0x0)
        Subject: C=US, ST=Virginia, O=CyberMerchants, CN=ourstore.com
        Subject Public Key Info:
            Public Key Algorithm: RSA Encryption
            Public Key:
                Modulus:
                    00:c3:2a:84:65:52:2c:db:ff:c6:cf:34:6f:0d:1a:
                    ff:51:a4:d6:a4:29:ec:80:9d:4b:34:32:57:76:5d:
                    cd:74:ed:e6:5d:3f:a0:db:46:b4:76:ab:be:c5:bd:
                    e9:c7:34:e3:5b:b2:ea:ca:05:18:ff:56:d6:07:96:
                    79:7c:64:d9:a3:ec:5f:9e:22:d1:23:80:17:18:37:
                    f6:c6:18:8b:1d:8f:fc:f1:2f:87:93:38:07:46:14:
                    b6:0a:71:c5:e3:be:99:cc:a1:b3:fc:9a:29:13:65:
                    e4:62:55:74:9e:fe:8d:9d:e1:e3:31:7b:59:05:70:
                    41:fe:de:0c:75:4d:1f:ef:e3
                Exponent: 3 (0x3)
    Attributes:
        a0:00
Signature Algorithm: MD5 digest with RSA Encryption
Signature:
    88:68:90:c7:2f:03:e8:bb:34:d5:e0:b6:ba:84:bc:87:89:5a:
    55:7f:26:71:17:ba:75:b3:9a:87:99:da:ac:c2:a2:55:74:2c:
    0a:34:44:cf:44:43:8d:df:3e:4a:d4:d0:c6:1a:a3:2e:da:12:
    6e:55:2a:86:ee:6d:f9:00:c7:61:a5:89:8b:fc:2c:a7:04:fb:
    d0:43:be:c0:7a:2e:46:55:ce:4b:c9:5f:3f:e0:2e:dc:e9:a0:
    5c:e9:db:7a:9b:a1:da:96:00:14:05:3b:4c:1f:9a:f8:8c:99:
    98:fd:65:36:f7:ab:b4:9b:ad:87:1e:e5:c5:9b:c2:72:35:38:
    db:39


Creating a temporary file for mail...
Headers generated. Converting binary request to ascii data...
Finishing mail message...
Done. The mail message contains:

To: netscape-cert@verisign.com
Subject: Certificate request
Reply-To: Webmaster@ourstore.com
```

Webmaster: Webmaster@ourstore.com
Phone: 703-754-0001

—-BEGIN NEW CERTIFICATE REQUEST—-
MIIBmjCCAQMCAQAwXDELMAkGA1UEBhMCVVMxETAPBgNVBAgTCFZpcmdpbmlhMSQw
IgYDVQQKExtFbGVjdHJvbmljIENvbWllcmNlIIFN5c3RlbXMxFDASBgNVBAMTC3d1
Ym1hhGwuY29tMIGdMAOGCSqGSIb3DQEBAQUAA4GLADCBhwKBgQDEKoR1Uizb/8bP
NG8NGv9RpNakKeyAnUsOM1d2Xc107eZdP6DbRrR2q77FvenHNONbsurKBRj/VtYH
1n18ZNmj7F+eItEjgBcYN/bGGIsdj/zxL4eTOAdGFLYKccXjvpnMobP8mikTZeRi
VXSe/o2d4eMxe1kFcEH+3gx1TR/v4wIBA6AAMAOGCSqGSIb3DQEBBAUAA4GBAIho
kMcvA+i7NNXgtrqEvIeJW1V/JnEXunWzmoeZ2qzColVOLAoORM9EQ43fPkrUOMYa
oy7aEm5VKobubfkAx2G1iYv8LKcE+9BDvsB6LkZVzkvJXz/gLtzpoFzp23qbodqW
ABQFOOwfmviMmZj9ZTb3q7SbrYce5cWbwnI10Ns5
—-END NEW CERTIFICATE REQUEST—-

Note that *this process does not actually mail the request to VeriSign*. I'm not sure why this is so, since most sites where this is performed will have an SMTP server that this could be mailed out of. Anyway, instead of mailing this, a temporary file is created (the browser page will tell you what the filename is) that you can then mail yourself to **netscape-cert@verisign.com**, or you can just cut and paste the message above (everything from the "To:" field on down) from your Web browser into your mail client to send them the request.

You need to do a couple more things before VeriSign will grant you a certificate. The next step, again not really documented sufficiently by Netscape, is to (as VeriSign calls it) document your server. This means proving (to VeriSign) that you have the right to use the name in the organization field of your distinguished name. Valid proof includes articles of incorporation, or partnership papers, or a business license. Fax this to (415) 508–1121 *and* mail it to: VeriSign, Inc., P.O. Box 2004, Belmont, CA 94002. Although they document it as a separate step, you may as well as fax payment information (a credit card number) to them at the same time. The certificate costs $290 for the first year.

Once VeriSign has processed your application you should receive mail with your server certificate, embedded inside BEGIN CERTIFICATE and END CERTIFICATE markers. Choose the **Install a certificate** item from the admin server page, and paste the text (include markers) into the text field allotted for it. Then click on **Make these changes** and the **ServerCert.der** file will be generated. You are now ready to activate security. Choose the **Activate security** item from the server admin page. Enable security by clicking on the **I'd like to run in secure mode** radio button. Then click on the **Make these changes** button. You should receive a "success!" page back, and you will need to restart your server from Control Panel Services to make the change take effect. When you restart your server, it will then be running in secure mode. You now need to access it as an **https** resource instead of http, since it is now using a secure http protocol rather than just http. Your server is now secure. Netscape browsers that access it transmit and receive information in encrypted form.

Once your server is running in secure mode, it's really running a different protocol than straight http. So now your home page can be accessed with the **https://**_prefix rather than the familiar **http://** prefix. Not only is this unfamiliar to some users, but actually precludes non-Netscape browser from accessing the content (they don't know how to interpret the https protocol. You will probably want to still allow users to access your server as, for example, *http://ourstore.com*. But provide a link from there to your secure server. For example:

```
Welcome to our cool store! If you are using Netscape, you may
access us with your information encrypted from prying Internet
eyes via our <A HREF="https://ourstore.com">secure server.</A>
```

Since your server is now secure, its URL begins with https. How do you provide a server to support the http address? Install Netscape again, but list the port number as 80 for the second installation, and leave the second installation not configured for secure access. The Netscape Admin program will recognize the two server sites and allow you to manage them both from the same first page. Alternatively, you can have another Web server for your nonsecure access (https, Purveyor, WebSite, or whatever), and let this Web server point to the same area for document content. Believe it or not, this works just fine, and actually gives you a reassuring level of redundancy, and an opportunity to test new Web technology on your non secure site, while leaving Netscape serving users with secure access.

Server Configuration

The Document Config page lets you change where your content is located, and what the name of your home page is. A new feature of Netscape Commerce Server 1.1 is multiple domain support. As discussed in the description of Purveyor, if you are hosting multiple home pages, this allows users to access the page with an URL such as **http://www.abc.com** and **http://www.xyz.com**, instead of **http://www.provider.com/ abc/abc.html** and **http://www.provider.com/xyz/xyz.html**. Netscape does this by allowing you to specify several IP address to document directory mappings. The one

Netscape http server will serve multiple IP addresses. Each supplied IP address will result in a different set of HTML content being displayed. This is shown in Figure 9.18.

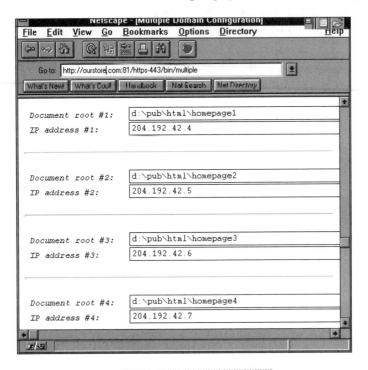

FIGURE 9.18 NETSCAPE DOMAIN CONFIGURATION

Of course, you must still have each of these IP addresses associated with domain names by having your Internet provider register the domain names for all of these IP addresses. Otherwise prospective Web browsers would have to enter IP addresses to reach your content.

Netscape allows you to maintain logical-to-physical URL mappings. Again, we've seen this feature in other Web servers covered. It lets you place some of your content on other drives or on the network while maintaining it as part of the same path hierarchy that all of your HTML content is located under. For example, you might have a listing of useful files that you wish to make available, but they are located on a network drive not in your HTML content directory hierarchy. For example, a list of files might be located in **H:\PATCHES**, but you wish it to be available with the URL **http://ourstore.com/patches**. Figure 9.19 illustrates how Netscape lets you do this.

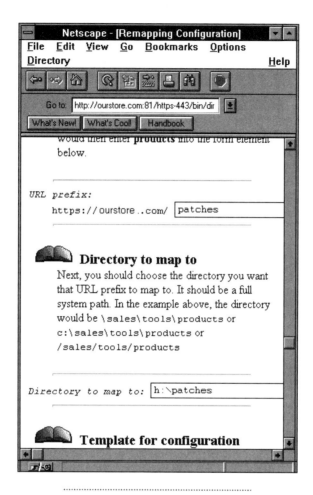

FIGURE 9.19 NETSCAPE REMAPPING CONFIGURATION

Netscape lets you establish user databases for access control. Note that unlike other servers reviewed, Netscape does not support user groups. However, since you can have multiple user databases, and you can restrict access using wildcard patterns to selected users from a database (such as * for all users), you can easily get functionality equivalent to allowing groups.

When establishing access control, you can restrict access to parts of your server with authentication of users, using one of these user databases. You can also restrict access to files on your server to only certain IP addresses of accessing browsers.

Evaluation

Netscape matches most of the features of other servers, while providing the huge benefit of secure access. It is a bit lacking in some of the add-on tools bundled with WebSite and, to a lesser extent, with Purveyor. Still for those who need secure access, all other factors pale in comparison. There are a few other unique features of Netscape including browser based administration. But the cost of Netscape Commerce Server ($2,995 at this writing) makes it only worthwhile if you truly need the Secure Sockets Layer capability. If you remove the secure server functionality, you would probably have to give the nod to WebSite for functionality. This makes the Communications Server, selling for $795, which lacks security features, a difficult sell, except perhaps for organizations that need some secure servers and other nonsecure servers, but want a consistent administrative interface.

SUMMARY

All of the servers that are reviewed here are very strong compelling products, that leverage the capabilities of Windows NT to provide industrial strength Web servers. Some of the most heavily visited Web sites (including early incarnations of the Microsoft site) are run on EMWAC's https on reasonably modest hardware (90 MHz Pentiums). https is free from EMWAC at the URL noted earlier, which makes it a good choice for those experimenting with or prototyping a site: no need to invest real money up front before the site is operational. As the site increases in volume and in its importance to the business, you will probably want to purchase one of the commercial Web servers, and it is easy enough to move your content and gateways to one of the other products, provided you follow the portability guidelines for HTML features and scripts presented in this chapter and Chapters 10 and 11.

Process Software's enhanced version of https, Purveyor, has many commercial-level features, such as extensive configurability and more information in logging, ODBC connectivity to SQL data, the ability to support multiple Web sites from one server, and user and group level access control. Since it evolved from https it is similar in many ways to that product. This makes a good upgrade path for those who began their webmastering with https. Purveyor's add-on utilities for content management and log analysis are not particularly well executed but the core product is very solid. Purveyor sells for $495 which is very reasonable given its depth of features.

Another server in the same price/feature ballpark is O'Reilly's WebSite. The server is configured very similarly to Purveyor, with many of the same features. WebSite's hierarchical HTML content manager, Web View is excellent, in stark contrast to Purveyor's Link Browser. WebSite ships with a Web browser, Enhanced Mosaic, an Image Map Editor, and a full text indexing utility, none of which are present in Purveyor. However, since all of these programs are available free on the Web (and we show you several sources for all of these classes of utilities in this book), this difference shouldn't be enough by itself to make you choose WebSite. The server functionality is still very similar, as is the $495 price tag. Overall, I would currently have to give the nod to WebSite, but if you are in the market for a commercial level http server, these products both merit careful evaluation before committing to one or another. Since both products have evaluation copies available over the Internet, this is relatively easy to do.

If you need a secure Web server for commerce, you should evaluate the Netscape Commerce Server. The lack of add-on tools and the price tag of the Netscape Communications Server make it less than ideal for sites that do not need the security of Netscape's Commerce Server. For sites conducting electronic commerce however, the Commerce Server is almost a requirement, and opens up a whole realm of possibilities for the enterprising webmaster.

## CHAPTER 10

Gateways: Converting Information to HTML On Demand

Earlier when we discussed HTML forms, I said that you would need to supply a program to process the input supplied by the user: the http server itself does not have this capability. Also, all of the Web content I have shown so far has been *statically authored*. That is, it is created before placing on the Web server for viewing. It is easy to imagine several cases where we might want to generate the information that the user views on-the-fly in response to user queries or actions. To do this you will need to use a *gateway*—a program that gives the http server a "gateway" to other information that can be invoked by the server in response to user actions or when the user clicks on a link that calls the gateway. Originally, each http server wrote its own method of accessing and supplying information to these external programs. The Common Gateway Interface or *CGI* attempts to standardize how these gateways worked.

CGI gateways provide realtime access to information, without the necessity of a priori conversion or the creation of an HTML text file. For example, a CGI gateway to a SQL server might retrieve current product price and availability information. Another CGI program might store data supplied in a form into a database format of choice.

CGI gateways conform to the *Common Gateway Interface* (hence the acronym). This standard allows these programs to interact with any Web server software. Details of the CGI standard are presented in Chapter 11. Despite the standard, there are differences in the details of gateways for different Web servers. I will try to enumerate those differences for the most common Windows NT-based servers.

I will then present some available CGI gateway programs and scripts for common Web server needs and for interacting with common data sources. In this chapter, I will not cover gateway programming. I assume that you have a finite job to do and would like to use existing software, commercial or freeware, to accomplish the task. In the next chapter, I cover Web gateway programming and other forms of programming for the Web. In this chapter, I present just enough information about CGI to integrate the existing CGI gateway software, but I will not overwhelm you with additional information necessary only if you are only going to create your own CGI programs.

Before presenting the various gateways, in order to allow you to test these gateways, I need to show you the format to use to embed references to gateways into your HTML documents:

```
<gateway> [/<supplementary path>][?<query>]
```

where *<supplementary path>* and *<query>* are optional arguments. Gateways can be configured to process form data as in the statement

```
<FORM METHOD=POST ACTION="cgi-bin/webdbc.exe/db/table/insert">
```

Read your particular gateway's documentation to see what format it expects its arguments in, and to view sample invocations of the gateway.

A brief reminder of how Web CGI gateways work is also probably in order. The scenario is as follows:

1. The user points browser at (or selects a link for) a URL which represents a program or script instead of an existing HTML page.
2. The http server identified in the URL invokes the program, with whatever arguments are supplied in the URL, and other information supplied by environment variables to the invoked program.
3. The program creates an HTML page on the fly and sends it back to the server.
4. The server sends the newly created page to the browser, which then displays the page.

The key thing to remember in the above discussion that is not always immediately obvious is that the user is clicking on an URL that causes *the server* to invoke the selected program. The user is not invoking these programs directly. The next chapter on gateway programming presents much more detail on this sequence and how to process data supplied to a gateway that you write. For now, let's go on to some existing gateways that you can integrate into your Web sites to perform various useful tasks.

GATEWAYS TO ACCESS TEXT INFORMATION SOURCES

One of the key challenges in electronic publishing via the Web is to provide an easy way of searching the potentially huge amount of information that one might make available. It is more difficult to browse through large volumes of information via a Web browser than it is to leaf through hundreds of pages of text or multiple issues of magazines. So in any case where a large amount of information needs to be accessible, some way of *searching* into that collection of information is very important. Also you now have an electronic interface that provides additional advantages over the print product.

There are two main types of text searching that take place from Web servers: searching the actual HTML document base that makes up the Web server content and searching a separate text database. Searching a separate text database can be very useful to make a large amount of information available from the Web server without having to convert it all into HTML and link each document into listing pages. However, besides being a lot of work for the HTML author, this approach is just plain unusable as the text base grows too large. Some information is not appropriately accessed from lists, even hierarchical ones that are possible with HTML. For a large class of information, the appropriate interface for retrieving the information is to do a full text search on it.

The method for performing the search with a Web browser and making the results available from the same interface is primarily with a WAIS server. *WAIS* stands for Wide Area Information Search, and it is a standard for performing full text searches for documents distributed over the Internet. As I discussed earlier, you may refer to WAIS servers from other sites by inserting *wais:* URLs within your HTML. If you wish to make your own text databases searchable you will want to set up your own WAIS server. In some cases, you may not need to set up an actual WAIS server. Just creating a WAIS database may be all that is necessary to make your information searchable from your Web pages. I will examine the process of creating WAIS-indexed databases and setting up WAIS servers for a few of the WAIS servers available for Windows NT.

EMWAC's WAIS Toolkit for Windows NT

This WAIS server from University of Edinburgh (just like https) has the advantage of tight integration with https. It also ships with the Microsoft Windows NT 3.5 Resource Kit, making it free for those who already have purchased the Resource Kit. It consists of the following executable components.

- WAISS.EXE   The WAIS Server service.
- WAISS.CPL   The Control Panel applet.
- WAISINDX.EXE   The WAISINDEX program.
- WAISLOOK.EXE   The searching program.
- WAISSERV.EXE   The Z39.50 searching program.

The two essential documentation files are WAISS.DOC and WAISTOOL.DOC. WAISS.DOC documents the "high level" interface of the WAIS Server service— WAISS.EXE and WAISS.CPL, the Control Panel applet. WAISTOOL.DOC documents the actual tools themselves WAISINDX.EXE, WAISLOOK.EXE, and WAISSERV.EXE. Unfortunately, you must read *both* documents to get your WAIS Server installed and operational. Some brief instructions here may alleviate the work of getting this product installed. Also I will start off just showing you what you need to make either your HTML document base (your Web server content) or a separate text database (i.e. other information that is not part of your Web server content) searchable from your Web pages. I will follow that by showing how to actually set up the full-fledged WAIS server.

Creating the WAIS Database: Making Your HTML Documents or a Text Database Searchable From Your Web Server

To begin, copy all of the components above to your \WINNT35\SYSTEM32 directory (or whatever your equivalent is on your Windows NT machine). Then, build the WAIS database with the WAISINDX program. If you are indexing your HTML content, this step is as simple as running the following from your Web server data directory:

```
WAISINDX -R -T HTML -EXPORT *.HTM
```

The *-R* option says to index all subdirectories recursively. *-T HTML* tells it that the data type of the files is HTML. WAISINDX then uses this information to determine what the "headline" of the document is when returning lists of matches. If the *-T* option is not given, text files are assumed, in which case no headline is supplied. For other formats which the indexer understands, see WAISTOOL.DOC, page 4. *-EXPORT* option includes the hostname and WAIS TCP port in the generated index, for use by WAIS clients of the WAIS server. *.HTM* determines what files are indexed. *.* would index all files including any images that might be present—probably not what is desired.

As another example, if you are just indexing text files in a subdirectory of your Web server data directory, and you were not planning on having external WAIS clients (that is you were just going to have your Web browser users search it) you would run the following command from that subdirectory (assuming all files in the subdirectory are text files):

```
WAISINDX *.*
```

These commands create several files, all with the base name of INDEX in the current directory where the command is invoked. The set of files comprises the WAIS database. The base name of the files and the directory where they are located can be changed with the *-D* option. For example, the last command could be modified with *-D WAISDIR/WAISDB* to place files with base name of WAISDB in the WAISDIR subdirectory of the Web server data directory from which the command is run.

Other options are available as documented in WAISTOOL.DOC. But you can create useful WAIS databases to start with by knowing the commands just described.

Now, test that the WAIS indexing occurred successfully by invoking the WAISLOOK tool with a search. For example:

```
WAISLOOK COMPUTER
```

This command returns the list of all documents in the WAIS database that contained the keyword computer. If the documents indexed were HTML documents, the list will include the titles of those documents.

Build an HTML page with the same base name as the one generated by the WAIS database, by default called INDEX, to allow searching of the created WAIS database. Include in that document the *<ISINDEX>* element to allow searching of the WAIS database.

For example, create INDEX.HTM to search a WAIS database created by either of the commands above (both databases are entitled INDEX by default). Place this document in the same directory as the WAIS database you created earlier. Link to this document from your home page or another suitable location within your documents.

Test your search document. From your Web browser, load up the search page (probably called INDEX.HTM) and enter some keywords. The documents that match should be returned to you in a list, with each list item linked to the matching document. Click on one of the items to insure that you can navigate to document.

That's it! That is all that's necessary to make your HTML documents or a separate text database searchable from your Web server. You may go on to make your WAIS database available to a true WAIS server as instructed in the following, but it's not necessary for achieving the goal of making your HTML documents or a separate text database searchable.

Setting up the WAIS Server

The following steps below finish the process of making your WAIS Server to be available to external WAIS clients.

From a command prompt in the directory above, install the WAISS Service by typing **WAISS -INSTALL**.

Now, start up **Control Panel.** Click on the **WAIS Server** icon and set the directory to the same name as your Web server data directory, if you are planning on making your Web content searchable. If you are planning on making another text base available to search, I suggest making it a subdirectory of your Web data directory, and setting the WAIS Server data directory to that subdirectory.

If you wish to enable logging, use the same directory that you have dedicated for your Web server logs. This makes it easier to build batch files to purge your logs.

Click on the **Services** icon of the Control Panel. Scroll down to the WAIS Server line. Click **Start** to start up the WAIS Service. Click on **Startup** and set the startup option to **Automatic** if you wish the WAIS Service to start on machine startup every time.

For further information on WAIS Server options, see the WAISS.DOC file. WAIS Server intricacies are really beyond the scope of this book. I just want you to use its basic capabilities to allow your HTML or a database of textual information to be searchable by users of our Web server.

WWWAIS

I covered EMWAC's WAIS server in detail since it is free (available with Windows NT), and, most importantly, due to its unique integration with https, you can create searchable text databases by creating a WAIS database (performing a WAIS indexing run) *only.* You don't need to actually bring up a WAIS Server or include a third party WAIS gateway.

To use other WAIS servers, you may need a gateway from your http server to the WAIS server. Once such gateway is WWWAIS. WWWAIS is a gateway that lets the freeWAIS and SWISH WAIS servers (discussed in subsequent sections) to be accessible from your Web server. WWWAIS has direct support for freeWAIS and SWISH so those are certainly the easiest WAIS servers to support. Nevertheless, full source is supplied, and, for those so inclined, it should be easy to add support for other WAIS servers.

It is worth pointing out that, even if you are not using an integrated http server/WAIS server combination such as EMWAC, a WAIS gateway may not always be necessary to incorporate that use of a WAIS server on your host. Most browsers incorporate support for accessing WAIS URLs, as implied in the earlier HTML chapters. If you know for a fact that all browsers accessing your true WAIS server support WAIS servers, you may not need a gateway. However, be sure that the browser will really support the WAIS server you have installed. As discussed in the following, to access SWISH, WWWAIS is required. Web browsers cannot directly access SWISH using the WAIS URLs discussed earlier, since SWISH is not a true WAIS server.

You can retrieve WWWAIS from **http://www.eit.com/software/wwwwais/**. Its also included on this book's CD-ROM. We will now cover some WAIS servers that can be integrated into our Web server using a gateway such as WWWAIS. FreeWAIS and SWISH are most commonly used with WWWAIS. Isite conforms to a newer standard for information retrieval that may supersede WAIS, though access to it from WAIS clients and http servers can still be achieved with gateways.

freeWAIS

FreeWAIS is, as the name implies, a free WAIS server from the Center for Networked Information Discovery and Retrieval (CNIDR). It is distributed in C source form, so it should be usable on whatever platform you are using. The following outlines the steps necessary to create an indexed, searchable text database with freeWAIS.

The first step in installing freeWAIS is to retrieve the source code and get it compiling on your host. freeWAIS is available via anonymous ftp at **ftp://ftp.cnidr.org/ pub/NIDR.tools/freeWAIS/freeWAIS-0.202.tar.Z**. It is also included on the CD-ROM accompanying this book (but the included source may not be current at this time).

Use the **waisindex** command as described previouslyin the section on EMWAC's waiss service to index your HTML or text based content. The command line switches and available text types are almost identical. With waisindex however, you will want to explicitly specify the generated WAIS database with the *-d* option.

Use the **waisq** command to test that your WAIS database is searchable.

Start up your WAIS server by moving to the directory containing the WAIS database (created with waisindex's *-d* option), and invoke the WAIS server to run on port 2010.

```
waisserver -p 2010 &
```

For detailed instructions, see the "Mosaic and WAIS Tutorial" on NCSA, **http://wintermute.ncsa.uiuc.edu:8080/wais-tutorial/wais.html**.

SWISH

If you feel that the WAIS servers discuss thus far have an unnecessary level of complexity to go through to just get searchable text databases, you will want to evaluate SWISH. The *Simple Web Indexing System for Humans* is written from the ground up to be an indexer accessible from Web servers, and also to do a particularly good job of indexing HTML files. It is also distributed with source code. Since the source code is relatively generic, this means you'll be able to use it on your platform of choice.

SWISH has just one executable, appropriate enough called "swish," for both indexing your content, and searching for information, which are invoked with different command line switches to get the different functionals. With SWISH, you *must* use the WWWAIS gateway to make it accessible by your Web browser users. It cannot be accessed with a WAIS URL reference, as freeWAIS can.

Details and source for SWISH are available at **http://www.eit.com/software/ swish/swish.html**. It is also included on the CD-ROM accompanying this book.

CNIDR ISite

The Center for Networked Information Discovery and Retrieval (CNIDR) is also the author of the previously mentioned freeWAIS server. Why two information servers? Early WAIS servers were compatible with a standard for networked information retrieval known as Z39.50-1988. The newer versions of Z39.50 (1992 and 1995) are not directly compatible with recent extensions to the WAIS protocol. CNIDR has built a new product called Zdist, a true Z39.50-1992 server. It can still be accessed from WAIS clients and http servers by means of a gateway. The example gateway that CNIDR provided was known as Zclient. Zclient was not intended for use by users directly, but Zclient can be used from http servers as a CGI gateway.

CNIDR distributes these programs through Isite. The Isite package consists of Zdist the Z39.50 version 2 server, Zclient the http gateway, Iindex which actually indexes the database, and Isearch which allows command line searching. Though Isite is not truly a WAIS server, I'm telling you about it so that you won't be confused (or will be less confused) by references to Z39.50. You'll also have a better idea about how to integrate other Z39.50 version 2 servers into your Web site (a gateway such as Zclient will be necessary).

Isite, available right now only for Unix platforms, is available at **http://vinca.cnidr.org/software/Isite/Isite.html**.

GATEWAYS TO ACCESS SQL DATABASES

For the applications that we are emphasizing in this book, Web servers for commerce, access to SQL databases is likely to be the most important type of gateway. If you wish to let your users search product catalogs, browse through advertisements selected by category, or look at their order history, retrieval from a relational database is a great way to provide this facility. Similarly if you want to allow users to place orders, post classified advertisements, request more information, register as members of an information service, or accept any other input from them which will be comprised of multiple fields, you will probably want to consider using a SQL database as the data store.

WWW servers are attractive because of the volume of users they can attract. But that very strength brings with it a problem. You could decide to keep your product catalog in text files and search it with WAIS gateways as shown in the last section. But as the popularity of your site increases and you have hundreds of simultaneous users searching through product databases, or entering orders, performance will quickly become unacceptable. As a commercial Web site becomes large (and thus needs to be searchable) and popular, it will inevitably need to use some high performance relational database, such as Oracle, Microsoft SQL Server, Sybase, or Informix, for many of its functions. Initially you may be able to do without a SQL gateway, but over time, if you are doing your job well, you will need to use a SQL gateway and a high-end relational database environment.

The best approach for storing large product catalogs that need to be accessed in varying ways (by category, by manufacturer, by price) is certainly to put them into SQL tables. Orders should probably be the next entity to be stored in tables. For other data stores, such as user registrations, the volume may be low enough to allow them to be stored as text files. At some point, however, you will want to be consistent about where your business's data is stored.

There's yet another advantage to using SQL databases for your data, and deploying gateways for access to to the data. It creates a tendency to *generate* your Web pages dynamically via gateways, rather than having your content stored statically as a set of HTML files. Why is this better? Your site is much more maintainable. If planned properly, you can create templates for information once, and data that fills in these templates can be maintained in the SQL tables. There are also security advantages to this approach. In a corporate team environment, you can use the facilities of your SQL database to limit access to tables to the appropriate individuals, and can implement varying levels of security for different database operations. Order databases containing customer credit card information need maximum protection, and a good SQL environment will allow you to provide that. Storing such customer data in a bunch of plain text files on the corporate network, even in secured directories, is a disaster waiting to happen.

Anyway, I'll go on to give you the information you need to build these solutions.

WebDBC

One of the best options for SQL connectivity to Web servers is WebDBC from Nomad Development Corporation of Seattle, Washington. WebDBC takes the approach of allowing connectivity to many different SQL backends by utilizing Microsoft's Open Database Connectivity (ODBC) standard, hence the name: WebDBC.

WebDBC is more than just connectivity to SQL databases, however. That in itself is quite useful. But WebDBC takes the state of the art in gateways a step further: it provides a mechanism for formatting the data that is returned from the SQL database for display to the user in a format consistent with the rest of your Web content. What WebDBC does is provide an enhanced HTML format that allows you to embed commands in HTML-like files (which they call "HTX" files) that define how data returned from the SQL database is embedded in the HTML document. Data retrieved by WebDBC is then placed in HTML in the locations specified by the HTX file. This mechanism is useful for more than just SQL rows. Any of the other types of data that you might want to retrieve (text documents, Notes documents, GIS information, or Excel spreadsheets) would benefit from this approach of embedding retrieval codes into HTML-like template documents. For now, WebDBC is among the few with this very powerful mechanism (a program called FORMSHOW that I present in the next chapter on gateway programming uses a similar technique).

WebDBC is currently available only for Windows NT, but a UNIX version is promised, perhaps available by the time you read this. This evaluation is based on Version 1.1 for Windows NT. I also used Microsoft SQL Server 6.0 in our evaluation of the sample applications. WebDBC provides ODBC connectivity from all commercially available Windows NT Web servers: EMWAC, Purveyor, WebSite, and Netsite. It provides connectivity to any database platform with a 32 bit ODBC driver. Platforms with such drivers include: Microsoft SQL Server, Oracle 7, Informix, Ingress, Progress, Unify, Sybase, Gupta, and SQL base. WebDBC also has support for connectivity to Microsoft Access.

WebDBCSetup

During the setup, based on the server that you tell it you are using, WebDBC determines where your Web data files are using the Web server's configuration information. The software also optionally installs ODBC drivers for some databases (e.g., SQL Server) to enable it to communicate with your backend database. Of course you may already have ODBC drivers installed, in which case it won't overwrite those drivers unless you ask it to. The SETUP program prompts you for a default database login to use for ODBC connections. The default they supply is WebDBC with password of "WebDBC." You will need to remember to create this database login (or whatever other name you use) in your database environment.

The WebDBC setup installs two main programs: WEBDBC.EXE, which performs the actual reading or writing of records from the ODBC databases, and WDBCCFG.EXE, the WebDBC administration program. If you have installed ODBC drivers, then an ODBC admin program will also be created in its own program group.

The SETUP program does not quite perform all the steps required to bring up a WebDBC application. There are enough steps involved in bringing up WebDBC against a particular database, that I highly recommend that you examine the sample applications before building your own applications. Besides the fact that they effectively document all of the components you need to integrate for building an application, the samples that Nomad provides are useful in their own right. Sample applications are provided for Microsoft SQL Server, Microsoft Access, and Oracle 7. The SQL Server samples include both a Classified Ads system and a Real Time chat system. The Microsoft Access sample is a merchant catalog system. All of these should be very relevant to the work I need to do. First of all, you need to self-extract the SAMPLES.EXE file that is in the SAMPLES directory, with the command **SAMPLES-D**. The setup program should of course perform this step for you, and this is promised for a future release.

After extracting the samples, you must still run a SQL script, **WEBDBC.SQL**, to set up some stored procedures and database users. The script is written to use a database called SAMPLES. Of course, if you wish to use it against this database, you will probably have to create this database first manually using SQL Enterprise Manager (if you are using SQL Server Version 6.0). This step is also not documented.

WebDBCAdministration

The first tab is the WebDBC Admin tabbed dialog that controls logging done with WebDBC. You can log problems, failed requests, all requests, or all SQL statements. Logging of errors is performed to the NT event log. Logging of information is performed to the log directory in a text file. The Locations tab controls locations for data files and temp files. The installation normally determines appropriate values for all of these options. You can also start and stop the Web Scavenger from this tab. Scavenger is an NT service that cleans up temp files used to create place SQL fields into the embeddable HTML templates (HTX files).

For each database that you decide to have WebDBC use, you need to set WebDBC options for it. Click on **New** to add a record for the database (this is not necessary for the database Samples, which already has a record). You should set the Name field to the ODBC source name, and the User Name and Password to use the database user defined for each data source. To allow setting permissions at a very granular level, you should probably create a different database user for each database. But if you do that, you will need to remember to create each of the users within your database environment as well.

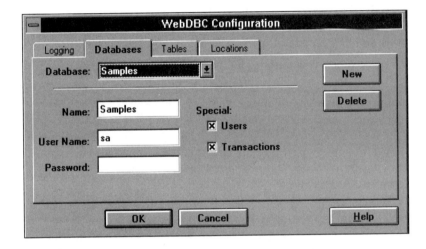

FIGURE 10.1 WEBDBC CONFIGURATION DATABASE TAB

The Users checkbox enables user authentication for the database, allowing only specified users to access the database. Of course, this is the actual end Web browser user, not database user defined for the ODBC connection. This option will not work unless you have run the SAMPLE.SQL script (modified to work on the database in question) to create some stored procedures and a *users* table for the database. Note that the documentation calls this the WEBDBC.SQL script, but there is no such file. The sp_deact_user stored procedure will allow you to disable a user and record the reason why. The users table also keeps track of times of the user's last vist. Nomad should also have allowed "number of visits" to be tracked for each user. This would be easy to do by modifying the the sp_makevisit stored procedure and the users table. That is one of the advantages of using stored procedures for functionality: easy modification by the Webmaster. You should consider making this modification if Nomad has not added this feature by the time you read this. The transactions checkbox enables transaction logging in of WebDBC level events (e.g., "download table contents"). It requires an *xact* table to be present which is created by the SAMPLE.SQL script (again not the WEBDBC.SQL file).

The Tables tab provides security to individual tables in the database by defining access levels that may perform various operations on the table. You will want to remember to create a Default table for your new database whose access levels will be used when the table does not appear in the list of tables. An example access level setting would be to set the **SELECT** operation access to **Any**, allowing all users to view information retrieved by a SQL SELECT statement. This setting is depicted in Figure 10.2.

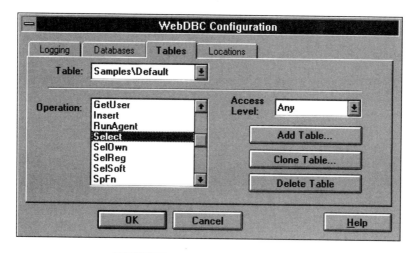

FIGURE 10.2 WebDBC Configuration Tables Tab

WebDBC Query Format

To use WebDBC in your HTML files the URLs you embed will need to conform to the CGI format for passing arguments, where WebDBC expects to receive the database, table, and SQL method in the *PATH_INFO*, and the variable names and values in the *QUERY_STRING*.

This means you will need to use the following format for embedded URLs:

```
http://<server>/webdbc.exe/<database>/<table>/<operation>/&/<result file>
?<variable name>=<value>&<variable name=<value> ...
```

> *<server>* represents your local server name, e.g. ourstore.com.
>
> *<database>* is the SQL (or Access) database with which you wish to work.
>
> *<table>* is the table with which you wish to work.
>
> *<operation>* is the SQL command or special WebDBC command that you wish to perform. Common commands used are Select, Insert, and Update. This argument can also be used to invoke to SQL stored procedures.
>
> *<result file>* is the file to place the result into, typically an HTX file.
>
> *<variable name>* The variable names are generally field names of the table specified in the *PATH_INFO*, prefixed with *d_*.

For example,

```
http://ourstore.com/webdbc.exe/samples/classifieds/select/&/results/
resfile.htx
?&d_state=CA&d_city=SF
```

This will result in the query:

```
select * from classifieds where state='CA' and city='SF'
```

Note that the values themselves must be URL-encoded, plus signs must be used for spaces, non-alphanumeric characters must be converted to hex representation with *%xx*. More details of URL-encoding are presented in the next chapter on gateway programming.

WebDBC Forms

You may wish to use Web-based forms to create the arguments to a WebDBC invocation. For example, you may want the user to enter the field values for a record, and have WebDBC create the record in the database. If so, you should list the form action program as everything up to the PATH_INFO but not the QUERY_STRING. That is, the format is:

```
http://<server>/webdbc.exe/<database>/<table>/<operation>/&/<result file>
```

Standard input is supplied to WebDBC by the Web browser by concatenating all of the field names and values on the form. For this to work properly, the field names in the form must be named properly. That is, they must be named with the same name as appears in the table, but prepended with *d_*. Also the form must be invoked with the POST method. If invoked with the GET method, the field names and values are supplied to WEBDBC.EXE as the QUERY_STRING, and WebDBC won't process them.

Below is an example form to submit an order:

```
<FORM ACTION="/bin/webdbc.exe/Catalog/Orders/insert/&/insok.htx"
METHOD="POST">
<PRE>
Product Name: <INPUT TYPE="TEXT" NAME="d_product"><BR>
Quantity:     <INPUT TYPE="TEXT" NAME="d_qty"><BR>
Special Instructions <TEXTAREA NAME="d_instructions">
</TEXTAREA><BR>
<INPUT TYPE="submit" VALUE="Place Order">
</FORM>
```

This form invokes WebDBC on the Catalog database in the Orders table with a SQL command to insert the data supplied and return the results using the insok.htx HTX file. At this point I'll describe just what an HTX file is.

HTX Files

WebDBC returns information resulting from a database query or operation based upon a user supplied HTML template as an HTX file. An HTX is just an HTML file with some extensions that allow you to specify where data returned from the database should be placed. All of the extension codes begin with <%.., so they are easy to identify in the file. WebDBC will replace the codes with data returned from a WebDBC operation (such as a SELECT query) and then generate HTML to be displayed to the user that contains all of the data retrieved. This provides a much more elegant way of displaying data than just spewing back the raw text resulting from the SQL command. You can bring back only the fields you are interested in, and format the data perfectly with all the power of HTML (tables, heading levels, text formatting, hypertext linking, embedded images) at your disposal to create really attractive page displays. This is far cry from the generated output of most CGI gateways.

The *<%R_fieldname>* code embeds the contents of the specified field returned from the operation into the generated HTML. The *<%F_fieldname.ext>* code places the contents of the specified field into a file (with extension *.ext*) and embeds a reference into the generated HTML. The *<%D_fieldname>* code is used to embed field values used in the query originally supplied to WebDBC not necessarily in the WebDBC result set. Other values can also be embedded into the generated HTML. See the WebDBC User's Guide for a complete list.

At this point I have given you not just enough information to evaluate a purchase of WebDBC, but also enough instructions to begin productively using the product. WebDBC is priced at $395 for a single user. A version capable of supporting ten concurrent users is $1,395. You should purchase the license that matches how your database server is licensed. For example, if you have a ten concurrent user SQL Server license, you need a ten user license for WebDBC. Further details about the licensing scheme and other information on WebDBC is available at **http://www.ndev.com**. Now I'll proceed to evaluate a newer entry in this product category.

Cold Fusion

Another tool that provides connectivity from Web servers to ODBC backends is Cold Fusion from Allaire.

The concept behind this product is very similar to that of WebDBC. That is, providing connectivity from Web servers through a gateway to any ODBC data source. They both do this with a program that can be supplied data from a form for two major functions: inserting records into a database and searching from a database for a record, and returning the data into an HTML template.

Setting up the ODBC connectivity works very similar to WebDBC's setup process. ODBC drivers are supplied for Access, dBase, FoxPro, Paradox, plain text, and Microsoft SQL Servers. Once an ODBC data source is configured within ODBC Setup, Cold Fusion requires the extra step of publishing the data source from the Cold Fusion Admin program so that it can be accessed by the Cold Fusion executable.

The essence of Cold Fusion is the DBML.EXE program. You insert references to DBML.EXE within your HTML, usually as the ACTION of a FORM statement. DBML.EXE expects an Action argument on the command line telling it what to do with the database: Insert, Update, or Query. If the Action is Query, it expects a Template argument telling it how to return the data from the query. Again this should seem very familiar from the earlier discussion. Notice that it needs command-line arguments, which are supplied by putting the arguments after a question mark following the program name. So to make Cold Fusion insert the values of a form's field into a new record, you would specify

```
<FORM ACTION="/cgi-shl/dbml.exe?Action=Insert" METHOD=POST>
```

A query for a record given the values supplied in a form, might appear as follows:

```
<FORM ACTION="/cgi-
shl/dbml.exe?Action=Query&Templates=results.dbm" METHOD=POST>
```

Notice that no extra "path information" is given after the DBML.EXE and before the question mark. That was the method that WebDBC used to specify the data source and table name to operate upon. The method that ColdFusion uses is a hidden field in the form. There are two special hidden field names that DBML uses to get the data source and table name, logically called "DataSource" and "Table Name." This approach probably creates more understandable forms. There a couple drawbacks to this approach: 1) it restricts use of DBML.EXE to form actions, and 2) it stops single forms from being reused in several contexts. An example of the hidden field specification appears below:

```
<INPUT TYPE="hidden" NAME="DataSource" VALUE="PUBS">
<INPUT TYPE="hidden" NAME="TableName" VALUE="Authors">
```

Another required hidden field is the NextPage field, which specifies the URL to go to (typically an HTML file) if the operation is successful. Note that if you are using the form to Update a record in the database, all of the fields comprising the primary key of the table must be supplied in the form. If you are displaying a form to a user to allow the user to change values and submit the changed values back to the database, it will often be appropriate to have the primary key embedded in the form as a hidden field. Also note that ColdFusion, unlike WebDBC, requires that the field names embedded in the HTML form be exactly the same as what they are in the database: no d_ or r_ prefixes are necessary or allowed, as we had with Nomad's product.

To build queries using ColdFusion, you can create a form frontend to prompt for the search criteria, and it will work just as described above. That is, the search fields will be the form fields, and the form action will just invoke DBML.EXE with Action=Query and Template of your template file. If you want to invoke the search capability as a simple HTML link, but that includes search criteria, list the field names and values as additional arguments to the program. For example,

```
<A HREF="cgi-
shl/dbml.exe?Action=Query&Template=results.dbm&Category=software"
METHOD=post>List software products</A>
```

Notice that in both this example and the form query example the data source and table name do not appear. With WebDBC, these are specified as additional path information after the executable name and before the question mark and command-line arguments. With Cold Fusion, the data source and table name are specified in the template file.

Template files are built as HTML with some additional tags created to assist in placing retrieved data into the HTML. WebDBC took the same approach and called the files HTX files. Cold Fusion calls the extended HTML syntax DataBase Markup Language or DBML. The essential first step in building a DBML template file is specifying the DBQUERY tag. The DBQUERY tag takes several attributes which define how data is retrieved. The NAME attribute names the query. The DATASOURCE attribute specifies the ODBC data source to retrieve from. The SQL attribute specifies the SQL statement to be used for retrieval. The SQL statement can use the field value supplied by the form or argument to DBML with *dynamic parameters*: the field names with surrounding pound signs ('#type#'). For example, DBQUERY tag that retrieves all of the titles in a certain category, might look something like:

```
<DBQUERY NAME="GetTitlesInCategory"
     DATASOURCE="PUBS"
     SQL="SELECT * FROM Titles WHERE Type = '#Type#'"
```

To present the results of a query in your output, use the DBOUTPUT tag. This tag takes a QUERY attribute naming what DBQUERY is the source of the output. It opens a DBOUTPUT element which must be closed with a </DBOUTPUT> tag. Within the DBOUTPUT element you will of course place references to the field values of the records returned, but also surrounding text, embedded images, links to other URLs: any valid HTML. The field value from the records returned by the query can be displayed by, again, by surrounding the field names with pound signs. To display the results of the DBQUERY listed above, you would place the DBOUTPUT element in your DBML template as shown below.

```
Title Price              Date
<DBOUTPUT QUERY="GetTitlesInCategory">
<I>#title#</I> $#price#    (c)#pubdate#
</DBOUTPUT>
```

In the preceding fragment, you might want to display the information in tabular format so that the columns line up below the headings. Fortunately, Cold Fusion supports that: both in "preformatted form" done with spaces, and with true HTML 3.0 style tables. Since many browsers (including Microsoft's Internet Explorer) *still* don't support HTML 3.0, it's good to have both options. With current Web browser technology in the field, you will probably want to stick with preformatted tables.

Tables are created with the DBTABLE element. The DBTABLE element begins with a DBTABLE tag which takes the following attributes (among others):

- QUERY—Names the source for the rows oof table data.
- COLHEADERS—Determines whether headers are printed.
- HTMLTABLE—Uses HTML 3.0 style tables.

Within the DBTABLE element, you also need to supply DBCOL tags. The DBCOL tag takes attributes of:

- HEADER—Necessary if COLHEADERS was chosen in the DBTABLE tag.
- WIDTH—The column width in character, which defaults to 20.
- ALIGN—LEFT, CENTER, or RIGHT.
- TEXT—Will typically have the field value reference (the field name enclosed in pound signs) but can include other text and even HTML links.

To redo the above example with DBTABLE for preformatted non HTML 3.0 tables:

```
<DBTABLE QUERY="GetTitlesInCategory" COLHEADERS>
<DBCOL HEADER="Title" TEXT="<I>#title#</I>" ALIGN=LEFT>
<DBCOL HEADER="Price" TEXT="$#price#" ALIGN=LEFTT>
<DBCOL HEADER="Date" TEXT="(c)#pubdate#" ALIGN=RIGHT>
</DBOUTPUT>
```

I am reluctant to say this, since I have used WebDBC from its inception, and Nomad did create the first product in this category, but, as you can see from this discussion, Allaire now leads in the feature department with its Web to ODBC gateway. It's also available for an uncomplicated $495 for any number of users license fee. This is likely to be cheaper than Nomad's fee for all but the smallest sites. Still, both products are well executed from creative enterprising companies. This is a feature battle that has no doubt just begun. You owe it to yourself to evaluate both products (evaluation versions are available over the Internet from both companies) before making a purchase decision. More information, and a downloadable evaluation copy of Cold Fusion, can be retrieved from Allaire's Web site at **http://www.allaire.com**.

GSQL

A discussion of CGI gateways to databases, such as WebDBC and ColdFusion, would not be complete without mentioning their forefather GSQL. The venerable GSQL was developed at NCSA in 1993, qualifying it as among the first Web gateways written.

GSQL is a good option for those webmasters running on UNIX platforms, or those who just want a free product (which GSQL is) versus a commercial product such as WebDBC, which can get expensive as the number of simultaneous users increases.

Compared with WebDBC, GSQL takes a minimalist approach, but it is straightforward and easy to understand. GSQL creates HTML forms that prompts the Web user for various fields. How does it do this? You specify the fields that you want to appear, what their prompts are, and how you want them to be mapped to a SQL statement component, in a PROC file. The PROC file format is somewhat idiosyncratic and rather than repeat it here, it is documented at **http://www.ncsa.uiuc.edu/ SDG/People/jason/pub/gsql/proc-fmt.html**.

This PROC file name can then be supplied as the argument to GSQL to create an HTML form on the fly.

The user is then prompted to fill in several fields, the prompts for which were defined in the PROC file. Also defined in the PROC file were how those fields were to be used to assemble a SQL statement. Once a user has entered all the fields in the form, and clicked on **Submit** to finish the form, the data from the fields are then assembled as specified in the PROC file into a single SQL statement.

This statement is then passed to a backend database program, which is just responsible for executing the statement. A sample backend program is provided that is just a few lines long. Depending on the RDBMS you are using, you may have to supply or modify this component to execute it with a different method or to pass back the information you think is appropriate as a result of the SQL call. But the amount of code necessary is likely to be very small. The SQL statement built can be a query (a Select statement) to retrieve a number of records based on some criteria that the user entered into the form. It can also be a record store call (an Insert statement). Needless to say, the backend program will have to be different in each case. The Insert statement program is fairly simple: it will only have to report back on the success or failure of the statement, and, ideally, provide a link back to the "calling page." The Select statement program is more complex: it will have to retrieve each of the rows, and then format the data in those rows into HTML for display back to the user. Since programming gateways is the topic of the next chapter, not this one, I won't go into further detail on that problem here.

You should now have a pretty good idea of how to go about integrating GSQL into your site. Note that the GSQL program itself is extremely database independent. It's just a way a specifying how form fields and widgets map to SQL statement components. The resulting SQL statement created when a user fills out a form, should be executable with any SQL server. The component of GSQL that will vary for each SQL implementation (Sybase, Oracle, MS) is the "backend database" program to execute the SQL statement and interpret the results. However, if the SQL statement is a record update (an Insert statement) such as might be generated from a product order or a user registration, the backend database program is trivial, and should require little or no modification from the sample backend program supplied. If a Select statement is generated, the backend program will be more complex, and it is fair to say it will require real programming to make it effective. This should help you decide if it is appropriate to deploy GSQL on your site or not.

GSQL is distributed in source form from **http://base.ncsa.uiuc.edu:1234/ gsqlsrc/gsql.tar**.

It has been used to interact with Oracle and Sybase databases on several platforms. More information on getting GSQL up and running is at **http://www.ncsa.uiuc.edu/ SDG/People/jason/pub/gsql/starthere.html**.

Notes

In the chapter on conversion tools, I discussed TILE, which converts Notes databases into HTML. In many businesses, Notes is the primary database where most data is located, and the database more people are comfortable creating content in. I recommended TILE for those companies to enable them to use Notes to create their content. I have already discussed the advantages of using a database to store information to be disseminated over the Web and to store user responses. Some companies will be more comfortable using Notes as their database for this, if they do not already have a relational database environment such as Oracle or MS SQL Server. This is especially true if TILE or another Notes-to-HTML converter is used to create content.

Ideally, I would like to see a gateway that would allow search for and extraction of Notes documents from Notes databases, and conversion to HTML on-the-fly. The gateway should also allow (potentially with a separate executable program), an HTML form's contents to be posted to a Notes database. One solution for this is FormGate (**http://www.mpi-sb.mpg.de/~brahm/formgate.html**), from the Planck Institute in Germany. Form Gate currently only addresses the latter need: posting form contents to databases. By the time you read this there should be other alternatives available to allow all of the functionality mentioned.

PROCESSING FORMS WITH CGI

One of the most common uses of the CGI interface is to process the results of user input forms. I stated earlier when discussing forms in the advanced HTML chapter that you would need to specify a program to process the form information, probably storing it in one data format or another In this chapter, promised you no programming or viewing code listingsjust useful off-the-shelf tools. So we'd like to give you some programs that you may reference within the FORM element that will store form information in a format you desire.

The problem: right now there aren't really a lot of tools written to store form information in a specified format. What does exist are lots of code libraries and source listings in C, C++, and Perl that show how to write CGI form processing applications, and can be easily modified or invoked to create full-fledged forms processing programs.

The solution: I will supply you with a program, called FORMSTOR.EXE, that will store the form information in as generic a format as we can think of for you to do with what you will. FORMSTOR.EXE takes two arguments, a file to store information to and an URL to provide a link back to when FORMSTOR reports its success or failure on an HTML page. FORMSTOR.EXE is supplied on the accompanying CD, and the source for it appears in the next chapter (remember I promised no source code in this chapter).

FORMSTOR appends all of the information in the form to a text file of comma-separated-value (CSV) records. Each form that is processed adds to the end of the text file. The resulting CSV file is importable into just about any database package or spreadsheet. At the same time that it adds to the CSV file, it adds to a log file called FORMSTOR.LOG, in a more verbose format of keyword-value pairs. All of the fields and values in the form are added as well as the value of several environment variables common to all CGI programs (see the next chapter's discussion of the CGI standard).

Following is the HTML for a sample form that incorporates FORMSTOR.EXE:

```
<FORM METHOD=POST ACTION="cgi-
bin/formstor.exe?orders.csv+products.htm">
<H2>Product Information</H2>
<PRE>
Product Name <INPUT SIZE=40 NAME="Product" VALUE="Ginsoo Knife">
Part Number  <INPUT SIZE=12 NAME="PartNum" VALUE="GS-001">
Price        <INPUT SIZE=12 NAME="Price" VALUE="$39.95">
</PRE>
<H2>Shipping Information</H2>
<PRE>
Name    <INPUT SIZE=20 NAME="Name">
Address <INPUT SIZE=30 NAME="Address">
City <INPUT SIZE=20 NAME="City"> State <INPUT SIZE=2 NAME="State">
Zip  <INPUT SIZE=10 NAME="Zip">
Phone <INPUT SIZE=15 NAME="Phone">
Email <INPUT SIZE=25 NAME="Email">
</PRE>
<HR>
<INPUT TYPE="submit" VALUE="Order Product"> <INPUT TYPE="reset"
VALUE="Clear Form">
</FORM>
```

The invocation of the FORMSTOR program is in the ACTION attribute of the FORM tag.

```
ACTION="cgi-bin/formstor.exe?orders.csv+products.htm"
```

This invokes FORMSTOR with command line arguments of *orders.csv* and *products.htm*. All of the form data is then supplied to FORMSTOR on standard input. The data is stored in file *orders.csv* and a link back to *products.htm* is supplied to the user. Details of how to write this program are presented in the next chapter.

Below is how this form would appear in Netscape after the user filled in the fields. Note that the first three fields (Product Name, Part Number, and Price) are filled in automatically with the Value attribute of the Input tag.

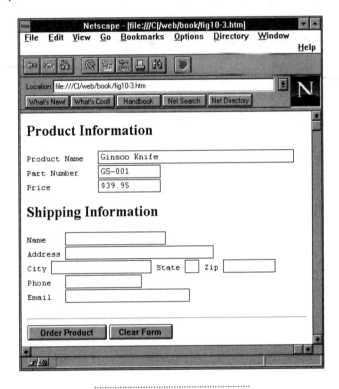

FIGURE 10.3 FORMSTOR FORM EXAMPLE

When the user fills in the information and clicks on the **Order Product** button all of the information will be appended as a row to the ORDERS.CSV file as shown below:

```
Ginsoo,GS-001,$39.95,John Doe, 123 Main Street,Anytown,VA,22222,
703-555-1234,jdoe@anyhost.com,
```

The following information will be appended to the FORMSTOR.LOG file:

```
ComSpec=C:\WINNT35\system32\cmd.exe
PATH=C:\WINNT35\system32;C:\WINNT35;
SystemRoot=C:\WINNT35
```

```
CONTENT_LENGTH=154
CONTENT_TYPE=application/x-www-form-urlencoded
GATEWAY_INTERFACE=CGI/1.1
HTTP_ACCEPT=*/*,image/gif,image/x-xbitmap,image/jpeg
QUERY_STRING=orders.txt+products.htm
REMOTE_ADDR=111.222.33.4
REMOTE_HOST=ourstore.com
REQUEST_METHOD=POST
SCRIPT_NAME=cgi-bin\formstor.exe
SERVER_NAME=ourstore.com
SERVER_PROTOCOL=HTTP/1.0
SERVER_PORT=80
SERVER_SOFTWARE=HTTPS/1.0
HTTP_REFERER=http://ourstore.com/ginsoo.htm
HTTP_USER_AGENT=Mozilla/1.1N (Windows; I; 32bit)
Product=Ginsoo
PartNum=GS-001
Price = $39.95
Name = John+Doe
Address = 123 Main Street
City = Anytown
State = VA
Zip = 22222
Phone = 703-555-1234
Email = jdoe@anyhost.com
argc = 3
argv[0] = cgi-bin\formstor.exe
argv[1] = orders.txt
argv[2] = products.htm
```

The upper entries in all caps are environment variables from the CGI interface. I will discuss them in detail in the next chapter on CGI gateways. The lower entries are the field names and values entered into the form, along with the arguments to the FORMSTOR program. The log provides a human-readable version of data processed by FORMSTOR to supplement the less readable CSV file used as the primary data store. The next chapter will discuss how the program was constructed and many other ways of processing form data. But in the meantime, this program will allow you to process and store form data without having to write any code.

REFERENCES FOR GATEWAYS TO INFORMATION SOURCES

- Nomad Development Corporation (**http://www.ndev.com**)
- GSQL (**http://www.ncsa.uiuc.edu/SDG/People/jason/pub/gsql/starthere.html**)
- How To Do a Searchable Database (**http://www2.ncsu.edu/bae/people/faculty/ walker/hotlist/html**)
- Yahoo Web Directory, Computers: World Wide Web: Gateways (**http://www.yahoo.com/Computers/World_Wide_Web/Gateways/**)

WEB PROGRAMMING
CGI GATEWAYS AND MORE

Should the CGI gateway programs presented in Chapter 10 not meet your needs, you will need to write your own programs. This chapter will cover gateway programming and programming for other aspects of Web development in detail.

THE CGI STANDARD

From the very first http servers, there was often the need for these servers to run external programs to store information from an HTML form, to retrieve information from an external database, or to create an HTML page dynamically. From the very beginning these programs were called gateways, but there was no standard for them. Each Web server—there were two primary Web servers at the time from NCSA and CERN—communicated with gateways differently.

The CGI interface standardized how information was communicated from servers to gateways, so that gateways could be written that functioned on more than one server. The CGI interface standard consists of a set of *environment variables* that are created by the server for each gateway invocation, a set of command-line arguments to the gateway program, and the input and output files to and from the program.

Also note that the term *standard* loosely, because that's just what CGI has become: a loose standard. Many of the environment variables in CGI are available on all servers, because they have to be. In general, however, each server has introduced its own environment variables for its own needs. Some servers don't implement parts of the documented standard. I will try to navigate this maze for you so that you can implement a workable subset of the standard that will make your gateway programs portable amongst the many popular Web servers. Where using a non-standard environment variable is necessary, the information presented in this chapter will help you include conditional logic in your program to check for the server used (through a CGI environment variable!), and to use the appropriate extension environment variable in each case, depending on which server the gateway is installed on.

CGI URLs

To begin the discussion of how CGI gateway programs are developed, first recall the earlier references to CGI URLs embedded in HTML files that were in discussed in the various off-the-shelf CGI gateways. The format again is:

```
<CGI gateway program> [ / <supplementary path information> ] [ ? <query> ]
```

<CGI gateway program> is a path to the CGI gateway itself, such as **http://ourstore.com/cgi-bin/order.exe** or just **cgi-bin/order.exe**. *<supplementary path information>* is an optional argument that follows the gateway name after an intervening slash (/). It can be retrieved from the PATH_INFO environment variable. It is often the name of a file that the gateway program operates upon; for example, /data/products.db. Recall from the WebDBC example, that it was the database and table name that WebDBC should work from, as well as the operation to be invoked.

The query is another optional argument that is appended to the gateway program and to the supplementary path info (if present). The query is available in URL-encoded form in the QUERY_STRING environment variable. If there is no equal (=) sign in the query, it will also be available in the command line arguments to the program.

Gateways are commonly used to process data from a form as in the following statement:

```
<FORM METHOD=POST ACTION="cgi-bin/order.exe/products.db?widget">
```

In this example, the gateway program is order.exe, the PATH_INFO is products.db, and the command line argument (and QUERY_STRING) is widget. Standard input is all of the form data (field names and values) in URL-encoded form.

Invocations of CGI gateways can also be embedded into your HTML with simple hypertext links. In this form, the method is always GET, and there is no standard input to the program.

```
<A HREF="cgi-bin/order.exe/products.db?widget">Order this Product</A>
```

Now lets go on to develop programs that process the input that you have specified with this format.

Input

If the CGI program has been invoked with the POST method, data will be supplied to your program via standard input. The CONTENT_LENGTH environment variable determines the size of the data. If the CGI program has been invoked with the GET method, this information appears in the QUERY_INFO environment variable (see the following section on CGI environment variables). Of course, the data is then limited to the size of environment variables, so this is not an ideal way to pass data to your program. Ideally your gateway should be prepared to handle data from either QUERY_INFO or standard input, determining at run time which is actually present. The REQUEST_METHOD environment variable determines from where to get the information.

The CONTENT_TYPE environment variable determines in what form this data is sent. Currently, the only standard content type used is application/x-www-form-urlencoded. This means that the information has been *URL encoded*: spaces have been replaced with plus signs (+), and non-alphanumeric characters have been replaced with %xx codes. You will have to URL decode this information to use it within your program. The following C function will decode a character buffer of URL-encoded information.

C++ code to decode URL-encoded text

```
    // decode URL-encoded text
    void UrlDecode(char *p)
    {
        char *p2 = p;
        while (*p) {
            if (*p == '%') {
                // next 2 chars are hex representation
                ++p;
                if (!isxdigit(p[0]) || !isxdigit(p[1]))
                    throw "corrupted hex encoding";
                char hold = p[2];
                p[2] = '\0';
                *p2++ = char(strtoul(p, 0, 16));
```

```
            p[2] = hold;
            p += 2;
        }
        else if (*p == '+') {
            *p2++ = ' ';
            ++p;
        }
        else
            *p2++ = *p++;
    }
    *p2 = '\0';
}
```

For form data, the input will be a series of field names and field values. Subsequent sections will present some reusable code to parse out this data format, and do useful things with it, such as store it in text files.

Command-Line Arguments

Command line arguments are often used in programs that are written to respond to ISINDEX queries, but they can also be used in other programs that take arguments, but little data. They aren't usually necessary for form processing programs which should interpret their data from standard input. However, They are useful in search programs, or programs that generate pages based on some criteria.

The query, all of the text following the question mark, is split at the plus signs (+), URL-decoded, and placed into successive command-line arguments. The query is also available in undecoded form in the QUERY_STRING environment variable. If the query contains any unencoded equal (=) signs, the query is only accessible from the QUERY_STRING environment variable.

Output

Output from the CGI program is returned to the user via standard output. Output should be in valid HTTP format. As mentioned earlier, HTTP is the Web transport protocol. Web browsers submit requests to Web servers via http, and receive responses back in http. As you start to write your own gateway programs to communicate back to the Web browser, you will need to generate output in http format. This is very similar to HTML with a few additional responsibilities as discussed in the following.

The output begins with a set of headers, which is terminated with a blank line.

Content-Length and Content-Type

First the gateway should tell the server and the client in what format the data is displayed. This is done with the Content-type: directive followed by the MIME type. Common values are text/html to return HTML, and text/plain for plain text. Content-length is a less necessary header but it may be supplied if you wish.

Status

Another common header is the status line. The status header is in the format *Status: <number> <text>*. A common response is *Status: 200 OK*. You should attempt to follow the conventions for reporting CGI program status. Available status codes are described in Table 11.1.

TABLE 11.1 CGI PROGRAM STATUS CODES

Code	Text	Meaning
200-204	**SUCCESS**	
200	OK	Succeeded
201	CREATED	Text part of response line indicates the URI by which the new document should be known.
202	ACCEPTED	Accepted for processing, but processing has not yet been completed. This is useful for asynchronous processing requests—the work is submitted but the user can continue with their Web browsing.
203	Partial Information	Returned information is not definitive or complete.
204	No Response	Server received request but there is nothing to send back. This allows script inputs without changing documents.

Code	Text	Meaning
300-304	**REDIRECTION**	
301	Moved	Data requested has been permanently moved. Header lines that follow show the new location(s) with URI: <url>
302	Found	Data requested has been found at the following other locations: URI: <url>
303	Method	Suggests client try different URL or method to access (for example POST rather than get): Method: <method> <url>
304	Not Modified	Client has performed condition GET but document has not been changed since the time specified in the If-Modified-Since field.
400-404	**CLIENT ERRORS**	
400	Bad Request	For example, bad syntax.
401	Unauthorized	Needs valid authorization header.
402	Payment Required	Client should respond with valid ChargeTo header.
403	Forbidden	Request will not be granted even with valid authorization or payment.
404	Not found	Could not find specified document, query, or URL.
500-503	**SERVER ERRORS**	
500	Internal Error	Server experienced internal error.
501	Not implemented	This particular server does not support function requested.
502	Service temporarily overloaded	Due to current high load on server, the service is temporarily unavailable.
503	Gateway timeout	If your gateway is using another gateway or service, that other service took longer to respond than you were configured to wait.

Other headers that may be supplied in your returned data include the following.

Expires

Indicates by what date the data is no longer valid.

Content-Encoding

You can return data in compressed form if the client has indicated that they can accept the particular content type (see the Accept-Encoded request header in Table 11.3).

Location

This is the location of a URL for the server to retrieve to present to the client. You can think of it as shorthand for you actually opening that file, reading all of the data in it, and outputting it for the client to read.

The server will check all of these headers for validity before returning the information to the client. If you wish to bypass this checking, begin your script name with *nph-* (no parse headers). There is little reason to do this with modern Web servers—the performance hit of the checking is not significant and the verification of your output is a worthwhile safety net.

Below is a short sample C++ program that returns a document to the Web browser user. Subsequent sections will show you how to install these programs on your server and how to invoke them in your HTML documents.

Sample Program Demonstrating CGI Output

```
// 11-2.CPP
// simple CGI output
#include <iostream.h>
void main()
{
    cout << "Content-type: text/html\n" // returning HTML
            << "Status: 200 OK\n"    // indicate success of gateway
            << "\n" // blank line indicates end of headers
            << "Order entered successfully!\n"
            << "Go back to <A HREF=\"http://ourstore.com\">"
            << "home page</A>\n"
            ;
}
```

Environment Variables

Table 11.2 documents the morass of available environment variables available on each of the popular Windows NT-based Web servers. If you are reading this chapter, you are familiar with what an environment variable is, but for the sake of completeness: it is a variable name and some text associated with that variable name. Each process or program in UNIX, MS-DOS, Windows, or Windows NT has an *environment* associated with it, which is just a collection of environment variables. Generally there is a global environment that contains environment variables such as PATH (the list of directories to look for an executable command in) and COMSPEC (the directory for the command processor). But each program or process can be supplied with additional environment variables that are only valid for it and its child processes. Environment variables are chosen to communicate information to CGI programs, since they are a simple mechanism to communicate of data to invoked programs available on all popular modern operating systems. (I emphasize simple and available since it is hardly the most advanced. If I assumed that everyone was using Windows NT or UNIX, I could use other techniques such as shared memory, but at the cost of the ability to write scripts that run on any platform.)

Generally in gateway programs you will use the contents of environment variables to get information from the server. In C or C++ that is performed with the getenv() run-time library command, and in Perl with the $ENV associative array. I will cover these details later as we show you how to create CGI programs in Perl and C++. Note in the above discussion that since there is a global environment, there will be environment variables that have nothing whatsoever to do with the gateway program or the http server that will nevertheless show up if a "dump" of the environment is performed. A dump of the environment can be performed with the following code in Visual C++. Note that the following code, unlike other examples presented is not portable to other platforms, due to the non-standard _environ array. If you aren't a programmer you should still be able to understand what is going on. (All the details of building and testing gateway programs in C++ or Perl will be presented in coming sections.)

Simple Program

```
// 11-3.cpp
// dump out contents of environment
#include <stdlib.h>
#include <iostream.h>
```

```
main()
{
    cout << "Content-type: text/html\n" // returning HTML
            << "Status: 200 OK\n"
            << "\n"; // indicate success of gateway
    for (int i=0;_environ[i];i++)
            cout << _environ[i] << "\n";
}
```

Such a dump will always result in the following environment variables on Windows NT: PATH, COMSPEC, and SystemRoot. You can use the contents of these environment variables if you wish, but be aware that they aren't really related to the Web, and haven't been generated for your use by the http server. That said, I'll go on to show you the variables that the http server has created for you to use. Please note that in the following table that WebSite has its own equivalents for most CGI standard options that appear in the WebSite CGI "profile" (see next section), and I attempt to note them in Table 11.2. ALL in the Availability column means "EMWAC, Purveyor, Netscape."

TABLE 11.2 CGI ENVIRONMENT VARIABLES.

VARIABLE	DESCRIPTION	EXAMPLE	AVAILABILITY	WebSite Windows CGI Equivalent
GATEWAY_INTERFACE	CGI/version, does not vary per invocation.	CGI/1.1	ALL	CGI version
PATH_INFO	Additional arguments following slash after the script name and before the question mark.	/document.htm	ALL	Physical Path
PATH_TRANSLATED	The translated physical path corresponding to a virtual path. Of course, doesn't exist on servers that do not provide path translation.	d:\docs\ document.htm	Netscape, Purveyor, WebSite (not EMWAC)	Logical Path

VARIABLE	DESCRIPTION	EXAMPLE	AVAILABILITY	WebSite Windows CGI Equivalent
QUERY_STRING	The arguments supplied to the gateway following the question mark. In some cases, the server may choose to send the information here on the command line as well. For safety, you may wish to have your script check the command line for information if QUERY_STRING is blank.	arg1+arg2+arg3	ALL	Query String
REMOTE_ADDR	IP address of remote host	192.177.42.2	ALL	Remote Address
REQUEST_METHOD	GET or POST	GET	ALL	Request Method
SCRIPT_NAME	Name of CGI gateway program. Useful for gateway program to create URLs that reference the current program or even current site.	cgi-bin\ formstor.exe	ALL	Executable Path
SERVER_NAME	Hostname or IP address,does not vary per invocation.	204.192.45.2	ALL	Server Name
SERVER_PROTOCOL	Name and revision format of gateway request, varies per invocation.	HTTP/1.0	ALL	Request Protocol
SERVER_PORT	Port that Web server was accessed from. Usually 80 by default. Sometimes 443 with Netscape's secure http server.	80	ALL	Server Port

VARIABLE	DESCRIPTION	EXAMPLE	AVAILABILITY	WebSite Windows CGI Equivalent
SERVER_SOFTWARE	Name/version of server, does not vary per invocation.	HTTPS/1.0	ALL	Server Software
REMOTE_HOST	The host corresponding to REMOTE_ADDR. Not set if server doesn't have this information.	http://users. host.com	Netscape and WebSite (not EMWAC or Purveyor) but is part of proposed standard	Remote Host
REMOTE_USER	If user authentication is performed, the remote user name will be supplied here.	jdoe		Authenticated Username
AUTH_TYPE	The type of user authentication performed (if user authentication was performed before invoking your gateway).		Netscape (not Emwac or Purveyor or WebSite)	Authentication Type
CONTENT_TYPE	If POST method is used to send data to our gateway, the MIME type used to send. Currently can only be: application/x-www-form-urlencoded.	application/ x-www-form- urlencoded	ALL	Content Type
CONTENT_LENGTH	Length of packet sent via POST method	156	ALL	Content Length
HTTP HEADERS				
HTTP_*	Any header lines received from the client are placed by the server into the environment for processing by the gateway, with the header name prepended with HTTP_as a direct pass-through. The complete list is shown in Table 11.3.		ALL	

VARIABLE	DESCRIPTION	EXAMPLE	AVAILABILITY	WebSite Windows CGI Equivalent
HTTP_REFERER	The name of the document that links to or invokes the gateway.	http://somewhere .else.com/ cool_links.html	ALL	Referer
HTTP_USER_AGENT	What Web browser the reader is using. Very useful for creating pages with content conditional on what browser they are using. For example, only display HotJava stuff if they are using a HotJava browser. *Worth noting*: Netscape shows up as Mozilla.	Mozilla/1.1N (Windows; I; 32bit)	ALL	[Extra Headers] section
HTTP_ACCEPT	Type/subtype. The MIME formats the client will accept. Useful for the gateway program to determine in what format to return information.	*/*,image /gif,image /x-xbitmap,image/ jpeg	ALL	[Accept] section
NETSCAPE EXTENSIONS				
SERVER_URL	The URL to access the server.	http://ourstore. com	Netscape only	
HTTPS	Whether or not the server is running in secure mode or not: ON or OFF.	ON	Netscape only	
HTTPS_KEYSIZE	Parameters for the Netscape secure mode server.	128	Netscape only	
HTTPS_SECRETKEYSIZE	Parameters for the Netscape secure mode server.	40	Netscape only	

HTTP REQUEST HEADERS

I have referred several times to HTTP request headers that may be supplied by the Web client, and passed through the server to be available to the gateway program you may write. Note in the table where it states: "Any header lines received from the client are placed by the server into the environment for processing by the gateway, with the header name prepended with *HTTP_* as a direct pass-through."

This includes the Referer, User_Agent, and Accept headers mentioned when discussing CGI environment variables. It also includes the Charge-To, Authorization, and If-Modified-Since headers mentioned in the status code table. For completeness, I will present all the HTTP request fields that you have available to you. *If the header is present,* that is; if it is created by the Web client, you should be able to use the contents of these headers by accessing the CGI environment variable that is the same name as the request header, but prefixed with *HTTP_*. Also note that the CGI environment variable will also be in all caps, and dashes (–) will be replaced with underscores (_).

Typically these headers are created by the http client, the Web browser. However, you can have a gateway program that you write to generate these headers for use by another gateway program. The headers below that are almost always created by a Web browser are: User-Agent (the HTTP_USER_AGENT environment variable), Referer (the HTTP_REFERER environment variable), and Accept (the HTTP_ACCEPT environment). However, you should not assume the presence of any of the headers in your programs.

TABLE 11.3 HTTP REQUEST HEADERS

HTTP Request Header	Description
From	Name of the requesting user (From keyword in WebSite profile)
Accept	List the types of output that the http client will accept in response to a request. http requests are generally accompanied by one or more accept directives.
	By default
	```Accept: text/plain, text/html```
	is assumed.
Accept-Encoding	Similar to Accept, but lists the Content-Encoding types which are acceptable in the response.

HTTP Request Header	Description
Accept-Language	Lists the Language values which are preferable in the response in ISO 3316.
User-Agent	The http client (the Web browser).
Referer	The URL of the page or program that refers to this gateway.
Authorization	Formats still emerging and being specified. For example, the user format: user username:password.
Charge-To	The account to which this will be charged (no browsers that we know of supply this header yet).
If-Modified-Since	This will have a date, and when invoked with a conditional GET, will not return the document if not modified since the supplied date.
Pragma	Used for extensions to this list. Only one pragma currently exists, no-cache. This should indicate to your program not to return any cached copy of the document the user requests. Pragma: no-cache

For a complete and current list of request headers, see **http://www.w3.org/ hypertext/WWW/Protocols/HTTP/HTRQ_Headers.html**

SERVER-SPECIFIC CGI INTERFACES

If the environment variable table and the rest of the previous discussion seemed complex—especially if you are attempting to write gateway programs that work with a variety of Web servers—I agree! In this section I will summarize the salient differences between the CGI interfaces of the various NT-based Web servers. UNIX-based Web servers (CERN's https and NCSA's httpd) for the most part comply closely with the standard, so there is less of a need to discuss their idiosyncracies here. I also describe how to install CGI scripts for each of these servers.

Netscape Commerce Server for NT

Most of Netscape's differences stem from its status as a *secure* Web server. There are several environment variables associated with Netscape's secure server scheme: HTTPS, HTTPS_KEYSIZE, HTTPS_SECRETKEYSIZE. You would not typically use HTTPS_KEYSIZE and HTTPS_SECRETKEYSIZE in your CGI programs. HTTPS is very useful and should be the variable that you use to determine whether you are running in secure mode. For example, you may want to check whether you are running securely before enerating a credit card number field in a CGI script generated form. The following code will set the variable secure to nonzero if the HTTPS variable is turned on.

```
char *p=getenv("HTTPS");
int secure=p&&!strcmp(p,"ON");
if (secure) {
        // do stuff only appropriate for secure mode
}
```

Netscape lets you set a particular directory for your CGI gateways, as shown in Figure 11.1. This makes use of the directory mapping capability that Netscape (and other servers) have. For example, you can configure all of the references to your CGI programs to be: **http://ourstore.com/cgi-bin/program.exe**, but you can make the physical directory in a place not a subdirectory of your HTML documents. For example, you may have your HTML documents all in C:\DOCS, and subdirectories thereof. But with directory mapping, you can place your CGI programs in a directory called D:\PROGRAMS, which of course means that the programs don't even have to be on the same machine—D:\PROGRAMS could be a network share on another machine. This is a very useful security feature. You can also configure Netscape to use a particular extension for all CGI scripts. For example, you can state that CGI scripts bear extension, .CGI.

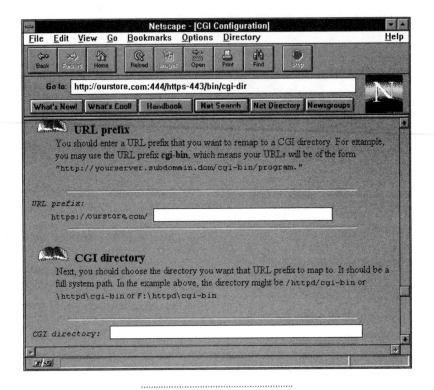

FIGURE 11.1 NETSCAPE CGI CONFIGURATION

EMWAC https for Windows NT

EMWAC is relatively minimalist regarding its CGI interface. You can't specify a directory to limit from where CGI is invoked, nor can you specify a CGI program extension. No path translation is offered as part of EMWAC, so the PATH_TRANSLATED environment variable is not present. None of the authentication related variables are implemented.

This leaves the following subset of environment variables supported by EMWAC HTTPS:

```
CONTENT_LENGTH
CONTENT_TYPE
GATEWAY_INTERFACE
HTTP_ACCEPT
```

```
PATH_INFO
QUERY_STRING
REMOTE_ADDR
REQUEST_METHOD
SCRIPT_NAME
SERVER_NAME
SERVER_PROTOCOL
SERVER_PORT
SERVER_SOFTWARE
```

If you want to write gateways that are portable across Web servers including EMWAC (and remember that EMWAC is free over the Internet, so it has a large installed base), you should have your gateway do reasonable things when environment variables beyond this set are not present. For example, it is alright to check for the environment variable HTTPS, but if it is not there, your program should do something reasonable, and continue operating. Your functionality shouldn't hinge on any of the variables not listed here. It may be affected by other variables, but it shouldn't need them.

The CGI interface for Purveyor is currently identical to Emwac so we do not review it separately. The previous discussion applies to version 1.0 of Purveyor.

O'Reilly WebSite

I will discuss the WebSite interface last, since they have diverged most from the original standard, at least in their Windows CGI interface. Instead of reading input from standard input, displaying it out to standard output, and reading CGI environment variables from the gateway programs inherited environment, WebSite creates a whole new way of passing data to and from gateway programs. WebSite also provides a conventional CGI interface to allow porting of existing scripts, but it is fairly generic so I won't discuss it at length here.

The Windows CGI interface peculiar to WebSite started when Bob Denny (author of WebSite) first ported NCSA httpd to Windows. Denny wanted the CGI gateway programs for httpd for Windows to be written in Visual Basic. Of course, Visual Basic has no standard input and standard output, so that left out using the standard. Denny introduced the convention of passing in a filename to identify the input and output files, and another file to contain what would have been placed in enviroment variables into a Windows-style profile file. It is not clear to me what advantage of the file for the CGI environment files has, but perhaps at the time it was perceived to be more Windows-like. Of course nowadays with the advent of Win32 programming and the move to Windows NT-based Web servers, this doesn't seem to be that much of an innovation after all. Options are not kept in profiles anymore but in the registry, so the profile file for CGI options seems like a bit of a throwback. I am not advocating storing CGI options in a registry (which would be absurd), but the good old-fashioned environment is actually more Win32-like than lugging around that profile file.

But the salient feature of Windows CGI is the input and output filename approach that allows VB developers into the CGI game, which is a good thing on the whole: it leverages a huge installed base of application programmers. Keep in mind, however, that the compliant CGI interface should be used for those willing to create NT console applications, which, as I demonstrate later, are pretty easy to create in Perl, C, or C++. The gateways shown later are all portable *between* Web servers with CGI compliant interfaces. They would all require significant (but reasonably localized) revision to work with WebSite's Windows CGI standard.

That said, here is the actual interface. WebSite calls gateway programs by supplying them with a profile file, followedby the filenames of the input and output files, followed by the arguments to the program. The CGI profile contains CGI standard (mostly) options in a CGI section of the code. Notice that the underscores have been removed from the standard names, and some new variables have been introduced.

```
[CGI]
CGI Version=
Request Protocol=
Request Method=
Executable Path=
Logical Path=
Physical Path=
Query String=
Content Type=
Content Length=
Server Software=
Server Name=
Server Port=
Server Admin=
Referer=
From=
Remote Host=
Remote Address=
Authenticated Username=
Authentication Method=
Authenticated Password=
Authentication Realm=
```

The last two options (Authentication Password and Realm) above are very specific to WebSite. That is, there is really no direct equivalent on other NT-based Web servers discussed here. Any gateway programs that use those options may not be able to have that specific functionality ported to other servers. For the other options, the equivalents on other Web servers are shown in Table 11.2.

The MIME types that the server will accept are identified in an [Accept] section with lines such as

```
[Accept]
text/plain=Yes
```

instead of the normal HTTP header environment variable such as HTTP_ACCEPT containing *text/plain,text/html*. Other options covered in the standard CGI with HTTP_ headers that have not been included in the CGI section of the profile may (this is left rather vague) appear in the [Extra Headers] section as keyword value pairs.

The URL-decoded values of form fields are placed in the [Form Literal] section of the profile, with the keyword as the field name, and the value as the field contents URL-decoded (plus signs and hex codes converted to spaces and special characters). This is a great feature and saves doing the URL decoding within the gateway. Large field contents are placed into [Form External] and [Form Huge] sections with references to external files.

Again, I presented this interface for the Visual Basic programmers among you, but I urge you not to use this interface if gateway programming in Perl, C, or C++ is an option. In this chapter, I present extensive material and examples that should assist you in those efforts. I don't provide VB examples using the WebSite special interface, but O'Reilly has thoughtfully included several good ones with the distribution.

More Information on CGI

The actual CGI specification can be found at **http://hoohoo.ncsa.uiuc.edu/ cgi/interface.html**, though from the variations shown above you can see that it may be of limited use in your day-to-day programming efforts. For a good general introduction to CGI gateways and programming, see Rob McCool's "The Common Gateway Interface" **http://hoohoo.ncsa.uiuc.edu/cgi/intro.html**. More information is available at **http://hoohoo.ncsa.uiuc.edu/cgi/overview.html**. All of this information is fairly old by now. (Rob McCool now works for Netscape, and NCSA doesn't seem to have substituted anyone else to fill his shoes and keep this information updated.) An example of the content worth tracking is the set of Netscape extensions to CGI environment variables. For another introduction to the subject, see **http://www.charm.net/~web/Tutorial/CGI**. However, you will want to use this to learn material, *not* to follow their example of HTML. It is atrociously formatted: all of the text is bold, and although they commendably have an <HTML> and <BODY> tag, they don't close them!

GATEWAY PROGRAMMING IN PERL

Perl, the Practical Extraction and Reporting Language, has become the almost the de facto tool for building Web CGI scripts. Notice that previously I have always referred to CGI gateways as programs, because in fact, that is really what they are. In many places, gateways are referred to offhandedly as scripts, but a good CGI gateway application is a full-fledged program. However, with Perl, much of the complexity of building CGI gateways is handled so intuitively and easily with Perl's powerful yet simple notation, that in fact, the script moniker becomes appropriate.

If you are a C or C++ programmer, you may ask "Why do I need to learn another language? I can already imagine writing these programs in C++. It shouldn't be too hard." Well, you're right. With a good set of classes, such as C++ iostreams libraries, input and output of the sort required by Perl becomes pretty easy. Combined with the C tools for CGI development that I will present later, it's even easier. Depending on the complexity of what you're trying to accomplish, if you're already a C++ programmer, you may want to do your gateway programming in C++. But you should make an informed decision to do so, *after* learning the merits of gateway programming in Perl. Despite our supply of C-based Web gateway functions, there are still more gateways and Web-related utilities already built in Perl.

Once you learn it, you will find it to be faster to modify interpreted Perl scripts than it will be for you to compile and link C based gateways. Just change the Perl code in place and it is ready to run with no more effort (though you could perhaps test it once or twice). Also, the interpreted environment is easier for testing and debugging, especially since it can be cumbersome to use a symbolic debugger on a C gateway program. The program is expecting to be called from the Web server and supplied with its data on standard input. You will have to rig up some kind of scaffolding to supply the program with the data as you run it in your debugger. That said, if you are a proficient C programmer and feel that your gateways will definitely require the power of C, feel free to skip ahead to the next section on C++ gateway development.

Perl is now also available for Windows NT in several forms. Perl 5.0 is included with the Microsoft Windows NT 3.51 Resource Kit. This version of Perl can control

OLE servers, making it a scripting tool for Win32 applications in general, a status previously reserved primarily for Visual Basic. O'Reilly's WebSite comes with a Perl port to NT performed by WebSite's author Bob Denny. DEC has a Perl 4.0 for NT that was one of the first implementations available.

As I traverse through the Perl describing its various elegant features, you may start to think that I'm a Perl zealot. Not really: I actually do most CGI development in C++, because C++'s capacity for abstraction is stronger. As programs get larger and larger, I find this ability to abstract out the fundamental objects in classes to be more and more important. Also, integration of third party DLLs and function libraries is more possible in C++ and when talking to other data formats that is sometimes important. Both Perl and C++ have their advantages for gateway programming. You will want to know the strengths of both tools so that you can make an informed decision about which tool to use for a given task. With that caveat out of the way, I'll go on to explain how to use this very valuable tool.

An Introduction to Programming in Perl

Covering all of the capabilities and nuances of Perl is far beyond the scope of this book. What I want to do here is teach you just enough Perl to be able to modify existing Perl-based CGI gateways, and to potentially write your own. I also want to give you a sense of the power and flexibility of the language, and in some cases its limitations, to help you to decide between Perl and C++ for various tasks in your gateway development.

An excellent book on Perl is O'Reilly's *Programming Perl* by Larry Wall (the creator of Perl) and Randal Schwartz. Another good book, more geared to the beginning programmer, is *Learning Perl* by Randal Schwarz. As good as these books are, they take their time in giving you the knowledge you need to program productively or to modify Perl scripts. For example in *Programming Perl*, to get the overview of all of Perl's capabilities, you have to wade through an extensive set of scenarios of Job using Perl to automate his camel farming operation. While these examples are well presented and entertaining, it may at times seem to knowledgeable programmers like a slow moving caravan across a desert of less-than-relevant problems. So informally I'll title my treatment, "Perl for the Impatient: Mastering Perl Without the Trials of Job."

I'll show you the significant elements of the language that you are likely to find useful and encounter in CGI scripts written by others, and I will bypass the more obscure portions of the language as well; as, in-depth nuances are not necessary to get your code written. I hope this introduction will help you to be productive in Perl very quickly. If you decide you need to know everything about the language you can pick up *Programming Perl* to expand your knowledge on individual topics.

Hello, Perl

Typically I will supply Perl with scripts that are written and stored in files. I then invoke Perl with an argument of the file name. All programming tutorials seem to begin with printing "Hello, world!", and who am I to buck tradition? So (presuming you have installed a Perl of your choice on your system), create a file called *hello.pl*. Place in the file the following text:

```
print "Hello, world\n";
```

Now run the program by invoking *perl hello.pl* from the command line. This assumes that you have made your Perl directory part of your path, which you should do anyway.

Data Types

Now let's look at the various data types that are available so that the program can start to process data. The first example showed the most common data type used in Perl: *strings*. Strings enclosed in double quotes (" ") as shown above may have escape sequences to operate on them and embedded variables will be replaced with their content. Strings inside apostrophes (' ') will have no substitutions done on them. Perl also has numbers in the form of integers (a string of digits with no decimal point), floating point (a string of digits containing a decimal point or in scientific notation), hex (prefixed with 0x), or octal (digits with a leading zero). Examples include:

'hello'	literal string
"hello\n"	string allowing escapes (such as "\n") and "variable interpolation"
100	integer
100.5	floating point

Complex data types include arrays that are represented as comma delimited sequences of values or variables inside parentheses. For example:

```
(1,2,3)
```

File handles in Perl are represented as a literal or variable inside angle brackets, for example, *<FILE>*. Predefined file handles include *<STDIN>*, the input supplied to the program on the command; *<STDOUT>*, the output of the program; *<STDERR>*, the error output of the program that always goes to the screen even if the standard output is redirected, and <ARGV> a special file handle that combines all files mentioned on the command line. For example, in the following invocation

```
PERL PROGRAM.PL ARG1.DAT ARG2.DAT <INPUT1.DAT >OUTPUT.DAT
```

<STDIN> contains the contents of the INPUT.DAT file. <STDOUT> writes out to OUTPUT.DAT and <STDERR> writes to the console. <ARGV> reads from ARG1.DAT until exhaused and then reads from ARG2.DAT. If input is not redirected to the program on the command line (for example, <INPUT1.DAT>) input is obtained by prompting the user.

Variables

In order to build useful programs, you'll need to use variables as well as data-type literals. Variables are prefixed with a dollar sign ($var1). All data types use the same notation for variable references. The data type of the variable is determined by its contents. For example,

```
$var1=1
```

makes the $var1 variable an integer. It can become a string as quickly as it is assigned

```
$var1="hello"
```

An array variable is referred to by prefixing the name with an at sign (@). Array items are referenced by subscripting the variable name in square brackets. The last item of an array can be accessed using the built-in value, #<arrayname>. In the example below, #array is 2, since an array is indexed beginning with zero.

```
# simple array manipulation example - note that # begins a comment line
@array=(5,10,15);
$firstitem=@array[0];
$lastitem=@array[#array];
```

The values of an array can also be treated as a list and Perl has several functions available to operate on the array as a list, which we I present shortly. Perl has a built-in array variable called @ARGV that contains all of the arguments to Perl that are present on the command line.

Perl also introduces a concept known as an *associative array*, an array that is retrieved by supplying the value of a key rather than an index. An associative array is referred to with a variable name prefixed with a percent sign (%). Individual elements are accessed by including the key value inside braces ({"key"}). The contents of an associative array are specified as a list of key, value pairs. For example

```
%capitals=("Israel", "Jerusalem",
                "Egypt", "Cairo",
                "Saudi Arabia", "Riyadh");
$city=%capitals{"Egypt"};
print $city;
```

This will print out Cairo. Perl has a built-in associative array called *%ENV* that has all of the environment variables available to the Perl program. Since environment variables play a prominent role in communication of information to CGI gateways, this is a very useful feature. The following code will retrieve the contents of the QUERY_STRING environment variable.

```
$query_string=%ENV("QUERY_STRING");
```

Special Variables

Perl has several built-in variables supplied for you which you do not need to declare or set values of. Table 11.4 shows some of the more important built-in variables.

TABLE 11.4 PERL SPECIAL VARIABLES

Variable	Description
$_	default inout
$@	error message from last *eval* or *do* command
$ARGV	name of current file
$&	string matched by last pattern match see pattern match section)
$'	string preceding match
$`	string following match
$+	last bracket matched by last search

Variable	Description
$1..$9	subpattern in parens from last match
@ARGV	command line arguments for script (not including script name)
@INC	where to look for Perl scripts (typically set by programmer)
%ENV	associative array of current set of environment variables and their values

Operators

The following operators are available in Perl to work on the data and variable types that I just described.

Numeric Operators

These operators work on numeric data types. You will want to restrict the bitwise and shift operators to work on integer data or variables. There are of course traditional arithmetic operators (+, -, /, *) and the modulo division remainder operator (%). Perl includes the exponentation operator (**) to raise the left hand argument to the right hand number power. Bitwise operators for or (|), and (&), and exclusive-OR (^), and for left and right shift (<< and >>) are also available.

Appending any of the preceding operators with and equal sign (=) assigns the resulting value to the left-side operand. For example

```
$a=1; $a += 2; print $a;
```

This will print out 3.

There are operators to perform comparison on numeric data types. ==, !=, <, >, <=, >=, <=>. The last operator returns a number depending on whether the first operand is less than one (–1), equal to zero (0), or greater than one (1) than the second operand. The ++ and — operators take a variable as argument and increment or decrement that variable. For example, $I++ increments the variable $I.

String Operators

String operators include the period (.) operator for string concatenation, and the various string comparison operators: eq, ne, lt, gt, le, ge, cmp. Like <=>, cmp returns –1, 0, or 1 based on the comparison between the strings on the left and right side of the operator.

Functions

Perl includes many built-in functions, though not nearly as many as those of you that are C and C++ programmers may be used to.

Time

There are time functions: time, taking no arguments, returns number of seconds since January 1, 1970. localtime() converts the value return by time into a nine element array representing seconds, minutes, hour, day of month, month, year, weekday, and Julian day of year, for the local time zone. An example use is:

```
@ltime=localtime(time);
$wday=@ltime[6];
```

Trig

There are trig functions (sin(), cos(), atan2()), logarithmic functions (exp(), log(), and sqrt()), random number generation (srand(), rand()). All of these functions take one argument, whose meaning is usually obvious from the purpose of the function.

String

There are functions to operate on strings which include a length() function, taking one argument and returning the number of characters in the expression. The chop() function takes off the last character of all elements of the supplied list, which may be just one variable. The index() function returns the position of the second string argument in the first string argument at or after the position specified in the optional third argument (which is the first element if left unspecified). As with all Perl strings, indices are zero-based. The substr() function returns the string given by an offset specified in the second argument, into the string specified in the first argument.

These can be used as in the following code:

```
$string="Hello, world.";
$indx=index($string,",");
$substring=substr($string,$indx);
print $len=length(chop $substring);
```

This will display the length of ", world" or 7.

There is also a special string function called eval(). It evaluates the argument and executes it as if it were Perl code. An alternate form of eval is invoked as eval followed by Perl code surrounded by braces ({ }). If there are runtime errors the $@ variable contains the error message.

List and Array Functions

There are several functions to operate on arrays and lists. As I mentioned, they are represented the same way in Perl, as array variables, but you can operate on them as either arrays, using subscripting to access individual elements or to set individual elements, or setting all of the values of the array variable by setting the variable equal to a parenthesized list of values.

But there is also a set of functions that treat an array more abstractly as a list. This allows us to perform list oriented operations, such as adding to the end of a list or to the beginning of a list, accessing and/or removing the first element of the list, reversing the order of the list, and sorting the list. This level of abstraction will save you a lot of code from having to do all of these operations with raw arrays.

The list functions that operate on array variables are as follows (square brackets indicate optional arguments):

- **push** (@array, list) This pushes the elements of list onto the end of @array, List can be a single item.
- **pop** (@array) Removes and return the last (#array-th) element of the array list.
- **shift** (@array) Removes and returns the first element of the array. For example to process the elements of the @ARGV array successively, you would use code such as the following:

```
while (@ARGV){
    $arg= shift @ARGV;
# do stuff with $arg
}
```

- **unshift** (@array,list) Adds the elements of list, which can be a single item, to the beginning of the array.
- **splice** (@array,offset,[length],[list]) Removes elements of @array specified by offset and length and replaces them with list (if present). You will rarely use this, but it's worth noting that the other list functions can be implemented with splice().
- **reverse** (list) Returns the list in reversed order.

- **sort** (list) Returns the sorted list
- **split** (pattern,expression) Splits expression (a string variable or literal) on specified pattern into a list which is then returned.
- **join** (expr,list) This "joins" all of the items in the list, separated by the value in expr, into one string which is returned.

An example of using various list operations appears below.

```
@fruits=split(',',"apple,orange,lemon,kumquat,mango");
push(@fruits,("tangerine",'kiwi',"lime"));
$lostfruit=pop(@fruits);
@fruits=reverse(sort(@fruits));
$firstfruit=@fruits(#fruits);
```

The first statement *splits* the literal string of fruit names and puts it into the @fruits list. The second statement *pushes* three fruits to the end of the list, by listing the three fruits in a parenthesized literal list. Note that the use of apostrophes or quotes in that list are interchangeable. The third statement *pops* the last item (lime) off of the list and puts the contents into the $lostfruit variable. The list is then sorted in reverse alphabetic order with the reverse() and sort() functions. Finally the $firstfruit variable is assigned the last item of the list, apple, using the #fruits subscript on the @fruits array.

Flow Control

Perl statements are delimited by semicolons and can be conditionally executed or repeatedly executed using a modifier such as *if*, *unless*, *while*, or *until*. For example,

```
$a=1 unless $b<>0
```

Multiple statements can be combined by surrounding them with braces. The same modifier can then precede the block of statements, and more looping modifiers are available. These include:

- **while** (<expression>) { <block of statements> }

  Among the statements that can be used are the continue statement which will skip to the top of the loop without executing the rest of the statements in the block. Typically continue is executed conditionally with an if or unless statement.
- **until** (<expression>) { <block> }

- **for** (<expression>;<expression>;<expression>) { <block> }

    The **for** statement operates just like its C equivalent. The first expression is executed only once when the statement is first encountered, and is typically used to initialize variables. The second expression is used to test whether to continue the loop. The block of statements will only be executed again if it returns true. The third expression is executed after each time through the block of statements. It is typically used to increment index variables for the next pass through the loop.

- **foreach** <variable> (<array reference>) { <block>}

    This construct loops over all items in the specified <array reference>. The <variable> is used to place each element of the array into on successive iterations.

- **do** { <block> } **while** <expression>

    This will execute the block of statements while <expression> is true.

- **do** { <block> } **until** <expression>

    This will execute the block of statement until <expression> is true.

Input and Output

As stated earlier, Perl gives you several file handles for free. The most common one to use is <ARGV>. This file handle will supply all of the contents of files specified on the Perl command line successively. Another file handle is <STDIN> which will read either from the user or from a file that is supplied to Perl as standard input. How do you read from a file handle? Just assign a variable to the input operator for the file handle ($arg=<FILEHANDLE>). Or evaluate the file handle reference by itself, as in the condition of a while loop. This will read the next line from the file and put it into the variable on the left hand side of the assignment, or just test if another line is available.

For example, the following code reads successive strings from the user until they enter a null string.

```
while ($_=<STDIN>){
    print;
}
```

The print with no argument actually prints $_, which was assigned to be the line supplied from standard input. The $_ variable is a special variable that is supplied by default to many operations that expect an argument or a variable to assign their result.

The operations that work with $_ include input from file handle. So the above loop can be written even shorter as:

```
while (<STDIN>) { print;}
```

Or even:

```
print while <STDIN>;
```

If the input operator is assigned to an array, an array will be built that contains the rest of the file handle contents, one line to an array item. For example, the following code will read the entire contents of all files supplied on the command line and make each line an item in @array.

```
@array=<ARGV>
```

This is often done inadvertently, and can lead to huge arrays that use up gobs of memory in places where it is not anticipated or needed. On Windows NT and UNIX, this will work, but your system may slow down significantly as it pages to make enough virtual memory available for the full contents of all the files.

There is also a special file handle called the *null filehandle* whose notation is <>. <> reads from the files specified on the command line, if there are any present. Otherwise it reads from standard input. So, assuming that no files are supplied on the command line, the previous code can be shortened (*print while <STDIN>;*) to:

```
print while <>;
```

To use the input operator on other files besides *<ARGV>* and *<STDIN>*, you should open the file with:

```
open(filehandle, filename);
```

If filename is not specified, it is obtained from a variable named $filehandle (whatever the filehandle name may be). Prefixing the filename (either in the variable contents or in the open statement) with a greater than sign (>) opens a file for output. Placing two greater than's (> >) in front of the name opens the file for append. For example the following code opens a log file to add information to it.

```
$LOG=">>RESULTS.LOG";
open(LOG);
```

Output can be written to an output filehandle with any of the following commands:

- **print** (filehandle, list)

  If the filehandle is not specified, then STDOUT is used by default.

- **printf** (filehandle, list)

  This assumes that the first element of the list is a C printf style format string, and allows you to create more formatted output. For example:

```
open(OUT,">OUTPUT.TXT");
@list=('Value in hex is: %x');
push(@array,16);
printf(OUT,@list);
```

The %x flag prints out a digit in hexadecimal format. For details of the available C printf format flags see any C manual.

- **write** (filehandle)

  Writes out a formatted record. The format is set for a filehandle with the format statement.

```
format <filehandle> = <formlist>
```

<filehandle> specifies which filehandle the format statement affects. If unspecified, it applies to STDOUT. *<formlist>* consists of a sequence of *picture lines* to format the output, and *argument lines* which supply values or variables to insert into the previous picture line. As in other Perl code, comment lines can be created beginning with **#**. The picture line will contain multiple **@** codes, one for each value to be placed on the line. The **@** code will be followed by a number of justification characters, the number of which determines the width of the field. Less than (<) indicates left justification, vertical bar (|) indicates centering, and greater than (>) indicates right justification. An example format statement is:

```
      format STDOUT =
@<<<<<<<<<<<<<<<<<<< @<<<<<<<<<<<<<<< @<<<<<<<< @>> @>>>>>>>> @>>>>>>>>>>>
  $name,              $address,        $city,    $st,$zip,     $phone
```

Note that since STDOUT was the default its presence was not necessary in the format statement above.

Pattern Matching

Perl's pattern matching capabilities for searching, text substitution, parsing input formats, and translation are one of its greatest strengths. You can write a parser for any text-oriented file format with a small fraction of the code that it would require in C or C++.

Perl incorporates all of the regular expression-based pattern matching and substitution capabilities that are present in various UNIX tools such as *awk, flex, sed,* and *vi.* Among the regular expressions available are:

.	any character
[a-z]	any character of set
[^a-z]	any character not in set
\d	digit
\D	non digit
\w	alphanumeric
\W	non-alphanumeric
\s	whitespace
\S	non-whitespace
\n	newline (any C backslash escape sequence is valid)
\t	tab
\0	null
\nnn	ASCII character of octal value
\xnn	ASCII character of hex value
\<character>	character itself (e.g. \(is left paren, \. is period)
(pattern)	any parenthesized portion of expression saved to be referred to later with $n, where n is order of subexpression in overall pattern
x?	0 or 1 x's
x*	0 or more x's
x+	1 or more x's
this|that	matches first pattern or second pattern
\b	word boundary
\B	non-word boundary
^	beginning of line
$	end of line

There are two pattern matching operators: the matching operator, m// which can also be invoked with just //, and the substitution operator, s///. The matching operator lets you test for matches to a regular expression, and if the match occurs, put matching parenthesized subexpressions into variables known as *backreferences* (number $1 through $n, where n is the order of the subexpression) that you can then access and manipulate. The matching operator can be invoked with the expression to be searched followed by the =~ operator followed by the matching operator (with or without the preceding m. If operating on the $_ default variable the =~ is unnecessary (as is the default variable itself).

For example the following code matches the $_ variable containing an email address.

```
if ( /(\w*)@([a-z\.]+)/ )
{
    $user=$1;
    $domain=$2;
}
```

This expression will match any string with alphanumerics followed by an at (@) sign followed by a sequence of letters or periods (\. specifies the literal period). The expression returns true or false depending on whether the pattern is matched in the $_ variable. The block within the *If* will only be executed if the pattern is matched. The backreferences are assigned in the order the parentheses are encountered. For example if $_ contains webmaster@www.ourstore.com, $1 is webmaster and $2 is www.ourstore.com.

The replacement operator works very similarly except that an additional pattern is specified after the second slash (/) which is to be used to replace the matching pattern in the original expression. To parse out the name and domain of the email address and create a string containing them, the following code would suffice.

```
$string =~ s/(\w*)@([a-z\.]+)/Name: $1, Domain: $2/g;
```

This will replace all strings in $string matching the pattern inside the first pair of slashes with the text between the second and third slash, and the trailing g will make it do so globally across $string's contents.

Subroutines

Perl creates subroutines with a *sub* keyword followed by the name of the subroutine, followed by the block of statements enclosed in braces. In naming your subroutines and trying to avoid naming conflicts, remember that Perl-reserved words are lowercase and that identifiers in Perl are case sensitive. For example

```
# prints contents of filename specified in $_ to stdout
sub print_file_contents
{
    open (INPUT,$_);
    # note that we don't use $_ default so we leave $_ intact
    while ($arg=<INPUT>)
    {
        print $arg;
    }
}
```

To invoke a subroutine, just supply the subroutine name prefixed with an ampersand (&). For example, *&print_file_contents* would display the contents of the file specified in the $_ variable. You can also call subroutines with the *do* command but this is less common.

To pass arguments to subroutines by value, make a local copy of the arguments. You should assign the argument list variable, @_, containing the list of actual arguments, to a list of variables representing the formal parameters using the *local* function. For example, the *local* statement in the source below assigns the arguments from the call to the *$src* and *$dest* variables.

```
sub file_copy
{
    local($src,$dest)=@_;
    open(SRC,$src);
    open(DEST,">".$dest);
    while (<SRC>)
    {
        print DEST $_ ;
    }
    close SRC;
    close DEST;
}
```

Call by value arguments only you use the values locally in the procedure. If you want the ability to modify the arguments that you pass, you will need to "call by name." The exact way that Perl does this is slightly different than "call by reference," which Perl also supports, but I don't need to drill into those details here, since use of true call by reference is deprecated in Perl. I wound not even explain call by name, except that you will often see it in some of the more popular publicly-available Perl code. I recommend avoiding the technique as much as possible in your own programs.

Call by name is performed by assigning the argument list (@_) to a *type glob*, which is an asterisk (*) followed by a name. The type glob can then be referenced later in the subroutine with at sign (@) followed by the name. For example, the following subroutine removes all trailing whitespace from the supplied argument, which is passed by name with the *local(*arg)=@_;* code.

```
# removes all trailing whitespace
sub rtrim
{
    local(*arg) = @_;
    while ($arg~=/.*\s/)
            chop $arg;
}
```

This function is invoked by passing the name of the variable used to the *rtrim* subroutine. The name is passed by supplying an asterisk preceding the variable to the subroutine call.

```
$x="a string with trailing whitespace            ";
&rtrim(*x);
print $x." chopped.\n";
```

In order to successfully reuse subroutines (which is the main purpose of writing them), you will need to have some way of including them from existing files. This mechanism is the Perl *require* statement. *require* takes an argument of a filename, and then executes all of the code found in the specified file. In that sense, it's very similar to the eval statement except that it works on a filename rather than a literal string, and it is smart enough not to execute code that has been required earlier. For example, to include the subroutine above and other related ones into a set of string subroutines, you could use them in other programs with the statement:

```
require "string.pl";
```

Perl has even more sophisticated tools for reuse and abstraction: *packages*. Packages provide a separate namespace for variables. Packages are created by simply invoking the package statement with the package name, as in:

```
package string_handling;
```

This provides a rudimentary form of data hiding: the variables associated with a package are not accessible to other routines unless they explicitly set their package to string_handling (which of course they shouldn't do). It also provides a tool that helps in building abstract data types, or that overused term *objects*. That is, building a related set of routines that all operate on the same data. The data is hidden from outside code (that is, well-behaved outside code), and is accessible only through the defined set of routines, usually called *methods*. The subroutines may each invoke the package statement, or be in a file with the package statement at the top. Data shared among package routines are referenced as if it was global data. This falls short of the protection mechanisms available in most object-oriented programming languages: you can't actually package all of the data into its own explicit object, and invoke the methods on the object directly. But it has more support for abstraction and reusability than you would expect in a scripting-oriented language.

Perl as an OLE Automation Controller

Windows NT Perl 5.001 as released on the Microsoft Windows NT Resource Kit allows Perl to control and utilize OLE Automation servers. This warrants extensive coverage here, since you will not find this documented in any other books at this point. If you aren't running Windows NT, you may want to skip on to the next section, since everything I discuss here is specific to this product and to Windows NT.

OLE Automation is the method under Microsoft's OLE 2.0 specification of a program exposing a set of capabilities (which might also be called methods) to other programs. I am not going to try to describe OLE here, a task far beyond the scope of this subject. However, you should know that all Microsoft desktop applications, and a large and growing set of applications from other vendors, are OLE automation servers. They expose capabilities that can be used by other programs and applications: including programs that you write. This means that you can write programs that, for example, grab information from Excel or Access through the OLE automation interfaces exposed by those programs. OLE automation controllers that do this can be written very easily in Visual Basic and Excel, and with a bit more work in Visual C++.

But as you've been reading this section, you may have started to like Perl for many scripting-like applications - a category that controlling an OLE automation server would probably fall into. Wouldn't it be great if Perl could be an OLE automation controller? Well, with NT Perl 5.001 for NT, this is now possible. In fact, NT Perl ships out of the box with Perl packages to control Excel, Word Basic, and Netscape. The Word Basic and Excel packages are particularly relevant. You could use the Excel package to grab selected parts of an Excel spreadsheet that is updated frequently and dump the contents to a Web page.

These Perl packages are created by a script called MkOLEx.BAT. MkOLEx can be supplied with just the object class of an OLE automation server that has been installed on your NT system, or with a type library. What does that mean? Well, the object class is the name of the class associated with the particular OLE automation server whose services you wish to access, such as Word.Basic or Excel.Application.

How do you find this out? Typically it can be found in your product documentation, but you can also use the Registry Editor to find it. In your \WINNT\SYSTEM32 directory is a program called REGEDT32.EXE. Launch REGEDT32.EXE. and you'll be surfing the NT registry. You'll want to use the Windows NT Resource Kit, or Jeffrey Richter's *Advanced Windows*, or another Windows NT-oriented book to understand all aspects of the registry. For now, we can help you find the class name of the application which you want to control from Perl. Go the HKEY_CLASSES_ROOT portion of the registry (using the Window command if necessary). Scroll down past all of the extensions listed (*.ASC, .AVI*). Then you'll see a bunch of class names that correspond to your applications with OLE automation interfaces. For example, if you have Microsoft Office installed, you'll see Access.Database.2, Excel.Application, and Word.Basic. You can run MkOLEx.BAT and supply it with any of the names of the classes in the registry, and it will determine the methods available for that program and create a Perl package that exposes the capabilities of that automation server. At the same time it creates an HTML document that describes the available methods of the package.

MkOLEx can also create Perl packages from type libraries. In this case, if you're not familiar with what that means, you probably can't use one. A type library is a file (typically with a .TLB extension, although groups of type libraries can appear in .OLB files) containing information about the methods and properties available for a class object. Most commercial software that provides an OLE automation server interface still does not ship with type libraries. Once installed however, the information that

MkOLEx needs is available in the registry, and the script can then be run with the class name as described. When would you use a type library? Possibly on your own OLE automation servers if you wanted to make manual changes to the .TLB files rather than the registry, and then quickly regenerate the Perl packages to correspond with this.

MkOLEx does not support every type of method, property, or parameter. However, it graciously reports those methods and properties which it cannot convert. MkOLEx is a very exciting capability: giving Perl the ability to control any OLE automation server. This truly opens up the door to access to all types of information from your Web server, without the necessity of writing a full-fledged special-purpose gateway program for each type of data you need to access. Now, when you encounter a new type of data that you need to make available, possibly dynamically, on your Web server, you can ask "is there an OLE automation server that can provide this data?" If so you can use NT Perl to serve that data directly to your Web clients.

Libraries for Web-Oriented Perl Programming

In writing CGI gateways, many of the tasks, such as the URL-decoding the information supplied by the user, creating fillout forms, parsing the user responses to those forms, creating HTML documents, and creating HTML URLs, are quite repetitive. This area is ripe for reuse with Perl libraries and packages. In this section I wull present several libraries

cgi-lib.pl

Let's start with the basics: a simple set of routines to process form input supplied to CGI scripts. Steve Brenner's "CGI Form Handling" page (**http://www.bio.cam.ac.uk/ web/form.html**) includes this set of Perl routines that takes a CGI form response and creates an associative array from the values, for easier processing. The code is small enough that I'll present it here.

The essential function is the *ReadParse()* routine. It takes the input from the user from the environment, URL decodes it, and places it into an associative array called *%in*, which can then be easily processed with your Perl code. Brenner processes it with his *PrintVariables* and other calls. As you can see, there's not much code here (see CGI-lib.pl), but it's beautiful in its simplicity. It is also a good demo of Perl's power, and should serve as a good example for your HTML Perl coding efforts. The *ReadParse* function you will probably leave intact and use it in your own CGI scripts, but the other functions for printing out the associative array and other tasks you will likely modify to suit the task at hand (respecting Brenner's copyright however to "use and modify this library so long as the copyright above is maintained, modifications are documented, and credit is given for any use of the library.")

cgi-lib.pl

```perl
sub ReadParse {
  local (*in) = @_ if @_;
  local ($i, $key, $val);
  # Read in text
  if (&MethGet) {
     $in = $ENV{'QUERY_STRING'};
  } elsif (&MethPost) {
     read(STDIN,$in,$ENV{'CONTENT_LENGTH'});
  }
  @in = split(/[&;]/,$in);
  foreach $i (0 .. $#in) {
     # Convert plus's to spaces
     $in[$i] =~ s/\+/ /g;
     # Split into key and value.
     ($key, $val) = split(/=/,$in[$i],2); # splits on the first =.
     # Convert %XX from hex numbers to alphanumeric
     $key =~ s/%(..)/pack("c",hex($1))/ge;
     $val =~ s/%(..)/pack("c",hex($1))/ge;
     # Associate key and value
     $in{$key} .= "\0" if (defined($in{$key})); # \0 is the multiple separator
     $in{$key} .= $val;
  }
  return length($in);
}


# PrintHeader
# Returns the magic line which tells WWW that we're an HTML document
sub PrintHeader {
     return "Content-type: text/html\n\n";
}


# MethGet
```

```perl
# Return true if this cgi call was using the GET request, false otherwise
sub MethGet {
  return ($ENV{'REQUEST_METHOD'} eq "GET");
}


# MethPost
# Return true if this cgi call was using the POST request, false otherwise
sub MethPost {
  return ($ENV{'REQUEST_METHOD'} eq "POST");
}


# MyURL
# Returns a URL to the script
sub MyURL {
  local ($port);
  $port = ":" . $ENV{'SERVER_PORT'} if $ENV{'SERVER_PORT'} != 80;
  return 'http://' . $ENV{'SERVER_NAME'} . $port . $ENV{'SCRIPT_NAME'};
}


# CgiError
# Prints out an error message which which contains appropriate headers,
# markup, etcetera.
# Parameters:
#  If no parameters, gives a generic error message
#  Otherwise, the first parameter will be the title and the rest will
#  be given as different paragraphs of the body
sub CgiError {
  local (@msg) = @_;
  local ($i,$name);
  if (!@msg) {
    $name = &MyURL;
    @msg = ("Error: script $name encountered fatal error");
  };
  print &PrintHeader;
  print "<html><head><title>$msg[0]</title></head>\n";
  print "<body><h1>$msg[0]</h1>\n";
  foreach $i (1 .. $#msg) {
    print "<p>$msg[$i]</p>\n";
```

```perl
  }
  print "</body></html>\n";
}
# CgiDie
# Identical to CgiError, but also quits with the passed error message.
sub CgiDie {
  local (@msg) = @_;
  &CgiError (@msg);
  die @msg;
}
# PrintVariables
# Nicely formats variables in an associative array passed as a parameter
# And returns the HTML string.
sub PrintVariables {
  local (%in) = @_;
  local ($old, $out, $output);
  $old = $*; $* =1;
  $output .= "<DL COMPACT>";
  foreach $key (sort keys(%in)) {
    foreach (split("\0", $in{$key})) {
      ($out = $_) =~ s/\n/<BR>/g;
      $output .= "<DT><B>$key</B><DD><I>$out</I><BR>";
    }
  }
  $output .= "</DL>";
  $* = $old;
  return $output;
}
# PrintVariablesShort
# Now obsolete; just calls PrintVariables
sub PrintVariablesShort {
  return &PrintVariables(@_);
}
1; #return true
```

Below is a minimal script example supplied with the library that uses ReadParse to process a form. *ReadParse* processes the user input and if successful prints out the input with the *PrintVariables* call. The script also generates the test form itself when first invoked.

```
require "cgi-lib.pl";
if (&ReadParse(*input)) {
   print &PrintHeader, &PrintVariables(%input);
} else {
   print &PrintHeader,'<form><input type="submit">Data: <input name="myfield">';
}
```

CGI.pm

A more ambitious and comprehensive package is Lincoln Stein's "Perl5 CGI Library." It's a great resource of Perl routines for creating HTML forms and interpreting their results. It uses the latest Perl standard and is a well thought-out effort to create an object-oriented reusable library of routines for various HTML tasks. To use it install the CGI.PM file in your Perl library path, and include *use CGI* at the top of your script.

Creating HTML Forms

You will normally begin outputting your form with the *header* call, which will generate Content-type: text/html.

```
print $query->header ;
```

The next call you will usually make in displaying a form is to create an HTML document template with *start_html*. *start_html*'s first argument is the title of the document, the second argument is the author of the document and the third argument is 'true' or 'false' and controls whether a BASE element is created that allows relative addresses to be converted to absolute addresses.

```
print $query->start_html('Order Form','webmaster@ourstore.com','true');
```

This will generate an HTML document that looks something like this:

```
<HTML><HEAD><TITLE>Order Form</TITLE>
<LINK REV=MADE HREF="mailto:webmaster@ourstore.com">
<BASE HREF="http://www.ourstore.com:80">
</HEAD><BODY>
```

The *startform* call generates a <FORM> tag. It takes arguments of the FORM method (GET or POST with default of POST) and the form action, which defaults to none. Since you will almost always want something to be done with your data, you shouldn't rely on the default of no action (though Lincoln Stein's example script does invoke *startform* with no arguments).

```
print $query->startform('GET','cgi-bin/formstor.exe');
```

There are methods to generate each field type: *textfield, checkbox, textarea, radio_group, popup_menu, scrolling_list*. Text input fields are created with the *textfield* call. The first argument is the name of the field. The second argument is the initial default value of the field. The third optional argument is the size of the field in characters. The fourth optional argument is the maximum number of characters the field will accept.

```
print $query->textfield('Part Number','123-001',40,80);
```

The *textarea* call is identical but the third and fourth argument specify the number of rows and columns.

```
print $query->textarea('Part Number','123-001',5,40);
```

The package also lets you create menus with the *popup_menu* call. The first argument names the menu, the second argument is an array reference with the available selections, and the optional last argument indicates the default choice.

```
print $query->popup_menu('Credit Card',
['Visa','MasterCard','Amex'],'Visa');
```

You can create multiple select lists with the *scrolling_list* call. The first argument is the field name, the second argument is the list of possible choices, the optional third argument is a list of selected items (or single selected item), the optional fourth argument is the size of the list, and the last argument enables multiple selection (it should be '*true*' if you wish to select multiple items).

```
     print $query->scrolling_list('Toppings',
['pepperoni','mushrooms','sausage',green peppers','hot peppers',
'onions','anchovies'],
['pepperoni','mushrooms'],7,'true');
```

An individual checkbox can be created with the *checkbox* call. The first argument specifies the checkbox name. The second argument indicates whether the checkbox is on by default. The third argument indicates the value that is set if the checkbox is on.

The last argument is the label used to prompt the user, which is just the checkbox name if not supplied.

```
print $query->checkbox('Mailing List','checked','ON',
'Would you like to be on our mailing list');
```

You can create a group of checkboxes with the *checkbox_group* call. The *scrolling_list* pizza topping example above translates to the following for a checkbox group. The first argument is the field name. The second argument is the list of checkbox values. The optional third argument is the list of checkboxes that are selected (default is none). The optional fourth argument is *'true'* if you wish line breaks to appear between the boxes (defaults to no line breaks). The optional fifth argument is an associative array that relates the checkbox values to labels for display to the user (defaults to labeling with the values themselves).

```
print $query->checkbox_group('Toppings',
['pepperoni','mushrooms','sausage','green peppers','hot peppers',
'onions','anchovies'],
['pepperoni','mushrooms'],'true');
```

Radio button groups can be created with the *radio_group* call, which has the same calling convention as the *checkbox_group,* with the exception that the third argument can only have one item selected.

```
print $query->radio_group('Credit Card',['Visa','MasterCard','Amex'],
'Visa','true');
```

Your form should include one submit field which will generate a submit button. It has optional arguments for the button label and a value that can be submitted to the form processing script.

```
print $query->submit('Order');
```

Processing HTML Forms

CGI.pm supports processing user responses from HTML forms. To begin processing a form, create a CGI form object with the *new* method in your Perl script that you create to process a form.

```
$query = new CGI;
```

$query will then contain the contents of the form filled out by the user. The names of the fields can be retrieved with the *$query->param* method.

```
@fieldnames = $query->param;
```

Individual field values can be retrieved by supplying the *param* method with a field name.

```
$emailaddr = $query->param('Email Address');
```

Field values can be set with by supplying the *param* call with additional parameters.

```
$query->param('Total amount',$totamt);
```

You can save the state of a form to a file with the *save* method.

```
$FORMSTORE='ORDER.TXT';
$query->save(FORMSTORE);
```

The values can be retrieved from the file with the *new* method.

```
$query->new(FORMSTORE);
```

An Example Form

The following code (cgi-lib.pl) is an example that uses most of the major calls of the library.

cgi-lib.pl example

```
use CGI;
$query = new CGI;
print $query->header;
print $query->start_html("Order Form");
print $query->startform('GET','FORMSTOR.EXE');
print $query->textfield('Name')
print $query->checkbox('Ship Overnight?');
print $query->submit('Order');
```

```
print $query->endform;
foreach $key ($query->param) {
        print "Field Name: $key, Value: ";
        @values = $query->param($key);
        print join(", ",@values),"<BR>\n";
}
print $query->end_html;
```

CGI.pm is presented in Appendix C in its entirety, and is provided on the CD accompanying this book. Current versions can be retrieved at **http://www-genome.wi.mit.edu/ftp/pub/software/WWW/cgi_docs.html**.

Other Packages

I have found the last two packages to be sufficient for almost all of my CGI scripting needs. Nevertheless there are at least two other interesting packages in the arena of Perl HTML libraries.

libwww-perl

Roy Fielding's package of routines for HTTP and HTML consist of several Perl scripts submitted by several authors for a variety of server-oriented tasks. I have not found it to be as useful as some of the other packages mentioned, but if the packages above don't suffice, you should take a look at this library. It is available at **http://www.ics.uci.edu/pub/websoft/libwww-perl/**.

PERLLib

This library consists of Web-related Perl routines. The most relevant package is probably *htgrep.pl*. This is a library of routines to search HTML files. You can find this at **http://iamwww.unibe.ch/~scg/Src/PerlLib/**.

Perl Programs

At this point, I have introduced you to the various elements of Perl, but haven't given you xtensive examples of Perl code. In lieu of writing Perl code that counts camels or some other artificial task, I'll present some programs for analyzing and processing your HTML code. I present a table of contents generator, a basic text to HTML converter, an HTML file cross referencer, and a Web "lint" that checks your HTML source for problems.

All of these tools are useful by themselves, whether or not you understand the Perl code or how to modify it. But the goal of this section is to teach you Perl programming, so I will also be present each of the programs and show you how they are structured. The full code for each of these programs appears in Appendix C, but I will present the essence of each program as an example of real Perl code in the sections below.

Table of Contents

The first two tools we examine create HTML source from other HTML and from plain text. They show off Perl's capability to easily generate HTML content. Earl Hood's *htmltoc* (see the htmltoc generate-toc() routine) creates a table of contents from (and for) a set of HTML documents. For some sites, especially large collections of other HTML content, potentially submitted by a number of other authors, this will save you from spending all of your time cataloging their contributions.

Invoke the script with the complete list of files you wish to catalog. For example, to create a table of :all the HTML files in a directory as the file ourtoc.htm, enter:

```
perl htmltoc *.htm -toc ourtoc.htm
```

The essence of the program is contained in the function *generate_toc*. This function takes as input the name of an array of parsed HTML elements. It also takes as arguments the name of an array of table of content elements and a revised array of HTML content elements. This is all specified with the line, *local(*html,*toc,*newhtml)=@_;*. The main loop reads one item of the HTML content array at a time, until the array is exhausted. *$item=shift @html* extracts an element from the array, *while($#html >= 0)* stops the process when there are no more elements left.

Each item is then checked to see if it is just content versus an HTML tag with *$item !~ /^</*. If it is a tag, it is checked to see if it is one of the Table of Contents-related tags with *foreach (keys %TOC) {*, where *keys %TOC* is the array of keys of the associative array of ToC related tags, currently just H1 and H2, but this can be extended to deeper heading levels. Inside the foreach loop the level of the tag, the level of the tag is recorded for use in generating the ToC array. An inner *while($#html>=0)* loop grabs the text inside the heading for use in generating the Table of Content name. The text is also put into the revised HTML file but labeled with a named anchor that the Table of Contents file is linked to. The last step in processing each heading tag is to add the heading to the table of contents file.

The htmltoc generate_toc() routine

```perl
##-----------------------------------------------------------##
##        generate_toc() reads the HTML specified by *html and adds to the
##        ToC specified by *toc. The new modified HTML is in *newhtml.
##
sub generate_toc {
    local(*html, *toc, *newhtml) = @_;
    local($content,$adone,$name,$level,$i,$title,$before,$after,$q
);
    while ($#html >= 0) {
        $item = shift @html;
        next if $item eq '';
        if ($item !~ /^</) { push(@newhtml,$item); next; }
        $level = 0; $title = 0;
        ## Check if tag included in TOC
        foreach (keys %TOC) {
            if ($item =~ /^<$_/i) {
                $tag = $_;
                $level = $TOC{$_};          # Level of significant element
                $endtag = $TOCend{$_};      # End tag of significcant element
                $before = $TOCbefore{$_};   # Before text in ToC entry
                $after = $TOCafter{$_};     # After text in ToC entry
                last;
            }
        }
    }
    if (!$level) { push(@newhtml,$item); next; }
    ## Insert A element into document
    $content = ''; $adone = 0; $name = $tocprefix . $_id;
    if ($tag =~ /title/i) {                 # TITLE tag is a special case
        $title = 1; $adone = 1;
    }
    push(@newhtml,$item);
    while ($#html >= 0) {
        $item = shift @html;
        next if $item eq '';
        if ($item !~ /^</) {                        # Text data
            $content .= $item;
            if (!$adone && $item !~ /^\s*$/) {
```

```perl
        push(@newhtml,qq|<A NAME="$name">$item</A>|);
        $adone = 1;
    } else {
        push(@newhtml,$item);
    }
} elsif (!$adone && $item =~ /^<A/i) { # Anchor
    if ($item =~ m/NAME\s*=\s*(['"])/i) {
        $q = $1;
        ($name) = $item =~ m/NAME\s*=\s*$q([^$q]*)$q/i;
    } else {
        $item =~ s/^(<A)(.*)$/$1 NAME="$name" $2/i;
    }
    push(@newhtml,$item);
    $adone = 1;
} else {                                        # Tag
    push(@newhtml,$item);
    last if $item =~ m|<$endtag>|i;
    $content .= $item
        unless $TEXTONLY || $item =~ m%</?(hr>|p>|a|img)%i;
}
}
$content =~ s/$ComMark//go;
if ($content =~ /^\s*$/) {      # Check for empty content
    warn "Warning: A $tag in $file has not content; $tag skipped\n";
    next;
} else {
    $content = $before . $content . $after;
}
## Update TOC
if ($level < $prevlevel) {
    for ($i=$level; $i < $prevlevel; $i++) {
        if ($OL && $i == 1) { push(@toc, "</OL>\n"); }
        else { push(@toc, "</UL>\n"); }
    }
} else {
    for ($i=$level; $i > $prevlevel; $i-) {
        if ($OL && $i == 1) { push(@toc, "<OL>\n"); }
        else { push(@toc, "<UL>\n"); }
    }
```

```
        }
        if ($title) { push(@toc, qq|<LI><A HREF="$file">$content </A>\n|); }
        else { push(@toc, qq|<LI><A HREF="$file#$name">$content </A>\n|); }
        $prevlevel = $level;
        $_id++;
    }
}
```

The entire source code is show in Listing 1 in Appendix C and on the accompanying CD-ROM. You can get an up-to-date copy on Earl Hood's Web site (which itself uses *htmltoc* to great advantage) at **http://www.oac.uci.edu/indiv/ehood/htmltoc.doc.html**.

Text to HTML Conversion

This script from Seth Golub of Washington University in St. Louis converts plain text files to a minimally formatted HTML. It makes several inferences about the HTML structure from the indentation, line lengths, blank lines, apparent list numbering, etc. The inferences are not always correct, and the resulting output often needs to have several edits made to match our true intentions. But it is a very useful tool, and simple enough to be a good example Perl script.

TXT2HTML is invoked with the name of the text file and options that determine the title of the HTML document (*-t <title>*), the number of dashes that determine an HRULE (*-r <number>*), whether or not mail addresses are converted to mail URLs (*-m/+m*), whether or not to append to the destination file (*-a/+a*), and when a line is short enough to assume that the next line is not part of the same paragraph (*-s <number>*). (See the TXT2HTML Option Handler code.)

The script starts off with a number of constant definitions, then all of the subroutine definitions, followed by the main program. The first subroutine called is *deal_with_options()* and the way they do this should be imitated in your programs.

The TXT2HTML option handler

```
sub deal_with_options
{
    while ($ARGV[0] =~ /^[-+].+/)
    {
        if (($ARGV[0] eq "-r" || $ARGV[0] eq "-hrule") &&
            $ARGV[1] =~ /^\d+$/)
        {
```

```
            $hrule_min = $ARGV[1];
            shift @ARGV;
            next;
        }
        if (($ARGV[0] eq "-s" || $ARGV[0] eq "-shortline") &&
            $ARGV[1] =~ /^\d+$/)
        {
            $short_line_length = $ARGV[1];
            shift @ARGV;
            next;
        }
# many options skipped here ...
        if ($ARGV[0] eq "-v" || $ARGV[0] eq "-version")
        {
            print
'$Header: /users/hilco/seth/projects/txt2html/txt2 html.pl
,v 1.10 1994/12/28 20:10:25 seth Exp seth $ ';
            print "\n";
            exit;
        }
        if ($ARGV[0] eq "-h" || $ARGV[0] eq "-help")
        {
            &usage;
            exit;
        }
        print STDERR "Unrecognized option: $ARGV[0]\n";
        print STDERR " or bad paramater: $ARGV[1]\n" if($ARGV[1]);
        &usage;
        exit(1);
    } continue {
        shift @ARGV;
    }
}
```

The *@ARGV* list is stepped through one option at a time. *$ARGV[0]* is tested against several option values. If it matches, the appropriate global parameter is set, and we move on to the next command line argument by invoking *shift @ARGV*. If the command line argument doesn't match any of the defined options, an error message is printed, and the script is exited.

The main processing loop steps through each of the lines in the file, with the $line variable, keeping a one line lookahead buffer in the $nextline buffer, and the previous line in the $prev buffer. Some conversions are done on every line before printing them out as HTML. For example, tabs are converted to whitespace, trailing spaces are removed. Other conversions are done conditionally. If a line contains a sequence of dashes, it is assumed to be equivalent to an HTML horizontal rule (<HR>). If a single letter or sequence of digits is followed by a colon, right paren, right brace, or period, and then followed by a string it is assumed this may in fact be a list item, and further processing is done to determine what type of list item it is. If the next line contains one or more equal signs, dashes, asterisks, periods, tildes or plus signs, then it is inferred that the current line is a heading and invoke the heading subroutine on the current line, that determines the heading level based upon the characters used to form the underline:

Heading Level	Character
1	*
2	=
3	+
4	-
5	~
6	.

TXT2HTML main loop is the main processing loop that shows this logic.

TXT2HTML main loop

```
do
    {
    $line =~ s/[ \011]*$//;      # Chop trailing whitespace
    &untabify;              # Change leading whitespace into spaces
    &hrule if !($mode & $PRE);
    &heading if (!($mode & $PRE) &&
            $nextline =~ /^\s*[=\-\*\.~\+]+$/)
    &liststuff if (!($mode & $PRE) &&
```

```
                !&is_blank($line));
        &paragraph if ((&is_blank($prev) || ($line_action & $END)) &&
                !&is_blank($line) &&
                !($mode & ($LIST | $PRE)) && # paragraphs in lists
                                        # *should* be allowed.
                (!$line_action ||
                ($line_action & ($CAPS | $END | $MAILQUOTE))));
        print $prev;
        $prev = $line;
        $line = $nextline;
        $nextline = <STDIN>;
    } until (!$nextline && !$line && !$prev);
```

Listing 11.2 in Appendix C is the complete code for TXT2HTML. The code also
appears on the accompanying CD.

Web Cross-Referencer

The next two tools check your HTML content, and provide good examples of how
easily Perl can parse HTML source, even without a third party library.

webxref, by Rick Jansen, identifies various types of references made in the HTML
file specified as the argument of the script. The essence of the logic appears in the
following *Get_Refs* routine. I have simplified the function to only look for *http*
references.

webxref Reference Retriever

```
sub Get_Refs {
# Get all referenced files from the file
local(%newlist);
local($file);
local($dir);
local($Old_Dir);
local($filename);
$dir=&Dir_Name($_[0]);
if ($dir eq "") {
    $dir = &Get_PWD;
}
```

```perl
$file=&Base_Name($_[0]);
#print "----------------------\n";
if ($debug) {
print "arg=$_[0]\n";
print "dir=$dir\n";
print "file=$file\n";
}
# http?
if ($_[0] =~ m/.*(http:.*)/i) {
   if (!defined($HTTPList{$1})) {
     $HTTPList{$1} = $_[1];
     }
   else {
     $HTTPList{$1} = "$HTTPList{$1} $_[1]";
   }
   return;
}
# directory reference?
if ($file eq "") {
   if ($debug) {
     print "$dir must be a dir, refd by $_[1]!\n";
   }
   if (-d $_[0]) {
     if (!defined($DirList{$_[0]})) {
       $DirList{$_[0]} = $_[1];
       }
     else {
       $DirList{$_[0]} = "$DirList{$_[0]} $_[1]";
     }
   }
   else {
     if (!defined($DirNotFoundList{$_[0]})) {
       $DirNotFoundList{$_[0]} = $_[1];
     }
     else {
       $DirNotFoundList{$_[0]} = "$DirNotFoundList{$_[0]} $_[1]";
     }
   }
   return;
}
```

The full source appears in Listing 3 in Appendix C and on the accompanying CD-ROM. Updated version of the script can be retrieved at **http://www.sara.nl/Rick.Jansen**.

WebLint

WebLint is a utility that finds problems and discrepancies in HTML files, similar in spirit to Lint, a program which checks C course code for problems. It checks for valid tags, attributes, empty container elements, and other features of "good" HTML. Since the general philosophy of most browsers is to handle bad or unknown tags as well as possible, this is a useful check that you are not likely to get by testing your HTML content with one browser.

The following shows the the main loop of the program, a good example of using Perl to apply various filters and tests on a line-by-line basis. The PAGE filehandle is opened earlier and the fragment begins looping through each line in the file. The code, *while ($line =~ /</o)*, searches for the beginning of a tag. *$tail* is set to the text following the tag. *$id* and *$tag* are set to the first string inside the tag. If *$id* is just white-space WebLint complains (*&whine($.,'unknown-element',$id)*). Then we skip a whole lot of processing to to check the attributes of the tag for duplicates and validity. I also skip over WebLint's check for empty elements (a closing tag just following the corresponding opening tag). Then I show WebLint's check for *$id* in the string of legal elements (*$legalElements*). WebLink will also announce if Netscape extension's have been used, or deprecated tags. Then there is a lot of checking that we skip below for balancing closing tags. Finally WebLint checks that each IMG element has an ALT tag, and the loop completes.

Main logic of weblint.pl

```
READLINE:
  while (<PAGE>)
  {
    $line .= $_;
    $line =~ s/\n/ /g;
    while ($line =~ /</o)
    {
      $tail = $'; #'
      undef $lastNonTag;
      $lastNonTag = $` if $` !~ /^\s*$/o;
      next READLINE unless $tail =~ /^(\s*)([^>]*)>/;
      $id = $tag = $2;
      $line = $';
```

```
      &whine($., 'unknown-element', $id),next if $id =~ /^\s*$/;
      # lots of other processing skipped
      #- whine about unrecognized element, and do no more checks —
      if ($id !~ /^($legalElements)$/io)
      {
          if ($id =~ /^($netscapeElements)$/io)
          {
              &whine($., 'netscape-markup', ($closing ? "/$id" : "$id"));
          }
          else
          {
              &whine($., 'unknown-element', ($closing ? "/$id" : "$id"));
          }
          next;
      }
          #-------------------------------------------------
          # check for tags which have been deprecated (now obsolete)
          #-------------------------------------------------
          &whine($., 'obsolete', $ID) if $ID =~ /^($obsolete Tags)$/o;
      }
      #----------------------------------------------------------
      #== inline images (IMG) should have an ALT argument :-)
      #----------------------------------------------------------
      &whine($., 'img-alt') if ($ID eq 'IMG'
                              && !defined $args{'ALT'}
                              && !$closing);
  } continue {
      $lastTAG = $TAG;
  }
  $lastNonTag = $line;
}
close PAGE;
```

The (quite long) full source is presented in Listing 4 in Appendix C and on the accompanying CD. You can retrieve the latest version at **ftp://ftp.khoral.com/ pub/perl/www/weblint.tar.gz**.

Perl CGI References

There really is an incredible amount of information available on creating CGI programs, but the signal-to-noise ratio is very high, even for the Web. Below are resources beyond the libraries listed above, on CGI programming in Perl.

- "Beyond Hypertext: Using the WWW for Interactive Applications" (**http://www.scu.edu.au/ausweb95/papers/hypertext/gleeson/**)

  Gleeson covers use of Perl to create CGI applications thoroughly and more self-contained (not necessarily a strength in the Web world) than other introductions, but the formal tone may put off some.

- "Programming Perl"

  (**http://gnn.com/gnn/bus/ora/catalog/pperl.desc.html**)

  This is the reference page for Larry Wall's *Programming Perl* book on the publisher's (O'Reilly's) Web site.

- "Learning Perl" (**http://gnn.com/gnn/bus/ora/catalog/lperl.html**)

  The page for Schwartz' *Learning* Perl book. This is a more approachable introduction to the subject.

- "CGI Form Programming in Perl" (**http://www.bio.cam.ac.uk/web/form.html**)

  Steven Brenner's page is brief, but it concisely summarizes how to build Perl scripts to process forms. Brenner is also the author of the *cgi-lib.pl* library of Perl routines for processing forms.

- "Forms in Perl" (**http://www.seas.upenn.edu/~mengwong/forms/**)

  Meng Wong builds upon Brenner's work on *cgi-lib.pl* with a routine to build a form: *generic.pl*.

- "perlWWW" (**http://www.oac.uci.edu/indiv/ehood/perlWWW/**)

  This is Earl Hood's (the author of the *htmltoc* Perl script mentioned earlier) attempt to concisely list links to important Web-related Perl programs and libraries. It's pretty good.

- "Web Developer's Virtual Library"

  http://WWW.Stars.com/Vlib/Providers/CGI.html

  Links to a variety of CGI programming resources.

GATEWAY PROGRAMMING IN C AND C++

Perl is excellent for CGI gateway development. It's strengths are in parsing information from files, its ability to create useful software in a short amount of readable code, and its interpretive nature make it easy to understand why it has become popular for CGI development.

Nevertheless, C and C++ have their own strengths for some gateway tasks. For processing-intensive tasks, compiled C programs tend to be faster. C++ provides better facilities in the form of classes, modern debugging environments, and use of existing C libraries that make it a good choice for more ambitious large gateway efforts. The API to most relational database packages is of course C or C++, so if you wish to access data on the fly from these likely repositories of corporate data this is a good choice.

In the discussion that follows, I assume that you know C. No gentle introduction to the language is provided as I did for Perl. If you are not an experienced programmer, you can still do plenty of things with gateways, but I recommend that you begin with Perl as shown earlier.

NCSA CGI Archive: Query and Post-query

The NCSA archive of CGI related code can be found at **ftp://ftp.ncsa.uiuc.edu/Web/ httpd/Unix/ncsa_httpd/cgi/**. It is a simple directory list of files with no annotation. So we'll show you one of the most useful packages for our purposes here. In the subdirectory called *cgi-src* is the source code and makefile for two programs: one called *query* and one called *post-query.*

query is a program that should be invoked when submitting forms or queries using the GET method. Of course you really should submit formdata with GET for reasons discussed earlier: the limitations on the amount of data that can be returned with GET. The more useful program for our likely applications is the *post-query* program (see the following). Since it is very short and a good example of just about the simplest CGI gateway you could write, the source, *post-query.c,* is presented below. I have left the code as it was originally written intact, but note that I would recommend changing the local entries variable presented below to static, to remove all of that data from the stack. In other words, if you're really going to use this, prepend that declaration with static. Also, note that the program makes use of a set of utility functions *makeword(), fmakeword(),* and *x2c()* found in a separate file in the same distribution. The full source appears in Listing 5 in Appendix C and on the accompanying CD-ROM.

postquery.c

```
#include <stdio.h>
#ifndef NO_STDLIB_H
#include <stdlib.h>
#else
char *getenv();
#endif
#define MAX_ENTRIES 10000
typedef struct {
    char *name;
    char *val;
} entry;
char *makeword(char *line, char stop);
char *fmakeword(FILE *f, char stop, int *len);
char x2c(char *what);
void unescape_url(char *url);
void plustospace(char *str);
main(int argc, char *argv[]) {
    entry entries[MAX_ENTRIES];
    register int x,m=0;
    int cl;
    printf("Content-type: text/html%c%c",10,10);
    if(strcmp(getenv("REQUEST_METHOD"),"POST")) {
        printf("This script should be referenced with a METHOD of POST.\n");
        printf("If you don't understand this, see this ");
        printf(
"<A HREF=\"http://www.ncsa.uiuc.edu/SDG/Software/Mosaic/Docs/fill-out-
forms/overview.html\">forms overview</A>.%c",10);
        exit(1);
    }
    if(strcmp(getenv("CONTENT_TYPE"),"application/x-www-form-urlencoded")) {
        printf("This script can only be used to decode form results. \n");
        exit(1);
    }
    cl = atoi(getenv("CONTENT_LENGTH"));
    for(x=0;cl && (!feof(stdin));x++) {
```

```
       m=x;
       entries[x].val = fmakeword(stdin,'&',&cl);
       plustospace(entries[x].val);
       unescape_url(entries[x].val);
       entries[x].name = makeword(entries[x].val,'=');
    }
    printf("<H1>Query Results</H1>");
    printf("You submitted the following name/value pairs:<p>%c",10);
    printf("<ul>%c",10);
    for(x=0; x <= m; x++)
        printf("<li> <code>%s = %s</code>%c",entries[x].name,
                entries[x].val,10);
    printf("</ul>%c",10);
}
```

URL decoding routines simply decodes (gets rid of the URL-encoding) the field data submitted by the user, and displays the keyword (field name), value (field data) pairs back to the user. The actual decoding is done by the *plustospace* and *unescape_url* routines that appear in the *util.c* file.

URL decoding routines

```
void unescape_url(char *url) {
    register int x,y;
    for(x=0,y=0;url[y];++x,++y) {
        if((url[x] = url[y]) == '%') {
            url[x] = x2c(&url[y+1]);
            y+=2;
        }
    }
    url[x] = '\0';
}
void plustospace(char *str) {
    register int x;
    for(x=0;str[x];x++) if(str[x] == '+') str[x] = ' ';
}
```

EGSCRIPT

The above program works fine, and could serve as the basis of some useful gateways you want to write. But wait. Didn't I say that the CGI standard was really a convention of what environment variables to create and use, and what information to store in them? The program above doesn't do anything with environment variables except get the REQUEST_METHOD, the CONTENT_TYPE, and the CONTENT_LENGTH. This is actually understandable because the *post-query* program actually predates the solidified CGI standard. Still if you are going to use a program as the basis of our C development efforts, I'd like one that shows us the available environment variables and how to access them.

A more complex, but still relatively straightforward, C-based CGI program can be found with the EMWAC http server, but can be used regardless of what server you are using. The *EGSCRIPT.C* is very similar in purpose and structure to the *post-query.c* program. It displays the field names and data back to the user along with the environment variables passed to the program. Note also that the URL-decoding process is a bit more sophisticated. For example, hex values are decoded into their actual characters.

EGSCRIPT.C should serve as an excellent basis for your development effort and for learning how CGI operates. Note that the example below is written in Microsoft C for Windows NT and contains a few non-portable constructs, notable the _environ array, and the _stricmp() function call. I would put conditional code in to fix this problem, but I don't want to tamper with the original effort.

EGSCRIPT.C

```
#include <stdio.h>
#include <stdlib.h>
#include <string.h>
#include <ctype.h>
char InputBuffer[4096];
/*
 * Convert all cOld characters in cStr into cNew characters
 */
void strcvrt(char * cStr,char cOld,char cNew) {
int i;
```

```
    i = 0;
    while (cStr[i]) {
        if (cStr[i]==cOld) cStr[i] = cNew;
        i++;
    }
}
/*
 * The string starts with two hex characters. Return an integer formed from them.
 */
static int TwoHex2Int(char *pC) {
int Hi;
int Lo;
int Result;
    Hi = pC[0];
    if ('0'<=Hi && Hi<='9') {
        Hi -= '0';
    } else
    if ('a'<=Hi && Hi<='f') {
        Hi -= ('a'-10);
    } else
    if ('A'<=Hi && Hi<='F') {
        Hi -= ('A'-10);
    }
    Lo = pC[1];
    if ('0'<=Lo && Lo<='9') {
        Lo -= '0';
    } else
    if ('a'<=Lo && Lo<='f') {
        Lo -= ('a'-10);
    } else
    if ('A'<=Lo && Lo<='F') {
        Lo -= ('A'-10);
    }
    Result = Lo + 16*Hi;
    return Result;
}

/*
 * Display all the environment variables
```

```
 */
void DisplayEnvVars(void) {
int i;
   i = 0;
   while (_environ[i]) {
      printf("%s\n",_environ[i]);
      i++;
   }
   printf("\n");
}


/*
 * Decode the given string in-place by expanding %XX escapes
 */
void urlDecode(char *p) {
char *pD;
   pD = p;
   while (*p) {
      if (*p=='%') {
         /* Escape: next 2 chars are hex representation of the actual character */
         p++;
         if (isxdigit(p[0]) && isxdigit(p[1])) {
            *pD++ = (char) TwoHex2Int(p);
            p += 2;
         }
      } else {
         *pD++ = *p++;
      }
   }
   *pD = '\0';
}


/*
 * Parse out and display field=value items. Don't use strtok!
 */
void DisplayField(char *Item) {
char *p;
   p = strchr(Item,'=');
   if (p==NULL) return;
```

```c
        *p++='\0';
        urlDecode(Item);
        urlDecode(p);
        strcvrt(p,'\n',' ');
        printf("%s = %s\n",Item,p);
    }
/*
 * Main program
 */
int main(int argc, char *argv[]) {
int ContentLength;
int x;
int i;
char *p;
char *pCGIVersion;
char *pRequestMethod;
    /* Turn buffering off for stdin */
    setvbuf(stdin,NULL,_IONBF,0);
    /* Tell the client what we're going to send */
    printf("Content-type: text/plain\n");
    /* If we are running CGI/1.1 or later, we can send a Status: header */
    pCGIVersion = getenv("GATEWAY_INTERFACE");
    if (pCGIVersion!=NULL) {
        if (_stricmp(pCGIVersion,"CGI/1.1")>=0) {
            printf("Status: 200 Orl Korrect\n");
        }
    }
    /* Finished sending headers */
    printf("\n");
    /* Print out command line variables */
    printf("argc = %d\n",argc);
    for (i=0;i<argc;i++) {
        printf("argv[%d] = %s\n",i,argv[i]);
    }
    printf("\n");
    /* Display the variables */
    DisplayEnvVars();
    /* What method were we invoked through? */
    pRequestMethod = getenv("REQUEST_METHOD");
```

```c
if (pRequestMethod==NULL) {
   return 0;
}
if (_stricmp(pRequestMethod,"POST")==0) {
   /* Read in the data from the client */
   p = getenv("CONTENT_LENGTH");
   if (p!=NULL) {
      ContentLength = atoi(p);
   } else {
      ContentLength = 0;
   }
   if (ContentLength>sizeof(InputBuffer)-1) {
      ContentLength = sizeof(InputBuffer)-1;
   }
   i = 0;
   while (i<ContentLength) {
      x = fgetc(stdin);
      if (x==EOF) break;
      InputBuffer[i++] = x;
   }
   InputBuffer[i] = '\0';
   ContentLength = i;
   p = getenv("CONTENT_TYPE");
   if (p==NULL) {
      return 0;
   }
   if (_stricmp(p,"application/x-www-form-urlencoded")==0) {
      /* Parse the data */
      p = strtok(InputBuffer,"&");
      while (p!=NULL) {
         DisplayField(p);
         p = strtok(NULL,"&");
      }
   } else {
      /* Display the data */
      printf("Input = %s\n",InputBuffer);
   }
} else
if (_stricmp(pRequestMethod,"GET")==0) {
```

```
/* Parse the data in the search term */
p = getenv("QUERY_STRING");
if (p!=NULL) {
    strncpy(InputBuffer,p,sizeof(InputBuffer));
    p = strtok(InputBuffer,"&");
    while (p!=NULL) {
        DisplayField(p);
        p = strtok(NULL,"&");
    }
}
}
return 0;
}
```

The Web Ordering System

Now I'd like to show you some examples of C-based CGI utilities, but also make sure these examples (like those in the Perl section) are immediately useful to you in your Web deployment efforts. In the remainder of this section we will look at a number of C programs to facilitate interactive Web sites: more importantly utilities to facilitate Web ordering. The programs are small, so they make good examples of CGI programs for you to turn to for reference, yet they should prove useful on your site in their own right.

Let's look at some tools that can be used directly to allow us to build a commercial Web site, by deploying an ordering system. In helping companies put together commercial Web sites, I found few existing tools in this area. I have tried to confine my discussions to existing, available tools as much as possible, and not make this a treatise on software development by developing a lot of my own custom utilities. In this case, however, I will need to show you some utilities I created to facilitate catalog-oriented sites.

Some commercial sites oriented to selling a variety of products may really be considered electronic catalogs. There is usually a page listing the variety of products, or potentially allowing searches for a product (if the amount of products is really large). Once the product is selected or searched for, a page will be retrieved showing all of the information on that product. That page will generally allow ordering of the product.

The database oriented tools I presented earlier lend themselves well to this paradigm. However, your product data may not be in a traditional relational database. And it may not be easy for you to take the generated orders from the relational database to disseminate to the responsible individuals. In order to give you tools that you can modify to read data from, and generate product orders to, *any* kind of data format, I present some tools that can read product data from a text database (a comma-separated value file), and generate orders to another text database. It should be straightforward to convert these programs to work with other data formats you may need to support.

formshow

The *formshow* utility looks up a record in a text database, and returns a Web page (usually an order form) displaying the retrieved information. The typical use is to embed the reference to *formshow* in the product listings or product search facility. The *formshow* utility is invoked with the name of an order form, a separate secure order form, databases to look for the product in, and the key value used to look up the product. The usage message is:

```
Usage: FORMSHOW <secure form> <nonnsecure form> <secure product database>
<insecure product database> <key to look for>
```

Why have two separate order forms and databases? If you are using the Netscape Commerce Server or another secure server, you will want to exploit the fact that some of your Web browsing customers will have secure Web browsers. That the channel is completely secure, so you can now prompt the user for credit card numbers and other information that you might not ask for over a nonsecure Internet connection. You may also want to have separate databases for secure and nonsecure access, because even the information that you display from the retrieved fields you may wish to vary for secure and nonsecure browsers. In general, most tools do not yet address this issue of dual class Web browsers. The issue is usually handled by the webmaster by creating separate pages and areas on their Web sites for secure and nonsecure access. Needless to say, that's a lot of work. In your own tool development, you may find that an approach of recognizing secure access and handling both nonsecure and secure access will save you a lot of duplicate content authoring.

As an example use of the utility, a list of products is displayed on an HTML page, one product to a line. When the user clicks on the product they are interested in, the *formshow* utility is invoked and displays an order form with more information about the product and pricing. The HTML for the line might appear as follows:

```
<A HREF=
"/cgi-bin/formshow.exe?secure.htm+order.htm+secprods.csv+products.csv+widget200"
>Widget 2.00</A>
```

The text following the question mark consists of the arguments to the *formshow* utility. The first two arguments are the secure and insecure order form template. The third and fourth arguments are the product databases, one for nonsecure access, the other for secure access. The last argument is the key used to retrieve the product information, often a product number. The order forms will contain all of the HTML you may wish to display, along with codes used to determine where the retrieved information will be placed. The following (secure Order Form Template—Secure.HTM) is an example order form, that could be used as SECURE.HTM in the *formshow* invocation above. Note that the full product name and price are retrieved from the secure products database (SECPRODS.CSV) and placed into the locations defined by %2 and %3 in the example below.

Secure Order Form Template—SECURE.HTM

```
<HTML>
<!- SECURE.HTM - order form to be used only with secure browsers ->
<HEAD><TITLE>Our Store Order Form</TITLE></HEAD>
<BODY>
<H1>Product Order</H1>
<FORM METHOD=POST ACTION=
"https://ourstore.com/cgi-bin/formstor.exe?orders.csv+default.htm">
<INPUT TYPE="hidden" VALUE="%1">
Full Product Name        <INPUT size=40 NAME="Product" VALUE="%2">
Price Per Unit           <INPUT size=12 NAME="Price" VALUE="%3">
<H2>Billing Information</H2>
<PRE>
Name    <INPUT size=20 NAME="Name">
Address <INPUT size=30 NAME="Address"> City <INPUT SIZE=20 NAME="City"> State
<INPUT SIZE=2 NAME="State"> Zip <INPUT SIZE=10 NAME="Zip">
Phone   <INPUT size=15 NAME="Phone "> Email <INPUT size=25 NAME="Email">
Credit card <SELECT NAME="CredCard">
<OPTION>VISA
<OPTION>MasterCard
<OPTION>American Express
</SELECT> Number: <INPUT SIZE=20 NAME="CredNum"> Expiration <INPUT SIZE=5
NAME="Expiration">
</PRE>
<INPUT TYPE="submit" VALUE="Order">
<INPUT TYPE="reset" VALUE="Clear Form"> <A HREF="/default.htm">Cancel Order</A>
```

```
</FORM>
<ADDRESS>
<A HREF="mailto:webmaster@ourstore.com">webmaster@ourstore.com</A>
</ADDRESS>
</BODY>
</HTML>
```

This example form has many elements that should be present in a Web-based order form whether or not you choose to use *formshow:*

- Buttons to submit the order, clear the form, or cancel the order.
- Name and address information in preformatted form
- Hidden fields for significant data that you would want to receive on the host side but that the user does not need to see (such as the product number).

Note that *formshow* can also be used from a searching interface as well as a list of products. This may be appropriate when the list of products is quite large. The method of doing this would be to make *formshow* the form action of the search form.

The databases that are referred to (SECPRODS.CSV and PRODUCTS.CSV in the examples above) are just comma-separated value files that can be created and imported by most database packages and spreadsheets. They may have as many fields as you wish, but require that the first field be the key field used for searching.

The Program

Below is the complete source for *formshow.* Note that this was built as a Win32 console application (no GUI interface) with Visual C++ 2.0, but it should compile under any C++ compiler. Feel free to use this program in your own efforts, but please maintain the original copyright.

There are few important things to notice about the code. First of all, note that access with the HTTPS environment variable created by the Netscape server, checking for a value of ON. Also, all significant information including the values of environment variables is logged. These log files are invaluable for both debugging and for monitoring activity on your Web site beyond what the server logs supply. For example, FORMSHOW.LOG stores a variety of information (everything available in the CGI standard) about users that retrieve order forms whether or not the user actually clicks on order. Also, even if you want to read from some other database format, you should be able to use much of the framework of code presented below.

FORMSHOW.CPP

```
// FORMSHOW.CPP
// CGI Script to display form with substitutable values, grabbed from a
// specified record file also will display different form depending on whether
// secure browser is detected Copyright (c) 1994, Adam Blum
#include <stdio.h>
#include <stdlib.h>
#include <string.h>
#include <ctype.h>
#include <iostream.h>
#include <fstream.h>

int strrepl(char *szLine,char *szPatt,char *szRepl,int maxsize);
int DisplayArgFile(char *szFileName,char *szArgs);
void LogEnvVars(void);
int GetNthLine(char *szFileName,int nLine,char *szArgs,int nMaxsize);
int FindInFile(char *szFileName,char *szKey,char *szArgs,int nMaxsize);
ofstream *pLog;
int main(int argc, char *argv[])
{
    /* Turn buffering off for stdin */
    setvbuf(stdin,NULL,_IONBF,0);
        if (argc<5)
        {
            cerr <<
"Usage: FORMSHOW <secure form> <nonnsecure form> <secure product database>
<insecure product database> <key to look for>\n";
            return 0;
        }
        pLog= new ofstream("FORMSHOW.LOG",ios::app);
        LogEnvVars();

        /* Tell the client what we're going to send */
    cout << "Content-type: text/html\n";
    /* If we are running CGI/1.1 or later, we can send a Status: header */
        char *pCGIVersion = getenv("GATEWAY_INTERFACE");
        if (pCGIVersion!=NULL) {
          if (_stricmp(pCGIVersion,"CGI/1.1")>=0) {
```

```
            cout <<"Status: 200 OK\n";
          }
        }
        cout << "\n";                    // end output of HTTP headers

        // decide which form to show user
        char szFormName[128];
        char szFileName[128];
        char *pszHttps;
        pszHttps=getenv("HTTPS"); // if HTTPS is set to ON then we're secure!
        if ((pszHttps!=NULL) &&!strncmp(pszHttps,"ON",2)) {
            strcpy(szFormName,argv[1]);
            strcpy(szFileName,argv[3]);
        }
        else {
            strcpy(szFormName,argv[2]);
            strcpy(szFileName,argv[4]);
        }
        char szArgs[1024];
        if (FindInFile(szFileName,argv[5],szArgs,sizeof szArgs))
            DisplayArgFile(szFormName,szArgs);
        else
            cout << "Could not find record.\n";
        delete pLog;
    return 0;
}
int FindInFile(char *szFileName,char *szKey,char *szArgs,int nMaxsize)
{
        ifstream is(szFileName);
        if (!is)
            return 0;
        char *pszBuf=new char[nMaxsize],*p;
        short nFound=0;
        while (is && !is.eof())
        {
            is.getline(szArgs,nMaxsize);
            strcpy(pszBuf,szArgs);
            if (p=strchr(pszBuf,','))
                *p='\0';
```

```
                    if (!strcmp(pszBuf,szKey)){
                        nFound=1;
                        break;
                    }
            }
            delete []pszBuf;
            return nFound;
    }
    int DisplayArgFile(char *szFileName,char *szArgs)
    {
            ifstream is(szFileName);
            if (!is || is.eof())
                return 0; // bad file
            char szLine[1024],szPatt[8],szRepl[1024],*p,*p2;
            while (is && !is.eof()){
                is.getline(szLine,sizeof szLine);
                p=szArgs;
                for (int i=1;p&&strlen(p);i++)
                {
                    //starting with %1 do a search and replace on all arguments
                    sprintf(szPatt,"%c%d",37,i);
                    strcpy(szRepl,p);
                    if(p2=strchr(szRepl,','))
                        *p2='\0';
                    strrepl(szLine,szPatt,szRepl,sizeof szLine-1);
                    p=strchr(p,',');
                    if (!p)
                        break;
                    p++;
                }
                cout << szLine << "\n";
            }
            return 1;
    }
    int strrepl(char *szLine,char *szPatt,char *szRepl,int maxsize)
    {
            char *p;
            char *pszDest=new char[maxsize],*pszAppend=new char[maxsize];
            strncpy(pszDest,szLine,maxsize);
```

```
            if (p=strstr(pszDest,szPatt)) // finds %n in line
            {
                strcpy(pszAppend,p+strlen(szPatt));
                *p='\0';
                if (strlen(pszDest)+strlen(szRepl)<(unsigned) maxsize)
                        strcat(pszDest,szRepl);
                if (strlen(pszDest+strlen(pszAppend))<(unsigned) maxsize)
                            strncat(pszDest,pszAppend,maxsize-strlen(pszDest));
            }
            strncpy(szLine,pszDest,maxsize);
            delete []pszDest;
            delete []pszAppend;
            return 1;
    }
    void LogEnvVars(void)
    {
            int i;
        i = 0;
        while (_environ[i]) {
            *pLog << _environ[i] << "\n";
            i++;
        }
        *pLog << "\n";
    }
```

formstor

You now have a utility, *formshow,* that can display product information to users as order forms, invoked either from explicit lists of products, or from a searchable catalog. But you still need a method of storing these orders. The *formstor* utility already presented in some detail in the chapter on gateways lets us do that. In the order form example presented above what the action for the order form was:

```
<FORM METHOD=POST ACTION=
"https://ourstore.com/cgi-bin/formstor.exe?orders.csv+default.htm">
```

The first argument to *formstor* is the CSV file database used to store the order. The second argument is the page to provide a link back to after informing the user of a successful order. *formstor* is similar to the other minimal CGI scripts presented earlier, such as *egscript* and *post-query* except that instead of displaying the field names and values back to the user, it stores the field values in a database file.

Below is the source for *formstor*, again originally developed as a Win32 console application under VC2.0, but eminently portable to other compilers and platforms. Again, you may wish to store your data in another form besides the CSV format used here, but you should find this a very useful base to start with for your programs that store order form values.

FORMSTOR.CPP

```cpp
// FORMSTOR.CPP
// CGI script to append contents of form as row in specified file
// Copyright (c) 1994, Adam Blum
#include <stdio.h>
#include <stdlib.h>
#include <string.h>
#include <ctype.h>
#include <iostream.h>
#include <fstream.h>
#include "html.h"
char InputBuffer[4096];
FILE *log;
ofstream *pData;
/*
 * Convert all cOld characters in cStr into cNew characters
 */
void strcvrt(char * cStr,char cOld,char cNew) {
int i;
   i = 0;
   while (cStr[i]) {
      if (cStr[i]==cOld) cStr[i] = cNew;
      i++;
   }
}
/*
 * The string starts with two hex characters. Return an integer formed from them.
 */
static int TwoHex2Int(char *pC) {
```

```
int Hi;
int Lo;
int Result;
   Hi = pC[0];
   if ('0'<=Hi && Hi<='9') {
      Hi -= '0';
   } else
   if ('a'<=Hi && Hi<='f') {
      Hi -= ('a'-10);
   } else
   if ('A'<=Hi && Hi<='F') {
      Hi -= ('A'-10);
   }
   Lo = pC[1];
   if ('0'<=Lo && Lo<='9') {
      Lo -= '0';
   } else
   if ('a'<=Lo && Lo<='f') {
      Lo -= ('a'-10);
   } else
   if ('A'<=Lo && Lo<='F') {
      Lo -= ('A'-10);
   }
   Result = Lo + 16*Hi;
   return Result;
}


/*
 * Display all the environment variables
 */
void DisplayEnvVars(void) {
int i;
   i = 0;
   while (_environ[i]) {
      fprintf(log,"%s\n",_environ[i]);
      i++;
   }
   fprintf(log,"\n");
}
```

```
/*
 * Decode the given string in-place by expanding %XX escapes
 */
void urlDecode(char *p) {
char *pD;
   pD = p;
   while (*p) {
      if (*p=='%') {
         /* Escape: next 2 chars are hex representation of the actual character */
         p++;
         if (isxdigit(p[0]) && isxdigit(p[1])) {
             *pD++ = (char) TwoHex2Int(p);
             p += 2;
         }
      } else {
         *pD++ = *p++;
      }
   }
   *pD = '\0';
}


/*
 * Parse out and display field=value items. Don't use strtok!
 */
void DisplayField(char *Item) {
char *p;
   p = strchr(Item,'=');
   if (p==NULL) return;
   *p++='\0';
   urlDecode(Item);
   urlDecode(p);
   strcvrt(p,'\n',' ');
   fprintf(log,"%s = %s\n",Item,p);
      *pData << p << ",";
}


/*
 * Main program
 */
```

```
int main(int argc, char *argv[]) {
int ContentLength;
     int x;
int i;
char *p;
char *pCGIVersion;
char *pRequestMethod;

     if (argc<3) {
          cerr <<
"Usage: FORMSTOR <file to append data from form to> <URL to link back to>\n";
          exit(0);
     }
  /* Turn buffering off for stdin */
  setvbuf(stdin,NULL,_IONBF,0);
     log=fopen("FORMSTOR.LOG","a");
     pData=new ofstream(argv[1],ios::app);
  /* Tell the client what we're going to send */
  cout << "Content-type: text/html\n";
  /* If we are running CGI/1.1 or later, we can send a Status:  header */
  pCGIVersion = getenv("GATEWAY_INTERFACE");
  if (pCGIVersion!=NULL) {
     if (_stricmp(pCGIVersion,"CGI/1.1")>=0) {
        cout <<"Status: 200 OK\n";
     }
  }
  /* Finished sending headers */
  cout <<"\n";

  /* Print out command line variables */
  fprintf(log,"argc = %d\n",argc);
  for (i=0;i<argc;i++) {
     fprintf(log,"argv[%d] = %s\n",i,argv[i]);
  }
  fprintf(log,"\n");
  /* Display the variables */
  DisplayEnvVars();
  /* What method were we invoked through? */
  pRequestMethod = getenv("REQUEST_METHOD");
```

```
            if (pRequestMethod==NULL) {
                    cout << "No request method\n";
                    fprintf(log,"No request method.\n");
                return 0;
            }
            if (_stricmp(pRequestMethod,"POST")==0) {
                /* Read in the data from the client */
                p = getenv("CONTENT_LENGTH");
                if (p!=NULL) {
                    ContentLength = atoi(p);
                } else {
                    ContentLength = 0;
                }
                if (ContentLength>sizeof(InputBuffer)-1) {
                    ContentLength = sizeof(InputBuffer)-1;
                }
                i = 0;
                while (i<ContentLength) {
                    x = fgetc(stdin);
                    if (x==EOF) break;
                    InputBuffer[i++] = x;
                }
                InputBuffer[i] = '\0';
                ContentLength = i;
                p = getenv("CONTENT_TYPE");
                if (p==NULL) {
                    cout << "CONTENT_TYPE is required.\n";
                    return 0;
                }
                if (_stricmp(p,"application/x-www-form-urlencoded")==0) {
                    /* Parse the data */
                    p = strtok(InputBuffer,"&");
                    while (p!=NULL) {
                        DisplayField(p);
                        p = strtok(NULL,"&");
                    }
                    *pData << "\n";
                } else {
                    /* Display the data */
```

```
          fprintf(log,"Input = %s\n",InputBuffer);
      }
  } /* end POST method *.
  else if (_stricmp(pRequestMethod,"GET")==0) {
      /* Parse the data in the search term */
      p = getenv("QUERY_STRING");
      if (p!=NULL) {
          strncpy(InputBuffer,p,sizeof(InputBuffer));
          p = strtok(InputBuffer,"&");
          while (p!=NULL) {
              DisplayField(p);
              p = strtok(NULL,"&");
          }
                  *pData << "\n";
      }
  }
  cout << "Successfully stored form information.<P>\n";
  HTLink ht(argv[2],"Back to calling page.");
  cout << ht.GetAnchor();
  cout << "<P>\n";
  delete pData;
  fclose(log);
  return 0;
}
```

Note that unlike Formshow, FORMSTOR needs to generate its own HTML dynamically.
To do this it uses the HTLink class. Below are the class definitions and C source file for
this class.

HTML.H—The HTLink Class

```
// HTML.H
// class definition for HTML class
#include <stdio.h>
#include <string.h>
#include <stdlib.h>
#include <iostream.h>
#include <strstrea.h>
```

```
#include <fstream.h>
class HTLink {
friend ostream& operator<<(ostream& os,HTLink& ht);
     char szType[8];
     char szServer[32];
     char szFile[128];
     char szPhrase[128];
     char szAnchor[256];
public:
     HTLink(char *szLink,char *szLinkPhrase);
     char *GetAnchor();
     ~HTLink(){}
};
ostream& operator<<(ostream& os,HTLink& ht);
```

HTML.CPP

```
// HTML.CPP
#include "html.h"
ostream& operator<<(ostream& os,HTLink& ht)
{
     return os << ht.GetAnchor();
}
HTLink::HTLink(char *szLink,char *szLinkPhrase)
{
     char *p;
     if (p=strstr(szLink,"://")){
         *p='\0'; // separate out resource type
         strcpy(szType,szLink);
         strcpy(szServer,p+3);
         if (p=strchr(szServer,'/')){
             *p='\0';
             strcpy(szFile,p+1);
         }
         else
             szFile[0]='\0';
     }
```

```
    else {
        strcpy(szType,"http");
        szServer[0]='\0';
        strcpy(szFile,szLink);
    }
    strcpy(szPhrase,szLinkPhrase);
}
char *HTLink::GetAnchor();
{
    strstream os(szAnchor,sizeof szAnchor,ios::out);
    os <<"<A HREF=\"";
    if (szServer[0])
        os << szType << "://" << szServer << "/";
    os << szFile;
    os << "\">" << szPhrase << "</A>";
    os.str();
    szAnchor[os.pcount()]='\0';
    return szAnchor;
}
```

With the combination of FORMSHOW and FORMSTOR, deployed and configured as I have described, you now have an immediately useful Web ordering system. You can then modify the source to use different formats for your product database and your stored orders. The programs are very brief, so you should find it easy to make such changes.

HotJava

A recent entry to the Web technology universe is Sun's HotJava browser. The concept behind HotJava is that you can write small programs (which they call "applets") in the Java language and any Web browser that supports Java will download the applet and run it locally. This idea opens up a whole new area of functionality to the Web. I have shown you that Web content can be static HTML text, images, or multimedia objects; or content created dynamically through the use of gateways. But the user always receives fixed content. Java lets you create applications that utilize the local machine for processing, enabling a new class of Web applications with a much greater degree of interactivity.

For example, in a product catalog database, the product might be shown rotating in three dimensions, and doing that perpetually until the user takes some actions. This is difficult to do with an MPEG video file due to the size of the file that is required, or with a gateway that created the images dynamically because the images have to be downloaded thus losing the desired effect of realtime motion. Further the basic idea of locally-executed programs opens more options because it would allow full knowledge of and participation with the applications running locally on the user's machine.

How to Incorporate Applets

You will first want to get a Java-compliant browser to test your Java-including HTML, such as Sun's own HotJava (available at **http://java.sun.com/installation-alpha2-nt-x86.html**). Netscape has announced Java support so by the time you read this, a Java-supporting Netscape browser may be available on Netscape's site (**http://home.netscape.com**).

To include a Java applet in your program, use the APP tag. Since non-Java supporting browsers will simply ignore this tag, this will allow browsers that don't support Java to still view your content. The APP tag has attributes of CLASS, SRC, ALIGN, IMG, HEIGHT, and WIDTH. The CLASS attribute specifies the name of the applet. The SRC attribute specifies the URL of the directory containing the classes subdirectory which contains the applet (instead of just referring to the compiled applet directly). There's a new resource type known as DOC that specifies the Java app. Instead of trailing the resource type with a colon and two slashes, there is only one slash. The net result is a strange looking URL such as doc://apps/. The ALIGN attribute allows you to specify that the image is lined up with the TOP, MIDDLE, or BOTTOM (the default) of the text following the APP tag. The HEIGHT and WIDTH attributes serve the same purpose as in the IMG tag, to accelerate the browser's page layout while waiting for the image to be downloaded. Other attributes are created on a per applet basis (the applet is written to check for specific attributes). For example, to incorporate the example ImageLoopItem applet that comes with the HotJava distribution, embed the following tag into your HTML:

```
<APP CLASS="ImageLoopItem" SRC="doc:/demo/" IMG="MyCartoon">
```

The ImageLoopItem applet is a particularly useful applet provided with HotJava that you may find uses for. *ImageLoopItem* performs animation by cycling through a sequence of images displayed in the user's browser. It is provided with the HotJava distribution. To incorporate it into your own content, create a series of GIF files, using Lview and other tools presented earlier. Name the successive files T1.GIF, T2.GIF, and so on. Place the GIF files in a subdirectory of the directory where your HTML content is located. Then include the applet in your HTML content with the code shown above.

Writing Java

To write your own Java applets, I'll need to show you a little bit about Java programming. Let's create a simple "Hello, world" app that shows the basic steps. First create a directory called *classes* off of your directory for HTML files. Then create the following simple Java program. Here's the example first program presented on the HotJava site.

```
import browser.Applet;
import awt.Graphics;
class HelloWorld extends Applet {
    public void init() {
        resize(150, 25);
    }
    public void paint(Graphics g) {
        g.drawString(&quot;Hello world!&quot;, 50, 25);
    }
}
```

Save the file as *HelloWorld.java* in the *classes* subdirectory. Then run *javac* (the Java compiler) on the file to compile it. *javac* is in the HotJava\bin directory, which you can place in your PATH or explicitly invoke. Then embed a reference to the Hello, World applet into your HTML.

```
<APP CLASS="HelloWorld">
```

Load the HTML into the HotJava or other Java-supporting browser. You should see the string "Hello, world" appear on the browser page. Of course, to take this much further, you'll need to review the Java language documentation.

Java is in many ways very similar to C++. Java's creators related that they have stayed as close to C++ as possible. In my opinion the major differences between C++ and Java, relevant to the Web applets that Java is a proposed mechanism for, are:

- Java is interpreted, allowing more rapid prototyping, and incremental changes. It also allows Java to be architecture neutral, since the object file format is not machine specific. Finally, and most importantly for the Web, it allows compact, efficient programs to be downloaded to a user's browser and run there.

- Java has intrinsic support for distributed applications, with language support to treat http and ftp resources as natively one would treat files in C++. This is also important for a role as a Web applet language.

- Java supports *interfaces*. In C++ the collection of public member functions to a class is often referred to as an interface, but this is stretching it. An interface is a set of methods that can be supported by any object that advertises support for that interface. The tying of interfaces directly to classes is a notorious problem in C++ and other OOP languages. Microsoft's OLE or COM technology was introduced to respond to this problem. OLE interfaces can be supported by many classes, and many different OLE servers. In fact, some interfaces must be supported by all OLE servers. Java has pushed this technique down to the language level. Interfaces solve other problems with OOP languages, such as version control. Objects can support new interfaces with additional methods, and still support the old interface. In the distributed environment of the Web, Java apps may begin to interface with other Java apps both locally on the user's browser and distributed to other servers. The packaging and interoperability issues solved by supporting true interfaces are significant.

- Java has a higher level of abstraction for handling memory: including automatic garbage collection, and true arrays that can't be given bad indexes, rather than pointers that can be referenced like arrays. This makes Java more robust to programming errors, and easier to program. This level of robustness is important when you are creating programs that are usually written fairly quickly, but that will run on your user's workstation rather than on your server.

SECURITY

Security issues are very important to the potential commercial Web site. Since I assume that many businesses will actually create their own Internet host, this opens the door to a variety of concerns. I have had the luxury of working in my many Web engagements with very knowledgeable security people that handled those issues, and in most cases I installed Web sites on existing Internet hosts, where a security policy was already in place. Since many of you will be bringing up new Internet hosts, a discussion of how to develop your own security policy is relevant. The topic of Internet security in general is not one that I'm comfortable tackling singlehandedly, so I'm enlisting the help of my colleagues, Matt Holmes and Noam Stopak, specialists in Internet security, to write this chapter. If you are creating your own new Internet host, you should be prepared to create your host's security policy by the end of this chapter.

The administrator of a Web site for commerce needs to be more concerned with the security of the http server's Internet host than a non-commercial webmaster. Many of the Web server software products that we presented earlier provided several important security features that go a long way toward making your Web server secure. Nevertheless, for some Web applications and depending on the software you use, relying on the Web server software's security alone may not be sufficient. Also, if you are truly performing electronic commerce via your Web server, you will want to have a more comprehensive understanding of the security issues facing your Internet host in general, and your Web server specifically. If this is the application you have in mind, your Internet host should have a comprehensive security policy defined, and you should deploy the tools necessary to effect that policy. To that end, this chapter will present an overview of Internet and Web server security issues. In particular, it will cover:

- The security threats your Internet Web site faces and how to address them.
- Firewalls and Routers, what they are and what they do.
- General http server security techniques.
- Theories of data encryption and their application to Web security.
- Buying, selling and trading information, how secure http servers work.
- Internet security organizations and standards.

This chapter will help develop, point by point, a sound security policy that the business webmaster may implement to foster a safe and profitable Web site. Each section of the security policy will be presented, addressing typical risks and threats with a policy prescription or security technique. At the end of the chapter, the entire policy will be summarized.

Most of the currently available security material only addresses UNIX-hosted Internet security requirements. Windows-NT products, and related technical material, are now just beginning to emerge, and have yet to identify specific network security problems or tools for Windows NT. We will try to present the material in an architecture-neutral fashion, so that it will be useful to you no matter what platform you choose.

The Internet consists of a large number of computers just like yours connected over a global network. These computers are owned by everyone: business, government(s), educational institutions. The strength of the Internet—its very inter-connectivity—is also unfortunately, its weakness. Computer security is very dependent on the strength of the weakest security link—once a single machine or account is compromised, it is often quite easy to attack other machines or accounts that "trust" the compromised link.

If you do not think that security is not an important issue, consider the following summary of a real attack on the computer systems of a business in New York City (Reported by George Kurtz and Andrew Toner in "Diary of a Tiger Team," *Infosecurity News*, May/June 1995):

1. The attackers program auto-dialing software to probe all telephone numbers in a range known to belong to the business. The software can detect which numbers are connected to modems. The attackers run the software overnight, and one of the probed numbers displays a login banner.

2. The banner identifies the type of computer system found, so the attackers try several "factory default" accounts and passwords. On this system, the default

accounts have been disabled. Next, the attackers try the default account for a data base system, which was successful.

3. The attackers log in, and download the /etc/passwd file (this is a UNIX system), which contains the account names and encrypted passwords for all users of this system. Then, they use a password-cracking program to break the security for several accounts with weak, obvious passwords.

4. One compromised account has created access to the business's customer data base.

Fortunately, this attack was arranged at the request of the business to test its internal computer security. Increasingly, these or similar tools are available and distributed via the Internet, and are available to an ever-widening array of computer hackers. The following short list represents only a small selection of the many online sources of information on monitoring, disrupting or compromising computer systems:

- **ftp://ftp.netcom.com/pub/br/bradleym/virus-source** (Source code listing for viruses).

- **http://www.-personal.engin.umich.edu/~jgotts/underground/hack-faq.html** (One of hundreds of hacker home pages, with tips on hacker culture and pointers to other hacker resources).

- **http://stud1.tuwien.ac.at/~e9125110/satan.html** (Tutorial on attacking your organization to improve its security).

There are legitimate uses for most of the security information and programs available on the Internet. Unfortunately, all of these tools may also be misused by individuals, and increasingly organizations such as criminal syndicates and business competitors, to attack computer sites. There are many general security related home pages available on the Web to address this growing threat. Here are a few starting points:

- **http://www.cis.ohio-state.edu/hypertext/faq/usenet/security-faq/faq.html** (A good general introduction to security issues).

- **http://www.iss.net/faq.html** (Information page with related FAQs on vendor security information and security-related operating system patches).

- **http://www.eecs.nwu.edu/~jmyers/bugtraq/index.html** (Security-related information and bug reports, including a searchable index).

- **http://www.alw.nih.gov/Security/first-papers.html** (List of papers on security and privacy related topics).

Some other sites also interested in aspects of security and privacy include the World Wide Web project at Cern, home of the WWW at **http://www.w3.org/hypertext/ WWW/TheProject**; The Electronic Frontier Foundation at **http://www.eff.org**; and a comprehensive technical reference at the Yahoo page at **http://www.yahoo.com/ Computers_and_Internet/Security_and_Encryption**.

DEVELOP A SECURITY POLICY

As the Table 12.1 shows, current industry security practice is focused primarily on virus prevention. Telephone and network communication security mechanisms are in place at barely half of the surveyed sites. Use of more advanced measures, required to defeat the state-of-the-art in intrusion technology, drops off rapidly.

TABLE 12.1 RANKING OF SECURITY MEASURES USED BY CORPORATIONS.

(FROM "TOP SECURITY THREATS," RUSSELL KAY, *BYTE MAGAZINE*, APRIL 1995)

Security Measure	Used by
Anti-virus software	91%
Dial-back or secure modems	54%
Firewalls	45%
File encryption	36%
PC hardware security devices	33%
Telecommunications encryption	22%
Message authentication encoding	17%

The governing body of the Internet is the Internet Engineering Task Force, the protocol engineering and development arm of the Internet. The IETF is a large open international community of network designers, operators, vendors, and researchers concerned with the evolution of the Internet architecture and the smooth operation of the Internet. It is open to any interested individual" (**http://www.ietf.cnri.reston.va.us/home.html**).

The IETF publishes defacto standards in the form of "Requests For Comments," which are not really requests at all, but rather documents that describe an Internet facility or service. Most of the popular Internet services that are taken for granted started as RFCs (TCP/IP, Telnet, and Simple Mail Transfer Protocol). For example, the paper describing Uniform Resource Locators—URLs like **http://xyz.com/**—is RFC #1650. The Internet as it is today exists because computers, and vendors, and users adhere to these RFCs.

An important RFC published by the IETF that describes the security responsibilities of an Internet site is *RFC 1281 November 1991 Security Guidelines*, which states in part: "Computer and network service providers are responsible for maintaining the security of the systems they operate. They are further responsible for notifying users of their security policies and any changes to these policies..." (see **http://hightop.nrl.navy.mil/docs/criteria/internet.txt**).

Some organizations, such as agencies of the U.S. government, are required by law to adhere to published security standards. Most corporations usually have a security policy—although not necessarily an articulated one. Whether required or not, a strong security policy just makes sense especially for those interested in electronic commerce.

NOTE   Computer security is a very complex and arcane business. This chapter cannot provide a comprehensive or authoritative reference to computer security—that would be the work of a book unto itself. What we try to do is to present enough information to enable the Webmaster to decide what kind of computer security is appropriate for a business http site. We then follow that up with pointers to printed or online reference materials and resources.

This chapter will help a business webmaster develop a security policy appropriate to his or her http site, by using a template. Each section of the chapter will introduce a section of the security policy and cover the technical ground addressed by the policy section.

The first section in the security policy is to define the orientation of the security policy.

Part 1. Security Policy. The security policy covers computer security issues. Current and proposed computer practices are addressed. The orientation of a security policy is either permissive or restrictive. A *permissive* policy addresses mandatory security issues, with issues not covered by the policy implicitly permitted. A *restrictive* policy also addresses mandatory security issues, but issues not covered are expressly prohibited. A valuable adjunct to any security policy is thorough and continuing education.

- Current practice / security survey
- Permissive versus restrictive operation
- Security education

The first step in developing a security policy is to survey current security practice and user expectations. This should cover both hardware and software, all network connections and dial-in modems, processes to manage user accounts, and electronic transfer packages such as electronic mail or file transfer. This includes all of your computers and networks not just those directly attached to the Internet. Any one user with a PPP or SLIP connection to the Internet from an internal node can unknowingly compromise the entire security plan. You should survey physical security policies as well: burglary and attacks from within cannot be ignored. Software programs that provide a communications capability also must be examined, in particular, file transfer packages and electronic mail.

The survey should measure the value of any intellectual property such as publications, databases, and proprietary information that will be at risk now that you are connected to the Internet. Beyond corporate data, an intruder may download or steal licensed or proprietary software installed on your system.

Security risks can never be eliminated only lessened. It is the role of the security policy to delineate and then address these risks. A good rule of thumb is to anticipate attacks in proportion to the perceived value of the assets stored on your system. Some organizations, such as military computer systems, simply attract more and more sophisticated hackers than the average Internet home page. Organizations that possess, maintain, or sell valuable data, such as mailing lists or credit card information, must be particularly alert.

Some general measures that should be covered by the security policy:

- Rights and responsibilities of local computer users.

- Network security policies governing computers on the local or corporate network.

- What corporate information will and will not be made public.

To illustrate the difference between the permissive and restrictive security approach, consider the rights and responsibilities of local computer users. A permissive security policy might address issues such the risk of loading personal files or shareware, and spell out anti-virus measures required before placing files onto computers from diskette. A restrictive policy might entirely forbid personal use of computer systems, or physically remove the floppy disk drives from personal computers. A balance must be established between security needs and the needs of end users.

There is an archive of security policies from various Internet and private sites located at **http://www.eff.org/pub/CAF/policies**. These policies and tools will help you modify the template to suit your unique needs.

Education about security is an ongoing requirement; hackers are not standing still, and new security holes are uncovered every day! See the references at the end of the chapter for several recommended texts, and for a list of security-related Usenet mailing lists that will help keep you up to date.

Internet Services

All Internet servers provide some communications protocols (or services), such as electronic mail, file transfer, and of course WWW information transfer using the http protocol. Each one of these services conveys information into and out of a computer system. Some services allow a user to run commands on the local computer from anywhere on the Internet. Most of the Internet services are bidirectional: they can be used by a local user going out over the network, and by a remote user coming into the local computer.

Most UNIX computers offer dozens of Internet services. This abundance of services is a traditional strength of the Internet from a networking perspective. Unfortunately, this proliferation of services is a weakness from the security viewpoint. Few of UNIX's Internet services were engineered with security as a goal. By contrast, most WindowsNT computers provide a minimum of Internet services—typically only FTP (although other non-Internet services are provided). WindowsNT was designed with security in mind.

Not all of these Internet services will be required for the typical business-oriented Web site. Each service connecting a system to the Internet must be analyzed before an informed decision can be made about its security vulnerability. Questions you should ask are: What does the service do? Is the service really necessary for my Web site? Is the service secure? Can it be made secure? The benefits of electronic mail, providing timely exchange of information between a Web site and its customers, usually outweigh security concerns. Providing an Internet login capability is harder to justify unless your company has many remote users who need access to some internal service.

Essential reading about Internet services can be found in the texts listed in the references at the end of the chapter. Details about security flaws in these services can be found at **http://www.eecs.nwu.edu/~jmyers/bugtraq/search.html**. In addition, information about automated risk analysis tools and security resources used to evaluate the security of various Internet servers can be found at **http://www.first.org/tools/tools.htm**.

Every service installed on your system exposes a potential security weakness. In addition, the very existence of a service that you rely upon opens a channel of attack: A denial of service attack is an attack that attempts to keep your server so busy that it cannot meet the needs of users. For example, a hacker might bombard a Web site with continuous http requests; during the attack legitimate users will experience sluggish or no response from the server. This type of attack can also be a prelude to a more sophisticated attack. By overwhelming a system with requests of a certain type, other security holes in the system can be exposed. An example is hacker Kevin Mitnick's successful attack against Tsutomu Shimomura, a noted Internet expert. For details, see the account at **http://underground.org/newswire/shimomura-attack.html**.

INTERNET SERVICES

The next section in the security policy examines Internet services. As noted above, there are many Internet services. The security policy specifies these services offered by the Web site. The policy must explain the risks and benefits of each service.

Part 2. Internet Services. The Internet offers many services: communications and data protocols that allow computers to exchange data. Most Internet services are not used in http processing, and may be disabled. Consider the risks of providing the following common Internet services:

- Finger
- NFS (Network File System
- Rexec/Rsh/Rlogin
- FTP (inbound, outbound, anonymous)
- Telnet
- SMTP
- WAIS
- http

Finger

Finger allows users to determine the user account status of other users over the Internet. If the user being "fingered" has registered personal information, that is relayed as well. From a security viewpoint, the service leaks valuable information—user account names and personal information. Some versions of the service will list all of the currently active users of a system. Finger can be used to gather account names; later an attacker can attempt to break in by guessing passwords for those accounts.

Risk: MEDIUM.

Business applicability: LOW.

Network File System Service

The NFS service provides the Network File System to share disks or file systems over the Internet. The service is very useful if files need to be shared by users on different host computers on a network. NFS provides security mechanisms that prevent unauthorized computer systems from accessing data. The chief danger posed by NFS is that the shared file systems will be unintentionally exported over the Internet. This can happen due to flaws in the implementation of the service (for example, one vendor's NFS will allow anyone access if the path name of the shared file systems exceeds a certain length).

> **Risk: MEDIUM.**
>
> **Business applicability: LOW.**

Rexec, Rsh, and Rlogin Services

The Rexec, Rsh, and Rlogin services provide a remote command execution and login protocol over the Internet. These commands are very useful for users who have accounts on several networked computers and who must frequently switch between accounts to work—typically at universities and software development companies. The remote command services are a poor security practice, as a penetration of one account can often cascade to all connected machines. While the remote command services can be configured to accept connection only from "trusted hosts," this is difficult to enforce because the *users*—not just the administrators—can also link machines. In addition, the very notion of a trusted host is suspect; if the trusted host is somehow mimicked or compromised, then network security is lost.

> **Risk: HIGH.**
>
> **Business applicability: LOW.**

FTP Service

The FTP service provides the File Transfer Protocol to transmit disk files over the Internet. This very useful service provides for both outbound and inbound transfer. FTP can be configured to provide anonymous transfer as well, to allow remote users without accounts to access a subset of the system. FTP raises some serious security issues. For example, the service allows local users to download software from many sites around the Internet. Often, this downloaded software is used without regard to licensing fees, and is rarely scanned for viruses. Worse, your site may be used to distribute unlicensed copies of software with the attendant liability risks.

Risk: MEDIUM

Business applicability: MEDIUM.

Telnet Service

Before the advent of high-speed local and wide-area networks, users accessed computers from terminals over telephone lines or serial connections. The Telnet service provides telephone network emulation to allow users to "dial up" machines over the Internet. This service is similar to the remote execution commands, but it uses the normal security access controls. In particular, a user cannot easily configure a machine to accept TELNET connections—only an administrator can. The chief security risk posed by TELNET, in the absence of other authentication techniques, is its vulnerability to password attacks.

Risk: HIGH

Business applicability: LOW.

SMTP Service

The SMTP service provides the Simple Mail Transfer Protocol to exchange electronic mail over the Internet. There are two major issues involving the heavily used SMTP service: the possibility of inadvertent or intentional revelation of proprietary or sensitive information, and the historical vulnerability of the service. Electronic mail packages make it simple for a user to send messages and documents to recipients around the world, sometimes by mistake. These messages are routed through many machines in their trip over the Internet. The supervisor of each machine can read the message, and probably the attachment, if desired.

One security vulnerability of the SMTP service for certain UNIX computers was exploited by the Internet Worm, which used flaws in SMTP's software design to gain access to the host computer. The Internet Worm temporarily crippled thousands of machines on the Internet. Privacy concerns can be addressed by encrypting messages and files prior to transmission, while education and training can cut down on the number of improperly addressed messages.

Risk: MEDIUM.

Business applicability: HIGH.

WAIS Service

The WAIS service provides the Wide Area Information Server to support information search and retrieval over the Internet. A site publishes data that may be searched by remote users with WAIS client programs. The WAIS service, used in conjunction with an http server, provides a lookup capability for searching databases over the Internet. Early versions of the WAIS service had security bugs—one version allowed a remote user to download any file on the system just by asking! It is difficult to evaluate the security status of the WAIS service, because it is public-domain software and is not officially supported by vendors.

> **Risk: MEDIUM.**
>
> **Business applicability: LOW-MEDIUM.**

http Service

The http service provides the Hyper-Text Transfer Protocol to exchange Web documents and files over the Internet. The http service's main security risk is through the Common Gateway Interface, which allows the server to run commands on behalf of remote users. These commands must be examined to ensure that they are secure (for example, that the information returned from the command is information that is allowed to be exported under the security policy).

> **Risk: MEDIUM**
>
> **Business applicability: VERY HIGH.**

NOTE Very few Internet services provide an adequate level of event logging, or any real mechanism detecting attacks. The TCP Wrapper software provides an increased level of logging, and some access controls, for the Internet services on UNIXmachines (this software has not yet been ported to Windows-NT, which has its own logging capabilities). This software is available from **ftp://cert.sei.cmu.edu/pub/network_tools/**.

USERS AND ACCOUNTS

The next section in the security policy addresses Users and Accounts. Internet http sites may be divided into two types: those sites that provide services for individual users, and those that do not. This section of the security policy is for those Web sites that differentiate services based upon user accounts.

Part 3. Users and Accounts. If a Web site supports local or remote accounts, care must be taken to ensure that only authorized persons gain access to the system. Each user granted access must understand the basic security policy. In particular, strong password security must be established.

- Account Management—only authorized users are given user accounts
- Strong Passwords—All accounts are protected by hard-to-guess passwords
- User Authentication—remote logins from unprotected networks are authenticated to prevent password-replay attacks

The basic security policy requires that only authorized users of the system have accounts. When a user no longer requires access, for example if he or she leaves the organization, the account should be terminated. Inactive accounts are targets for attackers because their passwords do not change, and because no one notices if the account is used. A related type of account, the system-type accounts created by the installation of vendor-supplied software, should be monitored closely. Some popular programs create user accounts with default names and passwords. Attackers always look for these known accounts, and can access a system using them, unless the name and password has been changed from the default.

A password provides an authentication mechanism, knowing the secret password proves that you are authorized access. All system accounts should be protected by passwords that are difficult to guess. Using good passwords, and changing them often, minimizes the chance of an attacker gaining access by masquerading as an authorized user. A good password is one that is not composed of a common word found in a dictionary, and uses numerals or punctuation (for example, **good4us** is a good password, and one that can be remembered). The use of simple passwords, such as common nouns or personal information like a birth date, must be discouraged. It is very easy for an attacker to mount a *dictionary* attack against weak passwords. The attacker first downloads the system password file; then each password is tested against common words (such as daisy or bamboo) from a dictionary file. A *crack* program that analyzes UNIX password files for vulnerabilities, is widely available (see **http://ciac.llnl.gov/ciac/ToolsUnixAuth.html**), as are utilities that generate "good" passwords.

Unfortunately, using good passwords is not always enough. The account and password are usually transmitted over the Internet without being encrypted and this information passes through many computers and routers in transit. The following output from the Traceroute command, which displays intermediate nodes between a source and destination address on the Internet is typical (network timing statistics were omitted):

```
traceroute to www.sunesis.com (204.156.144.35), 30 hops max, 40
byte packets
 1 gmuroute1.gmu.edu (129.174.40.1)
 2 gmu-cisco.ver.net (129.174.100.2)
 3 virginia-cisco.ver.NET (137.54.220.1)
 4 sura-gw.ver.NET (137.54.201.20)
 5 ctv1-uva-c3mb.sura.net (192.221.3.17)
 6 wtn8-ctv1-c3mb.sura.net (128.167.3.1)
 7 wtn9-wtn8-cf.sura.net (128.167.7.9)
 8 Net99-Mae-East01.net99.net (192.41.177.170)
 9 mae-w-pb-E0-0.SanJose.net99.net (204.157.38.2)
10 mae-west.best.net (198.32.136.36)
11 204.156.144.1 (204.156.144.1)
```

Each site that the network packet passes through may be examined and recorded. Later the attacker can access the system using the recorded user name and password. This type of attack is called a *sniffing attack*, because the technique is derived from the use of a network analyzer commonly called a sniffer. This kind of attack is similar to eavesdropping or tapping a telephone.

Sniffing is one of the most popular forms of attacks used by hackers. One special sniffer, called Esniff.c, is very small, designed to work on SunOS, and only captures the first 300 bytes of all telnet, ftp, and rlogin sessions. Sniffer was published in Phrack, one of the most widely read freely available underground hacking magazines (see **http://freeside.com/phrack.html** and **http://iss.net/iss/sniff.html**).

Such an attack often goes undetected, because it appears as though an authorized user is logging in with a correct password. Sniffing attacks are undetectable, the only defense is to require that network traffic be encrypted when transmitted over the Internet. If sniffing attacks are a concern (you should be concerned any time you allow the exchange of sensitive information over the Internet), stronger methods to authenticate a user are required.

Recent advances in technology have provided secure remote authentication mechanisms. These solutions use specialized hardware and software to generate passwords that are different *every* time the user logs in. A *one-time* password, as these are known, is very secure: it is worthless if it is compromised, because it is never used again. One type of system, S/Key, is a software-based password generator from Bellcore. It is based on a cryptographic algorithm that creates a list of one-time passwords from an initial encryption key. These passwords may be printed and distributed to remote users, or the S/Key software and encryption key can be distributed. Another system, SecureID, relies on a special hardware and cryptographic algorithms to generate a new one time-password every minute. This solution requires synchronization of the clocks on servers and remote smart cards (there are also cards with PIN capability). The Fortezza system uses PCMCIA smart card technology and public key cryptography to equip every user with a digital "certificate" or identity. The Fortezza system also supports on-card encryption. A very different system for user authentication and security, is the Kerberos system developed at MIT. The Sniffer FAQ has a comprehensive listing of strong user authentication systems.

Firewalls: Routers, Gateways and Proxies

A *firewall* is a defensive mechanism to block out unwanted intruders and to prevent the unauthorized disclosure of sensitive information from your Internet site. Firewalls are based on the concept of *defense-in-depth*—layers of security mechanisms, designed to detect and stymie intruders. A firewall works in several ways: by restricting connections or network traffic on certain ports or services by the application of rules (routers and gateways), or by replacing certain services completely with a "hardened" or secure implementation of that service (wrappers and proxy applications). A firewall includes one or more of the following components:

- screening routers
- host-based gateways
- proxy applications

Routers control the flow of information into and out of a system or network, regardless of the Internet service used. Gateways centralize mechanisms for security, access control, and logging. Proxy applications are Internet service programs designed with security in mind. Properly configured, these tools protect a Web site from access by undesired outsiders and prevent the unauthorized export of information from the inside. Improperly configured, the network can become unusable for local accounts, inaccessible for remote accounts, and probably not secure.

Not all Internet web sites need a firewall. A firewall should be considered if there are:

- internal users who need access to the Internet

- multiple machines on the local network, such as SQL for file servers

- special requirements, such as the security of financial data

If your site needs a firewall, please see the references at the end of the chapter for several texts that cover the details of firewall design and construction. These books cover the implementation details required to actually build a firewall, a topic that cannot be covered in a single chapter.

There are two basic types of firewalls. The *restrictive* firewall is configured to block all network services—only those services which are required for operation and that can be secured are then re-enabled. In the *permissive* firewall, the webmaster specifies and secures only those services that constitute a threat to the security of the system. There is a basic tradeoff between the two firewall types. Is the firewall in place to explicitly deny all services except those critical to the mission of connecting to the net, or is the firewall in place to provide a metered and audited method of "queuing" access in a non-threatening manner? There are degrees of paranoia between these positions; the final stance of your firewall may be more the result of a political than an engineering decision (see **http://www.greatcircle.com/firewalls/FAQ**).

Note that the restrictive firewall is considered more fail-safe, since it accepts that the administrator is ignorant of what TCP ports are safe, or what holes may exist in the manufacturers kernel or application. It is an admission of the fact that what you don't know can hurt you (see **http://www.greatcircle.com/firewalls/papers/ranum**).

There is a very active, and fairly technical mail list server for the firewall community. This list also receives crossposting from the major security organizations on the Internet. To subscribe to Firewalls, send **subscribe firewalls** in the body of a message (not on the Subject: line) to **Majordomo@GreatCircle.COM**.

For a sample of the type of messages on the list, see **http://firewalls.nexial.nl/cgi-bin/ firewalls,** a searchable archive. For a list of vendor-related security problems and solutions see the searchable archive **http://www.eecs.nwu.edu/~jmyers/bugtraq/search.html**.

SCREENING ROUTERS

The Web server, and any other internal computers, are connected to a router, which straddles the site's Internet connection. A router is a special computer or hardware device responsible for seeing that packet traffic addressed to the local network is transferred in, and packet traffic addressed to some external network (the Internet) is transferred out. The router is typically provided by an Internet Service Provider; a site may or may not have access to the configuration and setup of the supplied router. If access is permitted, the router may be configured as the first line of defense in a firewall.

The next section in the security policy is Routers.

> **Part 4. Routers**. The Web site's Internet router can be configured to filter network traffic to enhance the local security policy, by controlling the source, destination and data content of network connections.
>
> - Filtering by IP address
> - Filtering by service type
> - Filtering by connection direction

A screening router can be used to implement either of the two firewall security approaches—restrictive or permissive—by allowing or prohibiting Internet packets to pass into or out of the secured network. The router filters packets by applying rules to network traffic. These rules can be based on the IP address of the connecting and accepting addresses, the kind of data in the packet (the protocol or service used), and the direction of traffic flow (towards the Internet, or towards the internal network).

These rules can be combined to permit or eliminate most kinds of packet traffic between designated networks. Only those Internet services flagged in Part 2 of the security policy should be allowed through the router. Because router rules can be very difficult to implement and test, they should be used cautiously.

Some older routers cannot differentiate the physical source of network traffic. With these routers, network traffic from the Internet with a forged internal address cannot be distinguished from valid local traffic. These routers will simply transmit network traffic from the "impossible" location into the local network, without realizing that the traffic really arrived from outside the system. The router has been "spoofed" into accepting external traffic as local traffic and any security filters based on address are now compromised. This attack is made possible by the lack of security engineering in the Internet domain name service and routing protocols. There is a good explanation and reference list for spoofing attacks at **http://www.msen.com/~emv/tubed/spoofing.html**.

More recent routers and routing software can protect a network from "spoofing" attacks, by detecting and comparing the physical line or connection a packet arrives on with the packet's network address. Check with your vendor to determine what type of router is on your system.

Bastion Host and Dual-homed Gateways

The next section in the security policy is Gateways.

> **Part 5. Gateways.** A gateway can be configured to provide security by controlling user access to the resources of the network. A bastion host is a gateway configured as a network choke point; a dual-homed gateway is a more restrictive type of bastion host.
>
> • Bastion host
> • Dual-homed

A *bastion host* is a network firewall that is positioned at the local connection to the Internet. This machine is configured as the central point for the provision of network and Internet services and all remote users accessing the system must connect to this machine. The bastion host's logs must be monitored frequently to ensure that it is not compromised by intruders, and that all security mechanisms are working as planned. A good security package will automate the scanning of log files, and can be configured to send an alarm to the appropriate security personnel when an intruder or attack is detected.

A *dual-homed gateway* is a restrictive bastion host with two network adapters, one connected to the secure, internal network, and one connected to the unsecured, external network (the Internet). The dual-homed gateway is configured so that there is no default routing of network traffic between the two network adapters, and therefore no default routing of traffic between the secure and insecure networks. This "gap" is what makes the dual-homed gateway so secure. Instead of the free and possibly insecure flow of network traffic, proxy applications are configured to pass data between the two networks in a controlled manner.

The *air-gapped* system is the most secure, although it is not really a gateway at all. This type of system maintains an air gap—no physical connection of any kind—between the internal and external networks. Users must use this machine directly or through separate terminals to access the Internet. Most high-security government and military Internet sites use this technique.

PROXY APPLICATIONS

Dual-homed gateways require a specialized application to transfer network traffic from one network to the other for each Internet service supported by the security policy. From the "General Firewalls FAQ": A proxy server (sometimes referred to as an application gateway or forwarder) is an application that mediates traffic between a protected network and the Internet. Proxies are often used instead of router-based traffic controls, to prevent traffic from passing directly between networks. Many proxies contain extra logging or support for user authentication (see **http://www.cis.ohio-state.edu/hypertext/faq/usenet/firewalls-faq/faq.html**).

The next section in the security covers **proxy applications**.

> **Part 6. Proxy Applications.** Most Internet services were not designed for secure operation. Proxy applications, which replace standard services, have been engineered to provide secure Internet access.
>
> - "Access control" wrappers
> - Proxy applications
> - Generic proxies

With dual-homed gateways, a proxy application is installed for each desired protocol or service. The proxy application "connects" the two networks: the internal network and the Internet. For example, if users on the internal network wish to access Web sites on the Internet, an http proxy application must be installed on the dual-homed gateway. All http traffic passes through the proxy application. This gives the proxy an opportunity to decide if the data packets are permitted or not. The proxy application has been specifically engineered with security in mind, so it is more secure than the original Internet service. In addition, the proxy applications do not normally need to run as a privileged user.

For Web sites with internal users, there is an administrative cost to using proxies. Because each user can no longer reach the Internet directly, all access must be performed by proxy. For example, each internal user's HTML browser must be configured to access the proxy server, which will access the Internet on the internal user's behalf. For some types of Internet services, there might not be a specific proxy application available (in which case a custom proxy could be developed, or a generic proxy could be used, or the internal user could log into the gateway machine and use that service locally).

Popular Firewall Products

There are many firewall products available, both commercially and as public domain software. Some of the more popular ones are discussed below. Each product or kit has the URL of the vendor's Internet site, if available, a description, and some editorial comments.

The number of firewall products is growing daily. Table 12.2 shows representatives of the types of products available, but it is not comprehensive and should certainly not be considered an endorsement.

TABLE 12.2 ILLUSTRATIVE FIREWALL PRODUCTS BY TYPE

Vendor	Type	Description/URL
Gauntlet	Dual-Homed Gateway	Commercial and public domain versions of a firewall with application proxies. Supports third party authentication schemes. http://www.tis.com
Interlock	Dual-Homed Gateway	A commercial system that provides internal/external network security. Configurable on user or group level; also provides for multiple administrators.
Drawbridge	Screening Router	Public domain source code for a rules-based screening router. ftp://net.tamu.edu/pub/security/TAMU
Raptor	Dual-Homed Gateway w/Proxies	A nice feature is integrated internal/external network security: reportedly, 85 percent of computer crime is committed by insiders. http://www.raptor.com/prodinfo/ataglance/ataglance.html

Vendor	Type	Description/URL
CyberGuard	Dual-Homed Gateway w/Proxies	The gateway machine is built on a trusted operating system which provides a high degree of confidence. **http://www.hcsc.com/trusted/ cyberguard_bulletin.html**
Border	Dual-Homed Gateway	The gateway machine performs address translation so the internal network is completely hidden from the Internet. **http://www.border.com/contents.html**
Karlbridge	Screening Router	Commercial and public-domain versions of the Karlbridge are available. This PC-based router provides configurable network security and encryption.

See **http://www.greatcircle.com/firewalls/vendors.html**, for a listing of many more firewalls and related products. In addition, there are many public-domain and vendor-supplied programs that will test the security integrity of an Internet site. These include SATAN (Security Analysis Tool for Analyzing Networks), COPS (Computer Oracle and Password System), and ISS (Internet Security Scanner). SATAN bundles many security analysis tools previously available into a convenient package. COPS "examines a system for a number of known weaknesses and alerts the system administrator to them; in some cases it can automatically correct these problems" (see **http://www.first.org/tools// tools.htm**). ISS is a multi-level security scanner that checks a UNIX system for a number of known security holes such as problems with sendmail, improperly configured NFS file sharing, etc.

GENERAL HTTP SERVER SECURITY TECHNIQUES

The http server allows the configuration of some basic parameters that can control the security of the server. These parameters involve: the document directory root, directory access, protection of files by user name, protection of files by Internet address, CGI script execution, logging, and support for http protocol methods. The configuration of the http server will vary considerably from Web site to Web site, but there are a few general rules that will apply to most.

The next section in the security policy is General http Security.

Part 7. General http Security. http servers have parameters that can be configured to increase the security of the host system. These parameters must be evaluated and set as dictated by the security policy.

- Document root(s)
- Directory access
- Weak authentication
- IP filtering
- CGI scripts
- Logging

In addition to the following discussion, there is a general security overview on the WWW home pages at **http://www.w3.org/hypertext/WWW/Security/Overview.html**.

Document root(s)

This feature allows the webmaster to limit http server access only to files located in a particular directory or set of directories. This feature is very useful, as it allows the administrator to place all the HTML files for the server into a set location. If your Web site allows users to publish their own files, ensure that all such "public" information goes into a common area (e.g., /pub/users/name1). That way, you only have to maintain access permissions and monitor the contents of one directory. Use of this feature prevents remote users from stealing any sensitive files on your system.

Directory Access

This feature allows the webmaster to prohibit the http server from direct access to the server file system. The http server can be limited to opening disk files referenced within an HTML document. Or, the http server can have either unlimited or constrained access to the file system, using an access control list mechanism. There are two distinct issues involved:

- Does the http server have direct access to the files on the server?
- If so, which directories and files should be displayed?

If the http server is to be allowed access to the file system, limit the directory access to a subdirectory of the disk. Accidental exposure of other, sensitive documents not located in the subdirectory is then much less likely. Any files that are to be shared or exported can easily be linked or copied into this subdirectory.

Authentication/Password

This feature allows the webmaster to limit http access to selected disk files or directories based on a user account and password. This feature is useful for sites that want to limit access to certain sections or features of the Web site based on user account.

Names and passwords generally are not encrypted when transmitted, and are therefore vulnerable to playback attacks—a sniffing attack can record the name and password, and re-play it at a later time. Rely on this technique only for low-security situations. Some CGI scripts that aid in user authentication are at **http://hoohoo.ncsa.uiuc.edu/docs/tutorials/user.html**. Of course, if you are using the Netscape Commerce server or equivalent, then this feature may be safely used.

IP Filtering

This feature allows the webmaster to limit http access based on the remote user's network address. This feature is very useful—as it permits the webmaster to control access to a directory or file by the IP address of the remote user. When combined with the password protection feature described above, this feature becomes moderately secure.

The filter can be a *permit type*: anyone from a certain range of network addresses may access a file or directory. Or, the filter can be a *deny type*: no one from a range of network addresses can access a file or directory. As a word of caution, *IP spoofing*, asophisticated attack where the attacker pretends to be from a trusted Internet address, will defeat this method of access control. Rely on this technique for low to medium security situations, or on internal networks where spoofing attacks are less likely.

CGI Scripts

Most http servers allow the system administrator to control the permissions the http server has when serving user data or executing CGI programs. This feature is very useful on those systems whose operating systems control access to resources based on user account. Do not allow the http server to run as the administrator or root account. Create a special "WWW" account instead. That way, even if the http server is compromised, access and potential damage is limited to those areas accessible by the WWW user account.

In addition, all CGI scripts should be located in one directory (for example, /usr/local/etc/httpd/cgi-bin). Then restrict access to that directory. This precludes unauthorized changes or the addition of new scripts. In addition, centralization makes it easier to monitor the scripts for change. According to authors of the NCSA httpd server on CGI security: "Any time that a program is interacting with a networked client, there is the possibility of that client attacking the program to gain unauthorized access." Even the most innocent looking script can be very dangerous to the integrity of your system (see **http://hoohoo.ncsa.uiuc.edu/cgi/security.html**).

For example, be certain that CGI scripts do not have side effects, such as changing system security parameters or making copies of sensitive data into public areas.

Logging

Most http servers allow the system administrator to configure the amount and type of information that is logged when the server is processing http requests. These requests include: access logging, transfer logging, and script execution logging.

To be useful, this information should be reviewed periodically for indications of attack, especially access logging, which will record failed password guesses.

Theories of data encryption and their application to Web security

In this section, various cryptographic algorithms, systems, and techniques will be discussed in moderate depth. While this information is theoretical, many of the advanced security techniques for http servers depend on it. The topics covered are:

- symmetric key systems
- public key systems
- digital signatures
- key certificate authorities

Cryptographic algorithms are used everyday for sensitive electronic information. Various governments use cryptosystems to transmit diplomatic and military information. Banks and other financial institutions use cryptosystems to send and receive electronic transactions, including automated-teller transactions. Finally, many readily available electronic mail systems use cryptosystems to protect the privacy of email exchanged by users.

All the proposals to implement secure http servers incorporate one or all of the described crypto-systems.

Cryptographic algorithms are mathematical functions used for *encryption,* hiding a message; and *decryption,* restoring a message. *Plaintext* messages are encrypted using an encryption algorithm to produce *ciphertext.* Modern algorithms use a key which can take one of many values (the more the better) to change the behavior of the algorithm so that performing the encryption algorithm on a given plaintext will produce a different ciphertext for each key value.

Symmetric Key Cryptosystems

In some systems the encryption key and the decryption key are the same, or the keys can both be generated from a common value. These types of algorithms are called *symmetric* algorithms, also known as secret-key algorithms, single-key algorithms, or one-key algorithms. The sender and the receiver must agree upon a key (or a key must be sent via a secure channel) before messages may be exchanged. Note that for this scheme to be usable, the cost of sending the keys in a secure channel must be much less than the cost of sending one or more messages via the same secure channel. The security of a symmetric algorithm is dependent upon the security of the key. Anybody who knows the key can encrypt and decrypt messages using a symmetric algorithm.

One of the most commonly available symmetric key systems is the *Data Encryption Standard.* Developed by IBM and subsequently adopted as a U.S. federal encryption standard in 1976, DES is an iterated block cipher, meaning the algorithm is applied to a chunk of text, in this case 8 byte blocks, and repeated (iterated) a number of times, 16 in the case of DES. DES has held up nicely against attack over the years, but today its 56 bit key length is considered inadequate to protect valuable information against a determined or well equipped adversary. There is a variant of DES, called Triple-DES which, in its most common form, involves encrypting a message with one key, decrypting it with a second key, and then encrypting it once again with the first key. Decrypting is accomplished by decrypting with the first key, encrypting with the second, and finally decrypting with the first one final time. This form is called *DES-EDE* (for DES encrypt-decrypt-encrypt). DES-EDE has a 112-bit key, composed of two independent 56-bit keys and is currently considered safe from brute force attacks.

Public Key Cryptosystems

Public key algorithms operate differently. The encryption key is different from the decryption key, and the decryption key cannot be derived from the encryption key (or at least cannot be derived without a large effort over an extended period of time). Once keys have been generated, the encryption key, also known as the public key, is made available to those the key holder wishes to receive messages from. Often this is accomplished by posting it in a public place or including it in email messages or postings on bulletin boards. A number of key servers are maintained by universities and network providers as a public service.

Anyone can use the public key to encrypt a message to the recipient, who uses his or her private key to decrypt it. According to Philip Zimmerman, author of PGP: "No one but the owner of the private key can decrypt it because nobody else has access to the private key. Not even the person who sent the message can decrypt it."

The RSA public key algorithm, named for its developers (Rivest, Shamir and Adleman) is the defacto public key encryption standard. RSA was introduced in 1978 and, when used with a sufficiently long key length, at least 1024 bits, is thought to be secure from brute force attacks.

RSA public and private keys are calculated from a pair of large (100 to 200 digits at a minimum) prime numbers. It is believed that RSA derives its security from the difficulty of factoring large numbers. RSA is much slower than DES, and is typically used to encrypt symmetric keys which are later used to encrypt the bulk of a message. This technology is also employed in the digital signature applications as discussed in the following section.

Digital Signatures

Data stored electronically is vulnerable to tampering in many ways. Documents or photographs may be altered or completely replaced. Electronic mail return addresses may be forged. Many of the techniques used to determine the authenticity of paper-based documents, such as handwriting or chemical analysis of paper and ink for dating and evidence of tampering, are not applicable.

Digital signatures is an application of public key cryptography that provides a mechanism to address concerns about both the identity of the originator of a message and the integrity of the message. A digital signature is simply a short encoded message appended to a digital document. Unlike a handwritten signature, a digital signature is different for each document because a digital signature is really an encoding of some information derived from the document being signed. The digital signature ensures that 1) the document is known to be from the signer, or someone who knows his or her private key, and 2) it has not been altered. How can we be sure? Let's look a bit more closely at the process.

One-Way Hash Functions

A *one-way hash function* takes an arbitrary sized message and produces a small value, typically 16 or 20 bytes. While a cryptographer will be happy to prove to you that an infinite number of different messages will produce the same hash, in practice it is extremely difficult to produce two messages that have the same hash. This is the mark of a good hash function; that it is not practical to produce a message that hashes to a particular value, or equivalently to produce two messages that generate the same hash value.

Some popular one-way hash functions are MD2, MD4, and MD5 developed by Ron Rivest (see the IETF RFCs 1319, 1320, 1321 respectively). The Secure Hash Algorithm has been proposed by NIST and adopted as a United States Government standard (FIPS 180). The MDx functions produce a 128 bit hash, while SHA produces 160 bits.

Now that you understand a bit about one-way hash functions we can take a look at how digital signatures typically work. A *message digest*, a short block of data produced by running the document through a one-way hash function, is encrypted using the signer's private key. The signer's software computes the message digest, encrypts it using the signer's private key and appends the result to the document. To verify the signature, the recipient's software also computes the message digest. The encrypted digest from the sender is decrypted by the recipient using the sender's public key. The two message digests are then compared. If they are equal the recipient knows that the message was produced by the signer and has not been altered during transmission. The importance of the security of the one-way hash function used is now clear: if we were capable of producing another message with the same hash we could replace the signed document with our own message.

Public Key Repositories X.509/PKCS

Public key cryptography depends heavily upon the ability to trust the other party's public key. Keys are trusted when vouched for by some authority that the user trusts. The difficulty lies in finding authorities that can be trusted by all the systems involved. In everyday life, the government or a large institution such as a bank acts as the authority. In the electronic world all transactions are faceless; therefore a more elaborate, and secure, mechanism must be devised.

Public key and certificate exchange is governed by the ISO X.509 protocol and PKCS (Public Key Cryptography Standards). These standards and conventions are widely recognized, mostly because the ability to exchange certificate and encryption key information is very important to secure data exchange on the Internet.

A certificate is issued by a trusted party known as a *Certification Authority* or *CA*. CA's are certified by higher level CA's on up a chain with the highest level being the Internet PCA Registration Authority (IPRA). The IPRA certifies *Policy Certificate Authorities (PCA's)* who certify CAs which may certify other CAs. The idea is that signature certificates may be verified by following up the certificate chain until a common trusted link in the chain is found. If the signature is valid, and the signing key is certified by a CA that the recipient trusts then they can be sure of the origin and integrity of the message. If the message was encrypted, and the recipient's private key has not been compromised, then they can be reasonably sure that the privacy of the message was maintained in transit.

Buying and Selling: How Secure HTTP Servers Work

Secure http servers use the public/private key cryptology techniques discussed above to provide:

- **Data encryption services.** A unique session key is used to encrypt the "secure" HTML page or form before it is transmitted over the Internet.
- **Server authentication services.** The user can inspect the server's digitally signed certificate and be certain that the server is legitimate.

The secure http server encrypts data exchanged with users over the Internet. Anyone eavesdropping on this exchange would record only the encrypted network traffic. Decrypting this traffic is a very difficult task. Because the data is secure, high value information such as credit card numbers or proprietary information can be exchanged safely. Also, FORMS-based authentication techniques, such as requesting a name and password, can be safely used to control access, without fear of a captured password.

ADVANCED HTTP SECURITY

> **Part 8. Advanced http Security.** Some http servers may be configured to provide transaction security. To do so, the server must be registered with a key management service, and secure forms must be designed. In addition, the impact of import/export restrictions must be evaluated.
>
> • Netscape SSL
> • Secure http
> • Certification

The two major secure servers available today are the Netscape Commerce Server and EIT's Secure http Server. These two servers use a modified variant of the standard http protocol to achieve security. Each requires a specialized browser (NCSA Mosaic or Netscape Navigator) to participate in a secure conversation with the server. Currently, not all browsers and servers are interoperable, but it is likely that this issue will be resolved in the near term.

NOTE   The U.S. Government currently considers encryption technology a controlled item for export purposes. Essentially, this means that, for international commerce, a weaker version of the encryption software (key length less than 41 bits) must be used. For domestic commerce, there are no such restrictions.

Netscape Commerce Server (Secure Socket Layer)

The Netscape SSL (**http://www.mcom.com/newsref/ref/netscape-security.html**) uses the public key techniques discussed above to provide security. This includes both encryption and authentication services to provide a secure transaction. Whenever the Netscape (or SSL-compatible) browser decodes a URL with the https method, the following dialog with the server occurs:

1. The browser downloads the server's certificate and public key. The certificate is examined for authenticity using the Certificate Authority keys embedded in the browser.

2. The client generates unique session keys. The session keys are encrypted using the server's public key and sent to the server, along with a message.

3. The server decrypts the session keys with its private key. It then encrypts the message from the client with the session keys and sends it back.

4. The client verifies that the message from the server was encrypted using the session keys that it itself generated. The server is now authenticated, because the session keys could only have been decrypted by the server (refer to the section on public key cryptography above).

5. All data transmitted via the secure URL is encrypted with the unique session keys, and transmitted in encrypted format.

Implementations of SSL, for incorporation into existing programs, is available from both Netscape and the public domain. Because the security features are provided at the transport level, most third-party applications will not have to be changed to utilize them.

Netscape has announced that *interoperability* (the capability for a browser from one company to operate securely with a server from another company) will be supported for existing and future browsers.

The Netscape Navigator includes embedded Certificate Authority (CA) keys for certain CAs, including our test CAs. As new CAs come online, Netscape Corporation will embed their keys as well. These embedded keys allow the Netscape Navigator to verify the legitimacy of arbitrary servers. (For more information see **http://www.mcom.com/newsref/ref/netscape-security.html**).

Because both the Netscape Commerce Server and the NCSA Secure-http server use the same key certification technology (PKCS) and encryption techniques, interoperability is possible.

There is an Internet mailing list for SSL, whose purpose is to "discuss [the] secure sockets layer—Netscape's (and, increasingly, others') approach to providing encryption and authentication for IP-based services." See **http://www.iss.net/iss/maillist.html** for details on how to subscribe.

Secure http

Secure http provides for the secure transmission of data, as well as authentication of end users and servers. In addition, Secure http provides for the "non-reputability" of messages. This means that if you purchase something, the protocol precludes you from denying that fact later. Secure http is an application-layer protocol, which means that programs - and programmers - must be aware of its details to use the protocol successfully. See **http://www.eit.com/creations/s-http/** for more information and technical details.

There is an Internet mailing list for Secure http, whose purpose is to "allow people who are interested in potentially using Shttp to ask questions, air issues, express concerns and discuss the specification and reference implementation." See **http://www.iss.net/iss/maillist.html** for details on how to subscribe.

STANDARDS THAT WORK TOGETHER

Compatibility of security standards is a major issue for Web Internet sites. There is an IETF working group on security addressing this issue at **http://www-ns.rutgers.edu/www-security/wts-wg.html**. Because a uniform security standard has not been adopted by the IETF or the WWW project staff, many software vendors are incorporating both existing security methods in their own http servers and Web browsers. A consortium of leading Internet http vendors has formed, and a tool-kit to aid in this integration has been announced. The first product of the newly organized Terisa is a version of Terisa's SecureWeb(TM) toolkit that combines Secure http (HyperText Transfer Protocol) from EIT and SSL (Secure Sockets Layer) from Netscape, the two leading transaction security protocols on the market today, into a single development package (for more information see **http://www.terisa.com/pr/sept.html**).

Server Certification

To enable the advanced security features of a secure http server, a key certificate that vouches for the authenticity of the server's public key must be obtained. The procedures for obtaining the certificate are similar for both of the major secure http servers currently available (the Netscape Commerce Server and the Secure-HTTP server).

First, a *distinguished name,* one that uniquely identifies the server, is devised. CommerceNet, a certification authority for S-HTTP, uses this definition of a distinguished name

A Distinguished Name (DN) is a collection of attributes that assign a unique means of identification to an entity, in this case a secure server operated by your company. The DN for a server consists of the following attributes: Server URL, Organizational Unit, Organization, Country where the server resides.

Other information supporting the legal identity of the server is gathered, such as incorporation papers, name of the webmaster, and so on. RSA Data Security, the certification authority for Netscape, requires this information for certificates:

1. Identity the webmaster(s) of your organization.
2. State the formal name of your organization.
3. Present "proof of right to use" the proposed name contained in the Organization field of the Server Name request form (see **http://www.rsa.com/netscape/ letter.htm**).

Next, a public/private key pair for the server is generated, using the HTML browser supplied by the secure server vendor. The key pair and the supporting information are sent to a key certification authority. The certification authority verifies the information and creates a digitally signed certificate. Finally, the certificate is loaded into the http server. Secure forms can now be accessed by constructing a special URL using a secure "method" (for example, https://www.yourorg.com/secure.html); any browser that recognizes and trusts the certificate embedded in the server can access the form safely.

CONCLUSION

Internet security ia a very technical and complex subject. We have presented some of the major issues and problems touching on the business of running a Web site for commerce, such as protecting your computer networks and providing secure transactions. While doing so, we have ignored major topics in security, such as physical security, non-http data encryption, and many thorny legal issues. Finally, although we have provided pointers to the many security resources available today, we must point out that, ultimately, security is your business. Start your security plan today!

SECURITY POLICY DOCUMENT TEMPLATE

The security template can be used in conjuction with the resources and information presented in this chapter as a check list to help you derive and implement a security policy for your Web site.

Part 1. Security Policy. The security policy covers computer security issues. Current and proposed computer practices are addressed. The orientation of the security policy is either permissive or restrictive. A *permissive* policy addresses mandatory security issues, with issues not covered by the policy implicity permitted. A *restrictive* policy also addresses mandatory security issues, but issues not covered are expressly prohibited. The best security policy is thorough and continuing security education.

- Current practice
- Security survey
- Permissive/Restrictive operation
- Education

Part 2. Internet Services. The Internet offers many hundreds of services: communications and data protocols that allow computers to interchange data. Most Internet services are not used in http processing, and may safely be disabled. Consider providing the following common and useful services:

- Finger/Whois
- NFS
- Rexec/Rsh/Rlogin
- FTP (inbound, outbound, anonymous)
- Telnet
- SMTP
- WAIS
- http

Part 3. Users and Accounts. If a Web site supports local or remote accounts, care must be taken to ensure that only authorized persons gain access to the system. Each user granted access must understand the basic security policy. In particular, string password security must be established.

- Account Management
- Passwords
- Strong Authentication

Part 4. Routers. The Web site's Internet router can be configured to filter network traffic to enhance the local security policy, by controlling the source, destination and data content of network connections.

- Filtering by IP address
- Filtering by service type
- Filtering by connection direction

Part 5. Gateways. A gateway can be configured to provide security by controlling user access to the resources of the network. A bastion host is a gateway configured as a network choke point; a dual-homed gateway is a more restrictive type of gateway.

- Bastion host
- Dual-homed

Part 6. Proxy Applications. Most Internet services were not designed for secure operation. Proxy applications, which replace standard services, have been engineered to provide secure Internet access.

- "Access control" wrappers
- Proxy applications
- Generic proxies

Part 7. General http Security. HTTP servers have parameters that can be configured to increase the security of the host system. These parameters must be evaluated and set as dictated by the security policy.

- Document root(s)
- Directory access
- Weak authentication
- IP filtering
- CGI scripts
- Logging

Part 8. Advanced http Security. Some http servers may be configured to provide transaction security. To do so, the server must be registered with a key management service, and secure forms must be designed. In addition, the impact of import/export restrictions must be evaluated.

- Certification
- Secure FORMS

INTERNET SECURITY ORGANIZATIONS AND RESOURCES

The Computer Emergency Response Team

The CERT home page and FAQ (**http://www.sei.cmu.edu/SEI/programs/cert/ CERT.info.html**) "...was formed by the Defense Advanced Research Projects Agency (DARPA) in November 1988 in response to the needs exhibited during the Internet worm incident. The CERT charter is to work with the Internet community to facilitate its response to computer security events involving Internet hosts, to take proactive steps to raise the community's awareness of computer security issues, and to conduct research targeted at improving the security of existing systems."

Computer Incident Advisory Capability.

From the CIAC home page **http://ciac.llnl.gov/**: "CIAC is the U.S. Department of Energy's Computer Incident Advisory Capability. Established in 1989, CIAC provides computer security services to employees and contractors of the Department of Energy,..."

FIRST

FIRST maintains an impressive list of documents at **http://www.alw.nih.gov/ Security/first-papers.html** including some papers focusing on the cultural and legal implications of computer usage and security.

CommerceNet

CommerceNet is an organization dedicated to providing a secure venue on the Internet for electronic commerce. The security guide **http://www.commerce.net/cgi-bin/textit?/information/services/security.html**

"There are many different components to Internet security. Message (e.g., transaction), network, and host security are all vital if an organization is to transact business on the Internet. The Network Services Working Group has put together several documents which describe CommerceNet's perspective on transaction and Internet network security. Many CommerceNet members also provide message and/or network security solutions, and they are listed in the Security Contacts document."

Mailing Lists

There are many security-related Internet mailing lists. The following (with directions on how to subscribe) are taken from the Security Mailing Lists FAQ developed by Chris Klaus at **http://www.iss.net/iss/maillist.html**:

Eight Little Green Men. Group of hackers that periodically post scripts to exploit various UNIX bugs.

Best of Security. Fast-breaking computer security news.

Bugtraq. This list is for *detailed* discussions of UNIX security holes; what they are, how to exploit, and what to do to fix them.

Computer Underground Digest. Issues of the computer underground (also Usenet Netnews as **comp.security.cu-digest**).

Cypherpunks. The cypherpunks list is a forum for discussing personal defenses for privacy in the digital domain.

Firewalls. Useful information regarding firewalls and how to implement them for security.

Intruder Detection Systems. The list is a forum for discussions on topics related to development of intrusion detection systems.

Phrack. A hacker magazine which deals with phreaking and hacking.

Sneakers. The Sneakers mailing list is for discussion of LEGAL evaluations and experiments in testing various Internet "firewalls" and other TCP/IP network security products.

Virus. An electronic mail discussion forum for sharing information and ideas about computer viruses, which is also distributed via the Usenet Netnews as **comp.virus**.

URLs

CHAPTER 1

Web Home   http://www.w3.org/hypertext/WWW/
                         Consortium/Prospectus/

CHAPTER 2

Web Indexes

W3 Consortium   http://www.w3.org

Web Registry   http://www.w3.org/hypertext/DataSources/
                            WWW/Servers.html

WWW Virtual Library   http://www.w3.org/hypertext/DataSources/
                            bySubject/Overview.html

*NCSA Mosaic What's New   http://www.ncsa.uiuc.edu/SDG/Software/Mosaic/
and Starting Points Pages* Docs/whats-new.html

                            http://www.ncsa.uiuc.edu/SDG/Software/Mosaic/
                            StartingPoints/NetworkStartingPoints.html

Yahoo	http://www.yahoo.com
Open Market's Commercial Sites Index	http://www.directory.net/
EINet Galaxy	http://www.einet.net/galaxy.html
CUI W3 Catalog	http://cuiwww.unige.ch/w3catalog
World Wide Web Worm	http://www.cs.colorado.edu/home/mcbryan/ WWWW.html
Lycos	http://lycos.cs.cmu.edu/
Harvest	http://harvest.cs.colorado.edu/brokers/ www-home-pages/query.html
Web Crawler	http://webcrawler.com
Architext's Excite	http://www.excite.com

News and Information

San Jose Mercury News	http://www.sjmercury.com/
PCWeek	http://www.ziff.com/~pcweek/Welcome.html
PC Magazine	http://www.ziff.com/~pcmag/
HotWired	http://www.hotwired.com

Search Services

Table-of-Contents, Inc.	http://www.mag-browse.com/
Dow Vision WAIS Interface	http://dowvision.wais.net

Quote.Com	http://www.quote.com

Businesses on the Web

Finance

Aufhauser WealthWEB	http://www.aufhauser.com

Software

The Internet Software Store	http://software.net

Music

Sound Wire	http://soundwire.com/

Books

O'Reilly's Online Bookstore	http://www.ora.com/gnn/bus/ora/catalog/index.html

Food and Drink

Wine: Virtual Vineyards	http://virtualvin.com
Pizza Hut	http://www.pizzahut.com
Waiters on Wheels	http://www.sunnyside.com

Web Malls

NetMarket	http://www.netmarket.com
Internet Shopping Network	http://shop.internet.net/
Open Market	http://www.openmarket.com
CyberMalls	http://www.hardiman.com/malls/rmcm/#directory

CHAPTER 3

Content and Style Guidelines for Web Server Authoring

NCSA's listing of online Web style guides	http://union.ncsa.uiuc.edu:80/HyperNews/ get/www/html/guides.html
Tim Berners-Lee's "Style Guide for Online Hypertext"	http://info.cern.ch/hypertext/WWW/Provider/ Style/Overview.html
Yale C/AIM WWW Style Manual	http://info.med.yale.edu/caim/ StyleManual_Top.HTML
CERN Guide	http://info.cern.ch/hypertext/WWW/Provider/ Style/Introduction.html

CHAPTER 4

Background on HyperText Markup Language (HTML)

NCSA's "A Beginner's Guide to HTML"	http://www.ncsa.uiuc.edu/General/Internet/ WWW/HTMLPrimer.html
"HTML Documents: A Mosaic Tutorial"	http://fire.clarkson.edu/doc/html/htut.html
"The HTML Specification"	http://www.w3.org/hypertext/WWW/ MarkUp/MarkUp.html
"Web Etiquette"	http://www.w3.org/hypertext/WWW/Provider/ Etiquette.htm

CHAPTER 5

Forms Searching

ISINDEX Tag
http://www.utirc.utoronto.ca/HTMLdocs/
NewHTML/server-isindex.html

Clickable Image Maps and Image Processing

References for Image Maps

Graphical Information Map Tutorial
http://wintermute.ncsa.uiuc.edu:8080/
map-tutorial/image-maps.html

CERN Server Clickable Image Support
http://www.w3.org/hypertext/WWW/Daemon/
User/CGI/HTImageDoc.html

Information for Imagemaps
http://blake.oit.unc.edu/~duncan/mapex.html

Methods for Creating Style Sheets

Robert Raisch's style
sheet proposal
http://gummo.stanford.edu/html/hypermail/
.www-talk-1993q2.messages/443.html

ISO Document Style and Semantics
Specification Language (DSSSL)
http://www.falch.no/~pepper/DSSSL-Lite/

HTML+ (Hypertext
Markup Format)
http://www.w3.org/hypertext/WWW/
MarkUp/HTMLPlus/htmlplus_1.html

HTML 3.0 Specification
http://www.hpl.hp.co.uk/people/dsr/html3/
Contents.html

Netscape Extensions

Netscape's HTML 2.0 Extensions   http://home.mcom.com/assist/net_sites/
html_extensions.html

HTML Page Design   http://ncdesign.kyushu-id.ac.jp/howto/text/
html_design.html

Frame Basics   http://home.mcom.com/assist/net_sites/
frame_syntax.html

VRML (Virtual Reality Modeling Language)

Web Space from SGI   http://www.sgi.com/Products/WebFORCE/
WebSpace/

References on VRML   http://www.w3.org/hypertext/WWW/MarkUp/
VRML/

CHAPTER 6

Tools for HTML Creation

SoftQuad HoTMetaL   http://www.sq.com

HTML Writer   http://lal.cs.byu.edu/people/nosack/get_copy.html

HTMLed   ftp://tenb.mta.ca/pub/HTMLed/

HTML HyperEdit   ftp://info.curtin.edu.au/pub/internet/windows/
hyperedit/htmledit.zip

Sausage Software   http://www.sausage.com

Image Maps

MapEdit   http://sunsite.unc.edu/boutell/mapedit/
                                             mapedit.html

CHAPTER 7

HTML Converters: Creating HTML from Existing Sources

Microsoft Word Word   http://www.microsoft.com
Internet Assistant

ANT HTML   Jswift@freenet.fsu.edu

QuarterDeck's WebAuthor   http://www.qdeck.com

Information Analytics, Inc.   http://www.infoanalytic.com/webbldr/index.html
Web Builder

Image Conversion Tools

Lview   http://mirror.wwa.com/mirror/busdir/lview/
                                             lview.htm

Image Libraries

Daniel's Icon Archive   http://www.jsc.nasa.gov/~mccoy/Icons/index.html

The Bitmap Vault   http://www.cs.uwm.edu:2010/

W3 Org Icon Collection   http://www.w3.org/hypertext/WWW/Icons

Images, Icons, and Sounds   http://melmac.corp.harris.com/images.html

Yahoo: Computers: World
Wide Web: Programming: Icons

http://www.yahoo.com/Computers/
World_Wide_Web/Programming/Icons/

Chapter 8

Internet Access Providers

http://www.yahoo.com/Business_and_Economy/
Companies/Internet_Access_Providers

T1 channel service

http://www.kentrox.com/tserv.html

Mail Servers

NT Mail from Internet Shopper

http://www.net-shopper.co.uk/

http://www.net-shopper.co.uk/software/
ntmail/key.htm

Secure Payment Methods

CyberCash

http://www.cybercash.com

First Virtual

http://www.fv.com

PGP Software

ftp://ftp.csn.net/mpj/README.MPJ

Chapter 9

Web Server Software

HTTPS for Windows NT

http://emwac.ed.ac.uk

Purveyor WebServer for
Windows NT, Version 1.1

http://www.process.com

WebSite	http://website.ora.com
Netscape Communications' *Netscape Commerce and* *Communications Servers* *for Windows NT*	http://home.netscape.com/comprod/ netscape_commerce.html
Security keys	http://www.verisign.com/netscape/naming/ index.html

CHAPTER 10

Gateways: Converting Information to HTML On Demand

EMWAC's WAIS Toolkit *for Windows NT*	http://emwac.ed.ac.uk
WWWAIS	http://www.eit.com/software/wwwwais/
freeWAIS	ftp://ftp.cnidr.org/pub/NIDR.tools/freeWAIS/ freeWAIS-0.202.tar.Z
"Mosaic and WAIS Tutorial"	http://wintermute.ncsa.uiuc.edu:8080/ wais-tutorial/wais.html
SWISH (Simple Web *Indexing System for Humans)*	http://www.eit.com/software/swish/swish.html
CNIDR Isite	http://vinca.cnidr.org/software/Isite/Isite.html
WebDBC	http://www.ndev.com
GSQL	http://www.ncsa.uiuc.edu/SDG/People/jason/ pub/gsql/proc-fmt.html

	http://base.ncsa.uiuc.edu:1234/gsqlsrc/gsql.tar
	http://www.ncsa.uiuc.edu/SDG/People/jason/pub/ gsql/starthere.html
Nomad Development Corporation	http://www.ndev.com

Searching Databases

http://www2.ncsu.edu/bac/people/faculty/ walker/hotlist.html

Yahoo Web Directory, Computers: World Wide Web: Gateways

http://www.yahoo.com/Computers/ World_Wide_Web/Gateways/

Notes and gateways

FormGate　　　　　http://www.mpi-sb.mpg.de/~brahm/formgate.html

CHAPTER 11

CGI Standard

http://hoohoo.ncsa.uiuc.edu/cgi/interface.html
http://hoohoo.ncsa.uiuc.edu/cgi/overview.html.
http://hoohoo.ncsa.uiuc.edu/cgi/intro.html
http://www.charm.net/~web/Tutorial/CGI

Perl

CGI Form Handling　　　http://www.bio.cam.ac.uk/web/form.html

Creating HTML forms　　http://www-genome.wi.mit.edu/ftp/pub/ software/WWW/cgi_docs.html

CGI scripting

libwww-perl   http://www.ics.uci.edu/pub/websoft/libwww-perl/

PERLLib   http://iamwww.unibe.ch/~scg/Src/PerlLib/

Perl Programs

Earl Hood's htmltoc   http://www.oac.uci.edu/indiv/ehood/
                               htmltoc.doc.html

WebXref   http://www.sara.nl/Rick.Jansen

WebLint   ftp://ftp.khoral.com/pub/perl/www/weblint.tar.gz

Perl CGI References

"Beyond Hypertext: Using the   http://www.scu.edu.au/ausweb95/papers/
WWW for Interactive Applications" hypertext/gleeson/

"Programming Perl"   http://gnn.com/gnn/bus/ora/catalog/
                               pperl.desc.html

"Learning Perl"   http://gnn.com/gnn/bus/ora/catalog/lperl.html

"CGI Form Programming in Perl" http://www.bio.cam.ac.uk/web/form.html

"Forms in Perl"   http://www.seas.upenn.edu/~mengwong/forms/

"perlWWW"   http://www.oac.uci.edu/indiv/ehood/perlWWW/

"Web Developer's Virtual Library" http://WWW.Stars.com/Vlib/Providers/CGI.html

Gateway Programming in C and C++

NCSA CGI Archive: Query and Post-query	ftp://ftp.ncsa.uiuc.edu/Web/httpd/Unix/ncsa_httpd/cgi/

Incorporating Applets with Java

HotJava	http://java.sun.com/installation-alpha2-nt-x86.html
Netscape Java Support	http://home.netscape.com

Chapter 12

General Information: Security Issues	http://www.cis.ohio-state.edu/hypertext/faq/usenet/security-faq/faq.html
	http://www.iss.net.html
	http://www.eecs.nwu.edu/~jmyers/bugtraq/index.html
	http://www.alw.nih.gov/Security/first-papers.html
Electronic Frontier Foundation	http://www.eff.net
Comprehensive technical reference at the Yahoo page	http://www.yahoo.com/Science/Mathematics/Security_and_Encryption
Internet Engineering Task Force (IETF)	http://www.ietf.cnri.reston.va.us/home.html
RFC 1281 November 1991 Security Guidelines	http://hightop.nrl.navy.mil/docs/criteria/internet.txt
Archive of security policies from various Internet and private sites	http://www.eff.org/pub/CAF/policies

Details about security flaws in Internet services	http://www.eecs.nwu.edu/~jmyers/bugtraq/search.html
UNIX host and network security tools	http://www.first.org/tools/tools.htm
Hacker attacks	http://underground.org/newswire/shimomura-attack.html
Source code listing for viruses	ftp://ftp.netcom.com/pub/br/bradleym/virus-source
Tips on hacker culture and pointers to other hacker resources	http://www.-personal.engin.umich.edu/~jgotts/underground/hack-faq.html
Tutorial on attacking your organization to improve its security	http://stud1.tuwien.ac.at/~e9125110/satan.html

Software

http Service	ftp://cert.sei.cmu.edu/pub/network_tools/
Crack programs	http://ciac.llnl.gov/ciac/ToolsUnixAuth.html
Sniffer	http://iss.net/iss/sniff.html

Firewalls

http://firewalls.nexial.nl/cgi-bin/firewalls

http://www.eecs.nwu.edu/~jmyers/bugtraq/search.html.

http://www.greatcircle.com/firewalls/FAQ

http://www.greatcircle.com/firewalls/papers/ranum

Firewalls

To subscribe to the online newsletter Firewalls send email to **Majordomo@GreatCircle.COM**

Screening Routers	http://www.msen.com/~emv/tubed/spoofing.html
Proxy Applications	http://www.cis.ohio-state.edu/hypertext/faq/usenet/firewalls-faq/faq.html
Firewall products	http://www.greatcircle.com/firewalls/vendors.html
Gauntlet	http://www.tis.com
Drawbridge	ftp://net.tamu.edu/pub/security/TAMU
Raptor	http://www.raptor.com/prodinfo/ataglance/ataglance.html
CyberGuard	http://www.hcsc.com/trusted/cyberguard_bulletin.html
Border	http://www.border.com/contents.html
Karlbridge	http://www.greatcircle.com/firewalls/vendors.html
COPS	http://www.first.org/tools//tools.htm
General http Server Security Techniques	http://www.w3.org/hypertext/WWW/Security/Overview.html
User authentication scripts	http://hoohoo.ncsa.uiuc.edu/docs/tutorials/user.html
	http://hoohoo.ncsa.uiuc.edu/cgi/security.html
Public key encryption	
Netscape SSL	http://www.mcom.com/newsref/ref/netscape-security.html
	http://www.iss.net/iss/maillist.html

Secure http

http://www.eit.com/creations/s-http/

http://www.iss.net/iss/maillist.html

Standards

IETF working group on security addresses

http://www-ns.rutgers.edu/www-security/wts-wg.html

Terisa's SecureWe b(TM)

http://www.terisa.com/pr/sept.html

Information on Distinguished Names (DN)

http://www.rsa.com/netscape/letter.htm

https://www.yourorg.com/secure.html

HTML 2.0 SPECIFICATION

The following is sections 5 (document structure) through 8 (forms) of the latest Internet Draft of the HTML 2.0 specification, posted by Tim Berners-Lee to the W3 Consortium on September 22, 1995 (**http://www.w3.org/hypertext/WWW/MarkUp/ html-spec/html-spec.txt**).

Of all of the HTML references out there, this gives the closest approximation to a "standard" for HTML. As indicated in the earlier chapters on HTML, there is some divergence between HTML 3.0 and proprietary extensions such as Netscape's. HTML 2.0 is a minimum standard to which everyone currently claims adherence. If you remain within HTML 2.0, you HTML will be accepted almost universally. If you choose not to, you should at least be aware of the consequences of that decision. Though we attempted to cover what the HTML 2.0 implies in the chapters on HTML, Sections 5 through 8 of the specification should give you a more official reference to what that standard is.

[Sections 5 through 8 of HTML 2.0 Specification posted 9/22/95 to W3C by
Tim Berners-Lee]

Hypertext Markup Language - 2.0

5. Document Structure

An HTML document is a tree of elements, including a head and
body, headings, paragraphs, lists, etc. Form elements are
discussed in 8, "Forms".

5.1. Document Element: HTML

The HTML document element consists of a head and a body, much
like a memo or a mail message. The head contains the title and
optional elements. The body is a text flow consisting of
paragraphs, lists, and other elements.

5.2. Head: HEAD

The head of an HTML document is an unordered collection of
information about the document. For example:

```
<!DOCTYPE HTML PUBLIC "-//IETF//DTD HTML 2.0//EN">
<HEAD>
<TITLE>Introduction to HTML</TITLE>
</HEAD>
...
```

5.2.1. Title: TITLE

Every HTML document must contain a <TITLE> element.

The title should identify the contents of the document in a
global context. A short title, such as ``Introduction'' may be
meaningless out of context. A title such as ``Introduction to
HTML Elements'' is more appropriate.

NOTE - The length of a title is not limited; however,
long titles may be truncated in some applications. To
minimize this possibility, titles should be fewer than
64 characters.

A user agent may display the title of a document in a history list or as a label for the window displaying the document. This differs from headings (5.4, "Headings: H1 ... H6"), which are typically displayed within the body text flow.

5.2.2. Base Address: BASE

The optional <BASE> element provides a base address for interpreting relative URLs when the document is read out of context (see 7, "Hyperlinks"). The value of the HREF attribute must be an absolute URI.

5.2.3. Keyword Index: ISINDEX

The <ISINDEX> element indicates that the user agent should allow the user to search an index by giving keywords. See 7.5, "Queries and Indexes" for details.

5.2.4. Link: LINK

The <LINK> element represents a hyperlink (see 7, "Hyperlinks"). Any number of LINK elements may occur in the <HEAD> element of an HTML document. It has the same attributes as the <A> element (see 5.7.3, "Anchor: A").

The <LINK> element is typically used to indicate authorship, related indexes and glossaries, older or more recent versions, document hierarchy, associated resources such as style sheets, etc.

5.2.5. Associated Meta-information: META

The <META> element is an extensible container for use in identifying specialized document meta-information. Meta-information has two main functions:

* to provide a means to discover that the data set exists and how it might be obtained or accessed; and

* to document the content, quality, and features of a data

set, indicating its fitness for use.

Each <META> element specifies a name/value pair. If multiple META elements are provided with the same name, their combined contents—concatenated as a comma-separated list—is the value associated with that name.

> NOTE - The <META> element should not be used where a specific element, such as <TITLE>, would be more appropriate. Rather than a <META> element with a URI as the value of the CONTENT attribute, use a <LINK> element.

HTTP servers may read the content of the document <HEAD> to generate header fields corresponding to any elements defining a value for the attribute HTTP-EQUIV.

> NOTE - The method by which the server extracts document meta-information is unspecified and not mandatory. The <META> element only provides an extensible mechanism for identifying and embedding document meta-information — how it may be used is up to the individual server implementation and the HTML user agent.

Attributes of the META element:

HTTP-EQUIV
> binds the element to an HTTP header field. An HTTP server may use this information to process the document. In particular, it may include a header field in the responses to requests for this document: the header name is taken from the HTTP-EQUIV attribute value, and the header value is taken from the value of the CONTENT attribute. HTTP header names are not case sensitive.

NAME
> specifies the name of the name/value pair. If not present, HTTP-EQUIV gives the name.

CONTENT
> specifies the value of the name/value pair.

Examples

If the document contains:

```
<META HTTP-EQUIV="Expires"
     CONTENT="Tue, 04 Dec 1993 21:29:02 GMT">
<meta http-equiv="Keywords" CONTENT="Fred">
<META HTTP-EQUIV="Reply-to"
     content="fielding@ics.uci.edu (Roy Fielding)">
<Meta Http-equiv="Keywords" CONTENT="Barney">
```

then the server may include the following header fields:

```
Expires: Tue, 04 Dec 1993 21:29:02 GMT
Keywords: Fred, Barney
Reply-to: fielding@ics.uci.edu (Roy Fielding)
```

as part of the HTTP response to a `GET' or `HEAD' request for that document.

An HTTP server must not use the <META> element to form an HTTP response header unless the HTTP-EQUIV attribute is present.

An HTTP server may disregard any <META> elements that specify information controlled by the HTTP server, for example `Server', `Date', and `Last-modified'.

5.2.6. Next Id: NEXTID

The <NEXTID> element is included for historical reasons only. HTML documents should not contain <NEXTID> elements.

The <NEXTID> element gives a hint for the name to use for a new <A> element when editing an HTML document. It should be distinct from all NAME attribute values on <A> elements. For example:

```
<NEXTID N=Z27>
```

5.3. Body: BODY

The <BODY> element contains the text flow of the document, including headings, paragraphs, lists, etc.

For example:

```
<BODY>
<h1>Important Stuff</h1>
<p>Explanation about important stuff...
</BODY>
```

5.4. Headings: H1 ... H6

The six heading elements, <H1> through <H6>, denote section
headings. Although the order and occurrence of headings is not
constrained by the HTML DTD, documents should not skip levels
(for example, from H1 to H3), as converting such documents to
other representations is often problematic.

Example of use:

```
<H1>This is a heading</H1>
Here is some text
<H2>Second level heading</H2>
Here is some more text.
```

Typical renderings are:

H1

> Bold, very-large font, centered. One or two blank lines
> above and below.

H2

> Bold, large font, flush-left. One or two blank lines
> above and below.

H3

> Italic, large font, slightly indented from the left
> margin. One or two blank lines above and below.

H4

> Bold, normal font, indented more than H3. One blank line
> above and below.

H5

> Italic, normal font, indented as H4. One blank line
> above.

H6

Bold, indented same as normal text, more than H5. One
blank line above.

5.5. Block Structuring Elements

Block structuring elements include paragraphs, lists, and block
quotes. They must not contain heading elements, but they may
contain phrase markup, and in some cases, they may be nested.

5.5.1. Paragraph: P

The <P> element indicates a paragraph. The exact indentation,
leading space, etc. of a paragraph is not specified and may be a
function of other tags, style sheets, etc.

Typically, paragraphs are surrounded by a vertical space of one
line or half a line. The first line in a paragraph is indented
in some cases.

Example of use:

```
<H1>This Heading Precedes the Paragraph</H1>
<P>This is the text of the first paragraph.
<P>This is the text of the second paragraph. Although you do not
need to start paragraphs on new lines, maintaining this
convention facilitates document maintenance.</P>
<P>This is the text of a third paragraph.</P>
```

5.5.2. Preformatted Text: PRE

The <PRE> element represents a character cell block of text and
is suitable for text that has been formatted for a monospaced
font.

The <PRE> tag may be used with the optional WIDTH attribute. The
WIDTH attribute specifies the maximum number of characters for a
line and allows the HTML user agent to select a suitable font
and indentation.

Within preformatted text:

* Line breaks within the text are rendered as a move to the beginning of the next line.

> NOTE - References to the ``beginning of a new line'' do not imply that the renderer is forbidden from using a constant left indent for rendering preformatted text. The left indent may be constrained by the width required.

* Anchor elements and phrase markup may be used.

> NOTE - Constraints on the processing of <PRE> content may limit or prevent the ability of the HTML user agent to faithfully render phrase markup.

* Elements that define paragraph formatting (headings, address, etc.) must not be used.

> NOTE - Some historical documents contain <P> tags in <PRE> elements. User agents are encouraged to treat this as a line break. A <P> tag followed by a newline character should produce only one line break, not a line break plus a blank line.

* The horizontal tab character (code position 9 in the HTML document character set) must be interpreted as the smallest positive nonzero number of spaces which will leave the number of characters so far on the line as a multiple of 8. Documents should not contain tab characters, as they are not supported consistently.

Example of use:

```
<PRE>
Line 1.
        Line 2 is to the right of line 1.      <a href="abc">abc</a>
        Line 3 aligns with line 2.             <a href="def">def</a>
</PRE>
```

5.5.2.1. Example and Listing: XMP, LISTING

The <XMP> and <LISTING> elements are similar to the <PRE> element, but they have a different syntax. Their content is declared as CDATA, which means that no markup except the end-tag open delimiter-in-context is recognized (see 9.6 ``Delimiter Recognition'' of [SGML]).

> NOTE - In a previous draft of the HTML specification, the syntax of <XMP> and <LISTING> elements allowed closing tags to be treated as data characters, as long as the tag name was not <XMP> or <LISTING>, respectively.

Since CDATA declared content has a number of unfortunate interactions with processing techniques and tends to be used and implemented inconsistently, HTML documents should not contain <XMP> nor <LISTING> elements — the <PRE> tag is more expressive and more consistently supported.

The <LISTING> element should be rendered so that at least 132 characters fit on a line. The <XMP> element should be rendered so that at least 80 characters fit on a line but is otherwise identical to the <LISTING> element.

> NOTE - In a previous draft, HTML included a <PLAINTEXT> element that is similar to the <LISTING> element, except that there is no closing tag: all characters after the <PLAINTEXT> start-tag are data.

5.5.3. Address: ADDRESS

The <ADDRESS> element contains such information as address, signature and authorship, often at the beginning or end of the body of a document.

Typically, the <ADDRESS> element is rendered in an italic typeface and may be indented.

Example of use:

```
<ADDRESS>
Newsletter editor<BR>
J.R. Brown<BR>
JimquickPost News, Jimquick, CT 01234<BR>
Tel (123) 456 7890
</ADDRESS>
```

5.5.4. Block Quote: BLOCKQUOTE

The <BLOCKQUOTE> element contains text quoted from another source.

A typical rendering might be a slight extra left and right indent, and/or italic font. The <BLOCKQUOTE> typically provides space above and below the quote.

Single-font rendition may reflect the quotation style of Internet mail by putting a vertical line of graphic characters, such as the greater than symbol (>), in the left margin.

Example of use:

```
I think the play ends
<BLOCKQUOTE>
<P>Soft you now, the fair Ophelia. Nymph, in thy orisons, be all
my sins remembered.
</BLOCKQUOTE>
but I am not sure.
```

5.6. List Elements

HTML includes a number of list elements. They may be used in combination; for example, a <OL> may be nested in an <LI> element of a <UL>.

The COMPACT attribute suggests that a compact rendering be used.

5.6.1. Unordered List: UL, LI

The <UL> represents a list of items — typically rendered as a bulleted list.

The content of a <UL> element is a sequence of <LI> elements. For example:

```
<UL>
<LI>First list item
<LI>Second list item
```

```
    <p>second paragraph of second item
    <LI>Third list item
    </UL>
```

5.6.2. Ordered List: OL

The <OL> element represents an ordered list of items, sorted by sequence or order of importance. It is typically rendered as a numbered list.

The content of a <OL> element is a sequence of <LI> elements. For example:

```
<OL>
<LI>Click the Web button to open URI window.
<LI>Enter the URI number in the text field of the Open URI
window. The Web document you specified is displayed.
  <ol>
   <li>substep 1
   <li>substep 2
  </ol>
<LI>Click highlighted text to move from one link to another.
</OL>
```

5.6.3. Directory List: DIR

The <DIR> element is similar to the <UL> element. It represents a list of short items, typically up to 20 characters each. Items in a directory list may be arranged in columns, typically 24 characters wide.

The content of a <DIR> element is a sequence of <LI> elements. Nested block elements are not allowed in the content of <DIR> elements. For example:

```
<DIR>
<LI>A-H<LI>I-M
<LI>M-R<LI>S-Z
</DIR>
```

5.6.4. Menu List: MENU

The <MENU> element is a list of items with typically one line per item. The menu list style is typically more compact than the style of an unordered list.

The content of a <MENU> element is a sequence of <LI> elements. Nested block elements are not allowed in the content of <MENU> elements. For example:

```
<MENU>
<LI>First item in the list.
<LI>Second item in the list.
<LI>Third item in the list.
</MENU>
```

5.6.5. Definition List: DL, DT, DD

A definition list is a list of terms and corresponding definitions. Definition lists are typically formatted with the term flush-left and the definition, formatted paragraph style, indented after the term.

The content of a <DL> element is a sequence of <DT> elements and/or <DD> elements, usually in pairs. Multiple <DT> may be paired with a single <DD> element. Documents should not contain multiple consecutive <DD> elements.

Example of use:

```
<DL>
<DT>Term<DD>This is the definition of the first term.
<DT>Term<DD>This is the definition of the second term.
</DL>
```

If the DT term does not fit in the DT column (typically one third of the display area), it may be extended across the page with the DD section moved to the next line, or it may be wrapped onto successive lines of the left hand column.

The optional COMPACT attribute suggests that a compact rendering be used, because the list items are small and/or the entire list is large.

Unless the COMPACT attribute is present, an HTML user agent may

leave white space between successive DT, DD pairs. The COMPACT
attribute may also reduce the width of the left-hand (DT)
column.

```
<DL COMPACT>
<DT>Term<DD>This is the first definition in compact format.
<DT>Term<DD>This is the second definition in compact format.
</DL>
```

5.7. Phrase Markup

Phrases may be marked up according to idiomatic usage,
typographic appearance, or for use as hyperlink anchors.

User agents must render highlighted phrases distinctly from
plain text. Additionally, <EM> content must be rendered as
distinct from <STRONG> content, and <B> content must rendered as
distinct from <I> content.

Phrase elements may be nested within the content of other phrase
elements; however, HTML user agents may render nested phrase
elements indistinctly from non-nested elements:

```
plain <B>bold <I>italic</I></B> may be rendered
the same as plain <B>bold </B><I>italic</I>
```

5.7.1. Idiomatic Elements

Phrases may be marked up to indicate certain idioms.

> NOTE - User agents may support the <DFN> element, not
> included in this specification, as it has been deployed
> to some extent. It is used to indicate the defining
> instance of a term, and it is typically rendered in
> italic or bold italic.

5.7.1.1. Citation: CITE

The <CITE> element is used to indicate the title of a book or
other citation. It is typically rendered as italics. For
example:

He just couldn't get enough of <cite>The Grapes of Wrath</cite>.

5.7.1.2. Code: CODE

The <CODE> element indicates an example of code, typically rendered in a mono-spaced font. The <CODE> element is intended for short words or phrases of code; the <PRE> block structuring element (5.5.2, "Preformatted Text: PRE") is more appropriate for multiple-line listings. For example:

```
The expression <code>x += 1</code>
is short for <code>x = x + 1</code>.
```

5.7.1.3. Emphasis: EM

The <EM> element indicates an emphasized phrase, typically rendered as italics. For example:

```
A singular subject <em>always</em> takes a singular verb.
```

5.7.1.4. Keyboard: KBD

The <KBD> element indicates text typed by a user, typically rendered in a mono-spaced font. This is commonly used in instruction manuals. For example:

```
Enter <kbd>FIND IT</kbd> to search the database.
```

5.7.1.5. Sample: SAMP

The <SAMP> element indicates a sequence of literal characters, typically rendered in a mono-spaced font. For example:

```
The only word containing the letters <samp>mt</samp> is dreamt.
```

5.7.1.6. Strong Emphasis: STRONG

The <STRONG> element indicates strong emphasis, typically rendered in bold. For example:

`<strong>STOP</strong>`, or I'll say "`<strong>STOP</strong>`" again!

5.7.1.7. Variable: VAR

The `<VAR>` element indicates a placeholder variable, typically rendered as italic. For example:

```
Type <SAMP>html-check <VAR>file</VAR> | more</SAMP>
to check <VAR>file</VAR> for markup errors.
```

5.7.2. Typographic Elements

Typographic elements are used to specify the format of marked text.

Typical renderings for idiomatic elements may vary between user agents. If a specific rendering is necessary — for example, when referring to a specific text attribute as in ``The italic parts are mandatory'' — a typographic element can be used to ensure that the intended typography is used where possible.

> NOTE - User agents may support some typographic elements not included in this specification, as they have been deployed to some extent. The `<STRIKE>` element indicates horizontal line through the characters, and the `<U>` element indicates an underline.

5.7.2.1. Bold: B

The `<B>` element indicates bold text. Where bold typography is unavailable, an alternative representation may be used.

5.7.2.2. Italic: I

The `<I>` element indicates italic text. Where italic typography is unavailable, an alternative representation may be used.

5.7.2.3. Teletype: TT

The <TT> element indicates teletype (monospaced)text. Where a teletype font is unavailable, an alternative representation may be used.

5.7.3. Anchor; A

The <A> element indicates a hyperlink anchor (see 7, "Hyperlinks"). At least one of the NAME and HREF attributes should be present. Attributes of the <A> element:

HREF
> gives the URI of the head anchor of a hyperlink.

NAME
> gives the name of the anchor, and makes it available as a head of a hyperlink.

TITLE
> suggests a title for the destination resource — advisory only. The TITLE attribute may be used:
>
>> * for display prior to accessing the destination resource, for example, as a margin note or on a small box while the mouse is over the anchor, or while the document is being loaded;
>>
>> * for resources that do not include a title, such as graphics, plain text and Gopher menus, for use as a window title.

REL
> The REL attribute gives the relationship(s) described by the hyperlink. The value is a whitespace separated list of relationship names. The semantics of link relationships are not specified in this document.

REV
> same as the REL attribute, but the semantics of the relationship are in the reverse direction. A link from A to B with REL=``X'' expresses the same relationship as a link from B to A with REV=``X''. An anchor may have both REL and REV attributes.

URN

> specifies a preferred, more persistent identifier for
> the head anchor of the hyperlink. The syntax and
> semantics of the URN attribute are not yet specified.

METHODS

> specifies methods to be used in accessing the
> destination, as a whitespace-separated list of names.
> The set of applicable names is a function of the scheme
> of the URI in the HREF attribute. For similar reasons as
> for the TITLE attribute, it may be useful to include the
> information in advance in the link. For example, the
> HTML user agent may chose a different rendering as a
> function of the methods allowed; for example, something
> that is searchable may get a different icon.

5.8. Line Break: BR

The <BR> element specifies a line break between words (see 6,
"Characters, Words, and Paragraphs"). For example:

```
<P> Pease porridge hot<BR>
Pease porridge cold<BR>
Pease porridge in the pot<BR>
Nine days old.
```

5.9. Horizontal Rule: HR

The <HR> element is a divider between sections of text;
typically a full width horizontal rule or equivalent graphic.
For example:

```
<HR>
<ADDRESS>February 8, 1995, CERN</ADDRESS>
</BODY>
```

5.10. Image: IMG

The <IMG> element refers to an image or icon via a hyperlink
(see 7.3, "Simultaneous Presentation of Image Resources").

HTML user agents may process the value of the ALT attribute as
an alternative to processing the image resource indicated by the
SRC attribute.

> NOTE - Some HTML user agents can process graphics linked
> via anchors, but not <IMG> graphics. If a graphic is
> essential, it should be referenced from an <A> element
> rather than an <IMG> element. If the graphic is not
> essential, then the <IMG> element is appropriate.

Attributes of the <IMG> element:

ALIGN
> alignment of the image with respect to the text
> baseline.
>
> > * `TOP' specifies that the top of the image aligns
> > with the tallest item on the line containing the
> > image.
> >
> > * `MIDDLE' specifies that the center of the image
> > aligns with the baseline of the line containing the
> > image.
> >
> > * `BOTTOM' specifies that the bottom of the image
> > aligns with the baseline of the line containing the
> > image.

ALT
> text to use in place of the referenced image resource,
> for example due to processing constraints or user
> preference.

ISMAP
> indicates an image map (see 7.6, "Image Maps").

SRC
> specifies the URI of the image resource.
>
> > NOTE - In practice, the media types of image
> > resources are limited to a few raster graphic
> > formats: typically `image/gif', `image/jpeg'. In
> > particular, `text/html' resources are not
> > intended to be used as image resources.

Examples of use:

```
<IMG SRC="triangle.xbm" ALT="Warning:"> Be sure
to read these instructions.

<a href="http://machine/htbin/imagemap/sample">
<IMG SRC="sample.xbm" ISMAP>
</a>
```

6. Characters, Words, and Paragraphs

An HTML user agent should present the body of an HTML document
as a collection of typeset paragraphs and preformatted text.
Except for preformatted elements (<PRE>, <XMP>, <LISTING>,
<TEXTAREA>), each block structuring element is regarded as a
paragraph by taking the data characters in its content and the
content of its descendant elements, concatenating them, and
splitting the result into words, separated by space, tab, or
record end characters (and perhaps hyphen characters). The
sequence of words is typeset as a paragraph by breaking it into
lines.

6.1. The HTML Document Character Set

The document character set specified in 9.5, "SGML Declaration
for HTML" must be supported by HTML user agents. It includes the
graphic characters of Latin Alphabet No. 1, or simply Latin-1.
Latin-1 comprises 191 graphic characters, including the
alphabets of most Western European languages.

> NOTE - Use of the non-breaking space and soft hyphen
> indicator characters is discouraged because support for
> them is not widely deployed.

> NOTE - To support non-western writing systems, a larger
> character repertoire will be specified in a future
> version of HTML. The document character set will be
> [ISO-10646], or some subset that agrees with
> [ISO-10646]; in particular, all numeric character
> references must use code positions assigned by
> [ISO-10646].

In SGML applications, the use of control characters is limited in order to maximize the chance of successful interchange over heterogeneous networks and operating systems. In the HTML document character set only three control characters are allowed: Horizontal Tab, Carriage Return, and Line Feed (code positions 9, 13, and 10).

The HTML DTD references the Added Latin 1 entity set, to allow mnemonic representation of selected Latin 1 characters using only the widely supported ASCII character repertoire. For example:

Kurt Gödel was a famous logician and mathematician.

See 9.7.2, "ISO Latin 1 Character Entity Set" for a table of the ``Added Latin 1'' entities, and 13, "The HTML Coded Character Set" for a table of the code positions of [ISO 8859-1] and the control characters in the HTML document character set.

7. Hyperlinks

In addition to general purpose elements such as paragraphs and lists, HTML documents can express hyperlinks. An HTML user agent allows the user to navigate these hyperlinks.

A hyperlink is a relationship between two anchors, called the head and the tail of the hyperlink[DEXTER]. Anchors are identified by an anchor address: an absolute Uniform Resource Identifier (URI), optionally followed by a '#' and a sequence of characters called a fragment identifier. For example:

http://www.w3.org/hypertext/WWW/TheProject.html
http://www.w3.org/hypertext/WWW/TheProject.html#z31

In an anchor address, the URI refers to a resource; it may be used in a variety of information retrieval protocols to obtain an entity that represents the resource, such as an HTML document. The fragment identifier, if present, refers to some view on, or portion of the resource.

Each of the following markup constructs indicates the tail anchor of a hyperlink or set of hyperlinks:

* <A> elements with HREF present.

* <LINK> elements.

* <IMG> elements.

* <INPUT> elements with the SRC attribute present.

* <ISINDEX> elements.

* <FORM> elements with `METHOD=GET'.

These markup constructs refer to head anchors by a URI, either

absolute or relative, or a fragment identifier, or both.

In the case of a relative URI, the absolute URI in the address
of the head anchor is the result of combining the relative URI
with a base absolute URI as in [RELURL]. The base document is
taken from the document's <BASE> element, if present; else, it
is determined as in [RELURL].

7.1. Accessing Resources

Once the address of the head anchor is determined, the user
agent may obtain a representation of the resource.

For example, if the base URI is `http://host/x/y.html' and the
document contains:

```
<img src="../icons/abc.gif">
```

then the user agent uses the URI `http://host/icons/abc.gif' to
access the resource, as in [URL]..

7.2. Activation of Hyperlinks

An HTML user agent allows the user to navigate the content of
the document and request activation of hyperlinks denoted by <A>
elements. HTML user agents should also allow activation of
<LINK> element hyperlinks.

To activate a link, the user agent obtains a representation of the resource identified in the address of the head anchor. If the representation is another HTML document, navigation may begin again with this new document.

7.3. Simultaneous Presentation of Image Resources

An HTML user agent may activate hyperlinks indicated by <IMG> and <INPUT> elements concurrently with processing the document; that is, image hyperlinks may be processed without explicit request by the user. Image resources should be embedded in the presentation at the point of the tail anchor, that is the <IMG> or <INPUT> element.

<LINK> hyperlinks may also be processed without explicit user request; for example, style sheet resources may be processed before or during the processing of the document.

7.4. Fragment Identifiers

Any characters following a `#' character in a hypertext address constitute a fragment identifier. In particular, an address of the form `#fragment' refers to an anchor in the same document.

The meaning of fragment identifiers depends on the media type of the representation of the anchor's resource. For `text/html' representations, it refers to the <A> element with a NAME attribute whose value is the same as the fragment identifier. The matching is case sensitive. The document should have exactly one such element. The user agent should indicate the anchor element, for example by scrolling to and/or highlighting the phrase.

For example, if the base URI is `http://host/x/y.html' and the user activated the link denoted by the following markup:

```
<p> See: <a href="app1.html#bananas">appendix 1</a>
for more detail on bananas.
```

Then the user agent accesses the resource identified by `http://host/x/app1.html'. Assuming the resource is represented using the `text/html' media type, the user agent must locate the

<A> element whose NAME attribute is `bananas' and begin
navigation there.

7.5. Queries and Indexes

The <ISINDEX> element represents a set of hyperlinks. The user
can choose from the set by providing keywords to the user agent.
The user agent computes the head URI by appending `?' and the
keywords to the base URI. The keywords are escaped according to
[URL] and joined by `+'. For example, if a document contains:

```
<BASE HREF="http://host/index">
<ISINDEX>
```

and the user provides the keywords `apple' and `berry', then the
user agent must access the resource
`http://host/index?apple+berry'.

<FORM> elements with `METHOD=GET' also represent sets of
hyperlinks. See 8.2.2, "Query Forms: METHOD=GET" for details.

7.6. Image Maps

If the ISMAP attribute is present on an <IMG> element, the <IMG>
element must be contained in an <A> element with an HREF
present. This construct represents a set of hyperlinks. The user
can choose from the set by choosing a pixel of the image. The
user agent computes the head URI by appending `?' and the x and
y coordinates of the pixel to the URI given in the <A> element.
For example, if a document contains:

```
<!DOCTYPE HTML PUBLIC "-//IETF//DTD HTML 2.0//EN">
<head><title>ImageMap Example</title>
<BASE HREF="http://host/index"></head>
<body>
<p> Choose any of these icons:<br>
<a href="/cgi-bin/imagemap"><img ismap src="icons.gif"></a>
```

and the user chooses the upper-leftmost pixel, the chosen
hyperlink is the one with the URI
`http://host/cgi-bin/imagemap?0,0'.

8. Forms

A form is a template for a form data set and an associated
method and action URI. A form data set is a sequence of
name/value pair fields. The names are specified on the NAME
attributes of form input elements, and the values are given
initial values by various forms of markup and edited by the
user. The resulting form data set is used to access an
information service as a function of the action and method.

Forms elements can be mixed in with document structuring
elements. For example, a <PRE> element may contain a <FORM>
element, or a <FORM> element may contain lists which contain
<INPUT> elements. This gives considerable flexibility in
designing the layout of forms.

Form processing is a level 2 feature.

8.1. Form Elements

8.1.1. Form: FORM

The <FORM> element contains a sequence of input elements, along
with document structuring elements. The attributes are:

ACTION
> specifies the action URI for the form. The action URI of
> a form defaults to the base URI of the document (see 7,
> "Hyperlinks").

METHOD
> selects a method of accessing the action URI. The set of
> applicable methods is a function of the scheme of the
> action URI of the form. See 8.2.2, "Query Forms:
> METHOD=GET" and 8.2.3, "Forms with Side-Effects:
> METHOD=POST".

ENCTYPE
> specifies the media type used to encode the name/value
> pairs for transport, in case the protocol does not
> itself impose a format. See 8.2.1, "The form-urlencoded
> Media Type".

8.1.2. Input Field: INPUT

The <INPUT> element represents a field for user input. The TYPE attribute discriminates between several variations of fields.

The <INPUT> element has a number of attributes. The set of applicable attributes depends on the value of the TYPE attribute.

8.1.2.1. Text Field: INPUT TYPE=TEXT

The default value of the TYPE attribute is `TEXT', indicating a single line text entry field. (Use the <TEXTAREA> element for multi-line text fields.)

Required attributes are:

NAME
>	name for the form field corresponding to this element.

The optional attributes are:

MAXLENGTH
>	constrains the number of characters that can be entered into a text input field. If the value of MAXLENGTH is greater the the value of the SIZE attribute, the field should scroll appropriately. The default number of characters is unlimited.

SIZE
>	specifies the amount of display space allocated to this input field according to its type. The default depends on the user agent.

VALUE
>	The initial value of the field.

For example:

```
<p>Street Address: <input name=street><br>
Postal City code: <input name=city size=16 maxlength=16><br>
Zip Code: <input name=zip size=10 maxlength=10 value="99999-9999"><br>
```

8.1.2.2. Password Field: INPUT TYPE=PASSWORD

An <INPUT> element with `TYPE=PASSWORD' is a text field as
above, except that the value is obscured as it is entered. (see
also: 10, "Security Considerations").

For example:

<p>Name: <input name=login> Password: <input type=password
name=passwd>

8.1.2.3. Check Box: INPUT TYPE=CHECKBOX

An <INPUT> element with `TYPE=CHECKBOX' represents a boolean
choice. A set of such elements with the same name represents an
n-of-many choice field. Required attributes are:

NAME

        symbolic name for the form field corresponding to this
        element or group of elements.

VALUE

        The portion of the value of the field contributed by
        this element.

Optional attributes are:

CHECKED

        indicates that the initial state is on.

For example:

<p>What flavors do you like?
<input type=checkbox name=flavor value=vanilla>Vanilla
<input type=checkbox name=flavor value=strawberry>Strawberry
<input type=checkbox name=flavor value=chocolate checked>Chocolate

8.1.2.4. Radio Button: INPUT TYPE=RADIO

An <INPUT> element with `TYPE=RADIO' represents a boolean
choice. A set of such elements with the same name represents a
1-of-many choice field. The NAME and VALUE attributes are

required as for check boxes. Optional attributes are:

CHECKED

> indicates that the initial state is on.

At all times, exactly one of the radio buttons in a set is checked. If none of the <INPUT> elements of a set of radio buttons specifies `CHECKED', then the user agent must check the first radio button of the set initially.

For example:

```
<p>Which is your favorite?
<input type=radio name=flavor value=vanilla>Vanilla<br>
<input type=radio name=flavor value=strawberry>Strawberry<br>
<input type=radio name=flavor value=chocolate>Chocolate<br>
```

8.1.2.5. Image Pixel: INPUT TYPE=IMAGE

An <INPUT> element with `TYPE=IMAGE' specifies an image resource to display, and allows input of two form fields: the x and y coordinate of a pixel chosen from the image. The names of the fields are the name of the field with `.x' and `.y' appended. `TYPE=IMAGE' implies `TYPE=SUBMIT' processing; that is, when a pixel is chosen, the form as a whole is submitted.

The NAME attribute is required as for other input fields. The SRC attribute is required and the ALIGN is optional as for the <IMG> element (see 5.10, "Image: IMG").

For example:

```
<p>Choose a point on the map:
<input type=image name=point src="map.gif">
```

8.1.2.6. Hidden Field: INPUT TYPE=HIDDEN

An <INPUT> element with `TYPE=HIDDEN' represents a hidden field.The user does not interact with this field; instead, the VALUE attribute specifies the value of the field. The NAME and VALUE attributes are required.

For example:

```
<input type=hidden name=context value="12k3j412k3j412k3j41k23">
```

8.1.2.7. Submit Button: INPUT TYPE=SUBMIT

An <INPUT> element with `TYPE=SUBMIT' represents an input
option, typically a button, that instructs the user agent to
submit the form. Optional attributes are:

NAME
> indicates that this element contributes a form field
> whose value is given by the VALUE attribute. If the NAME
> attribute is not present, this element does not
> contribute a form field.

VALUE
> indicates a label for the input (button).

```
You may submit this request internally:
<input type=submit name=recipient value=internal><br>
or to the external world:
<input type=submit name=recipient value=world>
```

8.1.2.8. Reset Button: INPUT TYPE=RESET

An <INPUT> element with `TYPE=RESET' represents an input option,
typically a button, that instructs the user agent to reset the
form's fields to their initial states. The VALUE attribute, if
present, indicates a label for the input (button).

```
When you are finished, you may submit this request:
<input type=submit><br>
You may clear the form and start over at any time: <input type=reset>
```

8.1.3. Selection: SELECT

The <SELECT> element constrains the form field to an enumerated
list of values. The values are given in <OPTION> elements.
Attributes are:

MULTIPLE

>   indicates that more than one option may be included in
>   the value.

NAME

>   specifies the name of the form field.

SIZE

>   specifies the number of visible items. Select fields of
>   size one are typically pop-down menus, whereas select
>   fields with size greater than one are typically lists.

For example:

```
<SELECT NAME="flavor">
<OPTION>Vanilla
<OPTION>Strawberry
<OPTION value="RumRasin">Rum and Raisin
<OPTION selected>Peach and Orange
</SELECT>
```

The initial state has the first option selected, unless a
SELECTED attribute is present on any of the <OPTION> elements.

8.1.3.1. Option: OPTION

The Option element can only occur within a Select element. It
represents one choice, and has the following attributes:

SELECTED

>   Indicates that this option is initially selected.

VALUE

>   indicates the value to be returned if this option is
>   chosen. The field value defaults to the content of the
>   <OPTION> element.

The content of the <OPTION> element is presented to the user to
represent the option. It is used as a returned value if the
VALUE attribute is not present.

8.1.4. Text Area: TEXTAREA

The <TEXTAREA> element represents a multi-line text field.
Attributes are:

COLS

> the number of visible columns to display for the text
> area, in characters.

NAME

> Specifies the name of the form field.

ROWS

> The number of visible rows to display for the text area,
> in characters.

For example:

```
<TEXTAREA NAME="address" ROWS=6 COLS=64>
HaL Computer Systems
1315 Dell Avenue
Campbell, California 95008
</TEXTAREA>
```

The content of the <TEXTAREA> element is the field's initial
value.

Typically, the ROWS and COLS attributes determine the visible
dimension of the field in characters. The field is typically
rendered in a fixed-width font. HTML user agents should allow
text to extend beyond these limits by scrolling as needed.

8.2. Form Submission

An HTML user agent begins processing a form by presenting the
document with the fields in their initial state. The user is
allowed to modify the fields, constrained by the field type etc.
When the user indicates that the form should be submitted (using
a submit button or image input), the form data set is processed
according to its method, action URI and enctype.

When there is only one single-line text input field in a form,
the user agent should accept Enter in that field as a request to
submit the form.

8.2.1. The form-urlencoded Media Type

The default encoding for all forms is
`application/x-www-form-urlencoded`. A form data set is
represented in this media type as follows:

1. The form field names and values are escaped: space
characters are replaced by `+`, and then reserved characters
are escaped as per [URL]; that is, non-alphanumeric
characters are replaced by `%HH`, a percent sign and two
hexadecimal digits representing the ASCII code of the
character. Line breaks, as in multi-line text field values,
are represented as CR LF pairs, i.e. `%0D%0A`.

2. The fields are listed in the order they appear in the
document with the name separated from the value by `=` and
the pairs separated from each other by `&`. Fields with null
values may be omitted. In particular, unselected radio
buttons and checkboxes should not appear in the encoded
data, but hidden fields with VALUE attributes present
should.

> NOTE - The URI from a query form submission can be
> used in a normal anchor style hyperlink.
> Unfortunately, the use of the `&` character to
> separate form fields interacts with its use in SGML
> attribute values as an entity reference delimiter.
> For example, the URI `http://host/?x=1&y=2` must be
> written `<a href="http://host/?x=1&#38;y=2"` or `<a
> href="http://host/?x=1&y=2">`.

> HTTP server implementors, and in particular, CGI
> implementors are encouraged to support the use of
> `;` in place of `&` to save users the trouble of
> escaping `&` characters this way.

8.2.2. Query Forms: METHOD=GET

If the processing of a form is idempotent (i.e. it has no
lasting observable effect on the state of the world), then the
form method should be `GET`. Many database searches have no
visible side-effects and make ideal applications of query forms.

To process a form whose action URL is an HTTP URL and whose method is `GET`, the user agent starts with the action URI and appends a `?` and the form data set, in `application/x-www-form-urlencoded` format as above. The user agent then traverses the link to this URI just as if it were an anchor (see 7.2, "Activation of Hyperlinks").

> NOTE - The URL encoding may result in very long URIs, which cause some historical HTTP server implementations to exhibit defective behavior. As a result, some HTML forms are written using `METHOD=POST` even though the form submission has no side-effects.

8.2.3. Forms with Side-Effects: METHOD=POST

If the service associated with the processing of a form has side effects (for example, modification of a database or subscription to a service), the method should be `POST`.

To process a form whose action URL is an HTTP URL and whose method is `POST`, the user agent conducts an HTTP POST transaction using the action URI, and a message body of type `application/x-www-form-urlencoded` format as above. The user agent should display the response from the HTTP POST interaction just as it would display the response from an HTTP GET above.

8.2.4. Example Form Submission: Questionnaire Form

Consider the following document:

```
<!DOCTYPE HTML PUBLIC "-//IETF//DTD HTML 2.0//EN">
<title>Sample of HTML Form Submission</title>
<H1>Sample Questionnaire</H1>
<P>Please fill out this questionnaire:
<FORM METHOD="POST" ACTION="http://www.w3.org/sample">
<P>Your name: <INPUT NAME="name" size="48">
<P>Male <INPUT NAME="gender" TYPE=RADIO VALUE="male">
<P>Female <INPUT NAME="gender" TYPE=RADIO VALUE="female">
<P>Number in family: <INPUT NAME="family" TYPE=text>
<P>Cities in which you maintain a residence:
<UL>
<LI>Kent <INPUT NAME="city" TYPE=checkbox VALUE="kent">
```

```
<LI>Miami <INPUT NAME="city" TYPE=checkbox VALUE="miami">
<LI>Other <TEXTAREA NAME="other" cols=48 rows=4></textarea>
</UL>
Nickname: <INPUT NAME="nickname" SIZE="42">
<P>Thank you for responding to this questionnaire.
<P><INPUT TYPE=SUBMIT> <INPUT TYPE=RESET>
</FORM>
```

The initial state of the form data set is:

name
        ``''

gender
        ``male''

family
        ``''

other
        ``''

nickname
        ``''

Note that the radio input has an initial value, while the checkbox has none.

The user might edit the fields and request that the form be submitted. At that point, suppose the values are:

name
        ``John Doe''

gender
        ``male''

family
        ``5''

city
        ``kent''

city

```
            ``miami''

other
            ``abc\ndef''

nickname
            ``J&D''
```

The user agent then conducts an HTTP POST transaction using the
URI `http://www.w3.org/sample'. The message body would be
(ignore the line break):

```
name=John+Doe&gender=male&family=5&city=kent&city=miami&
other=abc%0D%0Adef&nickname=J%26D
```

PROGRAM LISTINGS

When programs referenced in the earlier text are long enough that display within the text would interrupt the flow, but the programs are nevertheless useful for reading and study, I present them here. These are complete program codes fragments appear in this appendix.

LISTING 1: HTMLTOC.PL

```perl
#! /usr/local/bin/perl
##--------------------------------------------------------------##
## File:
##     htmltoc
## Author:
##     Earl Hood          ehood@convex.com
## Description:
##     htmltoc is a Perl program to generate a table of contents for
##     HTML documents.
##--------------------------------------------------------------##
## Copyright (C) 1994  Earl Hood, ehood@convex.com
##
## This program is free software; you can redistribute it and/or modify
## it under the terms of the GNU General Public License as published by
## the Free Software Foundation; either version 2 of the License, or
## (at your option) any later version.
##
## This program is distributed in the hope that it will be useful,
## but WITHOUT ANY WARRANTY; without even the implied warranty of
## MERCHANTABILITY or FITNESS FOR A PARTICULAR PURPOSE.  See the
## GNU General Public License for more details.
##
## You should have received a copy of the GNU General Public License
## along with this program; if not, write to the Free Software
```

```perl
##   Foundation, Inc., 675 Mass Ave, Cambridge, MA 02139, USA.
##—————————————————————————————————————————-##

package main;

unshift(@INC, '.');
require "newgetopt.pl" || die "ERROR: Unable to require newgetopt.pl\n";

##—————————————————————————————————————————-##
## Store name of program ##
($PROG = $0) =~ s/.*\///;

$VERSION = "1.1.1";

%TOC = (                     # Default ToC entry elements
    'H1', 1,
    'H2', 2,
);
%TOCend = (                  # Default ToC entry element terminators
    'H1', '/H1',
    'H2', '/H2',
);
%TOCbefore = ();# Before text for ToC entries
%TOCafter = ();              # After text for ToC entries

$file = '';                  # Current file being processed
$_id = 0;                    # Link counter
$prevlevel = 0;              # Previous ToC entry level

@Comments = ();
$ComMark = "$;$;$;";

##—————————————————————————————————————————-##
##————————##
## Begin MAIN ##
##————————##
{
&get_cli_opts();
&read_tocmap()  if $TOCMAP;

local(@html,@newhtml,@toc,$i);

## Remove filename arguments in @ARGV that are part of the options
@ARGV = grep(!/^($HEADER|$FOOTER|$TOCFILE|$TOCMAP)$/, @ARGV);
die "ERROR: -inline valid for only a single file\n" if ($INLINE && $#ARGV > 0);

if (!$QUIET) {
```

```perl
        if ($USEORG) {
          print STDERR qq|Using ".org" file(s) as source.\n|;
        } elsif (!$NOORG) {
          print STDERR qq|Original file(s) will be renamed with a ".org" |,
                       qq|extension.\n|;
        }
    }

    ## Read files and create ToC
    print STDERR qq|Processing file(s) ...\n|  unless $QUIET;
    $i = 0;
    foreach $file (@ARGV) {
        &cp($file, "$file.org")                      # Backup original
          unless $USEORG && -e "$file.org";
        open(FILE, "$file.org") ||                   # Use backup as source
          die "ERROR: Unable to open $file\n";
        open(FILEOUT, "> $file") ||                  # Overwrite original to filename
          die "ERROR: Unable to open $file\n";
        @html = ();  @newhtml = ();
        &read_sgml(FILE, *html);                     # Read HTML into @html
        &generate_toc(*html, *toc, *newhtml);    # Add to ToC
        &put_back_comments(*newhtml);
        close(FILE);
        if (!$INLINE) {                              # Close FILEOUT only if no in-lining
          print FILEOUT @newhtml;
          close(FILEOUT);
        }
        $i++;
    }
    print STDERR "$i files processed.\n"  unless $QUIET || $INLINE;

    ## Close up open elements in ToC
    for ($i=$prevlevel; $i > 0; $i-) {
        if ($OL && $i == 1) { push(@toc, "</OL>\n"); }
        else { push(@toc, "</UL>\n"); }
    }

    ## Write ToC
    print STDERR "Writing Toc ...\n"  unless $QUIET;
    if ($INLINE) {
        if ($HEADER) {
          if (open(HEADER, $HEADER)) {
              print FILEOUT <HEADER>;  close(HEADER);
          } else {
              warn "Warning: Unable to open $HEADER\n"; }
        } else {
          while ((($i = shift @newhtml) !~ /<body>/i) &&
```

```
                    ($#newhtml >= 0)) { print FILEOUT $i; }
            if ($#newhtml < 0) {
                warn "Warning: No open BODY tag found\n"; }
            print FILEOUT $i, "\n";
            print FILEOUT "$TOCHEADER\n"  if $TOCHEADER;
        }
        print FILEOUT @toc, "\n";
        print FILEOUT @newhtml;
        close(FILEOUT);
    } else {
        if ($HEADER) {
            if (open(HEADER, $HEADER)) {
                print $TOCHANDLE <HEADER>;
                close(HEADER);
            } else {
                warn "Warning: Unable to open $HEADER\n";
            }
        } else {
            print $TOCHANDLE "<HTML>\n",
                             "<HEAD>\n";
            print $TOCHANDLE "<TITLE>$TITLE</TITLE>\n"  if $TITLE;
            print $TOCHANDLE "</HEAD>\n",
                             "<BODY>\n";
            print $TOCHANDLE "$TOCHEADER\n"  if $TOCHEADER;
        }
        print $TOCHANDLE @toc;
        if ($FOOTER) {
            if (open(FOOTER, $FOOTER)) {
                print $TOCHANDLE <FOOTER>;
                close(FOOTER);
            } else {
                warn "Warning: Unable to open $FOOTER\n";
            }
        } else {
            print $TOCHANDLE "</BODY>\n",
                             "</HTML>\n";
        }
    }

# Delete originals if specified
if ($NOORG) {
    print STDERR "Cleaning up ...\n"  unless $QUIET;
    foreach $file (@ARGV) {
        unlink ("$file.org");
    }
}
```

```
    exit 0;

}
##————————##
## End MAIN ##
##————————##
##————————————————————————————————————————————————————————————-##
##      get_cli_opts() retrieves all command-line options and intializes
##      global variables.
##
sub get_cli_opts {
    &Usage unless
    &NGetOpt(
        "prefix=s",         # Prefix for ToC IDs for linking  (def: "xtocid")
        "tocmap=s",         # ToC map file defining significant elements
        "toc=s",  # Output ToC file  (def: STDOUT)
        "title=s",          # Title for ToC  (def: "Table of Contents")
        "toclabel=s",       # HTML text that labels the ToC  (def: nil)
        "inline", # Put ToC in document
        "header=s",         # File containing header text for ToC
        "footer=s",         # File containing footer text for ToC
        "ol",               # Use an order list for level 1 ToC entries
        "noorg", # Delete backup original ".org" files on completion
        "useorg", # Use pre-existing ".org" files
        "textonly",         # Use only text content in significant elements
        "quiet", # Suppress informative messages
        "help"              # Print usage message
    );
    &Usage() if defined $opt_help;

    $tocprefix = ($opt_prefix ? $opt_prefix : 'xtocid');
      $tocprefix .= $$;   # Append pid to prefix
    $TOCMAP = ($opt_tocmap ? $opt_tocmap : '');
    $TITLE = ($opt_title ? $opt_title : 'Table of Contents');
    $TOCHEADER = ($opt_toclabel ? $opt_toclabel : '<H1>Table of Contents</H1>');
    $TOCFILE = ($opt_toc ? $opt_toc : '');
    $HEADER = ($opt_header ? $opt_header : '');
    $FOOTER = ($opt_footer ? $opt_footer : '');

    $INLINE = (defined($opt_inline) ? 1 : 0);
    $OL = (defined($opt_ol) ? 1 : 0);
    $NOORG = (defined($opt_noorg) ? 1 : 0);
    $USEORG = (defined($opt_useorg) ? 1 : 0);
    $TEXTONLY = (defined($opt_textonly) ? 1 : 0);
    $QUIET = (defined($opt_quiet) ? 1 : 0);
```

```
          if ($TOCFILE) {
            open(TOCFILE, "> $TOCFILE") || die "ERROR: Unable to create $TOCFILE\n";
            $TOCHANDLE = 'TOCFILE';
          } else {
            $TOCHANDLE = 'STDOUT';
          }
      }
##----------------------------------------------------------------------##
##     read_tocmap() reads the ToC mapfile.
##
sub read_tocmap {
      local(@array, @befaft);

      open(TOCMAP, $TOCMAP) || die "ERROR: Unable to open $TOCMAP\n";

      undef %TOC;  undef %TOCend;            ## Clear defaults
      while (<TOCMAP>) {
        next if /^\s*#/ || /^\s*$/;  # Skip comment/blank lines
        s/#.*$//;  s/\s//g;                # Remove eol comments and whitespaces
        @array = split(/:/, $_);     # Split line into fields
        if ($#array < 1) {           # Error checking
            die "ERROR: ToC mapfile error: less than 2 fields: line $.\n";
        } elsif ($array[1] !~ /^\d+$/ || $array[1] < 1) {
            die "ERROR: ToC mapfile error: 2nd field not a positive number: ",
                "line $.\n";
        }
        $TOC{$array[0]} = $array[1]; # Store ToC tag and level
        if ($array[2]) {             # Store end delimiter
            $TOCend{$array[0]} = $array[2];
        } else {
            $TOCend{$array[0]} = '/'.$array[0];
        }
        if ($array[3]) {             # Store before/after text
            @befaft = split(/,/, $array[3]);
            $TOCbefore{$array[0]} = $befaft[0];
            $TOCafter{$array[0]} = $befaft[1];
        }
      }
      close(TOCMAP);
}
##----------------------------------------------------------------------##
##     generate_toc() reads the HTML specified by *html and adds to the
##     ToC specified by *toc.  The new modified HTML is in *newhtml.
##
sub generate_toc {
      local(*html, *toc, *newhtml) = @_;
```

```perl
local($content,$adone,$name,$level,$i,$title,$before,$after,$q);

while ($#html >= 0) {
   $item = shift @html;
   next if $item eq '';
   if ($item !~ /^</) { push(@newhtml,$item); next; }

   $level = 0;  $title = 0;
   ## Check if tag included in TOC
   foreach (keys %TOC) {
       if ($item =~ /^<$_/i) {
           $tag = $_;
           $level = $TOC{$_};              # Level of signicant element
           $endtag = $TOCend{$_};                # End tag of signicant element
           $before = $TOCbefore{$_};              # Before text in ToC entry
           $after = $TOCafter{$_};                # After text in ToC entry
           last;
       }
   }
   if (!$level) { push(@newhtml,$item); next; }

   ## Insert A element into document
   $content = '';  $adone = 0;  $name = $tocprefix . $_id;
   if ($tag =~ /title/i) {                 # TITLE tag is a special case
       $title = 1;  $adone = 1;
   }
   push(@newhtml,$item);
   while ($#html >= 0) {
       $item = shift @html;
       next if $item eq '';
       if ($item !~ /^</) {                        # Text data
           $content .= $item;
           if (!$adone && $item !~ /^\s*$/) {
               push(@newhtml,qq|<A NAME="$name">$item</A>|);
               $adone = 1;
           } else {
               push(@newhtml,$item);
           }
       } elsif (!$adone && $item =~ /^<A/i) {       # Anchor
           if ($item =~ m/NAME\s*=\s*(['"])/i) {
               $q = $1;
               ($name) = $item =~ m/NAME\s*=\s*$q([^$q]*)$q/i;
           } else {
               $item =~ s/^(<A)(.*)$/$1 NAME="$name" $2/i;
           }
           push(@newhtml,$item);
```

```
                    $adone = 1;
            } else {                                          # Tag
                push(@newhtml,$item);
                last if $item =~ m|<$endtag>|i;
                $content .= $item
                    unless $TEXTONLY || $item =~ m%</?(hr>|p>|a|img)%i;
            }
        }
        $content =~ s/$ComMark//go;
        if ($content =~ /^\s*$/) {    # Check for empty content
            warn "Warning: A $tag in $file has not content;  $tag skipped\n";
            next;
        } else {
            $content = $before . $content . $after;
        }

        ## Update TOC
        if ($level < $prevlevel) {
            for ($i=$level; $i < $prevlevel; $i++) {
                if ($OL && $i == 1) { push(@toc, "</OL>\n"); }
                else { push(@toc, "</UL>\n"); }
            }
        } else {
            for ($i=$level; $i > $prevlevel; $i-) {
                if ($OL && $i == 1) { push(@toc, "<OL>\n"); }
                else { push(@toc, "<UL>\n"); }
            }
        }
        if ($title) { push(@toc, qq|<LI><A HREF="$file">$content</A>\n|); }
        else { push(@toc, qq|<LI><A HREF="$file#$name">$content</A>\n|); }

        $prevlevel = $level;
        $_id++;
    }
}
##-----------------------------------------------------------------##
sub put_back_comments {
    local(*array) = shift;

    if (@Comments) {
      foreach (@array) {
          s/$ComMark/shift @Comments/geo;
      }
    }
    @Comments = ();
}
```

```
##————————————————————————————————————————————————————————-##
##     cp() copies file $src to $dst;
##
sub cp {
    local($src, $dst) = @_;
    open(SRC, $src) || die "ERROR: Unable to open $src\n";
    open(DST, "> $dst") || die "ERROR: Unable to create $dest\n";
    print DST <SRC>;
    close(SRC);
    close(DST);
}
##————————————————————————————————————————————————————————-##
sub Usage {
    select STDOUT;
    print <<EndOfUsage;
Usage: $PROG [<options>] file ...
Options:
  -footer <file>: File containing footer text for ToC
  -header <file>: File containing header text for ToC
  -help                      : This message
  -inline              : Put ToC in document
  -noorg               : Delete backup original ".org" files on completion
  -ol                  : Use an ordered list for level 1 ToC entries
  -prefix <string>     : Prefix for ToC IDs for linking
                          (def: "xtocid")
  -quiet               : Suppress informative messages
  -textonly            : Use only text content in significant elements
  -title <string>      : Title for ToC
                          (def: "Table of Contents")
  -toc <file>          : Output ToC file
                          (def: STDOUT)
  -toclabel <string>,  : HTML text that labels the ToC
                          (def: "<H1>Table of Contents</H1>")
  -tocmap <file>: ToC map file defining significant elements
  -useorg              : Use pre-existing ".org" files
Description:
  $PROG generates a Table of Contents (ToC) for all HTML files specified.
  By default, the generated ToC goes to standard output (STDOUT).  If
  the -toc option is given, the ToC goes to the named file.  If the -inline
  option is specified, the ToC is inserted at the beginning of the processed
  document.  Read documentation for more information on all options.
Version:
  $VERSION
  Copyright (C) 1995  Earl Hood, ehood@convex.com
  htmltoc comes with ABSOLUTELY NO WARRANTY and htmltoc may be copied only
  under the terms of the GNU General Public License (version 2, or later),
```

which may be found in the distribution.

```
EndOfUsage
    exit 0;
}
##———————————————————————————————————————————————————-##
##     read_sgml() reads SGML markup.  The *array_r is the returned
##     array that contains tags separated from text.  I.e. read_sgml()
##     splits the markup tags from text.  Each array item is either a
##     markup tag or a text.  The order of tag/text items are the
##     order they appear in the text.
##
##     Argument descriptions:
##         $handle :     Filehandle containing the SGML instance.
##         *array_r :    Pointer to array variable to put splitted tag/text.
##
sub read_sgml {
    local($handle, *array_r) = @_;
    local($d) = $/;
    local($txt, $save, $tmp, $c);

    $/ = 0777;               # Slurps entire file
    $tmp = <$handle>;

    ## Delete comment declarations ##
    while ($tmp =~ s/^([^<]*<)//) {
      $txt .= $1;
      if ($tmp =~ s/^(!-)//) {
          $c = chop $txt;
          $save = $c . $1;
          $txt .= $ComMark;
          while (1) {
              $tmp =~ s/^([^>]*>)//;
              $save .= $1;
              last if $1 =~ /-\s*>$/ || !$tmp;
          }
          push(@Comments, $save);
      } else {
          $tmp =~ s/^([^>]*>)//;  $txt .= $1;
      }
    }

    $txt .= $tmp;
    @array_r = split(/(<[^>]*>)/, $txt);
    $/ = $d;
}
1;
```

LISTING 2: TXT2HTML.PL

```
# Configurable options
#

# [-s <n>    ] | [-shortline <n>                     ]
$short_line_length = 40;         # Lines this short (or shorter) must be
                                 # intentionally broken and are kept
                                 # that short. <BR>

# [-p <n>    ] | [-prewhite <n>                     ]
$preformat_whitespace_min = 5;   # Minimum number of consecutive leading
                                 # whitespace characters to trigger
                                 # preformatting.
                                     # NOTE: Tabs are now expanded to
                                     # spaces before this check is made.
                                     # That means if $tab_width is 8 and
                                     # this is 5, then one tab is expanded
                                     # to 8 spaces, which is enough to
                                     # trigger preformatting.

# [-pb <n>   ] | [-prebegin <n>                      ]
$preformat_trigger_lines = 2;    # How many lines of preformatted-looking
                                 # text are needed to switch to <PRE>
                                 # <= 0 : Preformat entire document
                                 #    1 : one line triggers
                                 # >= 2 : two lines trigger

# [-pe <n>   ] | [-preend <n>                       ]
$endpreformat_trigger_lines = 2; # How many lines of unpreformatted-looking
                                    # text are needed to switch from <PRE>
                                # <= 0 : Never preformat within document
                                #    1 : one line triggers
                                # >= 2 : two lines trigger
# NOTE for -prebegin and -preend:
# A zero takes precedence.  If one is zero, the other is ignored.
# If both are zero, entire document is preformatted.


# [-r <n>    ] | [-hrule <n>                      ]
$hrule_min = 4;                  # Min number of --s for an HRule.

# [-c <n>    ] | [-caps <n>                      ]
$min_caps_length = 3;            # min sequential CAPS for an all-caps line

# [-ct <tag> ] | [-capstag <tag>                 ]
```

```
$caps_tag = "STRONG";              # Tag to put around all-caps lines

# [-m/+m    ] | [-mail      / -nomail      ]
$mailmode = 0;                     # Deal with mail headers & quoted text

# [-u/+u    ] | [-unhyphenate / -nounhyphenate ]
$unhyphenation = 1;                # Enables unhyphenation of text.

# [-a <file> ] | [-append <file>              ]
# [+a        ] | [-noappend                   ]
$append_file = 0;                  # If you want something appended by
                                   # default, put the filename here.
                                   # The appended text will not be
                                   # processed at all, so make sure it's
                                   # plain text or decent HTML.  i.e. do
                                   # not have things like:
                                   #    Seth Golub <seth@cs.wustl.edu>
                                   # but instead, have:
                                   #    Seth Golub &lt;seth@cs.wustl.edu&gt;

# [-t <title>] | [-title <title>              ]
$title = 0;                        # You can specify a title.
                                   # Otherwise it won't put one in.

# [-ul <n>   ] | [-underlinelong <n>          ]
$underline_tolerance_long = 1;     # How much longer can underlines
                                   # be and still be underlines?

# [-us <n>   ] | [-underlineshort <n>         ]
$underline_tolerance_short = 1;    # How much shorter can underlines
                                   # be and still be underlines?

# [-tw <n>   ] | [-tabwidth <n>               ]
$tab_width = 8;                    # How many spaces equal a tab?

# [-iw <n>   ] | [-indent <n>                 ]
$indent_width = 2;                 # Indents this many spaces for each
                                   # level of a list

# [-/+e      ] | [-extract / -noextract       ]
$extract = 0;                      # Extract Mode (suitable for inserting)

# END OF CONFIGURABLE OPTIONS
######################################
```

```
#####################################
# Definitions  (Don't change these)
#
$NONE       =   0;
$LIST       =   1;
$HRULE      =   2;
$PAR        =   4;
$PRE        =   8;
$END        =  16;
$BREAK      =  32;
$HEADER     =  64;
$MAILHEADER = 128;
$MAILQUOTE  = 256;
$CAPS       = 512;

$OL = 1;
$UL = 2;

sub usage
{
    $0 =~ s#.*/##;
    local($s) = " " x length($0);
    print STDERR <<EOF;

Usage: $0 [options]

where options are:
        $s [-v        ] | [-version                      ]
        $s [-h        ] | [-help                         ]
        $s [-s <n>    ] | [-shortline <n>                ]
        $s [-p <n>    ] | [-prewhite <n>                 ]
        $s [-pb <n>   ] | [-prebegin <n>                 ]
        $s [-pe <n>   ] | [-preend <n>                   ]
        $s [-e/+e     ] | [-extract / -noextract         ]
        $s [-r <n>    ] | [-hrule <n>                    ]
        $s [-c <n>    ] | [-caps <n>                     ]
        $s [-ct <tag> ] | [-capstag <tag>                ]
        $s [-m/+m     ] | [-mail      / -nomail          ]
        $s [-u/+u     ] | [-unhyphen / -nounhyphen       ]
        $s [-a <file> ] | [-append <file>                ]
        $s [+a        ] | [-noappend                     ]
        $s [-t <title>] | [-title <title>                ]
        $s [-tw <n>   ] | [-tabwidth <n>                 ]
        $s [-iw <n>   ] | [-indent <n>                   ]
        $s [-ul <n>   ] | [-underlinelong <n>            ]
        $s [-us <n>   ] | [-underlineshort <n>           ]
```

More complete explanations of these options can be found in
comments near the beginning of the script.

EOF
}

```perl
sub deal_with_options
{
    while ($ARGV[0] =~ /^[-+].+/)
    {
        if (($ARGV[0] eq "-r" || $ARGV[0] eq "-hrule") &&
            $ARGV[1] =~ /^%d+$/)
        {
            $hrule_min = $ARGV[1];
            shift @ARGV;
            next;
        }

        if (($ARGV[0] eq "-s" || $ARGV[0] eq "-shortline") &&
            $ARGV[1] =~ /^\d+$/)
        {
            $short_line_length = $ARGV[1];
            shift @ARGV;
            next;
        }

        if (($ARGV[0] eq "-p" || $ARGV[0] eq "-prewhite") &&
            $ARGV[1] =~ /^\d+$/)
        {
            $preformat_whitespace_min = $ARGV[1];
            shift @ARGV;
            next;
        }

        if (($ARGV[0] eq "-pb" || $ARGV[0] eq "-prebegin") &&
            $ARGV[1] =~ /^\d+$/)
        {
            $preformat_trigger_lines = $ARGV[1];
            shift @ARGV;
            next;
        }

        if (($ARGV[0] eq "-pe" || $ARGV[0] eq "-preend") &&
            $ARGV[1] =~ /^\d+$/)
        {
```

```perl
        $endpreformat_trigger_lines = $ARGV[1];
        shift @ARGV;
        next;
    }

    if (($ARGV[0] eq "-e" || $ARGV[0] eq "-extract"))
    {
        $extract = 1;
        shift @ARGV;
        next;
    }

    if (($ARGV[0] eq "+e" || $ARGV[0] eq "-noextract"))
    {
        $extract = 0;
        shift @ARGV;
        next;
    }

    if (($ARGV[0] eq "-c" || $ARGV[0] eq "-caps") &&
        $ARGV[1] =~ /^\d+$/)
    {
        $min_caps_length = $ARGV[1];
        shift @ARGV;
        next;
    }

    if (($ARGV[0] eq "-ct" || $ARGV[0] eq "-capstag") &&
        $ARGV[1])
    {
        $caps_tag = $ARGV[1];
        shift @ARGV;
        next;
    }

    if ($ARGV[0] eq "-m" || $ARGV[0] eq "-mail")
    {
        $mailmode = 1;
        next;
    }

    if ($ARGV[0] eq "+m" || $ARGV[0] eq "-nomail")
    {
        $mailmode = 0;
        next;
    }
```

```perl
if ($ARGV[0] eq "-u" || $ARGV[0] eq "-unhyphen")
{
    $unhyphenation = 1;
    next;
}

if ($ARGV[0] eq "+u" || $ARGV[0] eq "-nounhyphen")
{
    $unhyphenation = 0;
    next;
}

if (($ARGV[0] eq "-a" || $ARGV[0] eq "-append") &&
    $ARGV[1])
{
    if (-r $ARGV[1]) {
        $append_file = $ARGV[1];
    } else {
        print STDERR "Can't find or read $ARGV[1].\n";
    }
    shift @ARGV;
    next;
}

if ($ARGV[0] eq "+a" || $ARGV[0] eq "-noappend")
{
    $append_file = 0;
    next;
}

if (($ARGV[0] eq "-t" || $ARGV[0] eq "-title") &&
    $ARGV[1])
{
    $title = $ARGV[1];
    shift @ARGV;
    next;
}

if (($ARGV[0] eq "-ul" || $ARGV[0] eq "-underlinelong") &&
    $ARGV[1] =~ /^\d+$/)
{
    $underline_tolerance_long = $ARGV[1];
    shift @ARGV;
    next;
}
```

```perl
    if (($ARGV[0] eq "-us" || $ARGV[0] eq "-underlineshort") &&
        $ARGV[1] =~ /^\d+$/)
    {
        $underline_tolerance_short = $ARGV[1];
        shift @ARGV;
        next;
    }


    if (($ARGV[0] eq "-tw" || $ARGV[0] eq "-tabwidth") &&
        $ARGV[1] =~ /^\d+$/)
    {
        $tab_width = $ARGV[1];
        shift @ARGV;
        next;
    }


    if (($ARGV[0] eq "-iw" || $ARGV[0] eq "-indentwidth") &&
        $ARGV[1] =~ /^\d+$/)
    {
        $indent_width = $ARGV[1];
        shift @ARGV;
        next;
    }


    if ($ARGV[0] eq "-v" || $ARGV[0] eq "-version")
    {
        print '$Header: /users/hilco/seth/projects/txt2html/txt2html.pl,v 1.10 1994/12/28
20:10:25 seth Exp seth $ ';
        print "\n";
        exit;
    }


    if ($ARGV[0] eq "-h" || $ARGV[0] eq "-help")
    {
        &usage;
        exit;
    }


    print STDERR "Unrecognized option: $ARGV[0]\n";
    print STDERR " or bad paramater: $ARGV[1]\n" if($ARGV[1]);

    &usage;
    exit(1);


} continue {
```

```perl
        shift @ARGV;
    }

    $preformat_trigger_lines = 0 if ($preformat_trigger_lines < 0);
    $preformat_trigger_lines = 2 if ($preformat_trigger_lines > 2);

    $endpreformat_trigger_lines = 1 if ($preformat_trigger_lines == 0);
    $endpreformat_trigger_lines = 0 if ($endpreformat_trigger_lines < 0);
    $endpreformat_trigger_lines = 2 if ($endpreformat_trigger_lines > 2);

    $underline_tolerance_long  = 0 if $underline_tolerance_long < 0;
    $underline_tolerance_short = 0 if $underline_tolerance_short < 0;
}

sub is_blank
{
    return $_[0] =~ /^\s*$/;
}

sub escape
{
    $line =~ s/&/&amp;/g;
    $line =~ s/>/&gt;/g;
    $line =~ s/</&lt;/g;
    $line =~ s/\014/\n<HR>\n/g;        # Linefeeds become horizontal rules
}

sub hrule
{
    if ($line =~ /^\s*([-_~=\*]\s*){$hrule_min,}$/)
    {
        $line = "<HR>\n";
        $prev =~ s/<p>//;
        $line_action |= $HRULE;
    }
}

sub shortline
{
    if (!($mode & $PRE) &&
        !&is_blank($line) &&
        ($line_length < $short_line_length) &&
        !&is_blank($nextline) &&
        !($line_action & ($HEADER | $HRULE | $BREAK | $LIST)))
    {
        $line =~ s/$/<BR>/;
```

```perl
        $line_action |= $BREAK;
    }
}

sub mailstuff
{
    if ((($line =~ /^\w*&gt/) ||  # Handle "FF> Werewolves."
       ($line =~ /^\w*\|/))&&  # Handle "Igor| There wolves."
       !&is_blank($nextline))
    {
      $line =~ s/$/<BR>/;
      $line_action |= $BREAK | $MAILQUOTE;
    } elsif (($line =~ /^[\w-]*:/) # Handle "Some-Header: blah"
           && (($previous_action & $MAILHEADER) || &is_blank($prev))
           && !&is_blank($nextline))
    {
      &anchor_mail if !($previous_action & $MAILHEADER);
      $line =~ s/$/<BR>/;
      $line_action |= $BREAK | $MAILHEADER;
    } elsif (($line =~ /^\s+\S/) &&    # Handle multi-line mail headers
           ($previous_action & $MAILHEADER) &&
           !&is_blank($nextline))
    {
      $line =~ s/$/<BR>/;
      $line_action |= $BREAK | $MAILHEADER;
    }
}

sub paragraph
{
    $prev .= "<p>\n";
    $line_action |= $PAR;
}

sub listprefix
{
    local($line) = @_;
    local($prefix, $number, $rawprefix);

    return (0,0,0) if (!($line =~ /^\s*[-=\*o]\s+\S/ ) &&
                    !($line =~ /^\s*(\d+|[a-zA-Z])[\.\)\]:]\s+\S/ ));

    ($number) = $line =~ /^\s*(\d+|[a-zA-Z])/;

    # That slippery exception of "o" as a bullet
    # (This ought to be determined more through the context of what lists
```

```perl
   # we have in progress, but this will probably work well enough.)
   if($line =~ /^\s*o\s/)
   {
      $number = 0;
   }

   if ($number)
   {
      ($rawprefix) = $line =~ /^(\s*(\d+|[a-zA-Z]).)/;
      $prefix = $rawprefix;
      $prefix =~ s/(\d+|[a-zA-Z])//;          # Take the number out
   } else {
      ($rawprefix) = $line =~ /^(\s*[-=o\*].)/;
      $prefix = $rawprefix;
   }
   ($prefix, $number, $rawprefix);
}

sub startlist
{
   local($prefix, $number, $rawprefix) = @_;

   $listprefix[$listnum] = $prefix;
   if($number)
   {
      # It doesn't start with 1,a,A.  Let's not screw with it.
      if (($number != 1) && ($number ne "a") && ($number ne "A"))
      {
         return;
      }
      $prev .= "$list_indent<OL>\n";
      $list[$listnum] = $OL;
   } else {
      $prev .= "$list_indent<UL>\n";
      $list[$listnum] = $UL;
   }
   $listnum++;
   $list_indent = " " x $listnum x $indent_width;
   $line_action |= $LIST;
   $mode |= $LIST;
}


sub endlist                            # End N lists
{
   local($n) = @_;
```

```perl
    for(; $n > 0; $n--, $listnum--)
    {
      $list_indent = " " x ($listnum-1) x $indent_width;
      if($list[$listnum-1] == $UL)
      {
          $prev .= "$list_indent</UL>\n";
      } elsif($list[$listnum-1] == $OL)
      {
          $prev .= "$list_indent</OL>\n";
      } else
      {
          print STDERR "Encountered list of unknown type\n";
      }
    }
    $line_action |= $END;
    $mode ^= ($LIST & $mode) if (!$listnum);
}

sub continuelist
{
    $line =~ s/^\s*[-=o\*]\s*/$list_indent<LI> / if $list[$listnum-1] == $UL;
    $line =~ s/^\s*(\d+|[a-zA-Z]).\s*/$list_indent<LI> /    if $list[$listnum-1] == $OL;
    $line_action |= $LIST;
}

sub liststuff
{
    local($i);

    local($prefix, $number, $rawprefix) = &listprefix($line);

    $i = $listnum;
    if (!$prefix)
    {
      return if !&is_blank($prev); # inside a list item

      # This ain't no list.  We'll want to end all of them.
      return if !($mode & $LIST);  # This just speeds up the inevitable
      $i = 0;
    } else
    {
      # Maybe we're going back up to a previous list
      $i-- while (($prefix ne $listprefix[$i-1]) && ($i >= 0));
    }

    if (($i >= 0) && ($i != $listnum))
```

```perl
      {
        &endlist($listnum - $i);
      } elsif (!$listnum || $i != $listnum)
      {
        &startlist($prefix, $number, $rawprefix);
      }

      &continuelist($prefix, $number, $rawprefix) if ($mode & $LIST);
  }

sub endpreformat
{
    if(!($line =~ /\s{$preformat_whitespace_min,}\S+/) &&
       ($endpreformat_trigger_lines == 1 ||
       !($nextline =~ /\s{$preformat_whitespace_min,}\S+/)))
    {
      $prev =~ s#$#\n</PRE>#;
      $mode ^= ($PRE & $mode);
      $line_action |= $END;
    }
}

sub preformat
{
    if($preformat_trigger_lines == 0 ||
      (($line =~ /\s{$preformat_whitespace_min,}\S+/) &&
       ($preformat_trigger_lines == 1 ||
        $nextline =~ /\s{$preformat_whitespace_min,}\S+/)))
    {
      $line =~ s/^/<PRE>\n/;
      $prev =~ s/<p>//;
      $mode |= $PRE;
      $line_action |= $PRE;
    }
}

sub make_new_anchor
{
    $anchor++;
    $anchor;
}

sub anchor_mail
{
    local($text) = $line =~ /\S+: *(.*) *$/;
    local($anchor) = &make_new_anchor($text);
```

```perl
    $line =~ s/(.*)/<A NAME="$anchor">$1<\/A>/;
}


sub anchor_heading
{
    local($heading) = @_;
    local($anchor) = &make_new_anchor($heading);
    $line =~ s/(<H.>.*<\/H.>)/<A NAME="$anchor">$1<\/A>/;
}


sub heading
{
    local($hindent, $heading) = $line =~ /^(\s*)(.+)$/;
    $hindent = 0;                       # This isn't used yet, but Perl warns of
                                        # "possible typo" if I declare a var
                                        # and never reference it.

    # This is now taken care of in main()
#    $heading =~ s/\s+$//;# get rid of trailing whitespace.

    local($underline) = $nextline =~ /^\s*(\S+)\s*$/;

    if((length($heading) > (length($underline) + $underline_tolerance_short))
       || (length($heading) < (length($underline) -$underline_tolerance_long)))
    {
      return;
    }

#    $underline =~ s/(^.).*/$1/;      # Could I do this any less efficiently?
    $underline = substr($underline,0,1);

    local($hlevel);
    $hlevel = 1 if $underline eq "*";
    $hlevel = 2 if $underline eq "=";
    $hlevel = 3 if $underline eq "+";
    $hlevel = 4 if $underline eq "-";
    $hlevel = 5 if $underline eq "~";
    $hlevel = 6 if $underline eq ".";
    return if !$hlevel;

    $nextline = <STDIN>;  # Eat the underline
    &tagline("H${hlevel}");
    &anchor_heading($heading);
    $line_action |= $HEADER;
}
```

```perl
sub unhyphenate
{
    local($second);

    # This looks hairy because of all the quoted characters.
    # All I'm doing is pulling out the word that begins the next line.
    # Along with it, I pull out any punctuation that follows.
    # Preceding whitespace is preserved.  We don't want to screw up
    # our own guessing systems that rely on indentation.
    ($second) = $nextline =~ /^\s*([a-zA-Z]+[\)\}\]\.,:;\'\"\>]*\s*)/; # "
    $nextline =~ s/^(\s*)[a-zA-Z]+[\)\}\]\.,:;\'\"\>]*\s*/$1/; # "
    # (The silly comments are for my less-than-perfect code hilighter)

    $line =~ s/\-\s*$/$second/;
    $line .= "\n";
}

sub untabify
{
    local($oldws) = $line =~ /^([ \011]+)/;
    local($oldlen) = (length($oldws));

    local($i, $column);
    for($i=0, $column = 0; $i < $oldlen; $i++)
    {
        if(substr($oldws, $i, 1) eq " ")
        {                               # Space
            $column++;
        } else {          # Tab
            $column += $tab_width - ($column % $tab_width);
        }
    }
    $line = (" " x $column) . substr($line, $oldlen);
}

sub tagline
{
    local($tag) = @_;
    $line =~ s/^\s*(.*)\s*$/<$tag>$1<\/$tag>\n/;
}

sub caps
{
    if($line =~ /^[^a-z<]*[A-Z]{$min_caps_length,}[^a-z<]*$/)
    {
        &tagline($caps_tag);
```

```
            $line_action |= $CAPS;
        }
    }


sub main
{
    &deal_with_options;

    if(!$extract)
    {
      print "<HTML>\n";
      print "<HEAD>\n";

      # It'd be nice if we could guess a title from the first header,
      # but even that would be too late if we're doing this in one pass.
      print "<TITLE>$title</TITLE>\n" if($title);

      print "</HEAD>\n";

      print "<BODY>\n";
    }

    $prev     = "";
    $line     = <STDIN>;
    $nextline = <STDIN>;
    do
    {
      $line =~ s/[ \011]*$//;       # Chop trailing whitespace

      &untabify;                    # Change leading whitespace into spaces

      $line_length = length($line); # Do this before tags go in

      &escape;

      &endpreformat if (($mode & $PRE) && ($preformat_trigger_lines != 0));

      &hrule if !($mode & $PRE);

      &heading    if (!($mode & $PRE) &&
                       $nextline =~ /^\s*[=\-\*\.~\+]+$/);

      &caps if  !($mode & $PRE);
```

```
&liststuff if (!($mode & $PRE) &&
               !&is_blank($line));

&mailstuff if ($mailmode &&
               !($mode & $PRE) &&
               !($line_action & $HEADER));

&preformat if (!($line_action & ($HEADER | $LIST | $MAILHEADER)) &&
               !($mode & ($LIST | $PRE)) &&
               ($endpreformat_trigger_lines != 0));

&paragraph if ((&is_blank($prev) || ($line_action & $END)) &&
               !&is_blank($line) &&
               !($mode & ($LIST | $PRE)) && # paragraphs in lists
                                        # *should* be allowed.
               (!$line_action ||
                  ($line_action & ($CAPS | $END | $MAILQUOTE))));

&shortline;

&unhyphenate if ($unhyphenation &&
                 ($line =~ /[a-zA-Z]\-$/) && # ends in hyphen
                 # next line starts w/letters
                 ($nextline =~ /^\s*[a-zA-Z]/) &&
                 !($mode & ($PRE | $HEADER | $MAILHEADER | $BREAK)));


# Print it out and move on.

print $prev;

if (!&is_blank($nextline))
{
    $previous_action = $line_action;
    $line_action     = $NONE;
}

$prev = $line;
$line = $nextline;
$nextline = <STDIN>;
} until (!$nextline && !$line && !$prev);

$prev = "";
&endlist($listnum) if ($mode & $LIST); # End all lists
print $prev;
```

```
    print "\n";

    print "</PRE>\n" if ($mode & $PRE);

    if ($append_file)
    {
      if(-r $append_file)
      {
         open(APPEND, $append_file);
         print while <APPEND>;
      } else {
         print STDERR "Can't find or read file $append_file to append.\n";
      }
    }

    if(!$extract)
    {
      print "</BODY>\n";
      print "</HTML>\n";
    }
}

&main();
```

LISTING 3: WEBXREF.PL: A WEB CROSS-REFERENCER

```perl
$debug = 0;

if ($debug) {
print "=================================================\n";
print "\n input file: $ARGV[0]\n";
}

$root = `pwd`;
chop($root);

print "\nChecking $ARGV[0]\n\n";
&Get_Refs($ARGV[0],"<none>");

&Print_Lists;

exit;

#————————————————————————--

sub Get_PWD {

# Get the pwd, make sure it ends with a slash

local($dir);

$dir = `pwd`;
$dir =~ s/\n//g;
if (!($dir =~ m#.*/$#)) {
  $dir = "$dir/";
}

return $dir;

}
sub Get_Refs {

# Get all referenced files a from the file

local(%newlist);
local($file);
local($dir);
local($Old_Dir);
local($filename);
```

```perl
$dir=&Dir_Name($_[0]);
if ($dir eq "") {
  $dir = &Get_PWD;
}
$file=&Base_Name($_[0]);
#print "———————————\n";
if ($debug) {
print "arg=$_[0]\n";
print "dir=$dir\n";
print "file=$file\n";
}


# http?
if ($_[0] =~ m/.*(http:.*)/i) {
  if (!defined($HTTPList{$1})) {
    $HTTPList{$1} = $_[1];
    }
  else {
    $HTTPList{$1} = "$HTTPList{$1} $_[1]";
  }
  return;
}


# ftp?
if ($_[0] =~ m/.*(ftp:.*)/i) {
  if (!defined($FTPList{$1})) {
    $FTPList{$1} = $_[1];
    }
  else {
    $FTPList{$1} = "$FTPList{$1} $_[1]";
  }
  return;
}


# telnet?
if ($_[0] =~ m/.*(telnet:.*)/i) {
  if (!defined($TelnetList{$1})) {
    $TelnetList{$1} = $_[1];
    }
  else {
    $TelnetList{$1} = "$TelnetList{$1} $_[1]";
```

```
    }
   return;
  }
  # gopher?
  if ($_[0] =~ m/.*(gopher:.*)/i) {
    if (!defined($GopherList{$1})) {
      $GopherList{$1} = $_[1];
      }
    else {
      $GopherList{$1} = "$GopherList{$1} $_[1]";
    }
    return;
  }
  # mailto?
  if ($_[0] =~ m/.*(mailto:.*)/i) {
    if (!defined($MailList{$1})) {
      $MailList{$1} = $_[1];
      }
    else {
      $MailList{$1} = "$MailList{$1} $_[1]";
    }
    return;
  }
  # news?
  if ($_[0] =~ m/.*(news:.*)/i) {
    if (!defined($NewsList{$1})) {
      $NewsList{$1} = $_[1];
      }
    else {
      $NewsList{$1} = "$NewsList{$1} $_[1]";
    }
    return;
  }

  # directory reference?
  if ($file eq "") {

    if ($debug) {
      print "$dir must be a dir, refd by $_[1]!\n";
    }
    if (-d $_[0]) {
      if (!defined($DirList{$_[0]})) {
        $DirList{$_[0]} = $_[1];
        }
      else {
        $DirList{$_[0]} = "$DirList{$_[0]} $_[1]";
```

```perl
      }
    }
    else {

      if (!defined($DirNotFoundList{$_[0]})) {
        $DirNotFoundList{$_[0]} = $_[1];
      }
      else {
        $DirNotFoundList{$_[0]} = "$DirNotFoundList{$_[0]} $_[1]";
      }
    }

  return;
}


# Move to the specified directory
$Old_Dir = &Get_PWD;
if ($debug) {
  print "Chdir to $dir\n";
}
chdir($dir);
$dir=&Get_PWD;
if ($debug) {
  print "Now in $dir\n";
}
$filename = $dir . $file;

print "Checking: $filename\n";

# Is it a reference to a specific section? (a file#section reference)
if ($filename =~ m/(.+)#(.+)/) {
  $filename = $1;
  $section = $2;
  $filename = "$1#$2";
  if (&CheckAnchor($1, $2) ) {
    #print "** Anchor $2 is present in file $1\n";

    # Add to the list of anchors
    if (!defined($AnchorList{$filename})) {
      $AnchorList{$filename} = $_[1];
      }
    else {
      $AnchorList{$filename} = "$AnchorList{$filename} $_[1]";
    }
  }
```

```
    else {
      print "xx Anchor $2 is NOT present in file $1\n";
      print "xx Referenced by: $_[1]\n";
      #print "Anchor filename: $filename\n";

      # Add to the list of lost anchors
      if (!defined($LostAnchorList{$filename})) {
        $LostAnchorList{$filename} = $_[1];
        }
      else {
        $LostAnchorList{$filename} = "$LostAnchorList{$filename} $_[1]";
      }

    }
    return;
  }


#
# Add to the list of already tested files
#

# Check if the file is a plain file
if (-d $filename) {
  #print "xx $filename is a directory, skipped.\n";
  return;
}

if (! -f $filename) {
  print "xx $filename cannot be found\n";
  print "xx Referenced by: $_[1]\n";

  # Add to list of lost files
  if (!defined($LostFileList{$filename})) {
    $LostFileList{$filename} = $_[1];
    }
  else {
    $LostFileList{$filename} = "$LostFileList{$filename} $_[1]";
  }

  return;
}

# Binary file? (pictures,...)
if (-B $filename) {
  if ($debug) {
    print "** Binary file added to images";
```

```perl
    }
    if (defined($ImageFileList{$filename})) {
      return;
    }
    if (!defined($ImageFileList{$filename})) {
      $ImageFileList{$filename} = $_[1];  # Define!
      }
    else {
      $ImageFileList{$filename} = "$ImageFileList{$filename} $_[1]";
    }
    if ($debug) {
      print "\n\nAdded: $filename to list of images\n";
    }

    return;
  }

# else it's a text (html)file
if (!defined($FileList{$filename})) {
  $FileList{$filename} = $_[1];  # Define!
  }
else {
  $FileList{$filename} = "$FileList{$filename} $_[1]";

  return;  # Already did this file
}
if ($debug) {
  print "** Added: $filename \n";
}


# World readable?
($dev,$ino,$mode) = stat($filename);
$readmode = ($mode & 4);
if ($readmode == 0) {
  # Not world readable, add to list
  #print "xx Warning: $filename is not world readable\n";
  if (!defined($UnreadableList{$filename})) {
    $UnreadableList{$filename} = $_[1];
    }
  else {
    $UnreadableList{$filename} = "$UnreadableList{$filename} $_[1]";
  }
}

$err = 0;
```

```
open(HTML, $filename) || ($err = 1);
if ($err) {
  print "xx Could not open file $filename\n";
  return;
}

while (<HTML>) {
  chop;

  # <a href=...
  if (/<a\s+.*href\s*=\s*/i) {
    s/^.*<a\s+.*href *=//i;       # <a href=  at start
    s/>.*<a\s+.*href *=/ /gi;     # sub other <a href's in that line by space
    s/>.*$//i;                # remove >'s
    s/"//g;                   # Unquote file names
    s/^\s*//;                 # Remove spaces at start
    s/\s*$//;                 # Remove spaces at end

    # Link to section within current document?
    if (m/^#.*/) {
      $file_w_anchor = $filename;
      $file_w_anchor =~ s#.*/##;
      if ($debug) {
        print "file_w_anchor: $file_w_anchor\n";
        print "Added to newlist: $file_w_anchor$_\n";
      }
      $newlist{"$file_w_anchor$_"} = 1;  # Check this file plus anchor later
    }
    # Link to another document?
    else {
      if ($debug) {
        print "added to newlist: $_\n";
      }
      $newlist{$_} = 1;
    }

  }

  # <img src=...
  # NB: <img and src= must be on same line
  if (/<img\s*.*src\s*=\s*(.*)\s*.*>/i) {
    $imagefile = $1;
    $imagefile =~ s/"//g;
    $imagefile =~ s/>.*//;
    $imagefile =~ s/\s.*$//;
```

```perl
    # Add file to the list
    $newlist{$imagefile} = 1;
  }

}

close(HTML);

chdir($Old_Dir);

if ($debug) {
  # List files
  print "\nNewlist:\n";
  foreach $file (keys(%newlist)) {
    print "$file \n";
  }
}

# Walk the list
foreach $file (keys(%newlist)) {
  # if file is //something insert a http:
  if ($file =~ m#^//.*#) {
    $file = "http:" . $file;
  }

  $Notlocal_file = $dir . $file;

  # if file is /something it's a reference from the root document
#print "file-$file\n";
  if ($file =~ m#^/.*#) {
    #print "xxx ROOT REF DOC - not implemented yet\n";
    #print "xxx Result: $root$file\n";
    $Notlocal_file = "$root$file";
  }

  $Notlocal_ref_filename = $filename;
  if ($debug) {
    $ppp=&Get_PWD;
    print "\nCalling GR with $Notlocal_file\n";
    print "Referenced by: $newlist{$file}\n";
  }
  &Get_Refs($Notlocal_file, $Notlocal_ref_filename);
}
} #sub


#————————————————————————————-
```

```
sub Base_Name {

# return basename,
# e.g. /home/sscprick/.WWW/Welcome.html
# returns: Welcome.html

$local_filename=$_[0];
$local_filename =~ s#.*/##;  # remove the directory name -> file name

$local_filename;
}

sub Dir_Name {

# return dirname,
# e.g. /home/sscprick/.WWW/Welcome.html
# returns: /home/sscprick/.WWW/

$local_filename=$_[0];
$local_filename =~ s#.*/##;  # remove the directory name -> file name
$local_dirname = $_[0];
$local_filename =~ s/(\W)/\\$1/g;
$local_dirname =~ s/$local_filename//; # wipe filename -> dir name

$local_dirname;
}


sub CheckAnchor {

# See if #section anchor is present in file

open(CH_HTML, $_[0]);
while (<CH_HTML>) {
  chop;
  $anchor = $_[1];
  $anchor =~ s/(\W)/\\$1/g;  # quote rexep chars
  if (/<a +name *= *"*$anchor"*/i) {
    close(CH_HTML);
    return 1;
  }
}

close(CH_HTML);
return 0;
```

```perl
} # sub CheckAnchor

#——————————————————-

sub Print_List {

local(%list, $header) = @_;
print "\n\n————\n$header\n";
@TheList=keys(%list);
@SortedList = sort @TheList;

foreach $file (@SortedList) {
  print "$file \n";
  @lost = split(/ /,$list{$file});
  @sortlost = sort @lost;
  print "  Referenced by:\n";
  foreach $lostfile (@sortlost) {
    print "  $lostfile\n";
  }
}

} # sub Print_List
sub Print_Lists {

# Print lists

# List all files found
&Print_List(%FileList,"Web documents found:");

# List of directories referenced
&Print_List(%DirList,"Directories:");

# List of images referenced
&Print_List(%ImageFileList,"Images:");

# List of mailto's
&Print_List(%MailList,"Mailto:");

# List of ftp's
&Print_List(%FTPList,"ftp:");

# List of telnets
&Print_List(%TelnetList,"telnet:");

# List of gophers
&Print_List(%GopherList,"gopher:");
```

```
# List of news
&Print_List(%NewsList,"News:");

# List of http's
&Print_List(%HTTPList,"External URLs:");

# List of name anchors
&Print_List(%AnchorList,"Name anchors found:");

# List of files that can't be found
&Print_List(%LostFileList,"Files not found:");

# List of files that are not world readable
&Print_List(%UnreadableList,"Files not world readable:");

# List of directories that can't be found
&Print_List(%DirNotFoundList,"Directories not found:");

# List of name anchors not found
&Print_List(%LostAnchorList,"Name anchors not found:");

} #sub Print_Lists
```

LISTING 4: WEBLINT.PL

```perl
$VERSION  = '1.011';
($PROGRAM = $0) =~ s@.*/@@;
$TMPDIR   = $ENV{'TMPDIR'} || '/usr/tmp';


#-------------------------------------------------------------------
# $usage - usage string displayed with the -U command-line switch
#-------------------------------------------------------------------
$usage=<<EofUsage;
  $PROGRAM v$VERSION - pick fluff off web pages (HTML)
      -d     : disable specified warnings (warnings separated by commas)
      -e     : enable specified warnings (warnings separated by commas)
      -stderr : print warnings to STDERR rather than STDOUT
      -i     : ignore case in element tags
      -l     : ignore symlinks when recursing in a directory
      -s     : give short warning messages (filename not printed)
      -t     : terse warning mode, useful mainly for the weblint testsuite
      -todo  : print the todo list for $PROGRAM
      -help
      -U     : display this usage message
      -urlget : specify the command used to get a URL
      -version
      -v     : display version
      -warnings
             : list supported warnings, with identifier, and enabled status
      -x     : specify an HTML extension to include (supported: netscape)

  To check one or more HTML files, run weblint thusly:
      weblint foobar.html
      weblint file1.html ... fileN.html
  If a file is in fact a directory, weblint will recurse, checking all files.

  To include the netscape extensions:
      weblint -x netscape file.html
EofUsage


#-------------------------------------------------------------------
# $todo - ToDo string displayed with the -T command-line switch
#-------------------------------------------------------------------
$todo=<<EofToDo;
                    $PROGRAM v$VERSION - ToDo list

    o Verbose option to give longer warnings with example syntax.
    o build list of external links, for optional check at end.
```

o   check if any file in a directory hierarchy is not referenced.
o   Misuse of meta-characters, such as <, >, and ".
                (Barry Bakalor <barry\@hal.com>)
o   check for http://foo.com/nar/tar.gz!
o   option to spell-check text (Clay Webster <clay\@unipress.com>)
o   option to specify level of HTML (0, 1, or 2)
o   option to understand server-side includes, e.g.:
                    <!inc srv "/Header.html">
o   entity checks (Axel Boldt).
o   a `pedantic' command-line switch, which turns on all warnings.
o   bad-link check gets confused if given a path with directories in it,
    such as foo/bar/fred.html (Barry Bakalor)
o   SUB and SUP take one set of attributes in MATH mode, and
                a different set when used outside MATH mode.
o   Use a DTD!
o   Option to spit out the HTML source annotated with SGML comments
    which contain any weblint warnings. Tom Neff <tneff\@panix.com>
    This will be: set message-style = inline — neilb
o   Support for weblint directives in SGML comments.
    Tom Neff <tneff\@panix.com>
o   A standardized "Weblint approved" snippet of HTML to put in pages.
    This would also be a link to the weblint home page.
    Tom Neff <tneff\@panix.com>
o   Flag places where use of <P> is redundant, and considered bad style;
    such as following a <H?>. See "Composing Good HTML".
o   Illegal context check, such as <P> appearing in <H1> ... </H1>
    Jokinen Jyke <jyke\@cs.tut.fi>, Axel Boldt.
o   Check for existence of files with:
                <IMG src="missing.gif" alt="Missing Image">
                <BODY background="missing.gif">
    as it already does with:
                <A HREF="missing.html">missing thing</A>
    (Barry Bakalor <barry\@hal.com>)
o   Give a more helpful message when <A NAME="..."> is not closed.
o   The following is legal HTML, but weblint complains:
                <img alt = "> FOO <" src = "foo.gif">
    Reported by Abigail <abigail\@mars.ic.iaf.nl>
o   Warn about leading and trailing whitespace in container contents,
    at least for anchors:
                <a href="url"> url </a>
    Richard Finegold <goldfndr\@eskimo.com>
o   Add a warning which suggests you set WIDTH and HEIGHT on IMG
    elements, since this can improved rendering time on some browsers.
    Richard Finegold <goldfndr\@eskimo.com>
EofToDo

```perl
*WARNING = *STDOUT;

# obsolete tags
$obsoleteTags = 'PLAINTEXT|XMP|LISTING|COMMENT';

$maybePaired  = 'LI|DT|DD|P|ROW|TD|TH|TR';

$pairElements = 'A|ABBREV|ABOVE|ACRONYM|ADDRESS|ARRAY|AU|'.
                'HTML|HEAD|BANNER|BAR|BELOW|BIG|BLOCKQUOTE|BODY|BOX|BQ|BT|'.
                'CAPTION|CREDIT|DDOT|DEL|DIV|DOT|'.
                'FIG|FN|H1|H2|H3|H4|H5|H6|HAT|INS|LH|OVERLAY|'.
                'B|I|U|TT|STRONG|EM|CODE|KBD|VAR|DFN|CITE|SAMP|Q|LANG|'.
                'UL|OL|DL|'.
                'MATH|MENU|DIR|FORM|NOTE|PERSON|ROOT|'.
                'S|SELECT|SMALL|SQRT|STRIKE|STYLE|'.
                'SUB|SUP|T|TABLE|TEXT|TEXTAREA|TILDE|TITLE|VEC|CODE|PRE|'.
                $maybePaired.'|'.
                $obsoleteTags;

# expect to see these tags only once
%onceOnly = ('HTML', 1, 'HEAD', 1, 'BODY', 1, 'TITLE', 1);

%physicalFontElements =
(
 'B',  'STRONG',
 'I',  'EM',
 'TT', 'CODE, SAMP, KBD, or VAR'
 );

# expect these tags to have attributes
# these are elements which have no required attributes, but we expect to
# see at least one of the attributes
$expectArgsRE = 'A';

# these tags can only appear in the head element
$headTagsRE = 'TITLE|NEXTID|LINK|BASE|META';

%requiredContext =
(
 'ABOVE',    'MATH',
 'ARRAY',    'MATH',
 'ATOP',     'BOX',
 'BAR',      'MATH',
 'BELOW',    'MATH',
 'BOX',      'MATH',
```

```
'BT',        'MATH',
'CAPTION',   'TABLE|FIG',
'CHOOSE',    'BOX',
'DD',        'DL',
'DDOT',      'MATH',
'DOT',       'MATH',
'DT',        'DL',
'HAT',       'MATH',
'INPUT',     'FORM',
'ITEM',      'ROW',
'LEFT',      'BOX',
'LH',        'DL|OL|UL',
'LI',        'DIR|MENU|OL|UL',
'OF',        'ROOT',
'OPTION',    'SELECT',
'OVER',      'BOX',
'OVERLAY',   'FIG',
'RIGHT',     'BOX',
'ROOT',      'MATH',
'ROW',       'ARRAY',
'SELECT',    'FORM',
'SQRT',      'MATH',
'T',         'MATH',
'TD',        'TR',
'TEXT',      'MATH',
'TEXTAREA',  'FORM',
'TH',        'TR',
'TILDE',     'MATH',
'TR',        'TABLE',
'VEC',       'MATH'
);

# these tags are allowed to appear in the head element
%okInHead = ('ISINDEX', 1, 'TITLE', 1, 'NEXTID', 1, 'LINK', 1,
            'BASE', 1, 'META', 1, 'RANGE', 1, 'STYLE', 1, '!-', 1);

# expect to see these at least once.
# html-outer covers the HTML element
@expectedTags = ('HEAD', 'TITLE', 'BODY');

# elements which cannot be nested
$nonNest = 'A|FORM';

$netscapeElements = 'NOBR|WBR|FONT|BASEFONT|BLINK|CENTER';

#
```

```
# This is a regular expression for all legal elements
# UPDATE: need to remove duplication in legalElements and pairElements
#
$legalElements =
    'A|ABBREV|ABOVE|ACRONYM|ADDRESS|ARRAY|ATOP|AU|'.
    'B|BANNER|BAR|BASE|BELOW|BIG|BLOCKQUOTE|BODY|BOX|BQ|BR|BT|'.
    'CAPTION|CHOOSE|CITE|CODE|CREDIT|'.
    'DD|DDOT|DFN|DEL|DIR|DIV|DL|DOT|DT|'.
    'EM|FIG|FN|FORM|H1|H2|H3|H4|H5|H6|HAT|HEAD|HR|HTML|'.
    'I|IMG|INPUT|INS|ISINDEX|ITEM|KBD|'.
    'LANG|LEFT|LH|LI|LINK|MATH|MENU|META|NEXTID|NOTE|'.
    'OF|OL|OPTION|OVER|OVERLAY|P|PERSON|PRE|Q|RANGE|RIGHT|ROOT|ROW|'.
    'SAMP|SELECT|S|SMALL|SQRT|STRIKE|STRONG|STYLE|SUB|SUP|'.
    'T|TAB|TABLE|TD|TEXT|TEXTAREA|TH|TILDE|TITLE|TR|TT|U|UL|VAR|VEC|'.
    $obsoleteTags;

# This table holds the valid attributes for elements
# Where an element does not have an entry, this implies that the element
# does not take any attributes
%validAttributes =
    (
    'A',          'ID|LANG|CLASS|HREF|MD|NAME|SHAPE|TITLE|REL|REV',
    'ABOVE',      'SYM',
    'ADDRESS',    'ID|LANG|CLASS|CLEAR|NOWRAP',
    'ARRAY',      'ALIGN|COLDEF|LDELIM|RDELIM|LABELS',
    'BANNER',     'ID|LANG|CLASS',
    'BASE',       'HREF',
    'BR',         'ID|LANG|CLASS|CLEAR',
    'BLOCKQUOTE', 'ID|LANG|CLASS|CLEAR|NOWRAP',
    'BODY',       'ID|LANG|CLASS|BACKGROUND',
    'BOX',        'SIZE',
    'BQ',         'ID|LANG|CLASS|CLEAR|NOWRAP',
    'BELOW',      'SYM',
    'CAPTION',    'ID|LANG|CLASS|ALIGN',
    'CREDIT',     'ID|LANG|CLASS',
    'DD',         'ID|LANG|CLASS|CLEAR',
    'DIV',        'ID|LANG|CLASS|ALIGN|NOWRAP|CLEAR',
    'DL',         'ID|LANG|CLASS|CLEAR|COMPACT',
    'DT',         'ID|LANG|CLASS|CLEAR',
    'FIG',        'ID|LANG|CLASS|CLEAR|NOFLOW|SRC|MD|ALIGN|WIDTH|HEIGHT|'.
                  'UNITS|IMAGEMAP',
    'FN',         'ID|LANG|CLASS',
    'FORM',       'ACTION|METHOD|ENCTYPE|SCRIPT',
    'H1',         'ID|LANG|CLASS|ALIGN|CLEAR|SEQNUM|SKIP|DINGBAT|SRC|MD|NOWRAP',
    'H2',         'ID|LANG|CLASS|ALIGN|CLEAR|SEQNUM|SKIP|DINGBAT|SRC|MD|NOWRAP',
    'H3',         'ID|LANG|CLASS|ALIGN|CLEAR|SEQNUM|SKIP|DINGBAT|SRC|MD|NOWRAP',
```

```
    'H4',        'ID|LANG|CLASS|ALIGN|CLEAR|SEQNUM|SKIP|DINGBAT|SRC|MD|NOWRAP',
    'H5',        'ID|LANG|CLASS|ALIGN|CLEAR|SEQNUM|SKIP|DINGBAT|SRC|MD|NOWRAP',
    'H6',        'ID|LANG|CLASS|ALIGN|CLEAR|SEQNUM|SKIP|DINGBAT|SRC|MD|NOWRAP',
    'HR',        'ID|CLASS|CLEAR|SRC|MD',
    'HTML',      'VERSION|URN|ROLE',
    'IMG',       'ID|LANG|CLASS|SRC|MD|WIDTH|HEIGHT|UNITS|ALIGN|ALT|ISMAP',
    'INPUT',     'ID|LANG|CLASS|TYPE|NAME|VALUE|DISABLED|ERROR|CHECKED|SIZE|'.
                 'MAXLENGTH|MIN|MAX|ACCEPT|SRC|MD|ALIGN',
    'ITEM',      'ALIGN|COLSPAN|ROWSPAN',
    'LH',        'ID|LANG|CLASS',
    'LI',        'ID|LANG|CLASS|CLEAR|SRC|MD|DINGBAT|SKIP',
    'LINK',      'HREF|REL|REV|URN|TITLE|METHODS',
    'MATH',      'ID|CLASS|BOX',
    'META',      'HTTP-EQUIV|NAME|CONTENT',
    'NEXTID',    'N',
    'NOTE',      'ID|LANG|CLASS|CLEAR|SRC|MD',
    'OL',        'ID|LANG|CLASS|CLEAR|CONTINUE|SEQNUM|COMPACT',
    'OPTION',    'ID|LANG|CLASS|DISABLED|ERROR|VALUE|SELECTED|SHAPE',
    'OVERLAY',   'SRC|MD|UNITS|X|Y|WIDTH|HEIGHT',
    'P',         'ID|LANG|CLASS|ALIGN|CLEAR|NOWRAP',
    'PRE',       'ID|LANG|CLASS|CLEAR|WIDTH',
    'RANGE',     'ID|CLASS|FROM|UNTIL',
    'ROW',       'ALIGN|COLSPAN|ROWSPAN',
    'SELECT',    'ID|LANG|CLASS|NAME|MULTIPLE|DISABLED|ERROR|SRC|MD|WIDTH|'.
                 'HEIGHT|UNITS|ALIGN',
    'STYLE',     'NOTATION',
    'TAB',       'ID|INDENT|TO|ALIGN|DP',
    'TABLE',     'ID|LANG|CLASS|CLEAR|NOFLOW|ALIGN|UNITS|COLSPEC|DP|WIDTH|'.
                 'BORDER|NOWRAP',
    'TD',        'ID|LANG|CLASS|COLSPAN|ROWSPAN|ALIGN|DP|VALIGN|NOWRAP|'.
                 'AXIS|AXES',
    'TEXTAREA',  'ID|LANG|CLASS|NAME|ROWS|COLS|DISABLED|ERROR|ALIGN',
    'TH',        'ID|LANG|CLASS|COLSPAN|ROWSPAN|ALIGN|DP|VALIGN|NOWRAP|'.
                 'AXIS|AXES',
    'TR',        'ID|LANG|CLASS|ALIGN|DP|VALIGN|NOWRAP',
    'UL',        'ID|LANG|CLASS|CLEAR|PLAIN|SRC|MD|DINGBAT|WRAP|COMPACT',
    );

%requiredAttributes =
    (
    'BASE',      'HREF',
    'FORM',      'ACTION',
    'IMG',       'SRC',
    'LINK',      'HREF',
    'NEXTID',    'N',
    'SELECT',    'NAME',
```

```perl
    'STYLE',    'NOTATION',
    'TEXTAREA', 'NAME|ROWS|COLS'
    );

%validNetscapeAttributes =
    (
    'ISINDEX',  'PROMPT',
    'HR',       'SIZE|WIDTH|ALIGN|NOSHADE',
    'UL',       'TYPE',
    'OL',       'TYPE|START',
    'LI',       'TYPE|VALUE',
    'IMG',      'BORDER|VSPACE|HSPACE',
    'BODY',     'BGCOLOR|TEXT|LINK|VLINK|ALINK',
    'TABLE',    'CELLSPACING|CELLPADDING',
    'TD',       'WIDTH',
    'TH',       'WIDTH'
    );

%mustFollow =
(
 'LH',        'UL|OL|DL',
 'OVERLAY',   'FIG',
 'HEAD',      'HTML',
 'BODY',      '/HEAD',
 '/HTML',     '/BODY',
 );

%variable =
(
 'directory-index',       'index.html',
 'url-get',               'lynx -source',
 'message-style',         'lint'
);

@options = ('d=s', 'e=s', 'stderr', 'help', 'i', 'l', 's', 't', 'todo', 'U',
            'urlget=s', 'v', 'version', 'warnings', 'x=s');

$exit_status = 0;

require 'newgetopt.pl';
require 'find.pl';

die "$usage" unless @ARGV > 0;

&ReadDefaults();
&GetConfigFile();
```

```perl
# escape the `-' command-line switch (for stdin), so NGetOpt don't mess wi' it
grep(s/^-$/\tstdin\t/, @ARGV);

&NGetOpt(@options) || die "use -U switch to display usage statement\n";

# put back the `-' command-line switch, if it was there
grep(s/^\tstdin\t$/-/, @ARGV);

die "$PROGRAM v$VERSION\n"          if $opt_v || $opt_version;
die "$usage"                        if $opt_u || $opt_help;
die "$todo"                         if $opt_todo;
&AddExtension($opt_x)               if $opt_x;
$variable{'message-style'} = 'short' if $opt_s;
$variable{'message-style'} = 'terse' if $opt_t;
$variable{'url-get'} = $opt_urlget  if $opt_urlget;
*WARNING = *STDERR                  if $opt_stderr;
&ListWarnings()                       if $opt_warnings;

# WARNING file handle is default
select(WARNING);

$opt_l = 1                  if $ignore{'SYMLINKS'};

# -d to disable warnings
if ($opt_d)
{
   for (split(/,/,$opt_d))
   {
      &enableWarning($_, 0);
   }
}

# -e to enable warnings
if ($opt_e)
{
   for (split(/,/,$opt_e))
   {
      &enableWarning($_, 1) || next;
   }
}

# -i option to ignore case in element tags
if ($opt_i)
{
   $enabled{'lower-case'} = $enabled{'upper-case'} = 0;
}
```

```perl
while (@ARGV > 0)
{
    $arg = shift(@ARGV);

    &CheckURL($arg), next if $arg =~ m!^(http|gopher|ftp)://!;

    &find($arg), next if -d $arg;

    &WebLint($arg), next if (-f $arg && -r $arg) || $arg eq '-';

    print "$PROGRAM: could not read $arg: $!\n";
}

exit $exit_status;

#============================================================
# Function:     WebLint
# Purpose:      This is the high-level interface to the checker.  It takes
#               a file and checks for fluff.
#============================================================
sub WebLint
{
    local($filename,$relpath) = @_;
    local(@tags) = ();
    local($tagRE) = ('');
    local(@taglines) = ();
    local(@orphans) = ();
    local(@orphanlines) = ();
    local(%seenPage);
    local(%seenTag);
    local(%whined);
    local(*PAGE);
    local($line) = ('');
    local($id, $ID);
    local($tag);
    local($closing);
    local($tail);
    local(%args);
    local($arg);
    local($rest);
    local($lastNonTag);
    local(@notSeen);
    local($seenMailtoLink) = (0);
    local($matched);
    local($matchedLine);
    local($novalue);
```

```perl
      local($heading);
      local($headingLine);
      local($commentline);
      local($_);


      if ($filename eq ' ')
      {
        *PAGE = *STDIN;
        $filename = 'stdin';
      }
      else
      {
        return if defined $seenPage{$filename};
        if (-d $filename)
        {
         print "$PROGRAM: $filename is a directory.\n";
         $exit_status = 0;
         return;
        }
        $seenPage{$filename}++;
        open(PAGE,"<$filename") || do
        {
         print "$PROGRAM: could not read file $filename: $!\n";
         $exit_status = 0;
         return;
        };
        $filename = $relpath if defined $relpath;
      }

     undef $heading;

  READLINE:
    while (<PAGE>)
    {
      $line .= $_;
      $line =~ s/\n/ /g;

      while ($line =~ /</o)
      {
       $tail = $'; #'
       undef $lastNonTag;
       $lastNonTag = $` if $` !~ /^\s*$/o;


          #------------------------------------------
          #== SGML comment: <!- ... blah blah ... ->
```

```perl
#────────────────────────────────────────
if ($tail =~ /^!-/o)
{

    $commentline = $. unless defined $commentline;

    # push lastNonTag onto word list for spell checking

    $ct = $';
    next READLINE unless $ct =~ /-\s*>/o;

    undef $commentline;

    $comment = $`;
    $line = $';

    # markup embedded in comment can confuse some (most? :-) browsers
    &whine($., 'markup-in-comment') if $comment =~ /<\s*[^>]+>/o;
    next;
}
undef $commentline;

next READLINE unless $tail =~ /^(\s*)([^>]*)>/;


&whine($., 'leading-whitespace', $2) if $1 ne '';

  $id = $tag = $2;
  $line = $';

  &whine($., 'unknown-element', $id),next if $id =~ /^\s*$/;

# push lastNonTag onto word list for spell checking

  undef $tail;
  undef $closing;
  undef %args;

  #- <!DOCTYPE ... > is ignored for now.
  next if $id =~ /^!doctype/io;

$closing = 0;
  if ($id =~ m@^/@o)
  {
    $id =~ s@^/@@;
  $ID = "\U$id";
```

```
        $closing = 1;
    }


#—————————————————————————————————
#== some seriously ugly code to handle attributes ...
#—————————————————————————————————
if ($closing == 0 && $tag =~ m|^(\S+)\s+(.*)|)
    {
        ($id,$tail) = ($1,$2);
      $ID = "\U$id";
      $tail =~ s/\n/ /g;

        # check for odd number of quote characters
        ($quotes = $tail) =~ s/[^"]//g;
        &whine($., 'odd-quotes', $tag) if length($quotes) % 2 == 1;

      $novalue = 0;
      $valid = $validAttributes{$ID};
      while ($tail =~ /^\s*([^=\s]+)\s*=\s*(.*)$/
              # catch attributes like ISMAP for IMG, with no arg
              || ($tail =~ /^\s*(\S+)(.*)/ && ($novalue = 1)))
      {
          $arg = "\U$1";
          $rest = $2;

            &whine($., 'unexpected-open', $tag) if $arg =~ /</;

          if ($arg !~ /^($valid)$/i && $ID =~ /^($legalElements)$/o)
          {
              if ($arg =~ /^($validNetscapeAttributes{$ID})$/i)
              {
                  &whine($., 'netscape-attribute', $arg, $id);
              }
              else
              {
                  &whine($., 'unknown-attribute', $id, $arg);
              }
          }

          #— catch repeated attributes.  for example:
          #—     <IMG SRC="foo.gif" SRC="bar.gif">
          if (defined $args{$arg})
          {
              &whine($., 'repeated-attribute', $arg, $id);
          }
```

```
        if ($novalue)
        {
            $args{$arg} = '';
            $tail = $rest;
        }
        elsif ($rest =~ /^'([^']+)'(.*)$/)
          {
            &whine($., 'attribute-delimiter', $arg, $ID);
            $args{$arg} = $1;
            $tail = $2;
          }
        elsif ($rest =~ /^"([^"]+)"(.*)$/
               || $rest =~ /^'([^']+)'(.*)$/
               || $rest =~ /^(\S+)(.*)$/)
          {
            $args{$arg} = $1;
            $tail = $2;
          }
        else
          {
            $args{$arg} = $rest;
            $tail = '';
          }
        $novalue = 0;
      }
    &whine($., 'unexpected-open', $tag) if $tail =~ /</o;
  }
else
{
    if ($closing && $id =~ m|^(\S+)\s+(.*)|)
    {
      &whine($., 'closing-attribute', $tag);
      $id = $1;
    }
    $ID = "\U$id";
}

$TAG = ($closing ? "/" : "").$ID;
if (defined $mustFollow{$TAG})
{
    $ok = 0;
    foreach $pre (split(/\|/, $mustFollow{$TAG}))
    {
      ($ok=1),last if $pre eq $lastTAG;
    }
```

```
    if (!$ok || $lastNonTag !~ /^\s*$/)
    {
        &whine($., 'must-follow', $TAG, $mustFollow{$TAG});
    }
}


#- catch empty container elements
if ($closing && $ID eq $lastTAG && $lastNonTag =~ /^\s*$/
    && $ID ne 'TEXTAREA')
{
    &whine($., 'empty-container', $ID);
}


#- special case for empty optional container elements
if (!$closing && $ID eq $tags[$#tags] && $lastTAG eq $ID
    && $ID =~ /^($maybePaired)$/
    && $lastNonTag =~ /^\s*$/)
{
    $t = pop @tags;
    $tline = pop @taglines;
    &whine($tline, 'empty-container', $ID);
    $tagRE = join('|',@tags);
}

    #- whine about unrecognized element, and do no more checks —
    if ($id !~ /^($legalElements)$/io)
{
    if ($id =~ /^($netscapeElements)$/io)
    {
        &whine($., 'netscape-markup', ($closing ? "/$id" : "$id"));
    }
    else
    {
        &whine($., 'unknown-element', ($closing ? "/$id" : "$id"));
    }
    next;
}

    if ($closing == 0 && defined $requiredAttributes{$ID})
    {
    @argkeys = keys %args;
    foreach $attr (split(/\|/,$requiredAttributes{$ID}))
    {
        unless (defined $args{$attr})
        {
            &whine($., 'required-attribute', $attr, $id);
```

```perl
      }
    }
  }
  elsif ($closing == 0 && $id =~ /^($expectArgsRE)$/io)
  {
      &whine($., 'expected-attribute', $id) unless defined %args;
  }


  #-------------------------------------------------------------
  #== check case of tags
  #-------------------------------------------------------------
  &whine($., 'upper-case', $id) if $id ne $ID;
  &whine($., 'lower-case', $id) if $id ne "\L$id";


  #-------------------------------------------------------------
  #== if tag id is /foo, then strip slash, and mark as a closer
  #-------------------------------------------------------------
  if ($closing)
  {
    if ($ID !~ /^($pairElements)$/o)
    {
      &whine($., 'illegal-closing', $id);
    }

    if ($ID eq 'A' && $lastNonTag =~ /^\s*here\s*$/io)
    {
      &whine($., 'here-anchor');
    }

  #- end of HEAD, did we see a TITLE in the HEAD element? -
  &whine($., 'require-head') if $ID eq 'HEAD' && !$seenTag{'TITLE'};

  #- was there a <LINK REV=MADE HREF="mailto:..."> element in HEAD?
  &whine($., 'mailto-link') if $ID eq 'HEAD' && $seenMailtoLink == 0;
  }
  else
  {
      #-------------------------------------------------------------
      # do context checks.  Should really be a state machine.
      #-------------------------------------------------------------

    if (defined $physicalFontElements{$ID})
    {
      &whine($., 'physical-font', $ID, $physicalFontElements{$ID});
    }
```

```perl
    if ($ID eq 'A' && defined $args{'HREF'})
    {
     $target = $args{'HREF'};
      if ($target =~ /([^:]+):\/\/([^\/]+)(.*)$/
          || $target =~ /^(news|mailto):/
          || $target =~ /^\//)
      {
      }
      else
      {
          $target =~ s/#.*$//;
          if ($target !~ /^\s*$/ && ! -f $target && ! -d $target)
          {
              &whine($., 'bad-link', $target);
          }
      }
    }

    if ($ID =~ /^H(\d)$/o)
    {
        if (defined $heading && $1 - $heading > 1)
        {
         &whine($., 'heading-order', $ID, $heading, $headingLine);
        }
        $heading     = $1;
        $headingLine = $.;
    }

#- check for mailto: LINK ─────────────
    if ($ID eq 'LINK' && $args{'REV'} =~ /^made$/io
        && $args{'HREF'} =~ /^mailto:/io)
    {
        $seenMailtoLink = 1;
    }

    if (defined $onceOnly{$ID})
    {
        &whine($., 'once-only', $ID, $seenTag{$ID}) if $seenTag{$ID};
    }
     $seenTag{$ID} = $.;

     &whine($., 'body-no-head') if $ID eq 'BODY' && !$seenTag{'HEAD'};

    if ($ID ne 'HTML' && $ID ne '!DOCTYPE' && !$seenTag{'HTML'}
        && !$whined{'outer-html'})
    {
```

```
      &whine($., 'html-outer');
      $whined{'outer-html'} = 1;
  }


#- check for illegally nested elements ----------------.
if ($ID =~ /^($nonNest)$/o && $ID =~ /^($tagRE)$/)
{
    for ($i=$#tags; $tags[$i] ne $ID; -$i)
    {
    }
    &whine($., 'nested-element', $ID, $taglines[$i]);
}


&whine($., 'unknown-element', $ID) unless $ID =~ /^($legalElements)$/o;

#-----------------------------------------------------
# check for tags which have a required context
#-----------------------------------------------------
if (defined ($reqCon = $requiredContext{$ID}))
{
    $ok = 0;
    foreach $context (split(/\|/, $requiredContext{$ID}))
    {
        ($ok=1),last if $context =~ /^($tagRE)$/;
    }
    unless ($ok)
    {
        &whine($., 'required-context', $ID, $requiredContext{$ID});
    }
}


#-----------------------------------------------------
# check for tags which can only appear in the HEAD element
#-----------------------------------------------------
if ($ID =~ /^($headTagsRE)$/o && 'HEAD' !~ /^($tagRE)$/)
{
    &whine($., 'head-element', $ID);
}

if (! defined $okInHead{$ID} && 'HEAD' =~ /^($tagRE)$/)
{
    &whine($., 'non-head-element', $ID);
}


#-----------------------------------------------------
# check for tags which have been deprecated (now obsolete)
```

```
#————————————————————————————————
        &whine($., 'obsolete', $ID) if $ID =~ /^($obsoleteTags)$/o;
}


#————————————————————————————————
#== was tag of type <TAG> ... </TAG>?
#== welcome to kludgeville, population seems to be on the increase!
#————————————————————————————————
if ($ID =~ /^($pairElements)$/o)
{
#— if we have a closing tag, and the tag(s) on top of the stack
#— are optional closing tag elements, pop the tag off the stack,
#— unless it matches the current closing tag
if ($closing)
{
    while (@tags > 0 && $tags[$#tags] ne $ID
            && $tags[$#tags] =~ /^($maybePaired)$/o)
    {
        pop @tags;
        pop @taglines;
    }
    $tagRE = join('|',@tags);
}

  if ($closing && $tags[$#tags] eq $ID)
  {
    $matched     = pop @tags;
    $matchedLine = pop @taglines;

    #— does top of stack match top of orphans stack? ——
    while (@orphans > 0 && @tags > 0
        && $orphans[$#orphans] eq $tags[$#tags])
    {
        &whine($., 'element-overlap', $orphans[$#orphans],
                $orphanlines[$#orphanlines], $matched, $matchedLine);
        pop @orphans;
        pop @orphanlines;
        pop @tags;
        pop @taglines;
    }
    $tagRE = join('|',@tags);
  }
elsif ($closing && $tags[$#tags] ne $ID)
{
    #— closing tag does not match opening tag on top of stack
    if ($ID =~ /^($tagRE)$/)
```

```
        {
            # If we saw </HTML>, </HEAD>, or </BODY>, then we try
            # and resolve anything inbetween on the tag stack
            if ($ID =~ /^(HTML|HEAD|BODY)$/o)
            {
                while ($tags[$#tags] ne $ID)
                {
                    $ttag = pop @tags;
                    $ttagline = pop @taglines;
                    if ($ttag !~ /^($maybePaired)$/)
                    {
                        &whine($., 'unclosed-element', $ttag, $ttagline);
                    }

                    #- does top of stack match top of orphans stack? -
                    while (@orphans > 0 && @tags > 0
                            && $orphans[$#orphans] eq $tags[$#tags])
                    {
                        pop @orphans;
                        pop @orphanlines;
                        pop @tags;
                        pop @taglines;
                    }
                }

                #- pop off the HTML, HEAD, or BODY tag ————
                pop @tags;
                pop @taglines;
                $tagRE = join('|',@tags);
            }
            else
            {
                #- matched opening tag lower down on stack
                push(@orphans, $ID);
                push(@orphanlines, $.);
            }
        }
        else
        {
            &whine($., 'mis-match', $ID);
        }
    }
    else
    {
        push(@tags,$ID);
        $tagRE = join('|',@tags);
```

```
                push(@taglines,$.);
            }
        }

        #------------------------------------------------
        #-- inline images (IMG) should have an ALT argument :-)
        #------------------------------------------------
        &whine($., 'img-alt') if ($ID eq 'IMG'
                                  && !defined $args{'ALT'}
                                  && !$closing);

    } continue {
        $lastTAG = $TAG;
    }
    $lastNonTag = $line;
}
close PAGE;

if (defined $commentline)
{
    &whine($commentline, 'unclosed-comment');
    return;
}

while (@tags > 0)
{
    $tag = shift(@tags);
    $line = shift(@taglines);
    if ($tag !~ /^($maybePaired)$/)
    {
        &whine($., 'unclosed-element', $tag, $line);
    }
}

for (@expectedTags)
{
    # if we haven't seen TITLE but have seen HEAD
    # then we'll have already whined about the lack of a TITLE element
    next if $_ eq 'TITLE' && !$seenTag{$_} && $seenTag{'HEAD'};
    push(@notSeen,$_) unless $seenTag{$_};
}
if (@notSeen > 0)
{
    printf ("%sexpected tag(s) not seen: @notSeen\n",
                    ($opt_s ? "" : "$filename(-): "));
    $exit_status = 1;
```

```
   }
}

#========================================================
# Function:      whine
# Purpose:       Give a standard format whine:
#                        filename(line #): <message>
#                The associative array `enabled' is used as a gating
#                function, to suppress or enable each warning.  Every
#                warning has an associated identifier, which is used to
#                refer to the warning, and as the index into the hash.
#========================================================
sub whine
{
   local($line, $id, @argv) = @_;
   local($mstyle)              = $variable{'message-style'};


   return unless $enabled{$id};
   $exit_status = 1;
   (print "$filename:$line:$id\n"), return                if $mstyle eq 'terse';
   (eval "print \"$filename($line): $message{$id}\n\""), return if $mstyle eq 'lint';
   (eval "print \"line $line: $message{$id}\n\""), return if $mstyle eq 'short';

   die "Unknown message style `$mstyle'\n";
}


#========================================================
# Function:      GetConfigFile
# Purpose:       Read user's configuration file, if such exists.
#                If WEBLINTRC is set in user's environment, then read the
#                file referenced, otherwise try for $HOME/.weblintrc.
#========================================================
sub GetConfigFile
{
   local(*CONFIG);
   local($filename);
   local($arglist);
   local($value);


   $filename = $ENV{'WEBLINTRC'} || "$ENV{'HOME'}/.weblintrc";
   return unless -f $filename;

   open(CONFIG,"< $filename") || do
   {
```

```
        print WARNING "Unable to read config file `$filename': $!\n";
        return 0;
    };

    while (<CONFIG>)
    {
        s/#.*$//;
        next if /^\s*$/o;

        #- match keyword: process one or more argument ——————————-
        if (/^\s*(enable|disable|extension|ignore)\s+(.*)$/io)
        {
          $keyword = "\U$1";
          $arglist = $2;
          while ($arglist =~ /^\s*(\S+)/o)
          {
              $value = "\L$1";
              &enableWarning($1, 1) if $keyword eq 'ENABLE';
              &enableWarning($1, 0) if $keyword eq 'DISABLE';
              $ignore{"\U$1"} = 1 if $keyword eq 'IGNORE';
              &AddExtension($1) if $keyword eq 'EXTENSION';
              $arglist = $';
          }
        }
        elsif (/^\s*set\s+(\S+)\s*=\s*(.*)/)
        {
            # setting a weblint variable
            if (defined $variable{$1})
            {
                $variable{$1} = $2;
            }
            else
            {
                print WARNING "Unknown variable `$1' in configuration file\n"
            }
        }
    }
    close CONFIG;

    1;
}

sub enableWarning
{
    local($id, $enabled) = @_;
    if (! defined $enabled{$id})
```

```
    {
       print WARNING "$PROGRAM: unknown warning identifier \"$id\"\n";
       return 0;
    }
    $enabled{$id} = $enabled;
    #
    # ensure consistency: if you just enabled upper-case,
    # then we should make sure that lower-case is disabled
    #
    $enabled{'lower-case'} = 0 if $_ eq 'upper-case';
    $enabled{'upper-case'} = 0 if $_ eq 'lower-case';
    $enabled{'upper-case'} = $enabled{'lower-case'} = 0 if $_ eq 'mixed-case';

    return 1;
}


#=============================================================
# Function:       AddExtension
# Purpose:        Extend the HTML understood.  Currently supported extensions:
#                       netscape  - the netscape extensions proposed by
#                                   Netscape Communications, Inc.  See:
#                       http://www.netscape.com/home/services_docs/html-extensions.html
#=============================================================
sub AddExtension
{
    local($extension) = @_;
    if ("\L$extension" ne 'netscape')
    {
       warn "$PROGRAM: unknown extension `$extension' - ignoring.\n";
       return;
    }
    #------------------------------------------------------------
    # netscape extensions
    #------------------------------------------------------------

    #- new element attributes for existing elements ---------------

    &AddAttributes('ISINDEX',  'PROMPT');
    &AddAttributes('HR',       'SIZE', 'WIDTH', 'ALIGN', 'NOSHADE');
    &AddAttributes('UL',       'TYPE');
    &AddAttributes('OL',       'TYPE', 'START');
    &AddAttributes('LI',       'TYPE', 'VALUE');
    &AddAttributes('IMG',      'BORDER', 'VSPACE', 'HSPACE');
    &AddAttributes('BODY',     'BGCOLOR', 'TEXT', 'LINK', 'VLINK', 'ALINK');
    &AddAttributes('TABLE',    'CELLSPACING', 'CELLPADDING');
    &AddAttributes('TD',       'WIDTH');
```

```perl
    &AddAttributes('TH',          'WIDTH');

    #- new elements ————————————————————————————-

    $legalElements .= '|'.$netscapeElements;
    $pairElements  .= '|BLINK|CENTER|FONT|NOBR';
    &AddAttributes('FONT',      'SIZE');
    &AddAttributes('BASEFONT', 'SIZE');
}

sub AddAttributes
{
    local($element,@attributes) = @_;
    local($attr);
    $attr = join('|', @attributes);
    if (defined $validAttributes{$element})
    {
        $validAttributes{$element} .= "|$attr";
    }
    else
    {
        $validAttributes{$element} = "$attr";
    }
}


#========================================================
# Function:     ListWarnings()
# Purpose:      List all supported warnings, with identifier, and
#               whether the warning is enabled.
#========================================================
sub ListWarnings
{
    local($id);
    local($message);
    foreach $id (sort keys %enabled)
    {
        ($message = $message{$id}) =~ s/\$argv\[\d+\]/.../g;
        $message =~ s/\\"/"/g;
        print WARNING "$id (", ($enabled{$id} ? "enabled" : "disabled"), ")\n";
        print WARNING "    $message\n\n";
    }
}

sub CheckURL
{
    local($url)          = @_;
```

```perl
    local($workfile)       = "$TMPDIR/$PROGRAM.$$";
    local($urlget)         = $variable{'url-get'};

    die "$PRORGAM: url-get variable is not defined - ".
        "don't know how to get $url\n" unless defined $urlget;

    system("$urlget $url > $workfile");
    &WebLint($workfile, $url);
    unlink $workfile;
}


#==============================================================
# Function:    wanted
# Purpose:     This is called by &find() to determine whether a file
#              is wanted.  We're looking for files, with the filename
#              extension .html or .htm.
#==============================================================
sub wanted
{
    if (-d $_ && ! -f "$_/$variable{'directory-index'}")
    {
        &whine('*', 'directory-index', "$arg/$_", $variable{'directory-index'});
    }

    /\.(html|htm)$/ &&               # valid filename extensions: .html .htm
        -f $_ &&                     # only looking for files
        (!$opt_l || !-l $_) &&       # ignore symlinks if -l given
        &WebLint($_,$name); # check the file
}


#==============================================================
# Function:    ReadDefaults
# Purpose:     Read the built-in defaults.  These are stored at the end
#              of the script, after the __END__, and read from the
#              DATA filehandle.
#==============================================================
sub ReadDefaults
{
    local(@elements);
    while (<DATA>)
    {
        chop;
        s/^\s*//;
        next if /^$/;

        push(@elements, $_);
```

```
            next unless @elements == 3;

            ($id, $default, $message) = @elements;
            $enabled{$id} = ($default eq 'ENABLE');
            ($message{$id} = $message) =~ s/"/\\"/g;
            undef @elements;
        }
    }

    __END__
upper-case
        DISABLE
        tag <$argv[0]> is not in upper case.
lower-case
        DISABLE
        tag <$argv[0]> is not in lower case.
mixed-case
        ENABLE
        tag case is ignored
here-anchor
        ENABLE
        bad form to use `here' as an anchor!
require-head
        ENABLE
        no <TITLE> in HEAD element.
once-only
        ENABLE
        tag <$argv[0]> should only appear once.  I saw one on line $argv[1]!
body-no-head
        ENABLE
        <BODY> but no <HEAD>.
html-outer
        ENABLE
        outer tags should be <HTML> .. </HTML>.
head-element
        ENABLE
        <$argv[0]> can only appear in the HEAD element.
non-head-element
        ENABLE
        <$argv[0]> cannot appear in the HEAD element.
obsolete
        ENABLE
        <$argv[0]> is obsolete.
mis-match
        ENABLE
        unmatched </$argv[0]> (no matching <$argv[0]> seen).
```

img-alt
    ENABLE
    IMG does not have ALT text defined.
nested-element
    ENABLE
    <$argv[0]> cannot be nested – </$argv[0]> not yet seen for <$argv[0]> on line
$argv[1].
mailto-link
    DISABLE
    did not see <LINK REV=MADE HREF="mailto..."> in HEAD.
element-overlap
    ENABLE
    </$argv[0]> on line $argv[1] seems to overlap <$argv[2]>, opened on line $argv[3].
unclosed-element
    ENABLE
    no closing </$argv[0]> seen for <$argv[0]> on line $argv[1].
markup-in-comment
    ENABLE
    markup embedded in a comment can confuse some browsers.
unknown-attribute
    ENABLE
    unknown attribute "$argv[1]" for element <$argv[0]>.
leading-whitespace
    ENABLE
    should not have whitespace between "<" and "$argv[0]>".
required-attribute
    ENABLE
    the $argv[0] attribute is required for the <$argv[1]> element.
unknown-element
    ENABLE
    unknown element <$argv[0]>.
odd-quotes
    ENABLE
    odd number of quotes in element <$argv[0]>.
heading-order
    ENABLE
    bad style - heading <$argv[0]> follows <H$argv[1]> on line $argv[2].
bad-link
    DISABLE
    target for anchor "$argv[0]" not found.
expected-attribute
    ENABLE
    expected an attribute for <$argv[0]>.
unexpected-open
    ENABLE
    unexpected < in <$argv[0]> – potentially unclosed element.

```
required-context
      ENABLE
      illegal context for <$argv[0]> - must appear in <$argv[1]> element.
unclosed-comment
      ENABLE
      unclosed comment (comment should be: <!- ... ->).
illegal-closing
      ENABLE
      element <$argv[0]> is not a container - </$argv[0]> not legal.
netscape-markup
      ENABLE
      <$argv[0]> is netscape specific (use "-x netscape" to allow this).
netscape-attribute
      ENABLE
      attribute `$argv[0]' for <$argv[1]> is netscape specific (use "-x netscape" to
allow this).
physical-font
      DISABLE
      <$argv[0]> is physical font markup - use logical (such as $argv[1]).
repeated-attribute
      ENABLE
      attribute $argv[0] is repeated in element <$argv[1]>
must-follow
      ENABLE
      <$argv[0]> must immediately follow <$argv[1]>
empty-container
      ENABLE
      empty container element <$argv[0]>.
directory-index
      ENABLE
      directory $argv[0] does not have an index file ($argv[1])
closing-attribute
      ENABLE
      closing tag <$argv[0]> should not have any attributes specified.
attribute-delimiter
      ENABLE
      use of ' for attribute
```

Listing 5: UTIL.C

```c
/* This C source is used by the post-query program and all of the  interactive Web site
utilties presented. */

#include <stdio.h>

#define LF 10
#define CR 13

void getword(char *word, char *line, char stop) {
    int x = 0,y;

    for(x=0;((line[x]) && (line[x] != stop));x++)
        word[x] = line[x];

    word[x] = '\0';
    if(line[x]) ++x;
    y=0;

    while(line[y++] = line[x++]);
}

char *makeword(char *line, char stop) {
    int x = 0,y;
    char *word = (char *) malloc(sizeof(char) * (strlen(line) + 1));

    for(x=0;((line[x]) && (line[x] != stop));x++)
        word[x] = line[x];

    word[x] = '\0';
    if(line[x]) ++x;
    y=0;

    while(line[y++] = line[x++]);
    return word;
}

char *fmakeword(FILE *f, char stop, int *cl) {
    int wsize;
    char *word;
    int ll;

    wsize = 102400;
    ll=0;
```

```
        word = (char *) malloc(sizeof(char) * (wsize + 1));

        while(1) {
            word[ll] = (char)fgetc(f);
            if(ll==wsize) {
                word[ll+1] = '\0';
                wsize+=102400;
                word = (char *)realloc(word,sizeof(char)*(wsize+1));
            }
            -(*cl);
            if((word[ll] == stop) || (feof(f)) || (!(*cl))) {
                if(word[ll] != stop) ll++;
                word[ll] = '\0';
                return word;
            }
            ++ll;
        }
    }

    char x2c(char *what) {
        register char digit;

        digit = (what[0] >= 'A' ? ((what[0] & 0xdf) - 'A')+10 : (what[0] - '0'));
        digit *= 16;
        digit += (what[1] >= 'A' ? ((what[1] & 0xdf) - 'A')+10 : (what[1] - '0'));
        return(digit);
    }

    void unescape_url(char *url) {
        register int x,y;

        for(x=0,y=0;url[y];++x,++y) {
            if((url[x] = url[y]) == '%') {
                url[x] = x2c(&url[y+1]);
                y+=2;
            }
        }
        url[x] = '\0';
    }

    void plustospace(char *str) {
        register int x;

        for(x=0;str[x];x++) if(str[x] == '+') str[x] = ' ';
    }
```

```c
int rind(char *s, char c) {
    register int x;
    for(x=strlen(s) - 1;x != -1; x-)
        if(s[x] == c) return x;
    return -1;
}

int getline(char *s, int n, FILE *f) {
    register int i=0;

    while(1) {
        s[i] = (char)fgetc(f);

        if(s[i] == CR)
            s[i] = fgetc(f);

        if((s[i] == 0x4) || (s[i] == LF) || (i == (n-1))) {
            s[i] = '\0';
            return (feof(f) ? 1 : 0);
        }
        ++i;
    }
}

void send_fd(FILE *f, FILE *fd)
{
    int num_chars=0;
    char c;

    while (1) {
        c = fgetc(f);
        if(feof(f))
            return;
        fputc(c,fd);
    }
}

int ind(char *s, char c) {
    register int x;

    for(x=0;s[x];x++)
        if(s[x] == c) return x;

    return -1;
}
```

```
void escape_shell_cmd(char *cmd) {
    register int x,y,l;

    l=strlen(cmd);
    for(x=0;cmd[x];x++) {
        if(ind("&;`'\"|*?~<>^()[]{}$\\",cmd[x]) != -1){
            for(y=l+1;y>x;y--)
                cmd[y] = cmd[y-1];
            l++; /* length has been increased */
            cmd[x] = '\\';
            x++; /* skip the character */
        }
    }
}
```

THE WEBMASTER'S TOOLBOX

The CD that accompanies *Building Business Web Sites* contains a variety of software to assist you in building and maintaining your http server. We hit all of the categories that you need to effectively author content, host it on a Web server, build gateways to your existing data, and program utilities for other needs that arise. Most of the software packages included are evaluation copies of commercial products with some exceptions: https from EMWAC is freeware as are the majority of the Perl scripts. Should you adopt any of the commercial tools for your daily work, you should register the software with the vendor.

Path	Software	Vendor	Description
\EDITORS			
\HOTDOG	HotDog	Sausage Software	HTML editor
\WEBAUTHO	WebAuthor	Quarterdeck Software	Word-based HTML editor
\CONVRTRS			
\WEBBLDR	Web Builder	Information Analytics	Access-based authoring environment
\LVIEW	LView Pro	Lawrence Loureiro	BMP to GIF converter and image manipulator
\SERVERS			
\WEBSITE	WebSite	O'Reilly	full featured NT-based http server
\HTTPS	https	EMWAC	free NT-based http server
\GATEWAYS			
\SQL			
\COLDFUSN	Cold Fusion	Allaire	CGI gateway to ODBC provides access various SQL data sources
\GSQL	GSQL	NCSA	simple CGI gateway to SQL servers available free from NCSA
\WAIS			
\WAISS	WAISS	EMWAC	NT-based WAIS server integrates well with EMWAC's https
\PROGRAMS			
\PERL			
\NTPERL	NT Perl 5.001	Hip Communications	very good port of Perl 5 to NT, supports OLE Automation
\CGI.PM	CGI.pm Perl subroutine package	Lincoln Stein CGI development	package of Perl routines useful in Perl
\SCRIPTS	• htmltoc	none	Perl scripts that assist in various aspects of HTML authoring and verification
	• webxref		
	• txt2html		
	• WebLint		
	• htmlchek		
\CPP	• post-query.c	none	C utilities for various common Web tasks
	• util.c		
	• egscript.c		
	• guestboo.c		
	• count.c		
	• addlink.c		
	• formpost.c		
	• formshow.cpp		
	• formstor.cpp		
\UTILS			
\UNPACK	• tar111.exe (GNU Tar)	GNU	NT versions of utilities useful in unpacking and decompressing various software downloaded from the Internet
	• gzip.exe (GNU Zip)		
	• compress.exe		
\SMTP	NT Mail	Internet Shopper	Internet SMTP mail server for NT